CONFRONTING STRAVINSKY

CONFRONTING STRAVINSKY:
Man, Musician, and Modernist

EDITED BY JANN PASLER

UNIVERSITY OF CALIFORNIA PRESS
Berkeley • Los Angeles • London

Frontis. Igor Stravinsky. Photographer: Irving Penn. Courtesy *Vogue.* Copyright © 1948 (renewed 1976) by Condé Nast Publications, Inc.

University of California Press
Berkeley and Los Angeles, California

University of California Press, Ltd.
London, England

Printed in the United States of America

1 2 3 4 5 6 7 8 9

Library of Congress Cataloging in Publication Data
Main entry under title:

Confronting Stravinsky.

Includes index.
1. Stravinsky, Igor, 1882–1971. I. Pasler, Jann.
ML410.S932.C75 1986 780′.92′4 85–8426
ISBN 0–520–05403–2 (alk. paper)

Contents

Illustrations

Figures

Plates

Introduction

Issues in Stravinsky Research

ONE HUNDRED years after Stravinsky's birth, questions that puzzled the composer's contemporaries during his lifetime continue to intrigue us. From the beginning of his career in 1909 to his death in 1971, Stravinsky's refusal to become identified with a particular style stirred critical debate. Although his stylistic metamorphoses resulted in one of the most varied and important bodies of work in this century, they presented a continual challenge to his contemporaries and forced critics to come to grips with ever-shifting conceptual issues. Given on the one hand Stravinsky's unchanging prominence in twentieth-century culture and on the other new perspectives that have developed in recent years, we should not be surprised that the critical re-evaluation of Stravinsky's work continues.

In order to examine current trends in Stravinsky scholarship and open new avenues of research, numerous Stravinsky friends and scholars convened at the International Stravinsky Symposium, the first of its scope ever held, on 10–14 September 1982 at the University of California, San Diego. As its director, I conceived of the symposium as a gathering that would be both international and interdisciplinary—Stravinsky scholars have too long been isolated from one another by the boundaries of geography or discipline. Specialists from Europe and Asia were brought into discussions with Americans in the hope of bringing attention to varying analytical and methodological perspectives and repairing possible biases of those who knew Stravinsky only in his American period. The theoretical analysis that has dominated Stravinsky scholarship in recent years was balanced with points of view derived from cultural history, aesthetics, performance practice, painting, and dance. The inclusion of these broader approaches was intended to reflect the extent to which Stravinsky worked with all kinds of artists throughout his life and his important role in the formation of twentieth-century culture. By creating a lively context for the interchange of ideas, we hoped to arrive at a new understanding of the composer and his work through the cross-fertilization of ideas and methodologies from different parts of the world and from many disciplines.

This book grew out of the International Stravinsky Symposium and the papers commissioned for it. The participants' new insights fall into three broad categories. First, there are those of a general nature that shed light on some of the central aesthetic issues of our time, as reflected in Stravinsky's music. Second, there are those that lead to a more precise understanding of the different periods of Stravinsky's career and the forces operating within them. Third, there are those that reveal threads of continuity that permeate Stravinsky's entire oeuvre. Studies in this last category—attempts to define why "Stravinsky remains Stravinsky" despite his astonishing stylistic diversity—represent the newest tendency in Stravinsky research. Because the idea of unity in Stravinsky's music has been largely an intuitive one, the demonstration of specific kinds of recurrence is beginning to fill what is perhaps the greatest lacuna in Stravinsky scholarship.

Restless Multiplicity

One cannot study Stravinsky without first recognizing the stature of his work as a cultural symbol. As W. H. Auden said, the composer was "the great exemplary artist of the twentieth century, and not just in music."[1] His genius voraciously consumed anything that could become material for musical reflection, whether from the immediate or distant past, whether from musical or nonmusical sources. And what of any importance was he *not* exposed to? He traveled everywhere, assumed three nationalities, worked with and befriended countless writers, poets, and painters, and took a serious interest in whatever seemed new and interesting in his day, from Paul Valéry's lectures on poetry and abstract thought at the Collège de France to ragtime, big bands, film, and television. The plurality of his music is paradigmatic of this century's restless multiplicity of styles.

Although this plurality is the most characteristic aspect of his oeuvre, it remains its most perplexing one. How could Stravinsky change significantly so many times and yet, as in his *Poetics of Music*, deny being a revolutionary? How could he fail to perceive those metamorphoses as radical acts from a historical point of view? In his essay in this anthology, Milton Babbitt points to a certain attitude toward history that helps to explain this paradox. Babbitt writes that Stravinsky's "sense of historical position never burdened him, never obliged him to manufacture a history of music (both past and present) to which he could define his own relation in the most favorable way." Stravinsky often said, "I can only know what the truth is for me today."[2] This focus on the present gave Stravinsky great freedom and independence. His continually renewed sense of the present, moreover, suggests one reason he never worked to define and enshrine any one particular style.

Stravinsky's inclination toward continual metamorphosis also results from

---

1. W. H. Auden, quoted in Robert Craft, *Stravinsky: Chronicle of a Friendship, 1948–1971* (New York, 1972), p. 395.

2. Igor Stravinsky, *An Autobiography* (New York, 1936), p. 176. When such a statement was preceded by the claim, "I myself don't compose modern music at all nor do I write music of the future," as cited in chapter 19, appendix 2, it roused the ire of contemporaries such as Schoenberg, who felt personally attacked by such an attitude.

his attitude toward tradition. Babbitt remarks that Stravinsky never characterized composers as his predecessors; for Stravinsky, a tradition was "a living force that animates and informs the present."[3] Likewise many traditions could invigorate the present simultaneously. In *The Rake's Progress*, Stravinsky's allusions extend from the Orpheus myth to Faust, from Monteverdi to Broadway musical comedy. Traditions did not serve as norms for his systematic exploration but as various possibilities, at times almost like games, each having its own set of rules—another reason Stravinsky, unlike Schoenberg, never founded a school of his own.

This borrowing from many diverse traditions raises numerous questions. First, because Stravinsky gave little thought to acknowledging his sources, ascertaining the effect of specific traditions on his works and on his development as a composer has been difficult. Furthermore, Stravinsky's substantial deformation of his borrowed materials has thwarted efforts to detect them. Even the composer's own explanation of these details in his later years has proved troublesome, for he had new concerns and a memory that sometimes failed him.

Two essays in this book reveal sources of Stravinsky's work that have been almost entirely overlooked, largely because they lie outside musical traditions. Simon Karlinsky and Richard Taruskin demonstrate that Stravinsky's revolutionary Russian ballets borrow significant elements from Russian folk theater and folk art. Karlinsky points out that each of Stravinsky's major works from 1910 to 1918 integrates models borrowed from Russian preliterary theater and constructs a history of the rituals, folk plays, characters, and even instruments to which Stravinsky refers. He shows where Stravinsky may have learned these traditions and how he adapted them for his own ends. Even if Stravinsky was reluctant to admit the role of such folklore in his early works, Richard Taruskin sees folk sources as perhaps *the* most important factor in the formation of Stravinsky's modernist language and aesthetic. Though originally neither a nationalist nor a modernist, Stravinsky changed his attitude toward native Russian art when he met the "World of Art" circle around Diaghilev, which encouraged him to think of folk materials not as a source of subject matter but of artistic style. Taruskin suggests that the composer went even further than these painters in raising a "phoenix" from folk sources by synthesizing folkloristic (diatonic) and modernist (chromatic) musical elements.

These essays not only bring new information to light, but demonstrate how fruitful the study of Stravinsky's cultural and historical background can be. Similarly, Stravinsky's musical sources deserve close investigation. This anthology focuses particular attention on two kinds of borrowed material: pre-existent tunes and general techniques of composition. As he ponders what led Stravinsky to return to a traditional treatment of folk tunes after the extended experiments in his Russian works, Lawrence Morton detects direct quotations—two folk tunes in

3. Igor Stravinsky, *Poetics of Music* (Cambridge, 1942), p. 57.

the Sonata for Two Pianos and, in contradiction to Stravinsky's disclaimer, three tunes taken from Grieg in *Four Norwegian Moods.* Along with Elmer Schönberger and Louis Andriessen, Glenn Watkins points to how the tradition of canon served as an important general model for Stravinsky, especially in his late works. This development must be traceable to Stravinsky's fascination with Bach and Webern in the 1950s, they remark, and it also suggests the possible influence of Josquin and the other serialists. All of Stravinsky's sources need study, those mentioned in his writings and interviews and those remaining unacknowledged.[4] What led the composer to examine one set of sources rather than another, to borrow certain elements rather than others? What role did these traditions play in the development of his innovations?

Stravinsky's exploitation of the past also raises a second, more general question, namely, the relationship between innovation and academicism in his music. At the symposium, the Belgian music theorist Célestin Deliège pointed to two contradictory but omnipresent impulses in the composer's life—the necessity for constant self-renewal and a pronounced interest in academic formulas.[5] Deliège suggested that, under the influence of scholastic philosophy, Stravinsky turned to conventions from the past for the logic they could provide his music; hence his neoclassicism. Stravinsky's interest in canon, which Watkins calls "emblematic of a rigorously learned style," reinforces this point, as does the composer's dictum, "The person who is loath to borrow these forms when he has need of them clearly betrays his weakness." In later life, according to Lawrence Morton, the composer said he used the serial method, which he considered academic, because he found it interesting to "experience" (Stravinsky's word).

The whole question of borrowed material brings up a third issue as well—the idea of a work of art in the twentieth century. Stravinsky's use of various traditions reflects a distance toward his compositions and an interest in exploring the various contexts in which ideas can appear—timbral, rhythmic, and formal—rather than in transforming ideas themselves. In this way, his music shares important similarities with cubist collages, Picasso paintings, and Duchamp readymades in which "found" objects were assimilated and played with as whimsically as if they were free inventions.

The idea of a composition as a construction consisting primarily of formal relationships was always basic to Stravinsky's aesthetic. In my article, I propose that Stravinsky developed this formalist approach by working to create a new kind of total theater in *Petrushka* and *The Rite of Spring* and that the latter ballet laid

---

4. Philip Gossett (personal communication, fall, 1983) points to a little-known Stravinskyan source: "In *Oedipus,* which Stravinsky acknowledges has an important Verdian basis, Jocasta's aria, the cabaletta,is taken almost precisely from the cabaletta of the Act III trio in *Otello.* And there can be no doubt but that the cagey Stravinsky meant it—if you look at the texts in *Otello.* They are singing, this is a spider's web where Otello will be caught, suffer, and die. And, of course, Jocasta sings about that same problem for Oedipus. One-for-one."

5. See also his "Le leg du 1912," in *Stravinsky: Etudes et témoignages,* ed. François Lesure (Paris, 1982), pp. 149–191 and *Les Fondements de la musique tonale* (Paris, 1984).

the foundation for his turn to neoclassicism in the 1920s. Other articles in this anthology suggest further ramifications of the formalist aesthetic. Gilbert Amy points to the nonrepresentational character of Stravinsky's religious works; Boris Schwarz notes the nonemotive kind of performance his music requires; Babbitt and Charles Wuorinen and Jeffrey Kresky discuss the consequences of Stravinsky's fascination with relations of order rather than content in his music.

For Stravinsky, moreover, the artwork was never absolutely fixed. Traditions were living forces, so were his own and others' compositions. His frequent tinkering with otherwise finished pieces goes hand in hand with his use of borrowed material and often took the form of transcriptions or revisions. Several contributors to this collection focus on the composer's motivation for transcribing certain works and on how his transcriptions differ from the originals. Rex Lawson discusses the composer's work for pianola; Schwarz outlines how Stravinsky and Dushkin collaborated in adapting Stravinsky's orchestral works for the violin; and Watkins explains the circumstances that led Stravinsky to add a voice to two Gesualdo motets. Although the reasons for making these transcriptions varied from needing to complete a concert program to wanting to enhance the repertoire of certain instruments, the composer's friend Morton points to what was no doubt the most practical one. Citing Stravinsky's confession, "If I can't work, I want to die," he recalls how transcriptions from *The Well-Tempered Clavier* kept Stravinsky going when his health began to fail at the end of his life.

Louis Cyr's study of the many revisions in the scoring and orchestration of *The Rite of Spring* reveals the extent to which Stravinsky considered his own compositions works in process.[6] The different versions of this work (and of many others) point to Stravinsky's ambivalence with regard to his "text." While he disdained the performer's interpretative role and sought to limit it (as Rex Lawson shows in his study of the pianola music and as Leonard Stein cites in Stravinsky's 1925 interview[7]), Stravinsky permitted many variants in his own recordings, performances, and editions of the score. Cyr attempts to sort out which changes were motivated by the composer's evolving perception of his work and which were instigated by conductors and performers interested in correcting Stravinsky's "mistakes." Such an analysis underlines the necessity for critical editions of all Stravinsky's works.

Stylistic Periods

Although a division of Stravinsky's career into three periods—"Russian," neoclassical, and serial—cannot be dated exactly, one can understand this division

6. This study complements those by Robert Craft published in 1977, 1978, and 1982, and cited in note 1, chapter 9 in this volume.

7. In this interview, Stravinsky claimed, "Music absolutely has to be realized exactly as it is notated." See chapter 19 in this volume.

when problems specific to each period are defined. Some essays in this anthology clarify influences on Stravinsky at particular times; others demonstrate elements of continuity within the music of a given period that clearly differentiate it from that of the next period. The essays raise many issues that deserve future investigation, including some that are pointed to incidentally in them and others that I mention here only in passing.

A major difficulty in studying Stravinsky's first period arises from a lack of documentation. This collection's translations and analyses of previously unknown or unexamined criticism from both Russian and French sources of the period clarify the significant, although very different, roles of both cultures in the composer's early development. In Russia, according to critics cited by Malcolm Brown and Taruskin, Stravinsky was seen as heir to the nationalists and, surprisingly, as less oriented toward the future than either Maximilian Steinberg or Sergei Prokofiev. But, while Prokofiev's appreciation of the programmatic aspects of *Petrushka* led him to question the nature of the music itself, French critics (whom I quote) regarded the close relationship between music and scenario in Stravinsky's ballets as one of the composer's most significant innovations. The very different critical reception given the composer in France undoubtedly contributed to Stravinsky's decision to emigrate.

The extensive stylistic transformations from one work to the next within Stravinsky's "Russian" period also made it difficult to explain the intuitive sense of unity that they give to most listeners and critics. Several contributors address this question. Pieter van den Toorn and Taruskin demonstrate that the frequent presence of the octatonic scale, used previously by Rimsky-Korsakov and Scriabin, contributes significantly to the pervasive "Russianness" of this music. Allen Forte shows how much of this early music is based on melodic configurations and harmonic successions derived from recurring and interlocking tetrachords and other pitch-class sets, which, in the ballets, often function as leitmotifs associated with distinct personae.

But many questions regarding the music of this period remain to be answered. Karlinsky suggests investigating Alexei Remizov's *Follow the Sun*, Velimir Khlebnikov's poems, and Nikolai Roerich's essays and paintings as possible sources for *The Rite*, as well as looking to Nikolai Findeizen, editor of the *Russian Music Gazette*, for background information on *Les Noces* and *Renard*. Taruskin suggests studying whether Stravinsky knew Larionov and Goncharova in Russia at a time when their neoprimitivist ideas might have affected him. Takashi Funayama opens an entirely new field of inquiry, the possible effect of the turn-of-the-century fascination with *Japonisme* on the composer. One might also explore how much contact Stravinsky had with French music before he came to Paris and with French musicians during his first years there, what kind of influence Parisian artists and poets had on him, what the major influences during his Swiss years were, and whether fame in the West played any role in his compositional development.

Stravinsky's middle-period compositions still resist classification. Although, as Ernst Krenek points out, they introduced the style that came to dominate composition for thirty years,[8] scholars continue to view the neoclassical repertory in relationship to works in the preceding and subsequent periods rather than as a second period of maturity. At the time, these works aroused harsh criticism. Few of Stravinsky's contemporaries saw in the composer's works after *Mavra* a power or brilliance comparable with that of his earlier masterpieces. Schoenberg entered into a feud with his Russian contemporary in the 1920s because of this new style.

Yet in spite of much negative critical response, Stravinsky continued to experiment in new and unforeseen ways during his years in Paris between the two wars. Of particular interest is his special use of tonality in the works of this period. Wuorinen and Kresky, Jonathan Kramer, and van den Toorn posit this as characteristic of his neoclassical style. Aiming to show that these compositions are more than just "various distorting mirrors held up to the functional relationships of genuine tonal music," Wuorinen and Kresky point to a concept of tonality in which entire scales assume the role normally associated with the tonic note or triad. Kramer posits that Stravinsky stripped tonal sounds of their kinetic implications in this music in order to use the background motion of sections to create movement. Van den Toorn suggests that Stravinsky's interest in tonality during this period led him to use a major scale (C scale) in combination with octatonicism in his neoclassical works, in place of the modal (D-scale) type preponderant in his "Russian" works.

Even with these technical explications, however, the great diversity inherent in music based on numerous different models leaves many questions unresolved. For example, did the borrowed traditions leave any imprint on Stravinsky's style? Certainly jazz played a role, for in the 1925 interview Stein quotes, Stravinsky says it was the only modern music worth his attention. But what role exactly? And what about his other sources? It would be interesting, furthermore, to know if the pianola had any influence on Stravinsky's method of composition because, as Lawson shows, Stravinsky was fascinated by this instrument from 1914 through the 1920s and wrote several pieces for it. Stravinsky's prolonged association with Nadia Boulanger's circle during this period likewise merits study; in her apartment, according to Robert Craft, the composer sightread many scores of early music in transcriptions by German musicologists. Can the old masterpieces have shed light on his stylistic development at the time? Conversely, does Stravinsky's music reveal any new or striking perspectives on the early music?

At present, Stravinsky's late compositions are undergoing the most serious re-evaluation. They are now seen to occupy a different historical site than the

8. Ernst Krenek was unable to attend the symposium but sent a short note to the editor about Stravinsky subsequent to the symposium.

"Russian" or neoclassical works and can no longer be considered "a disappointing experimental dotage." According to Babbitt, Stravinsky himself claimed that *Movements* for Piano and Orchestra was "the most advanced music from the point of construction of anything he had composed." For him, these works define a different position for Stravinsky vis-à-vis the music that preceded them, both his own and that of others. Wuorinen and Kresky predict that Stravinsky's serial works one day may be viewed as his most significant in their influence on subsequent generations.

Along with re-examining the historical importance of the late works, this collection provides firsthand information about the composer during his American years.[9] Stein, the director of the Schoenberg Institute, traces the history of "kleine Modernsky's" relationship with his Viennese counterpart, particularly during the years when they lived only ten miles apart in Los Angeles and belonged to two different émigré communities. Morton, who met Stravinsky in 1941, organized twelve premiere performances of his works for the Los Angeles concert series "Evenings on the Roof," and was a regular visitor in the Stravinsky household during the 1950s and 1960s, offers a personal portrait of the composer. Stravinsky's librarian, Edwin Allen, here writes for the first time of his activity within the Stravinsky household.

Probably the most puzzling question arising from Stravinsky's late years is his turn to serialism after Schoenberg's death. Did he gravitate to the serial method in his search for increasing discipline in his musical materials, as Stein and Watkins suggest? Or did he use serial techniques to extend his own approach to composition, as Babbitt and Wuorinen and Kresky posit? The result was indeed a great discovery: by combining notions of pitch-class ordering and pitch-class interval through the use of "verticals,"[10] Stravinsky could extend and elaborate Schoenberg's own procedures and suggest a new way of using the system itself. But whether Stravinsky's use of serialism is taken as providing composers with a technique they themselves can extend, or whether it is seen as causing a dissociation of sensibility between the intellectual and the sensuous in his music, as Roger Shattuck fears, Stravinsky himself predicted that music would probably retreat from the "luxuriant complexity" that engaged him during this period, perhaps all the way back to the style of his *Fireworks*.

---

9. Other composers, musicologists, and friends who should be approached for information on Stravinsky include Arthur Berger, Luciano Berio, Lenox Berkeley, Sir Isaiah Berlin, Leonard Bernstein, Elliott Carter, Don Christlieb, Edward T. Cone, Aaron Copland, John Crosby, Dr. Max Edel, Lukas Foss, William Glock, Alexander Goehr, Christopher Isherwood, Lincoln Kirstein, Boris Kochno, Zorina Lieberson, Serge Lifar, Igor Markevitch, Paul Sacher, Kiriena Siloti, Pierre Souvtchinsky, Stephen Spender, Claudio Spies, and Beveridge Webster, as well as Stravinsky's sons Théodore and Soulima, daughter Milene Marion, grandson John Stravinsky, and granddaughter Katharine Gellatchitch. The films and recorded interviews with Stravinsky and a number of his friends should likewise be studied in detail.

10. Wuorinen defines "verticals" as the chords obtained by reading vertically in the chart of rotationally produced forms, or "verticalizations of corresponding order positions of all the rotations."

Threads of Continuity

With Stravinsky's late works now seen as his second period of maturity, we must reconsider the composer's oeuvre as a whole and try to understand its overall coherence. In this anthology, specialists investigate important kinds of recurrence in Stravinsky's music and explore several sources of unity in it. Much more work remains to be done in this regard.

Interestingly, despite the numerous characteristics differentiating the music of Stravinsky's three periods, the roots of the composer's aesthetic inclinations and even certain technical innovations can sometimes be found in his earlier music. For example, although an orientation toward the past is generally thought to have arisen only in Stravinsky's neoclassical period, Brown reveals that as early as 1914 the Russian critic Asafiev perceived Stravinsky's ability "to grasp with an intuitive perspicacity the spirit and sense of any preceding epoch and to stylize it by means of the most ingenious techniques at his disposal."[11] Similarly, Forte and van den Toorn show how the pitch organization of Stravinsky's neoclassical repertoire bears striking resemblances to that of his "Russian" works. Several authors in this collection give particular attention to the rarely performed Three Pieces for String Quartet (1914). Although the work predates his neoclassical ones by several years, it provides significant clues as to what motivated Stravinsky's stylistic evolution from his first period to his second.

As for links between Stravinsky's serial techniques and his earlier music, orchestral sonorities can be found in works of both periods, Amy points out, and so can Stravinsky's method of "slicing and intercalating continuities," developed in his "Russian" music. Even his verticals, which have no predecessor in other serial compositions, follow directly from Stravinsky's attitude toward chords as sonic rather than functional entities. Finding a foretaste of the serial method in Stravinsky's orientation toward order relationships in his "Russian" and neoclassical works, as well as remnants of tonal thinking in his more content-oriented approach to serial composition, Wuorinen and Kresky view Stravinsky's serial works as synthesizing tonal and twelve-tone traditions.

Larger, more sweeping kinds of unity in Stravinsky's work result from the influence of the composer's recurring preoccupations. Among the most important of these was his interest in visual images. As one might expect from a composer who had almost become a painter and who remained involved with the theater throughout his life, his visual imagination played a significant role in his composition. Many Stravinsky works originate with a visual image, sometimes more images than he revealed, as Jean-Michel Vaccaro demonstrated at the symposium in his discussion of the Hogarth illustrations that underlie *The Rake's Progress.* In *The Rite of Spring,* visual images can even be seen motivating some of Stravinsky's unusual musical techniques. Stravinsky's interest in visual images,

11. See note 14, chapter 3 in this volume.

however, can be regarded as only one aspect of the concern for the physical embodiment that his musical ideas receive in the gestures of dancers and instrumentalists in performance. Roger Shattuck argues that the corporal element in Stravinsky's music incorporates both the visual and aural modes and therefore is primary. Shattuck further suggests that the maestro's own physicality, described by many who watched him conduct or perform (including Morton and Allen), significantly influenced his musical language.

Throughout his life, Stravinsky was fascinated by the musical potential of syllables. Funayama describes the syllabic structure that intrigued the composer in the texts of his *Three Japanese Lyrics* (1912–1913) and that resulted in the continuous eighth-note pattern in which he sets them. Amy points out that syllabification of a Latin text is Stravinsky's most common procedure in his religious works, most of which use chorus. Even in his late works, Morton recollects, Stravinsky was still composing to the syllable—the basic row of *Threni* derives from its opening words. Although symbolist sources can be found for this abstract attitude toward text, one wonders whether the fact that Stravinsky worked with poets more than with singers had any effect on the tenacity with which he maintained this orientation toward the syllable.[12]

Other unifying factors are present in his work as well. Individual genres such as Stravinsky's music for religious chorus, violin, and pianola bear characteristic traits, as Amy, Schwarz, and Lawson point out. Stravinsky had a lifelong concern for correct harmony, Morton and Babbitt remind us, even if it meant cheating the row while composing serial works. Voice-leading techniques, here discussed by Forte and Schönberger and Andriessen, also recur throughout his music. Perhaps the most sweeping notion of unity discussed in this collection is Kramer's proposal that the composer used proportional relationships throughout his life to organize his musical forms. Kramer traces Stravinsky's increasing use of specific proportional consistencies between *Symphonies of Wind Instruments* (1920) and *Agon* (1953–1957), perhaps, as he suggests, as a consequence of the composer's classical aesthetic. If future scholars pursue such issues and if there is more international and interdisciplinary communication, they may initiate a new era in Stravinsky scholarship.

The essays presented in this book were only one aspect of the International Stravinsky Symposium. The event also involved many media and performances and collaboration between the university and the San Diego community. For vari-

12. I am indebted to William Austin for pointing to Stravinsky's apparent lack of substantial collaboration with singers throughout his career and for bringing up the question of its possible effect on his music.

ous reasons, many of the papers in this collection appear in a somewhat different form from that in which they were delivered at the symposium; other papers were inappropriate or impossible to include in the book. Rex Lawson and Charles Rosen presented recitals as well as lectures in which they discussed the works performed. David Hockney showed many slides, of which the illustrations in this book are only a few examples. A number of interviews and personal reminisences provided a lively opportunity for both technically untrained enthusiasts and specialists to learn more about the composer and his music. In addition to the organized discussions, there were a number of exhibitions and concerts. The videotapes of Stravinsky's ballets, the audiotapes of Stravinsky conducting his music, the exhibition of manuscripts, drawings, photographs, and other Stravinsky memorabilia, and the screening of Tony Palmer's four-hour BBC documentary, *Stravinsky,* all enhanced the diversity and breadth of the symposium and provided a context for informal discussions. The event can also claim some modest historical status in that a few of Stravinsky's small piano works and the Bach Fugue in C♯ Minor, which Stravinsky transcribed just before his death, were performed publicly for the first time.

The symposium and this book would not have been possible without the kind encouragement and assistance of Robert Craft, Théodore Strawinsky, Soulima Stravinsky, and Lawrence Morton, as well as the numerous Stravinsky friends and scholars in Europe and America who received me during the summer or fall of 1981 and shared their ideas about Stravinsky research. The National Endowment for the Humanities and the California Council for the Humanities, together with the University of California at San Diego, its Department of Music and its Chancellor's Associates, and many private individuals and foundations provided the necessary financial support to bring the participants together at the International Stravinsky Symposium. I am particularly grateful for the interest, enthusiasm, and generosity of many San Diegans, especially William Arens, Richard Atkinson, Danah Fayman, Kathi Howard, Irwin Jacobs, Nancy MacHutchin, George Mitrovich, Will Ogdon, Manny Rotenberg, and Ramona Sahm. The Committee on Research of the University of California at San Diego provided support at the lengthy editing stage. Through their generous contributions, Richard Chase and Robert Tobin, together with Sue Heller and Fran Luban, made possible the color reproductions in this book. I wish to thank especially Frantisek Deak, Joseph Kerman, Jonathan Kramer, Will Ogdon, and Robert Winter for their reading of individual essays; Nancy François for her sensitive translation of the Amy article; Bonnie Harkins for her transcriptions and tireless typing; Doris Kretschmer for her continuous encouragement and vision; and, most of all, David Reid for his unending generosity, sense of humor, and dedication while helping with the mammoth task of editing the papers.

Jann Pasler
Solana Beach, California
August 1984

Russian Background

1 Igor Stravinsky and Russian Preliterate Theater

SIMON KARLINSKY

AT THE BEGINNING of *Petrushka,* a tune is heard first in the bass at rehearsal number **2** and then in the full orchestra at **5**, with the stage direction: "There passes, dancing, a small crowd of drunken carousers." Western sources, such as Eric Walter White's *Stravinsky: The Composer and His Works,* identify this tune as "an Easter Song known as the 'Song of the Volochebniki' from the province of Smolensk."[1] This information is correct, though confusingly expressed. The *volochebniki,* also known as the *lalyn'shchiki,* were people who went around Belorussian villages on the Monday after Easter Sunday singing *volochebnye pesni,* that is, Easter carols. The cited identification is thus tautological because it says "an Easter song known as the 'Song of the Singers of Easter Carols.' "

In Russian, the carol is known as "Dalalyn'." A look at its lyrics as cited by Irina Vershinina reveals the humorous implications of Stravinsky's placement of the tune in *Petrushka.*[2] The passing carousers have to be out-of-towners because

N. B. For the convenience of the reader, a uniform style of reference has been imposed on these essays. In most cases, English language titles have been preferred, with the exception of works that are most commonly known to Anglo-Americans in French, such as *Histoire du soldat* [The soldier's tale] and *Les Noces* [The Wedding]. [Editor's note]

1. Eric Walter White, *Stravinsky: The Composer and His Works* (Berkeley and Los Angeles, 1966), p. 162. White cites Stravinsky's sources from Frederick W. Sternfeld, "Some Russian Folk Songs in Stravinsky's *Petrushka,*" which initially appeared in *Music Library Association Notes* (March 1945) and was reprinted in the Norton Critical Scores edition of *Petrushka* (New York, 1967). The same identifications are also cited in Vera Stravinsky and Robert Craft, *Stravinsky in Pictures and Documents* (New York, 1978). All these authors repeat Sternfeld's out-of-focus translations of Russian song titles ("Song of the Volochebniki" instead of "Easter Carol" and "Down in the Petersky" instead of "Along the St. Petersburg Road") and cite his nonexistent geographical locations ("Totemsk" and "Tombosk" instead of the correct Tot'ma and Tambov; the spurious forms are attributable to the inability to distinguish Russian nouns from their adjectival derivations). Sternfeld and those who rely on his identifications fail to distinguish between rural folk songs of anonymous origin and the urban popular ditties whose authorship can be established and that Stravinsky also quotes in his score. Thus, the organ-grinder's melody, first stated in a disjoined form by clarinets in octaves two measures after **10** and at **12** and then fully at **15**, is the sentimental *romans,* "Toward Evening, in Rainy Autumn," whose text was written by Alexander Pushkin (at the age of fifteen). The music was composed by Nikolai Titov (1798–1843).

2. Irina Vershinina, *Rannie balety Stravinskogo* [Stravinsky's early ballets] (Moscow, 1967), p. 73. Stravinsky found this song in Nikolai Rimsky-Korsakov's collection of arrangements for voice and piano *One Hundred Russian Folk Songs,* where it appears as no. 47. The translation of the cited portion of the text, with ellipses filled out in brackets, is: "Easter carol, Easter carol! [Give us] each an Easter egg! Christ is arisen." In the remainder of the text, the singers threaten to harm the livestock of those who fail to offer them gifts of holiday foods. See Rimsky-Korsakov, *Sto russkikh narodnykh pesen* [100 Russian folksongs], Opus 24 (Moscow and Leningrad, 1951), pp. 90–91 (originally published in 1877).

Example 1.1. An Easter Carol in *Petrushka.* Taken from Nikolai Rimsky-Korsakov, *Sto russikikh narodnykh pesen* (St. Petersburg, 1877)

the custom of Easter caroling existed only in Belorussia, in areas bordering on Poland, and was unknown in St. Petersburg, where the action of *Petrushka* takes place. In their drunken state, they are disoriented both geographically, thinking they are in their native Belorussian village, and chronologically, confusing the pre-Lenten carnival with the Monday after Easter Sunday, still six weeks away, on which their announcement that Christ has arisen and request for Easter eggs would be customary and appropriate.

This very small example illustrates how familiarity with Russian cultural background can enhance our understanding of Stravinsky's music. I had occasion to realize the truth of this during the twelve years it took me to write a survey of Russian drama from its prehistoric beginnings to the age of Pushkin. In studying indigenous forms of Russian drama, I kept stumbling on phenomena that were familiar from Stravinsky's oeuvre between 1910 and 1918. Conversely, examining his output dating from that period, I saw that his stage works from *Petrushka* to *Histoire du soldat* [The soldier's tale] add up to a compendium of the native theatrical genres of old Russia.

Prior to the introduction of literary drama, in the form of amateur theatricals in Orthodox religious seminaries (school drama) and at the court of Tsar Alexis (German-derived court drama) during the last quarter of the seventeenth century, dramatized rituals and folk entertainments that can be collectively described as Russian preliterary theater had existed in postbaptismal Russia. With some allowance for mutual contamination between categories, this theater existed in the following forms: (1) enactments of surviving pagan rituals that dated back to pre-Christian times, initially had agrarian significance, were timed to the change of seasons, and were usually (though not always) disguised as Christian holidays or ceremonies; (2) highly dramatized village customs of betrothal, wedding, and postwedding celebration, which also combined pre-Christian and postbaptismal elements; and (3) performances by itinerant folk entertainers, the *skomorokhi,* Russian minstrels who also doubled as buffoons, musicians, and animal impersonators.

In addition to these three forms of folk theater that go back to Kievan Russia and earlier, there existed in post-Petrine Russia the institution of (4) pre-Lenten carnival *(maslenitsa, maslenichnoe gulianie),* with its bearded carnival barkers, puppet shows, masked mummers, and trained bears, and (5) the performances of orally transmitted folk plays about peasants, devils, and foreign royalty that were put on by illiterate soldiers and by convicts in Siberian penal settlements. If we consider Stravinsky's major works for the period 1910–1918, we can see that *The Rite of Spring* [Vesna sviashchennaia, Le sacre du printemps] is a musical dramatization of the first of these categories—a pagan seasonal agrarian rite; *Les Noces* [Svadebka, The wedding] sets to music the second of our categories; *Renard* [Baika pro lisu] is, as most Soviet commentators have realized, a modern revival of the spirit of the *skomorokhi; Petrushka,* apart from its protagonist's drama, is a catalogue of *maslenitsa* customs; and *Histoire du soldat,* despite its Swiss disguises, shares features with the soldier and convict folk drama.

Why this musical innovator chose to compose some of his most revolutionary works on subjects taken from archaic and, by his day, mostly defunct preliterary dramatized folklore is a fascinating problem in creative psychology. The years 1907 to 1917 were the time of a great wave of new interest in native Russian art, stripped of the hybridization with Western themes and forms that had predominated in the nineteenth century. Pushkin could write his Russian fairy tales "The Tale of the Fisherman and the Fish" and "The Golden Cockerel" on subjects borrowed from the Brothers Grimm and Washington Irving, respectively. His "Ruslan and Ludmila," ostensibly a folktale about Kievan Russia, combines Russian folklore elements with themes drawn from Western chapbook romances and with stylistic mannerisms borrowed from Voltaire and Evariste Parny, just as the opera Glinka based on this poem weds Russian and Tatar folk songs to musical textures borrowed from Rossini and Weber. A not-dissimilar procedure was followed, *mutatis mutandis,* in the pseudo–folk operas, such as *Sadko* or *The Snow Maiden,* by Stravinsky's teacher, Rimsky-Koraskov. All this is said not to disparage the artistic quality of Pushkin or Glinka or even Rimsky-Korsakov, but to pinpoint the difference between their view of folklore and the one embodied in the work of Stravinsky and his contemporaries, the symbolist and postsymbolist poets and Russian modernist painters of the first two decades of the twentieth century.

Considered from this angle, Stravinsky's first ballet, *The Firebird* [Zhar-ptitsa, L'oiseau de feu], is a product of the nineteenth-century aesthetic. The libretto mingles themes from Russian folklore with elements drawn from Tchaikovsky's *Swan Lake* and Fyodor Sologub's play *Nocturnal Dances,* for which Mikhail Fokine did the choreography one year before he staged *The Firebird* and which had a plot based on a Brothers Grimm tale. The folk songs in *The Firebird* come from a reputable folk song collection and are cited verbatim.[3] They have been selected for their exotic beauty and are couched in the most advanced and elegant musical idiom of the time, French impressionism, just as Glinka and Rimsky-Korsakov used to set tastefully selected folk melodies in internationally approved musical styles of their day.

3. Vershinina, *Rannie balety* pp. 50–52, 58–59.

The use of musical folklore in *Petrushka* could not be more different. As Irina Vershinina has pointed out, Stravinsky's Russian contemporaries were actually shocked by what they saw as his lack of selectivity.[4] Trained musicologists were needed to identify the folk melodies in *The Firebird* (and later in *The Rite*), but any Russian child could recognize the tunes that accompany the street dancers, the coachmen, or the nursemaids in *Petrushka* because they were as familiar as "Home on the Range," "Three Blind Mice," or "When Irish Eyes Are Smiling." Combined with street vendors' cries, barrel organ ditties, the humorous use of an old Easter carol, and hackneyed waltzes by Lanner, this struck the early Russian listeners of *Petrushka* as a gaudy, tasteless mixture, leading the young Sergei Prokofiev to qualify the musical materials of *Petrushka* as "rotten trash" (*trukha*).[5]

In *Petrushka*, Stravinsky had turned his back on both the ethnographic approach and the Western-style sugarcoating of folklore that were implicit in the nineteenth-century Russian musical aesthetic. This process was deepened in *The Rite*, where, in line with the archaist conception, the musical folklore utilized was largely Lithuanian, that is, not only non-Russian, but non-Slavic (the Balts and the Slavs supposedly had common origins in ancient times). But Stravinsky deformed both the Lithuanian and Slavic materials with a sovereign freedom in a manner that may be termed cubistic. Lawrence Morton's and Richard Taruskin's best detective efforts were required to discern them at all.[6]

By the time he came to compose *Les Noces*, *Renard*, and the remarkable peasant songs and choruses of 1914–1919, Stravinsky no longer needed either to cite or to deform folk tunes or popular melodies because he had internalized the structural, modal, and melodic properties of Russian folk music. Pianist Alexei Liubimov declared that, in these works, "archaism of melodies and dynamism of rhythms create an extraordinary impression of a natural grasp of the spirit and style of ancient peasant folklore."[7] All that Stravinsky needed from the folk tradition at this point was the words (usually substandard or in phonetically transcribed dialect) and the subject matter in order to create dazzlingly original Russian music that was free of both ethnography and stylization.

Stravinsky's gradual internalization of Russian musical folklore, traceable from *The Firebird* to *Les Noces*, had a linear progression. The resultant manner had clear parallels in internalization of folklore observable in the work of other Rus-

---

4. Ibid., pp. 81–82.

5. Prokofiev's letter to Nikolai Miaskovsky in S. Prokofiev, *Materialy, dokumenty, vospominaniia* [Materials, documents, memoirs] (Moscow, 1961), p. 645. Cited in Vershinina, *Rannie balety*, p. 74.

6. Lawrence Morton, "Footnotes to Stravinsky: 'Le Sacre du printemps,' " *Tempo* (March 1979): 9–16; Richard Taruskin, "Russian Folk Melodies in *The Rite of Spring*," *Journal of the American Musicological Society* 23 (Fall 1980): 501–43.

7. Alexei Liubimov on the jacket of Lydia Davydova's recording of Stravinsky's songs, *Melodiia* Stereo 33 C 10–08133–4.

sian artists of the period—the paintings of Natalia Goncharova and Marc Chagall, for example, or the narrative poetry of Velimir Khlebnikov and Marina Tsvetaeva.[8] Stravinsky's utilization of folk theater forms during the same period does not follow a linear or chronological pattern, and it may therefore be more convenient to examine each individual case, beginning with the most ancient of these forms and going up to the more modern.

The Rite of Spring and Agrarian Vernal Rites

When the Grand Prince Vladimir decreed the imposition of Christianity as the state religion of Kievan Russia in A.D. 988, he lacked the power and the communication network to compel all his subjects to abandon their earlier Slavic religion. Christianization was followed by many centuries of *dvoeverie*, literally, "dual religion," and pagan survivals lingered on in the countryside well into modern times. With the nineteenth-century introduction of anthropology and ethnography, a wide array of seasonal folk customs and games was easily identified as direct descendants of ancient rituals for welcoming the springtime and expelling the winter, such as had been common since prehistory among various Indo-European tribes. The cults of sun gods Yarilo and Kostroma (who may have been of Slavic, Finnic, or Scandinavian origin) and of the mischievous river nymphs (*rusalki*) and ceremonies of welcoming or expelling them at the onset of spring were practiced in more or less disguised form well into the nineteenth century.

As Vladimir Propp points out, the surviving vernal rites for either welcoming the solar gods or expelling the river nymphs (*rusalia*, the object of which was either to make the local bodies of water safe for a summer of swimming or, because the *rusalki* represented water, to move them from rivers and lakes to the fields and thus assure an ample harvest) followed a similar format.[9] There would be ceremonial songs and processions followed by honoring the central figure, *velichanie*, which corresponds to the episode *Velichanie izbrannoi* in the second part of *The Rite*, usually translated as "Glorification of the Chosen One." The sun god or the river nymph could be impersonated by people or represented by effigies. Whether the honored entity was welcomed or expelled, the effigy was put to ritual death, either by burning or by tearing to shreds. Vladimir Propp compares this to ancient cults of dying and resurrected divinities, which symbolized the return of springtime. Other examples are Osiris in Egypt and Adonis and Persephone in ancient Greece. To read the descriptions of the Yarilo, Kostroma, and

8. See Taruskin's essay in this anthology.

9. V. Ya. Propp, *Russkie agrarnye prazdniki* [Russian agrarian holidays] (Leningrad, 1963).

rusalia ceremonies in V. Vsevolodsky-Gerngross's *History of Russian Theater* (1929), in *The Russian Folk Theater* by Elizabeth A. Warner (1977), and in Propp's cited book is to understand the long-range origins of the theme and the action of *The Rite*.[10]

Its immediate, short-range sources are to be sought in the great interest in prehistory and early Slavic religion in Russian arts in the years that immediately precede the composition of that ballet. The Soviet Stravinsky specialist Valery Smirnov in his 1970 book and Lawrence Morton, apparently independently in 1979, pointed out Sergei Gorodetsky's cycle of poems about Yarilo, written in 1905–1907, as a source of the idea and imagery of his ballet.[11] This is certainly plausible, but there are several other claimants: Alexei Remizov's book about seasonal changes and ancient games connected with them, *Follow the Sun* (Posolon', 1907), for example, or the leading futurist poet Velimir Khlebnikov's series of visionary narrative poems about stone age Russia, published in 1911 and 1912, especially *I and Ye*, in which a stone age maiden is caught in a competition between two rival tribes and condemned to be sacrificed to pagan gods. Another source that would bear more detailed investigation is the essays and paintings of the set designer for *The Rite*, Nikolai Roerich. He was involved in the project since its inception, and some of his earlier paintings bear titles or depict scenes that are reminiscent of certain episodes in the ballet.

Les Noces and Russian Village Weddings

The earliest native historical source, the *Primary Chronicle*, reports the existence of "pagan play acting" and dancing at the weddings of ancient East Slavic tribes. A sixteenth-century text, the *Stoglav* [The book of hundred chapters], complains of the enduring contamination of Christian weddings by pagan survivals. In the 1850s and 1860s, six volumes of *Ethnographic Studies* containing numerous transcribed wedding ceremonies from various regions were published by the Imperial Geographic Society. "The obviously theatrical character, as we understand it, of, for example, the wedding ceremony has enabled many ethnographers to re-

10. Vsevolod Vsevolodsky-Gerngross, *Istoriia russkogo teatra* [A history of Russian theater] (Leningrad, 1929), vol. 1, chap. 2, pp. 99–191, contains a detailed account of dramatically enacted pagan rituals that existed in Russian culture well into modern times. Elizabeth A. Warner, *The Russian Folk Theater* (The Hague, 1977), contains accounts of Kostroma, Yarilo, and *rusalia* ceremonies and their later survivals and transformations. Its bilingual format (Russian texts are copiously cited without translation) makes its use by nonspecialists in Slavic studies problematic.

11. V. V. Smirnov, *Tvorcheskoe formirovanie I. F. Stravinskogo* [Igor Stravinsky's artistic development] (Leningrad, 1970), p. 87. Morton, "Footnotes," pp. 9–16.

cord it in the form of theatrical play . . . "the entire ceremony abounded in magic spells, incantations and, in general, obvious traces of paganism."[12]

With a few individual adjustments, the betrothal ceremony, the *devishnik* (a kind of bridal shower, with unbinding of the tresses and the bride's lament for the loss of her freedom), the blessing of the groom by his parents, and the wedding feast were not spontaneous transactions but enactments of a prearranged, prerehearsed script that had been traditional in that particular village for centuries. As Tatiana's nurse puts it in Pushkin's *Eugene Onegin*: "They unbound my tresses with weeping/And led me to the church with songs." The actual marriage ceremony, which was a prescribed Christian rite, was the only part of the entire wedding not covered by the local ritual. The ritual's potential for theatrical adaptation has been realized since the eighteenth century, when two of the more successful Russian comic operas incorporated scenes of unbinding the bride's tresses, with texts similar to the one used in Stravinsky's ballet-cantata.[13] In 1875, a company of noted Russian actors and actresses brought to Paris an opulent staging of a transcript of a village wedding. In 1923, the State Experimental Theater presented in various cities of the Soviet Union a production called *The Russian Folk Wedding Ceremony*, an entire evening performance that reproduced the same ritual. That was, of course, the year Igor Stravinsky completed the instrumentation of his *Svadebka* (for some reason still known in this country under its French title of *Les Noces*).

What Stravinsky got from Pyotr Kireevsky's collection of folk texts was not a group of songs to be set to music, but a complete script of a ritual that was actually a folk play. He then trimmed and rearranged it to suit his purposes. The version he chose was less riddled with pagan survivals than some other recorded versions (for example, there is no part for the Guard or the Polite One, euphemism for a shaman who took over the priestly functions once the church ceremony was completed).[14] Still, when the Virgin Mary is commanded to bless the wedding and help comb the bridegroom's hair (at **44**) and then is given a direct order by the divided bassos (*Pod' na svad'bu*, which is roughly "Off to the wedding with you!"), we realize that the mother of the Savior is here replacing some ancient fertility goddess. In monotheistic religions, divinities do not get ordered about, but in *The Iliad*, a warrior could order Aphrodite off the battlefield.

---

12. Vsevolodsky-Gerngross, *Istoriia russkogo teatra*, pp. 81–82.

13. *The Miller Who Was a Wizard, a Cheat and a Matchmaker* (1979), with text by Alexander Ablesimov and with a pastiche of popular folk tunes arranged by Mikhail Sokolovsky, and *The St. Petersburg Bazaar* (1782), text and original music by Mikhail Matinsky, better known from the later score recomposed by Vasily Pashkevich. The wedding customs depicted in these eighteenth-century works and subsequently reflected in Stravinsky's masterpiece continued in certain areas in postrevolutionary times. A number of such traditional songs and ceremonies were collected by Soviet folklorists between 1920 and 1960 and published in *Lirika russkoi svad'by* [Russian wedding songs], ed. N. P. Kolpakova (Leningrad, 1973).

14. Vsevolodsky-Gerngross, *Istoriia russkago teatra*, pp. 81–82.

Renard and the *Skomorokhi*

In the early sketches for *Les Noces,* there was to be a role for a *skomorokh,* the minstrel-buffoon. *Skomorokhi* used to provide the entertainment at both royal and peasant weddings and are often mentioned in wedding songs. In the final score, **16** of the first scene, there is mention of a "dashing little *skomorokh,* running in from another village" to distract the bride from her lamentations. In the C. F. Ramuz translation, a singing bird replaces the clown. Ramuz's French translations of the three works of Stravinsky that are most closely connected with the lore and spirit of the *skomorokhi—Pribaoutki, Les Noces,* and especially *Renard—* systemically deprive them of that connection.

Renard is perhaps Stravinsky's least understood work among Western commentators. One gets to read in program notes that this is an Aesopian fable about barnyard animals, and Stravinsky gets praised for his clever imitation of these beasts. Soviet critics, from Boris Asafiev (Igor Glebov) in the early 1920s to Mikhail Druskin in the 1970s, invariably call *Renard* a *skomorosh'e deistvo,* a minstrel show or buffoon comedy. At its basic level, *Renard* depicts four *skomorokhi* in a pre-Petrine village who put on animal masks to perform a satirical, anticlerical skit about the victimization of a wealthy peasant (the Cock) by a con woman disguised as an itinerant nun (the Fox is a Vixen in the Russian text). The Cock's two fellow-peasants, the Tomcat and the Ram, rescue him twice. Then the peasants kill the predator and blame the murder on the hounds of the local noblemen, whereupon the performers remove their masks and demand a payment of a crock of butter for their performance.

The *skomorokhi* are mentioned in chronicles and sermons since the beginning of recorded Russian history. Despite clerical denunciations, they enjoyed a great popularity as purveyors of humor and satire in old Russia. They ceased to exist as a social class due to Tsar Alexis's edicts, which outlawed them in 1648 and, in even harsher terms, in 1657. But they were remembered for centuries in folk songs, folk poetry, wedding rituals, drama, and opera. Their history has been studied by a number of scholars, most authoritatively by the musicologist Nikolai Findeizen, Stravinsky's friend and correspondent.[15] His work has been supple-

15. See Nikolai Findeizen, *Ocherki po istorii muzyki v Rosii* [Studies in the history of music in Russia] (Moscow, 1928), 1:145–70. In addition to being the founder of *Russkaia muzykal'naia gazeta* [Russian music gazette] (published 1894–1918), Findeizen was an important music historian who published monographs on Glinka, Dargomyzhsky, Grieg, Anton Rubinstein, and books on early Russian music. Perhaps his most important work is the posthumous two-volume history of Russian music from antiquity to the eighteenth century.

The Russian text of Stravinsky's letter to him, written in 1912, about the plan of *The Rite of Spring* (apart from a deleted postscript) appears in *I. F. Stravinskii: Stati'i materialy* [I. F. Stravinsky: Essays and documents], ed. L. S. D'iachkova and Boris Yarustovsky (Moscow, 1973). Portions of the letter appeared in translation in Igor Stravinsky and Robert Craft, *The Rite of Spring Sketches 1911–1913* (London, 1969). Various excerpts cited by Craft, Vershinina, and Yarustovsky are all from the same letter. Yarustovský seems to imply there might be other correspondence between Stravinsky and Findeizen at the Saltykov-Shchedrin Library in Leningrad.

mented recently by two very good books on the *skomorokhi* by Anatoly Belkin and Russell Zguta.[16]

The instruments associated with the *skomorokhi* were the *gudok* (a vertically held fiddle), *volynka* (bagpipes), and *gusli* (the Russian psaltery). Stravinsky was fascinated with the sound of *gusli*. In early sketches for *Les Noces*, he intended to impersonate it with harpsichords and cimbaloms. Cimbalom as *gusli* is of course central to the conception of *Renard* (where this instrument is also prominently featured in the Russian text, but not in translations). Stravinsky's most realistic orchestral representation of *gusli* is in the piano and harp duet in the first trio of *Scherzo à la russe* (1944; this combination follows the example of Glinka's *Ruslan and Ludmila*). He was to return to the *gusli* sound once more in the 1954 instrumentation of Four Songs (taken from two earlier sets of songs), where the flute, harp, and guitar suggest a *skomorokhi*-like bagpipe and *gusli* accompaniment.

Folk Theater in *Petrushka*

The folk theater components in *Petrushka* are not as ancient in origin as the ones so far discussed. They date mostly no earlier than the eighteenth century, and they are also far more accessible to Western audiences. There are two points in this regard that I have not seen discussed. One is the importance of the figure of the long-bearded carnival barker, *balagannyi ded*, rather lamely translated as *le compère de la foire*, who appears in the first tableau. These barkers, whose job it was to entertain the crowd and to lure them into the *balagany* (the makeshift barracks where the various performances took place) spoke in lines of rhymed prose of unequal length, known as *raëshnik*. The syncopated, limping rhythms of the *raëshnik* (rather similar in form to the poetry of Ogden Nash, with its wildly varying line lengths) are conveyed in the flute and oboe figure when the curtain goes up (at **4**) in the first tableau of *Petrushka*. *Raëshnik* is also the rhythm of the subsequent passages, marked stringendo at **7**, **17** and **22**. They usually alternate with the cries of the coal vendor (*uglei! uglei!*) that open that tableau.[17]

16. A. A. Belkin, *Russkie skomorokhi* [Russian minstrels] (Moscow, 1975), and Russell Zguta, *Russian Minstrels. A History of the Skomorokhi* (Philadelphia, 1978).

17. The identification of the motive of fourths as "*uglei! uglei!*" ("there's some charcoal!") was made in Vershinina, *Rannie balety*. The author cites Alexander Kastalsky's notations of street vendors' cries, selling coal, herring, and marinated apples, all either jumping up a fourth or filling a downward fourth with lesser intervals. Vershinina demonstrates the derivation from these vendors' cries of the rhythm and the intervals of the opening flute motive and also of the theme of the four cellos at **1** and the oboe solo at bar six of **2.** As to the return of the initial motive in the "Dance of the Nursemaids," someone seems to be selling coal and pickled apples while the nannies are dancing.

Example 1.2. *Raёshnik* Rhythms in *Petrushka*

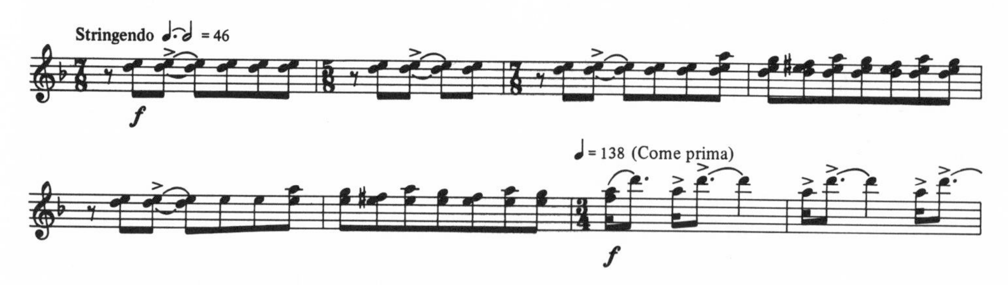

Raёshnik was also the standard verse of the oral folk theater of soldiers and convicts. Ramuz closely imitated its form in his text for *Histoire du soldat*, which makes for an interesting connection between that work and *Petrushka*. The other point concerns the episode of the maskers in the fourth tableau—men disguised as a devil, a pig, a goat, and (added in Fokine's choreography, though not indicated in the score), a woman. These masks, as both Propp's and Zguta's research suggests, go further back in history than the other customs depicted in *Petrushka*.[18] These particular masks indicate connections with both old pagan rites and the usages of the *skomorokhi*.

Histoire du soldat and Oral Folk Theater

The connection of the works so far mentioned with preliterate theater is self-evident. Stravinsky had during the gestation of these works friends and associates who encouraged this interest and could provide him with necessary expertise. The respective roles of Alexandre Benois and Nikolai Roerich in the creation of *Petrushka* and *The Rite* were, as we now know, far more fundamental than Stravinsky remembered when he reminisced about those collaborations in *Conversations with Igor Stravinsky*.[19] The possible connection of Findeizen with the subject matter of *Les Noces* and *Renard* is a topic that will bear investigation.

18. See Propp, *Russkie agrarnye*, pp. 111 (on the significance of animal disguises) and pp. 116– (on cross-dressing of the sexes during winter holidays); and Russell Zguta, "Origins of the Russian Puppet Theater: An Alternative Hypothesis," *Slavic Review* 33 (December 1974): 712 (on the antiquity of these forms of disguise).

19. In Igor Stravinsky and Robert Craft, *Conversations with Igor Stravinsky* (1959; rpt. Berkeley and Los Angeles, 1980), the sections on Roerich, pp. 94–95, and on Benois, pp. 97–98, create the impression that Stravinsky selected these artists to design his ballets after his conception of the two works was formed and his music was almost completed. But, as Stravinsky's letters to Roerich dating from 1910–1912 and Valery Smirnov's essay on the role of Benois in the genesis of *Petrushka* conclusively demonstrate, the two artists participated in creating the ballets they designed from their very inception. Each contributed important ideas for the stage action and musical realization of *The Rite* or *Petrushka*, respectively. See Igor Stravinsky's letters to Nikolai

Things may seem more dubious in the case of *Histoire du soldat*. After all, the only folkloric component here is the tale from Alexander Afanasiev's collection, which Stravinsky and Ramuz turned into a musical play and moved the setting to Switzerland. Ramuz, who in his memoirs could not even recall Afanasiev's name and who had no knowledge of any Russian traditions, could not have been familiar with the institution of the oral folk theater of soldiers and convicts, which arose in Russia in the eighteenth century in imitation of literate, professional theater and which still existed in the early twentieth century.[20]

Yet the similarities of *Histoire du soldat* to plays of this genre cannot be overlooked. In Chapter II of Part One of his semiautobiographical novel *Notes from the House of the Dead,* Fyodor Dostoevsky described a performance by convicts in a Siberian penal colony of a folk play based on plays and operas about Don Juan, a performance he had actually witnessed in the late 1840s. The play was accompanied by a raucous little orchestra of squeaky violins and balalaikas, and it featured a virtuoso contribution by a tambourine player. Other plays of this type were collected and described in the early twentieth century. Alexei Remizov, the influential writer, who may have had a hand in the libretto of *The Firebird* and whom Stravinsky helped out financially in Paris in the 1930s,[21] based his very successful *Comedy of the Devils* (1907) on such plays. He later adapted the most famous play of this genre, *Tsar Maximilian,* popular for almost two centuries in peasant amateur theatricals. Other twentieth-century playwrights, such as Zamyatin and Sologub, also drew on this type of play, whose logic, as Remizov remarked, is the logic of dreams.

Typical of this theater are deformations of foreign legends (*Histoire du soldat* is a deformation of the Faust legend, just as the play Dostoevsky saw was a deformation of Don Juan); interactions of common Russian folk (soldiers or peasants) with foreign, non-Russian royalty; the juxtaposition of everyday mundane reality of military barracks or peasant life with the supernatural, usually represented by the devil; and an anachronistic mixture of a fairy tale world with ultramodern realia, such as the stock exchange, the telephone, tango, and ragtime in *Histoire du soldat*. Combined with the French versification that seems to imitate the *raëshnik* of Russian folk dramas, these features indicate that the Russian oral folk theater connections of *Histoire du soldat* deserve to be investigated in greater depth.

Roerich, introduced and annotated by Irina Vershinina, in *Sovetskaia muzyka,* no. 8 (August 1966): 57–63 and V. Smirnov, "A. N. Benua—librettist 'Petrushki' " [Alexandre Benois, the librettist of *Petrushka*], in D'iachkova and Yarustovsky, *I. F. Stravinskii,* pp. 155–62.

20. C. F. Ramuz, *Souvenirs sur Igor Stravinsky* (Paris, n.d.), p. 79. Pierre Meylan in his book on the collaboration between Ramuz and Stravinsky, *Une amitié célèbre* (Lausanne, 1962), denies that *Histoire du soldat* owes anything to Russian folklore (p. 65). Unaware of its Russian ties, Meylan attempts to derive its dramatic conception from French medieval *fabliaux*. His book repeatedly implies that Ramuz was the author rather than the translator of the texts of *Les Noces* and *Renard,* though Meylan is clearly aware of the true facts.

21. Stravinsky and Craft, *Pictures and Documents,* p. 642, n. 10.

Conclusions

In a telling footnote to *Stravinsky in Pictures and Documents*, Robert Craft expressed regret that "Stravinsky never explained the anthropological background of *Les Noces* . . . the rituals and cultural traditions of which Western audiences are largely unaware."[22] The regret is of course also applicable to the rest of Stravinsky's oeuvre of the second decade of this century. When he was creating these epochal scores, he was addressing a Russian audience, for which such explanations would have been redundant. Foreign audiences, with whom these works were not yet established, might have been put off by too much ethnography or anthropology in program notes. In later years, Stravinsky was reluctant to discuss the folklore sources of his earlier compositions, not due to snobbery or reactionary politics, as has sometimes been suggested, but because his artistic tastes had undergone a complex evolution that caused him to lose interest in that whole sphere and also because he had forgotten a great deal. Just how much he forgot can be seen in his discussion in *Expositions and Developments* of his *Podbliudnye* [Dish-divination songs]. Stravinsky not only mistranslates the title of *Saucers* but gets the method of divination all wrong, the method that is described quite precisely in Pushkin's *Eugene Onegin*, Chapter 5, viii, where the text of the first of these songs is also quoted.[23] Speaking of *Renard* in the same book, Stravinsky can-

22. Ibid., p. 619, n. 236.

23. As outlined by Propp, *Russkie agrarnye*, p. 108, dish-divination songs were sung during Yuletide by young women in rural areas as an accompaniment to a special fortune-telling game. The game consisted of placing on the table a large dish filled with water in which each participant would put her ring, comb, or some other small trinket, after which the dish was covered with a towel. Next came the singing of the *podbliudnye* (literally, "in the presence of the dish") songs, whose texts dealt with allegorical descriptions of agricultural activities, gigantic symbolic animals, and possession of gold, jewels, and other treasures. Most of these songs featured the obligatory refrain of *slava!* or *slavna!* ("glory!" or "glorious!"). During the singing, the trinkets were extracted one by one from under the towel over the dish, and as each trinket was withdrawn, its owner's fortune was predicted in accordance with the imagery of the line being sung.

In addition to studies by folklorists, such as Propp, this divination game was described in two of the best-known Russian literary works of the early nineteenth century: *Eugene Onegin* and Vasily Zhukovsky's much-anthologized romantic ballad "Svetlana" (1812). Stravinsky himself, after completing his four dish-divination choruses (composed between 1914 and 1917), returned to this genre once more in 1919 in the third of his Four Russian Songs for voice and piano, which bears the title *Podbliudnaia* and has the typical refrain of *slavna!* Yet, discussing these choruses with Robert Craft in *Expositions and Developments* (1962; rpt. Berkeley and Los Angeles, 1981), pp. 118–119, Stravinsky stated: "Choruses of this sort were sung by the peasants while fortune-tellers read their fingerprints on the smoke-blackened bottoms of saucers."

This is either an aberration of memory or an *ad hoc* invention. No such method of fortune telling is associated with *podbliudyne* songs by any Russian poet or student of folklore (nor does it seem likely that reading fingerprints was known to Russian peasants in the eighteenth and nineteenth centuries). The saucers, whose mention by Stravinsky has saddled these choruses with their unsuitable English title, may have come from his confusing the Russian word for "dish," *(bliudo)* with the one for "saucer" *(bliudtse)*. Or Stravinsky may have been thinking that the English "saucer" had the same meaning as the French *saucière*. Be that as it may, the statement in *Expositions and Developments* has added further cultural barriers to appreciation in the West of this lovely

not remember the Russian title of this work and confuses the Russian *gusli* with the Yugoslav bowed instrument, the *guzla*.[24]

While Stravinsky was sharing his reminiscences with Robert Craft, his energies were still occupied with creating more new music. If the choice were between total recall of his "Russian" period and the composition of *Agon, The Flood*, and *Requiem Canticles*, we would all surely choose music over documentation and memories. But now that Igor Fyodorovich is gone, those of us who know something about Russian culture must try to supply the missing pieces.

---

choral work, made even more attractive by Stravinsky's 1954 rearrangement of it for voices and four horns.

Even a person as close to Stravinsky as Robert Craft is quite at sea about what the titles of the individual choruses should be. He calls the first of them "Saints' Day in Chigisakh" or "Christ in Chigisakh" or "Chigisakh Across Yauza" in *Pictures and Documents*, p. 604. In all three versions, the name of the village Chigisy appears in the locative case, which suggests that Mr. Craft's informants did not know Russian grammar. This is the song cited in *Eugene Onegin*. In his commentary to his translation of this novel, Vladimir Nabokov (vol. 2, p. 497) includes the correct translation of the title, which is "In Our Saviour's Parish in Chigisy Beyond the Yauza," and of the entire text. There is no way of knowing from the existing English translations that the song opens with a description of a brick church built in 1485 and ends with a portent of death, information that Nabokov supplies.

The 1932 J. & W. Chester edition of *Podbliudyne* accompanies the title of the second chorus, "Ovsen'," with a note that this is "A beneficient solar deity honoured in Russian mythology." White repeats this information in *Stravinsky*, p. 211, though no study of pre-Christian Russian mythology mentions any such being. Robert Craft, *Pictures and Documents*, calls this chorus "Autumn," apparently because his informants have confused "Ovsen" with *osen'*, which indeed means autumn. This is a particularly absurd mistake because a check with Vladimir Dahl's standard *Dictionary of the Great Russian Language*, shows that *ovsen'* (known in some areas as *avsen'* or *tausen'*) was the name of the first day of spring in the pre-Christian Russian calendar, according to which the new year began on the first day of March. Although the meaning was lost in later centuries, the word remained in some peasant songs as an exclamation that conveyed the hope for a good harvest (see Propp, *Russkie agrarnye*, pp. 38–39).

24. The Russian title of *Renard*, printed in recent editions of the score, is *Baika* (a regional word for "story" or "fairy tale"). The first edition had a more extended title that means "The Story of the Vixen, the Cock, the Tomcat, and the Ram." In Craft, *Expositions and Developments*, p. 119, Stravinsky, claiming to cite the original Russian title of this work, begins with a different word for "fairy tale," *skazka* (which is the first word in the Russian title of *Histoire du soldat*), and follows it with a wrong preposition, which puts the four animals (with the Cock preceding the Fox) in a different grammatical case from the one they were in in the first edition. The South Slavic *guzla* (possibly suggested to Stravinsky by Propser Mérimée's volume of faked Yugoslav poetry, *La guzla*, which Pushkin translated into Russian) has nothing to do with the Russian psaltery, *gusli*, which inspired the sonority of *Renard*.

2 From Subject to Style: Stravinsky and the Painters

RICHARD TARUSKIN

IN A PREVIOUS study of Stravinsky's use of authentic Russian folk material in *The Rite of Spring*, I ended by contrasting his approach with that of his teacher.

> The difference . . . was that Rimsky-Korsakov sought in the songs of Russian folk ceremonial only thematic material, which he then subjected to a treatment in the style of the mainstream of European art music that became, as his career wore on, increasingly conventional, even academic. Stravinsky, by seeking in folk songs something far more basic to his musical vocabulary and technique, was to use them as part of his self-liberation from that artistic mainstream, and as things turned out, its downright subversion.[1]

With this went the observation that the folk tunes in *The Rite* were not displayed as Rimsky might have displayed them. Instead, Stravinsky absorbed them into the fabric of his music until they became utterly concealed as specific entities, retaining at best only a generalized stylistic identity while contributing to some of the most startlingly novel musical constructs in the ballet.

All this was unprecedented in Russian music, and basic questions began to nag: Why Stravinsky? Why only Stravinsky? What impelled him to take this new approach, and what guided him in realizing his new aims? A search for the answers to these questions led straight out of music and into the visual arts, where experiments like Stravinsky's had by the time of *The Rite* a forty-year tradition in Russia and were just reaching a radical new phase uncannily akin to Stravinsky's breakthrough in his famous "neoprimitive" ballet. I propose, then, that the main aesthetic impulse behind the masterpieces of Stravinsky's "Russian" period—*The Rite, Les Noces, Renard*, and all those wonderful "Swiss" songs—lay in the so-called "neonationalist" trend of late nineteenth-century Russian fine and applied arts; that Stravinsky was the only Russian composer fully to realize the implications of this tendency in music; and that it was a most important—perhaps *the* most important—factor in the formation not only of his modernistic musical lan-

1. Richard Taruskin, "Russian Folk Melodies in *The Rite of Spring*," *Journal of the American Musicological Society* 23 (Fall 1980): 543.

guage, but also of his modernist aesthetic. Antecedents to the specific musical means of this realization may be found in a revolution that was taking place in musical folkloristics itself around the time of Stravinsky's early maturity and in Stravinsky's brilliant and original synthesis of the folkloristic and modernistic traditions of Russian art music—two strains that had previously been cultivated in parallel, always coexisting but never meeting.

I

When Mily Balakirev died in 1910, musicians in Russia sensed the closing of an epoch. Although one *kuchkist*, César Cui, still lived and would actually survive the Revolution, no one took any notice of him any longer.[2] To all intents and purposes, the "heroic generation" of Russian composers, and all that it had stood for, was now a thing of the past. In his obituary for the old warrior in the "advanced" arts journal *Apollon*, the critic Viacheslav Karatygin came eagerly to bury Balakirev, not praise him, sounding meanwhile a sententious death knell for Russian musical nationalism as a whole:

> Before our eyes there has occurred, or rather there is occurring, a new revolution in Russian music. There is taking place a certain denationalization of it alongside a noticeable invasion of it by elements of Western European "impressionism." Debussy and Ravel, Reger and Strauss have taken the place of Schumann and Berlioz in our musical history. . . . But in order for a new fertilization of Russian musical thought with the aid of Western European creative achievements to take place painlessly and without the eventual loss of our musical physiognomy, it was necessary that in preparation that physiognomy be shown fully. And this was the task accomplished by the members of the "New Russian School."[3]

2. "Kuchkist" from *Moguchaia kuchka*, the Russian sobriquet for the group known in English as the Mighty Five.

Cui was poignantly aware of his neglect. In public, he bore it with a widely admired dignity, but letters during his late years abound with raillery against Karatygin in particular ("a modernist with little talent but a high opinion of himself") and modernism in general ("instead of music they have sounds; instead of beauty they have deformity; instead of sense, nonsense; instead of talent, impudence and effrontery; instead of elegance, crudity"). Because his views accorded so well with those of Soviet leadership in the late Stalin period, these letters were published in a lavish edition (Tsezar Antonovich Kiui, *Izbrannye pis'ma* [Selected letters] [Leningrad, 1955]; the foregoing citations are from pp. 455, 469). Together with Stasov's late criticism, Cui's letters shed an interesting sidelight on the development of Russian modernism.

3. Viacheslav Karatygin, "Milii Alekseevich Balakirev 1837–1910," *Apollon*, no. 10 (September 1910): 54.

Seen this way, the *kuchkist* period had merely been a kind of adolescence Russian music was now happily on the point of outgrowing. And who were the "denationalizers"? Scriabin, obviously, above all, but also the "young Russian composers" to whom Karatygin devoted an admiring article in the very next issue of *Apollon*. Leading the pack were the two outstanding pupils of Rimsky-Korsakov's last years:

> I think I will not be mistaken if I begin my little list of the most significant contemporary Petersburgers with the names of [Maximilian] Steinberg and Stravinsky. Neither of them, it is true, is as yet a mature creative artist, but both of them are finished musicians in complete command of the craft of their art, willing to tackle and easily able to solve new problems of technique and color, freely and to a considerable extent originally and convincingly working their changes upon those basic matters of form, thematic content, harmony, polyphony, and sonority which are of lively current interest.[4]

Karatygin goes on to give the most complete characterization ever made in print of the pre-*Firebird* Stravinsky:

> The essential features of his talent are these: an inclination toward "major" moods—brisk, cheerful, at times humorous—and also a striving to achieve a general exterior smartness and splendor in his music. Stravinsky's ideas are always natural; they flow and develop very freely, as untouched by the slightest vulgarity as they are by the dubious means so often resorted to by composers of small gifts: harmonic caprice, artificial angularity, tendentiousness of line and color.[5]

This is pretty faint praise. The picture that emerges from Karatygin's description is that of a well-behaved composer with conventional and superficial aspirations—reminiscent, in fact, of Stravinsky's unfriendly recollections of Glazunov. Indeed, as Karatygin continues, he noticeably cools to his subject. About the Symphony in E♭, he complains that "for all [its] significant musical merits, the general impression it makes is rather external." Finally, there is this perhaps knowingly delivered coup de grace:

> However highly we may value the musical wit of Stravinsky's latest works—the *Scherzo fantastique* and especially the orchestral fantasia *Fireworks*, a piece dedicated to Steinberg and absolutely dazzling in its immense richness of harmonic and coloristic invention—still and all one must admit that from the point of view of musical interest and profundity of musical ideas, Stravinsky's work is much inferior to Steinberg's.[6]

---

4. Viacheslav Karatygin, "Molodye russkie kompozitory" [Young Russian composers], *Apollon*, no. 11 (October–November 1910): 36.

5. Ibid., p. 40.

6. Ibid.

We need look no further than this assessment—which, by all accounts, echoed Rimsky's own—to find at least one powerful motivation for Stravinsky's modernist revolt,[7] not to mention the fuming jealousy that remained so astonishingly alive in Stravinsky's recollections of Steinberg in *Expositions and Developments* a half-century later.[8]

Up to 1910, however, Stravinsky remained a docile Beliaevetz, that is, a member of the school of St. Petersburg composers trained by Rimsky-Korsakov, Glazunov, and Liadov and supported by the generosity of the millionaire timber merchant Mitrofan Beliaev. Although he died in 1903, Beliaev left endowments that kept his famous publishing house (which issued Stravinsky's *Faun and Shepherdess* in 1908), his series of Russian Symphony concerts, and his annual Glinka Prize (won by Stravinsky in 1909 with the *Scherzo fantastique*) all going strong. Beliaev, in fact, succeeded where Anton Rubinstein had failed in setting up an establishment governing all aspects of musical creation and performance, which provided composers willing and able to conform to its standards and ideals with a kind of cradle-to-grave career insurance. Few rebelled from within, though many taunted from without. An example that has a certain ironic appeal where Stravinsky is concerned is an attack on Beliaev published in Diaghilev's journal *Mir iskusstva* [The world of art] during its first year of existence. Signed with the typical "Miriskusnik" pseudonym Silenus, after the leader of the satyrs, the article, entitled "The Musical Artel," was the work of Alfred Nurok, soon to be a founder of the maverick concert series Evenings of Contemporary Music and an important early Stravinsky mentor after Rimsky-Korsakov's death. Chiefly devoted to a review of one of the Beliaev-sponsored Russian Symphony concerts, the article contains a withering general assessment of the great patron's effect on Russian musical life that might have gone straight into Stravinsky's *Autobiography* some thirty-seven years later.

> Mr. Beliaev's Maecenas activities bear a very special imprint. His undeniably lavish patronage of Russian music of the newest variety does not, unfortunately, so much facilitate the development of the talents of gifted but as yet unrecognized composers, as it encourages young people who have successfully completed their conservatory course to cultivate productivity come what may, touching little upon the question of their creative abilities. Mr. Beliaev encourages industry above all, and under his aegis musical composition has assumed the character of an artel, or even a crafts industry. The music of Messrs. [Fyodor] Akimenko [1876–1945, Stravinsky's first theory teacher], [Alexander] Kopylov [1854–1911], [Konstantin] Antipov [1859–19?], [Nikolai] Art-

7. For evidence of Rimsky's favoritism toward Steinberg, see Vasilii Yastrebstev, *Moi vospominaniia o Nikolae Andreeviche Rimskom-Korsakove*, vol. 2 (Leningrad, 1960), pp. 403, 441, 456, 485–86, 487, etc.

8. ". . . one of these ephemeral, prize-winning, front-page types, in whose eyes conceit for ever burns, like an electric light in daytime" (Igor Stravinsky and Robert Craft, *Expositions and Developments* [1962; rpt. Berkeley and Los Angeles, 1981], p. 45).

> sybushev [1858–1937], and the rest of these handicraftsmen-composers all possess the same dubious virtues and manifest the same creative impotence.[9]

Thanks largely to Beliaev, the same ironic transformation had occurred in Russian musical life as had taken place in the art world under the patronage of Tsar Alexander III, whose reign happened to commence the same year as Beliaev's publishing activity (1882): the radical mavericks of the 1860s became the entrenched and reactionary establishment of the nineties. Ossified *kuchkism* took its place alongside ossified *peredvizhnichestvo* in the rear guard of artistic creativity.[10] Both movements had originated as nationalistic upsurges against a neoclassical academicism. They now became academic styles themselves, every bit as rigid as those against which they had rebelled, though in both cases a huge amount of lip service continued to be paid to national character, particularly by their great tribune, the aging Vladimir Stasov (1824–1906). This national character, however, had far less to do with style than with subject matter and what might be described as ethos.[11] Folklore as such held little interest for latterday *kuchkists* and *peredvizhniki*, and folk art was positively scorned. You could pay a *peredvizhnik* no greater insult than to describe his work as *lubochnyi*. To compare his work with a peasant woodcut (*lubok*) was to call it technically inept and aesthetically crude.[12] Similarly, when Russian composers of the Beliaev circle affected a folkloristic idiom, they imitated the cultivated style of Balakirev and Rimsky-Korsakov, not the original model.[13] And they did it more and more rarely; by 1880, Rimsky-Korsakov had become aesthetically so remote from actual folk music that he was among those most hostile to the efforts of Iulii Melgunov (1846–1893), a young Moscow ethnographer who had made the first attempts to transcribe "Russian Songs Directly from the Voices of the People," to quote the title of his first publication.[14] "Barbaric," sniffed Rimsky on seeing these primitive heterophonic harmonizations, unwittingly echoing the judgment made only about a dozen years earlier by some unnamed German pedagogue in Prague who

---

9. Silèn [Alfred Nurok], "Muzykal'nyi artel' " [The musical artel], *Mir iskusstva*, no. 21–22 (1899): 79.

10. "Peredvizhnichestvo" from *peredvizhniki*, the nickname of the radical realist painters who seceded from the Academy in 1863 and later formed the *Tovarishchestvo peredvizhnykh khudozhestvennykh vystavok* [Association of traveling art exhibits]. These painters are often called the "Wanderers" in English, but that gives the wrong impression that they were nomads.

11. The best source for an understanding of late *kuchkist* and *peredvizhnik* aesthetics is Stasov's synoptic *Iskusstvo XIX veka* [Art in the XIX century], originally published in 1901. Rpt. in Vladimir Vasilievich Stasov, *Izbrannye sochineniia* [Selected works], vol. 3 (Moscow, 1952), pp. 485–755.

12. Elizabeth Valkenier, *Russian Realist Art* (Ann Arbor, 1977), p. 122.

13. For a detailed characterization of this style, see Richard Taruskin, "How the Acorn Took Root: A Tale of Russia," *19th-Century Music* 6 (Spring 1983): 189–212.

14. Iulii Nikolaevich Melgunov, *Russkie pesni neposredstvenno s golosov naroda i s ob'iasneniiami izdannye* [Russian songs directly from the voices of the people published with explanatory notes] (Moscow, 1879).

was shown that *kuchkist* article of faith, Balakirev's folk song anthology of 1866: "*Ganz falsch*."[15]

Stravinsky was heir to these attitudes and prejudices. Of his pre-*Firebird* compositions, only the Symphony in E♭ incorporates folk material, in two stereotypically conventional places: the trio of the scherzo, where a tune later to find a famous home in *Petrushka* makes a preliminary, plushly packaged, Glazunovian appearance, and the finale, where the allusion to the Jackdaw Song (*Chicher-Yacher*) is little more than an in-joke, hardly meant to be noticed by anyone not meant to share it. Not that the symphony lacks national character! On the contrary, its every bar proclaims its Russianness. But by the time Stravinsky was coming of age, Russian art music had developed a whole barrage of distinctive mannerisms and clichés, and it was to this tradition that the young Stravinsky owed fealty. Even in his Gorodetzky songs of 1907–1908, the texts of which are imitation folk poems (albeit of a rather recherché symbolist type), the music keeps a safe distance from the soil, getting no closer than Musorgskian tintinnabulations out of *Boris Godunov*—a Russian art-music cliché if ever there was one. When Stravinsky aimed at a folklike lyricism in these songs, the music came out sounding like Grieg. Clearly this was a composer who knew little native folk music and may have wished to know even less. His attitudes mirrored perfectly those of his peer group and of the historical moment in Russian music as defined by Karatygin. He was as unlikely a nationalist at this point as he was a modernist.[16]

It was when his peer group underwent a radical change that Stravinsky's stylistic orientation followed suit. This new peer group was, of course, the latterday *Mir iskusstva* circle around Diaghilev, who had commissioned *The Firebird* with what still seems uncanny prescience after hearing the *Scherzo fantastique* in 1909. The new circle into which Stravinsky eagerly moved contained scarcely a musician, unless one wants to count Nurok or Walter Nouvel. It was a world of artists and dancers, one that took the dimmest possible view of the ossified *kuchkist* traditions in which Stravinsky had been brought up and had a radically different attitude toward the folk heritage. For a preliminary assessment of their impact on the young composer, we may look to the very same issue of *Apollon* that contained Karatygin's obituary for Balakirev. There we may read a review by the art critic Yakov Tugenhold of the 1910 *Saison russe* in Paris, which had included the premiere of *The Firebird*, a work as yet unheard in Russia and therefore unknown to Karatygin. Tugenhold's description of the ballet—and luckily, because he was an art critic, he describes much more than the music—gives a strong sense of the

15. Cf. Alfred J. Swan, *Russian Music and Its Sources in Chant and Folk Song* (New York, 1973), p. 136; Edward Garden, *Balakirev* (New York, 1967), pp. 57–58.

16. Not even the harmonic effects in *Fireworks* are really modernist. Stravinsky was merely playing with the "few flimsy enharmonic devices" he had learned from his teacher in a particularly concentrated and systematic way (see Igor Stravinsky and Robert Craft, *Memories and Commentaries* [1959; rpt. Berkeley and Los Angeles, 1981], p. 59).

new attitude toward folklore and its role in the renovation of the visual arts in Russia.

> Despite all the cosmopolitanism of our art, one already sees the beginnings of a new and long hoped-for style in Russian archaism. The folk, formerly the object of the artist's pity, is becoming increasingly the source of artistic style. To its inexhaustible living mine music has returned, and now art is returning along with choreography. *The Firebird,* this ballet based on Slavonic myth, these ballet numbers (*tantsy*) transformed into folk dance (*plias*), this music, suffused with folk melodies, this painting by Golovine, brocaded with antique patterns (even to the point of being *too* patterned and honey-caked)—is this not the very latest attainment of our art? Before us are not official Stasovian cockerels nor even a showpiece ballet divertissement like *Le Festin,* no patriotic display of our "national countenance," but a serious longing for the open spaces of folk mythology (*toska po vol'noi stikhii narodnogo mifotvorchestva*).[17]

Stravinsky's music, however powerfully it may have contributed to the ballet's effectiveness, was far less deserving of these specific accolades than the visual aspects of the work. Conventional and derivative in its use of folklore, the score harked back in this, as in so many other ways, to the immediate precedent set by Rimsky-Korsakov and the remoter example of Glinka.[18] But the aesthetic tendency represented by *The Firebird* as a whole is captured to perfection in Tugenhold's description, particularly in his marvelously succinct sentence about the artist's pity versus artistic style. It sums up a whole generation of controversy between those who looked back upon the Russian artists of the sixties as philistines whose work was "one big slap in the face of Apollo," in the words of Benois, and those who regarded the younger generation as "spiritual beggars," to quote the title of Stasov's anguished review of the first four issues of *Mir iskusstva.*[19]

II

How ironic, then, that if we should attempt to locate the source of the new attitude toward folk art as the stylistic inspirer of modern art, or what has been aptly

17. Yakov Tugenhold, "Russkii sezon' v Parizhe" [Russian season in Paris], *Apollon,* no. 10 (1910): 21. *Le Festin* was a "suite of dances" presented in Paris in 1909, to music by Rimsky-Korsakov, Glinka, Tchaikovsky, Glazunov, and Musorgsky. In it, the "Blue Bird" pas de deux from *The Sleeping Beauty* (arranged for small orchestra in 1941 by Stravinsky on commission from Kirstein and Balanchine) was presented under the title "The Firebird."

18. See Richard Taruskin, "From *Firebird* to *The Rite:* Folk Elements in Stravinsky's Scores," *Ballet Review* 10 (Summer 1982): 74–76.

19. Alexandre Benois, "Vrubel'," *Mir iskusstva,* no. 10 (1903): 40. "Nishchie dukhom" in Stasov, *Izbrannye sochineniia,* vol. 3, pp. 232–38.

called the "professional assimilation of . . . tendencies inherent in Russian folk art,"[20] we are led straight to the work of Stasov himself, to the very apostle of *kuchkism* and *peredvizhnichestvo*.

At the invitation of the St. Petersburg Society for the Advancement of Art, Stasov prepared a substantial essay, the first of its kind in Russia, on "Russian Folk Ornament," which was published in 1872 in a lavish edition incorporating 215 illustrations on 75 plates.[21] This was an ambitious compendium of ornamental motifs systematically culled from embroideries, lace, wood and bone carvings, and handicrafts in metal, ceramics, enamel, and glass. Special attention was paid to capitals in old manuscripts (especially valuable from the archaeological point of view in that they were datable), where many of the same motifs were encountered as in the peasant handicrafts. Stasov sorted these motifs into four basic thematic categories: (1) geometrical figures (stars, crosses, intersecting lines), (2) flora (stylized floral patterns, garlands, branches, trees), (3) fauna (birds and beasts, often mythological, fantastic, two-headed, and so forth), and (4) human figures. All, even the last, were often stylized to the point of abstraction. Stasov typically devoted much space to the question of ethnic purity and was quick to conclude that many, if not most, Russian ornamental patterns were borrowed from the East.[22]

From our point of view, the most important aspect of Stasov's treatise is that he did not limit his view of the significance of the material he was presenting to archaeological or documentary values, but saw in it a potentially direct stimulus for contemporary art:

> If one looks upon Russian folk designs from the purely artistic, aesthetic point of view, then one cannot help but find here intriguing and very tasteful models of such a play of lines, such a masterly deployment of the patterns themselves and of their interstitial backgrounds, as must testify to a highly developed artistic sensibility and proficiency, and must prove a precious guide and counsel to our contemporary artist, when he shall wish to create in the area and in the character of our national art.[23]

---

20. John Bowlt, *Russian Art 1875–1975* (New York, 1976), p. 7.

21. Vladimir Vasilievich Stasov, *Russkii narodnyi ornament* [Russian folk ornament] (St. Petersburg, 1872). It had been anticipated by the work of a German scholar, Felix Lay, *Sudslavische Ornament* (Vienna, 1871). But this book dealt not with Russian but with Balkan artifacts. In 1887, Stasov reworked and expanded the essay into an imposing monograph entitled *Slavianskii i Vostochnyi Ornament* [Slav and Eastern ornament], "famous and unequalled" to this day in the estimation of a leading Western expert (Bowlt, *Russian Art*, p. 23).

22. In a like manner, Stasov had sought to rock the world of Russian ethnography a few years previously with his treatise *Proiskhozhdenie russkikh bylin* [The origin of the Russian byliny] (1868). This was a facile and shallow attempt to jump on the "Benfeyist" bandwagon then fashionable in folkloristic studies, which sought to trace anything and everything to India. See Richard Taruskin, *Opera and Drama in Russia* (Ann Arbor, 1981), p. 245.

23. *Sobranie sochinenii V. V. Stasova* [Collected works of V. V. Stasov] vol. 1 (St. Petersburg, 1894), col. 187.

Stasov probably had nothing more in mind than authenticity of detail, and he certainly had no inkling of the huge development of neonationalist art that was to take place beginning almost before his ink was dry. But his work undeniably provided the first powerful nudge in that direction.

The next name that deserves mention is that of Viktor Gartman (1834–1873) of *Pictures at an Exhibition* fame. A friend and protégé of Stasov, he was among the earliest Russian artists regularly to employ authentic Slav ornament in his architectural designs and handicrafts.[24] His mixture of media could be naively indiscriminate, as in his most famous design, the Great Gate at Kiev, whose dominant motifs were adapted from masculine and feminine headdresses, well meriting the sally directed at early "neo-Russian" architecture—that it was a matter of "marble towels and brick embroideries."[25] But Gartman was perhaps the earliest Russian artist on whom folk art exerted the kind of direct stylistic influence predicted by Stasov; in fact, his work was very likely foremost in Stasov's mind when he made the prediction.

Gartman is a particularly indispensable link in our chain because in 1873 his architectural services were engaged by the railroad tycoon Savva Mamontov (1841–1918), who was to be for neonationalist art what the textile merchant Pavel Tretiakov had been to the realist school. Besides designing four buildings for the Mamontov estate at Abramtsevo, Gartman became the first supervisor of the art colony and crafts workshop founded there under the influence of William Morris and the English arts and crafts movement. By common consent among art historians, this was the "cradle of modern art in Russia."[26] Gartman died suddenly the same year he was hired. He was succeeded by the brothers Vasnetsov, the Polenovs (husband and wife), and Valentin Serov, the composer's son, later (in Stravinsky's words) the "conscience" of the World of Art movement and the Ballets Russes, who literally grew up at Abramtsevo.[27]

After the state monopoly on theaters was abrogated in 1882, Mamontov branched out and founded his Private Opera Troupe in 1885. The very first production—Rimsky-Korsakov's *Snow Maiden* [Snegurochka] designed by Viktor Vasnetsov—was a milestone in the development of neonationalist art for many reasons: for the dazzling success with which folk ornamental motifs and color harmonies were assimilated into the designs, for the integration of the whole production into a fairly self-conscious Slavonic *Gesamtkunstwerk*, and in particular for

24. Examples of Gartman's neonationalist work may be seen in the illustrations to Alfred Frankenstein, "Victor Hartmann and Modeste Musorgsky," *Musical Quarterly* 25, no. 3 (1939): 268–91, and in the International Music Publishers edition of *Pictures at an Exhibition* (New York, 1952).

25. N. Sultanov, "Vozrozhdenie russkogo iskusstva" [The Renaissance of Russian art], *Zodchii* [The architect], no. 2 (1881): 11. Quoted in Bowlt, *Russian Art*, p. 26.

26. Camilla Gray, *The Russian Experiment in Art 1863–1922* (London, 1962), p. 9.

27. See Igor Stravinsky and Robert Craft, *Conversations with Igor Stravinsky* (1959; rpt. Berkeley and Los Angeles, 1980), p. 97, and Stravinsky and Craft, *Expositions and Developments*, p. 25.

establishing the tradition of collaboration between musicians and artists that made the musical stage the main "theater of operations," so to speak, of the neonationalist movement. This provided a powerful precedent and stimulus to the later Diaghilev enterprises through which Stravinsky met his destiny.[28]

By the 1890s, others were emulating Mamontov's patronage of neonationalist art and artists. Princess Maria Tenisheva (1867–1928), who around 1895 set up an arts colony and workshop on an estate called Talashkino near Smolensk in central Russia, with the avowed purpose of "doing better than Abramtsevo," eventually surpassed Mamontov.[29] Her upbringing, unlike Mamontov's, had been aristocratic, and her tastes were self-consciously highbrow. The artists she attracted no longer had attenuated connections with the *peredvizhniki*, but were inclined toward the art nouveau trends in the West, even as they continued to nurture an intense interest in, and derive inspiration from, the same Russian crafts and antiquities cultivated at Abramtsevo. The artists of the Talashkino circle—Golovin, Korovin, Maliutin, Bilibin, Roerich, Vrubel, Somov, Grabar, Serebriakova—formed the nucleus (along with the leaders Benois and Bakst) of the soon-to-be-born World of Art. They were the creators of an authentic Russian *Jugendstil*, and their patroness became known as the "mother of decadence" in Russia.[30]

With the founding of Diaghilev's *Mir iskusstva* in 1898, at first under the joint patronage of Mamontov and Tenisheva, neonationalism—now irrevocably allied with Beardsleyan "decadence"—achieved a position of great prominence in the world of Russian art. In its pages, folk art, both antique and as fabricated at Abramtsevo and Talashkino, were featured alongside modern art both Western and native. Photographs of peasant shoes, furniture, and embroidery vied for pride of place with reproductions of Puvis de Chavannes and Gustave Moreau. And peasant art was celebrated from an explicitly modernist perspective in articles by leading painters and sculptors who dabbled (some quite competently) in archaeology. The two greatest such connoisseurs were Nikolai Roerich, whose Stravinskyan connections are well known if underestimated, and Ivan Bilibin (1876–1942), best remembered today as an illustrator of *skazki* (fairy tales), includ-

28. The musical quality of the production was execrable, but that did not prevent the association of Rimsky-Korsakov and the Mamontov company from being a lasting one. They gave three Rimsky-Korsakov premieres, the most important being *Sadko* (1897), with sets and costumes by artists soon to be associated with *Mir iskusstva* (Konstantin Korovin and Sergei Maliutin). The title page of the vocal score published by Beliaev is a veritable paradigm of the decorative neonationalism of the period. The letters of the title were adapted from the decorative fourteenth-century Novgorodian initials first published in Stasov's 1872 monograph. (Very appropriately, the middle letter of the title, "D," around which the whole design was centered, took the shape of a *gusli* player like Sadko himself.)

29. M. Tenisheva, *Vpechatleniia moei zhizni* [Impressions of my life] (Paris, 1933), p. 388. Quoted in John Bowlt, *The Silver Age: Russian Art of the Early Twentieth Century and the "World of Art" Group* (Newtonville, Mass., 1979), p. 40.

30. Tenisheva, *Vpechatleniia*, p. 276, quoted in Bowlt, *The Silver Age*, p. 41.

ing a marvelous series on the legend of the Firebird.[31] In one of the last issues of Diaghilev's short-lived journal, Bilibin contributed a lively article on the folk art of the Russian north, a topic on which he was a recognized expert. The exordium and the peroration to this survey are a perfect passionate summation of neonationalist ideals. He begins:

> Only very recently, like an America, we discovered the ancient Rus' of art, maimed by vandals, covered with dust and mold. But even under the dust she was beautiful, so beautiful that one can easily understand the first sudden rush that seized the discoverers: Come back, come back. . . . So now nationalist artists are faced with a task of colossal difficulty: they, by using this rich and ancient heritage, must create something new and serious that logically follows from what has survived. . . . We will await this and, losing no time, we will collect and collect everything that still remains of old in our peasants' huts, and we will study it and study it. We shall try to let nothing slip from our attention. And perhaps, under the influence of this passion for bygone beauty, there may even be created, at last, a new, completely individual Russian style with nothing of tawdriness about it.[32]

In concluding his article, Bilibin removed all doubt as to the kind of art he was envisioning and the real aesthetic significance of Russian peasant antiquities to him and his confreres:

> And so, let us then rummage about amid old rags on which decaying threads trace ancient patterns, and amid half-rotted inlaid boards, amid all that is old, turned to dust and ashes, and let us try to believe that from these ashes there will fly up a risen phoenix.[33]

Bilibin had ended, as we now say, with a buzzword. The image of the risen bird was the prime symbol of *l'art pour l'art* in the Russia of the "silver age," whether the Firebird herself (clearly a programmatic choice of subject for the first wholly original ballet to be created under Diaghilev); the "light-winged, benevolent, free bird" that symbolized poetic inspiration for Alexander Blok; or, closest to home, the famous woodcut Léon Bakst had created as emblem for *Mir iskusstva* itself, to show (in the artist's words) that "the 'World of Art' is above all earthly

---

31. For an evaluation of Roerich's contributions to *The Rite of Spring*, see Richard Taruskin, "The Rite Revisited: The Idea and Sources of the Scenario," *Music and Civilization: Essays in Honor of Paul Henry Lang*, ed. Maria Rika Maniates and Edmond Strainchamps (New York, 1984), pp. 183–202. It is surely not without significance that Stravinsky's conferences with Roerich in 1911 took place in Talashkino.

32. Ivan Bilibin, "Narodnoe tvorchestvo russkogo severa" [The folk art of the Russian North], *Mir iskusstva*, no. 11 (1904): 317.

33. Ibid., p. 318.

things, above the stars [reigning] proud, secret, and lonely as on a snowy peak."[34]

This was what lay behind the *Mir iskusstva* artists' recognition of their kinship with folk art, particularly with the applied and decorative arts as practiced by peasant architects and embroiderers and as first systematically described a generation earlier by Stasov, now their archenemy. These were arts devoid of any "subject" beyond their intrinsic beauty. Approached simply for itself (rather than as an expression of "the people's spirit") and apprehended directly (rather than metaphorically, as evidence of "the people's condition"), folk art was seen as an aesthetically autonomous World of Art that shared and in large part inspired the new movement's qualities of exuberant fantasy, transcendence of sensory reality, and, perhaps above all, cool, rarefied—shall we call it "classical"?—impersonalism. This was the "real art" of Russia, as Diaghilev put it a dozen years later in an interview with Olin Downes during his one visit to America. Asked to explain the genesis of the Ballets Russes' aesthetic innovations, he replied: "In objects of utility (domestic implements in the country districts), in the painting on sleds, in the designs and the colors of peasant dresses, or the carving around a window frame, we found our motives, and on this foundation we built."[35]

III

These aesthetic tenets surrounded Stravinsky as soon as he cast in his lot with the Ballets Russes. From his works themselves we know how potent a stimulus they were. But still, a gap remains. Was there absolutely no musical precedent? What guided Stravinsky from the general stimulus to the specific, brilliant musical responses?

The passion for discovering an America in the Russia of old touched musicians little. There were no composers to put beside the neonationalist artists at Abramtsevo and Talashkino, except perhaps the Rimsky-Korsakov of *Sadko* and *Kitezh* as a kind of musical counterpart to Vasnetsov, who was the neonationalist with the strongest ties to the older *peredvizhnik* traditions. But a small flurry of exploratory activity may be traced among musical ethnographers, and it leads eventually to Stravinsky, the first composer to respond with enthusiasm to their work. This was the movement initiated by Melgunov, already mentioned, to transcribe without prejudice the so-called *podgoloski*, or "undervoices," of Russian folk song—that is, to notate not only the main tune of a given song but also

34. See D. S. Mirsky, *A History of Russian Literature* (New York, 1947), p. 457, and Gray, *The Russian Experiment*, p. 48.

35. Quoted in Richard Buckle, *Diaghilev* (New York, 1979), p. 300.

the heterophonic aspects of its performance practice. Where, with a few negligible exceptions, previous Russian field transcribers had collected songs from individual informants, Melgunov (1879, 1885) and, following him, Nikolai Palchikov (1888) took them down from groups of singers, that is, as the peasants actually sang them.[36] This type of singing has been succinctly described by Alfred Swan, one of the very few non-Russians to have personally recorded and transcribed it, as follows:

> Starting with a solo intonation (*zapevalo*), the ensemble of singers would without any warning split into parts, each of which was also a self-sufficient melody not too divergent from the one that could conceivably be termed "principal." In actual fact there was *no* principal melody. Each singer could contend with justice that he was giving the basic contours of the song. The resultant tonal image converged into unison only at the very end, while the bulk of the song—always excepting the solo opening—was intoned in a kind of unfixable, yet new and baffling harmony.[37]

As Swan points out, collecting *podgoloski* presented almost insuperable problems to transcriber and informants alike, because when asked to perform each variant in turn for the transcriber, "the singers, unaccustomed to sing separately, complied with difficulty" and with many distortions.[38] The early attempts at polyphonic transcription could hardly be called an unqualified success.

The problems were solved with the aid of the phonograph. The first collector in Russia to use this revolutionary tool was Evgeniia Linyova, who began her ethnographic activities in 1897 and who published three sensational sets of polyphonic song transcriptions, totaling sixty-five, between 1904 and 1909. Her work was considered so important that it was even published in Russia in English translation.[39] Stravinsky's knowledge of the Linyova publications, and his enthusiasm for them, is well documented.[40] One is easily tempted to speculate that Lin-

---

36. For a fascinating account of the tribulations involved in transcribing *podgoloski* before the advent of the phonograph, see Nikolai Palchikov, "O muzykal'nom zapisyvanii russkikh narodnykh pesen s golosa krest'ian" [On the musical transcription of Russian folksongs from the voices of peasants], *Izvestiia imp. russkogo geograficheskogo obschchestva* [Newsletter of the Imperial Russian Geographical Society] 24, no. 19 (1888).

37. Swan, *Russian Music*, p. 25.

38. Ibid., p. 26.

39. Linyova's publications with music are as follows: "Opyt zapisi fonografom ukrainskikh narodnykh pesen" [An experiment in the phonographic transcription of Ukrainian folk song], *Trudy muzykal'no-ètnograficheskoi kommissii* [Works of the musical-ethnographic commission], vol. 1 (Moscow, 1906), pp. 221–66; *Velikorusskie pesni v narodnoi garmonizatsii*, 2 vols. (St. Petersburg, 1904–1909). The English translation is entitled *The Peasant Songs of Great Russia As They Are in the Folk's Harmonization: Collected and Transcribed from Phonograms by Eugenie Lineff* (St. Petersburg, 1905–1912).

40. He wrote to his mother on 10/23 February 1916: "Send me please, and as quickly as possible . . . the folk songs of the Caucasian peoples that have been *phonographically* transcribed. Others, non-phonographic, you needn't pick up. And while you're at it, if Jurgenson has any other

yova's transcriptions may have had a direct influence on the harmonic style of such works as *Les Noces* or *Renard*, and in fact the folklorist and composer Alexander Kastalsky (1856–1926) made the point as early as 1923 (though he made it in the process of attacking Stravinsky for his distortions).[41] To follow this up would be properly the subject of another essay, as would the proper tracing of the relationship between Linyova's handling of meter—and, even more particularly, her lengthy comments on the rhythms and versification of Russian folk songs—and what Stravinsky called his "rejoicing discovery" that "the accents of the spoken verse are ignored when the verse is sung," a discovery that influenced his settings of all languages throughout his career.[42]

Let these for now be merely teasers. Here I wish to emphasize Linyova's place within the general cultural background I have been tracing. In her lengthy prefaces, she makes point after point that fit right into the neonationalist scheme—and she was, moreover, the only musician up to then to do so. On the basic matter of the value of the phonograph as a collecting tool, she goes much further than merely asserting its usefulness as an aide-mémoire or as a documentational device:

> With the principle *(s nachalom)* of studying folk song from *authentic materials*—and I especially insist upon the use in practice of only the most utterly authentic materials, obtained directly from singers in the field and recorded with the aid of the phonograph, the best possible notebook for a collector—and with the application of the *comparative method,* the artistic significance of folk song is vastly increased, since the possibility presents itself of gaining a closer acquaintance with the *musical form of folk songs* of various nationalities, which must have a great influence on the work of composers and, generally, on the future development of music.[43]

Thanks to the phonograph, then, preserving and assimilating a musical artifact in the way a visual artifact is preserved was possible for the first time. Only now, Linyova implies, could musicians even aspire to a neonationalist style. She goes on to make quite a prophecy in this regard—one that will remind us of Bilibin's passionate harangue and which the young Stravinsky may have found inspiring:

---

phonographically transcribed folk songs, get them as well. Keep in mind that I already have the first installment of 'Great Russian Songs in Folk Harmonization' (as transcribed phonographically by Linyova)." See *I. F. Stravinskii: Stat'i i materialy* [I. F. Stravinsky: Essays and documents], ed. L. S. D'iachkova and Boris Yarustovsky (Moscow, 1973), p. 488. That he knew the 1906 Ukrainian collection as well seems clear because street vendors' cries that appear at the very beginning of *Petrushka* were published by Alexander Listopadov in the same issue of the *Trudy muzykal'no-ètnograficheskoi kommissii.*

41. A. D. Kastalsky, "Iz zapisok" [From my notes], in D'iachkova and Yarustovsky, *I. F. Stravinskii,* pp. 207–213.

42. Stravinsky and Craft, *Expositions and Developments,* p. 121.

43. Linyova, *Velikorusskie pesni,* vol. 2, p. lxxii, including an author's footnote.

> It is probable that in spite of many unfavorable conditions, folk song, in the process of disappearing in the countryside, will be reborn, transformed, in the works of our composers. It will be reborn not only in the sense of borrowing melodies from the folk—that is the easiest and least gratifying means of using it; no, it would be reborn in the sense of *style*: free, broad and lyric; in the sense of bold and complex voice leadings, the voices interlacing and separating, at times fused with the main melody, at times departing radically from it. A rebirth of this kind . . . we await in interesting and bold compositions by musical innovators, both at home and abroad.[44]

We may obtain a better focus on the neonationalist implications of Linyova's remarks by comparing them with the reactions of the eighty-year-old Stasov. Linyova sent that great and venerable figure a complimentary copy of her 1904 publication and received a typically garrulous, deliriously enthusiastic response, which, just as typically, missed the point by a mile:

> In my opinion, right here, in these works of yours, the dawn is beginning of some sort of powerful musical revolution in music [*sic*] (above all, in Russian music). Particularly in choruses. Dargomyzhsky, Musorgsky took huge steps forward in the area of a new, and the only proper, form of singing and expression in opera (Russian, that is). Their comrades, men of talent and genius, seized upon and mightily continued the revolution begun by them. But *choruses* remained in their former, backward, false state of artificiality, convention and complete implausibility (in spite of all the beauty and originality they often contained). But now things are stirring even here, and even with choruses there is bound to take place a complete revolution and upheaval in opera. And, evidently, this revolution is reserved for Russia, for the Russian musical school. Convention and implausibility must disappear; truth and naturalness are approaching even in choruses. They will stop being sung nicely and conventionally; they will begin to be performed with all the truth, caprice, irregularity one finds on the lips of the people, with all the changes in the quantity of the *singing personnel,* from among whom some enter and join in, others fall silent for a few seconds and start up again when they're good and ready, still others keep the music rolling along straight through without stopping; and also with all kind of shifts in *rhythm, tempo,* and even *mood,* such as characterize real people, feeling and creating something "all their own" in the chorus, quite oblivious of any commanding, considering, or devising author.
>
> Such will be, in my view, the operatic choruses of the *future.*
>
> It is long since time, long since time that the old, stiff, frozen forms of chorus were smashed to smithereens. How long have I been dreaming of something like this. How long ago have I spoken of this revolution—with Musorgsky. He agreed with me, intended to make a start, to try his hand at something of the

---

44. Ibid., p. lxxv.

> sort—but he didn't make it, for he died too early. All the same, a few attempts by him do exist in the "Prologue" or "Introduction" to *Boris Godunov:* "The people on the Kremlin Square."[45]

Such a letter from such a patriarch would be a coup in anyone's book, so of course Linyova proudly published it in hers. But this last gasp of *kuchkism* had little or nothing to do with her aesthetic concerns. Stasov is still shadowboxing with specters from the 1860s—still insisting on his peculiar rosy meliorism, still defending realism against Italianate and academic convention, still sounding a clarion call to Russian messianism, all the while oblivious that realism had become the academic style of the moment or that conventional Russianisms had become a cliché. The extent of the aesthetic gulf that separated Stasov from the true import of Linyova's publication can best be measured where he speaks of individualizing each member of the chorus. This was the great shibboleth of sixties art criticism—the individualized crowd, whether portrayed in music by a Musorgsky or on canvas by a Perov.[46] It was still kicking around at the Moscow Art Theater and other pockets of unregenerate realism. Chernyshevsky, the archdeacon of Russian realist theory, had defined folk song as "natural singing," as being in its origins the spontaneous outpouring of individually experienced joy and sorrow.[47] But true ethnographers like Linyova knew better, and their writings gave considerable aid and comfort to the theorists of aesthetic modernism. For Linyova, the folksinger was not a person at all while in the act of singing, but a vessel. In her prefaces, she included many vivid excerpts from the diaries she kept in the course of her fieldwork that testify to the essentially emotionless quality of folk performance, the "profound gravity and cool inevitable intention" noted by many twentieth-century ethnographers.[48] That Linyova calls this quality classical will certainly ring a Stravinskyan bell for us, but it was a common idea among the artists in whose company Stravinsky came to his artistic maturity.[49] Linyova describes a particularly memorable field experience involving a peasant woman she refers to only as Mitrevna, the patronymic form of address used by peasants with their peers:

---

45. Ibid., p. lxxiv. Even this letter may have had its effect on Stravinsky, for he made a piano arrangement in 1918 of the very chorus Stasov mentions. (It was given its first public performance at the International Stravinsky Symposium, 13 September 1982.)

46. I do not select these names at random. Cf. Stasov, "Perov i Musorgskii" (1883) in *Izbrannye sochineniia,* vol. 2: 133–52.

47. See N. G. Chernyshevsky, "The Esthetic Relations of Art to Reality," in *Selected Philosophical Essays* (Moscow: Foreign Languages Publishing House, 1953), pp. 346–47. This conception of folk song had influenced not only the composers of the *kuchka,* but also the plays of Ostrovsky. See Taruskin, *Opera and Drama in Russia,* pp. 169–70.

48. Jeffrey Mark, "The Fundamental Qualities of Folk Music," *Music and Letters* 10, no. 3 (1929): 288.

49. See, for example, Léon Bakst, "Puti klassitsizma v isskustve" [The ways of classicism in art], *Apollon,* nos. 2, 3 (1909), in which the primitivism of Gauguin is seen as a cleansing and classicizing force.

> She started singing my favorite song, "Luchinushka," which I had been looking for everywhere, but had never succeeded in recording. Mitrevna took the main melody. She sang the *zapevalo* in a deep sonorous voice, surprisingly fresh for a woman so old. In her singing there were absolutely no sentimental emphases or howlings. What struck me was its elegant simplicity. The song flowed evenly and clearly, not a single word was lost. Despite the length of the melody and the slowness of the tempo, the expression with which she invested the words of the song was so great that she seemed at once to be singing and speaking the song. I was amazed at this pure, classical strictness of style, which went so well with her serious face.[50]

Linyova's account is strewn with quotations from what was said at her recording sessions. One that she emphasized particularly was the oft-heard condemnation of what the peasant singers called *vertikuly*, which we might as well render as "verticules" (that is, purely spontaneous, self-expressive embellishments). "Oh, that's terrible the way your voice is wagging," a singer would complain if one of her partners began expressing herself. "Get rid of those verticules; just say the song straight."[51] A singer whom Linyova particularly admired sang a song that had relevance to a recent, intense personal tragedy, but nonetheless "from the external standpoint the song was simple, strictly rhythmical, and not for a minute did it exceed the limits of artistic truth."[52] "Could it be," wondered Linyova, "that the un-self-conscious art of the people, in its purely classical simplicity of performance, surpasses even the highest level of training worked out by professional artists? Precisely because the folksinger makes the song himself, it flows as if involuntarily and artlessly."[53] How close this is to the concepts of depersonalization and dehumanization, so central to the theory of modern art,[54] not to mention the aesthetic distancing and abstraction we find in all of Stravinsky after *Petrushka*. Hearing Linyova's peasants talk, we seem to hear familiar Stravinskyan raillery against "interpretation."

IV

Accounts of cultural background can all too easily imply a false causality; I do not mean to suggest that Stravinsky read Linyova, shouted "Eureka!" and wrote *The*

50. Linyova, *Velikorusskie pesni*, vol. 2, pp. xxv–xxvi.

51. Ibid., p. xxiv (n.).

52. Ibid., p. xxvi.

53. Ibid., pp. xxiv–xxv.

54. The words are borrowed, respectively, from T. S. Eliot, "Tradition and the Individual Talent" (1919), in *Selected Prose of T. S. Eliot*, ed. Frank Kermode (New York, 1975), pp. 37–44, and Jose Ortega y Gasset, "The Dehumanization of Art" (1925), in *The Dehumanization of Art and Other Essays on Art, Culture and Literature* (Princeton, 1968), pp. 3–56.

Rite of Spring. Between imaginative stimulus and artistic realization exists a gap only genius can bridge. Linyova's transcriptions and prefaces did not provide Stravinsky with his modernistic style readymade. They were merely among the various factors that gave him an inkling of his goals, or as he might have preferred to put it, that helped limit his choices.

For an example of the kind of leap of genius I have in mind, consider the harmony of *The Rite*, described thoroughly by Allen Forte and more briefly but very penetratingly by Pieter van den Toorn and Robert Moevs.[55] Studying Stravinsky's stylistic evolution in terms of his historical background and cultural environment can contribute much to our understanding of his harmonic usages in that great watershed of a piece.

Over the seventy years separating Stravinsky's ballet from Glinka's *Ruslan and Ludmila*, St. Petersburg composers had mined two main lodes of harmonic innovation. One we might call the folkloristic-diatonic genre, the other, the fantastic-chromatic. The first was mainly cultivated during the 1860s, following the lead of Balakirev and to a smaller extent Alexander Serov. Its main technical innovation consisted in establishing methods of harmonizing folk songs that did not adulterate their modal structure with modern Western admixtures. In particular, this involved preserving the pure natural minor and of what Balakirev called the "Russian minor," that is, what we loosely call the Dorian mode.[56] By the end of the 1860s, the essential work had been done in this area; continued conspicuous employment of these harmonizing methods was more or less a sign of epigonism by the turn of the century. The fantastic-chromatic style, on the other hand, was still going strong. It was essentially a huge exploration of symmetrical third relations beginning with Glinka's whole-tone evil sorcerer music in *Ruslan*, leading through all kinds of common-tone progressions, and culminating in Rimsky-Korsakov's seemingly exhaustive manipulations in his late operas of what he called the "tone-semitone scale" (which is what we, since Arthur Berger's seminal 1963 essay, have been calling the "octatonic scale").[57] This, too, was evil sorcerer music, brought to its fullest development by Rimsky in *Kashchei the Deathless* (1902) and carried perhaps one step further by Stravinsky in the "ladder of thirds" that characterizes *his* Kashchei in *The Firebird*.

These two lines of development had proceeded strictly in parallel. Never, for example, were folk tunes harmonized in a "fantastic" manner. On the contrary, it

55. Allen Forte, *The Harmonic Organization of The Rite of Spring* (New Haven, 1978); Robert Moevs, review of Forte in *Journal of Music Theory* 24, no. 1 (1980): 97–107; Pieter van den Toorn, "Some Characteristics of Stravinsky's Diatonic Music," *Perspectives of New Music* 14, no. 1 (1975): 104, and 15, no. 2 (1977): 58. Since this article was written, van den Toorn's comprehensive monograph, *The Music of Igor Stravinsky* (New Haven, 1983) has appeared.

56. For a further discussion of these methods and some examples of Balakirev's harmonizations, see Richard Taruskin, " 'Little Star': An Etude in the Folk Style," in *Musorgsky: In Memoriam 1881–1981*, ed. Malcolm H. Brown (Ann Arbor, 1982), pp. 57–84.

57. See Arthur Berger, "Problems of Pitch Organization in Stravinsky," in *Perspectives on Schoenberg and Stravinsky*, ed. Benjamin Boretz and Edward Cone (Princeton, 1968), pp. 123–55.

was a commonplace in Russian opera ever since Glinka to contrast them baldly: to use the folkloristic-diatonic idiom for human characters and the fantastic-chromatic for supernatural ones. Nowhere, of course, had this cliché been more obediently invoked than in *The Firebird*. And Stravinsky still observed it in *Petrushka*, basing the outer tableaux on the folkloristic-diatonic style and the second tableau on new octatonic explorations, now involving superimpositions of octatonically related triads and seventh-chords previous Russian composers had juxtaposed.

But faced with a subject that epitomized the depersonalized Russian archaism so beloved of the neonationalists, and in fact at least in part supplied by one of the movement's leaders, Stravinsky sought a new approach.[58] Having drawn much of his thematic material from the most archaic stratum of surviving folk music (that is, the so-called "calendar songs") and having therefore adopted a number of themes and motives that were restricted in their melodic compass to the tones of the minor tetrachord (that is, T-S-T), Stravinsky made the astounding yet logical discovery that two such tetrachords pitched a tritone apart yield the tone-semitone scale.[59]

Example 2.1. x and y tetrachords

This was the first time anyone had partitioned the scale in a fashion that emphasized neither triadic derivations nor harmonic rotations by thirds. It was a discovery very nearly prefigured in *Petrushka* at **7** in the first tableau.

Example 2.2. *Petrushka*, "First Tableau." **7**

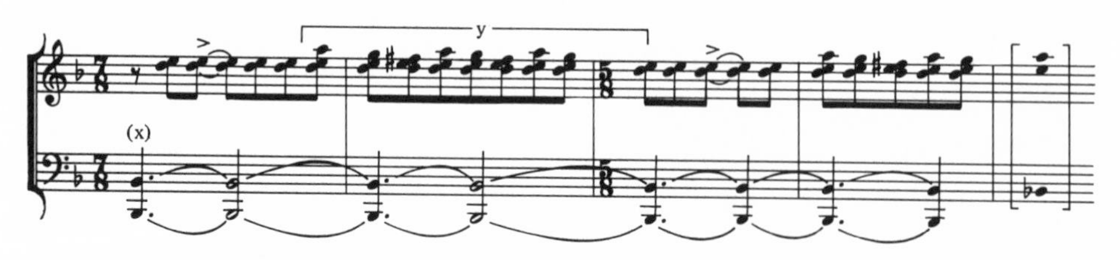

58. The movement's leader was Roerich. See note 31.

59. See Taruskin, "Russian Folk Melodies," esp. pp. 513–15. Such tetrachordal/tritonal oppositions had been prefigured in the choral prologue to Borodin's *Prince Igor* and in Rimsky's *Kaschei the Deathless*, but never as a vertical juxtaposition generating "polytonal" harmony.

In *The Rite,* it became a *Grundgestalt.* Here are a few of its many manifestations. One of the clearest and most vivid occurs when the "Procession of the Sage" overtakes the "Games of the Rival Tribes":

Example 2.3. *The Rite of Spring,* "Games of the Rival Tribes"

Another is the harmonization of the main theme of the "Ritual Action of the Ancestors," which I have shown elsewhere to be an authentic *vesnyanka* or springtime invocation:

Example 2.4. *The Rite of Spring,* "Ritual Action of the Ancestors"

If we take the *Petrushka* configuration as a kind of harmonic embryo of this new-style octatonicism, we may posit a kind of three-note harmonic source-chord consisting of the outer notes of the upper tetrachord "accompanied" by the lowest note of the lower tetrachord. This harmonic "cell" is then filled out in *The Rite* in a number of famous ways:

Example 2.5.

(a) Source chord

(b) Part 1, "Dances of the Young Girls"

(c) Part 2, "Sacrificial Dance"

What we have in effect is the harmonic content of the fantastic-chromatic genus (which in Rimsky's day meant modernism) expressed in terms of melodic configurations endemic to the folkloristic-diatonic. The ancient dichotomy is transcended and the two elements fused in an unprecedented way—both meanwhile being fundamentally transformed. As I pointed out in my earlier discussion of folk melodies in *The Rite,* they are invariably distorted and hidden rather than displayed, absorbed to the point where, without the evidence provided by Stravinsky's sketchbook, their presence could only be "felt," never proved. The same is true of the octatonic derivation of much of the harmony. In most of the examples given, it is effectively concealed by diatonic doublings or additives or by partitions that emphasize diatonically intersecting constituents, all of which until recently has always led to the assumption (eagerly abetted by Stravinsky) that an arbitrarily inspirational polytonalism had been the sole guide in constructing them.

Whence this rage to cover the tracks? But of course it is fundamental—the impulse to transform subject matter into style that lay at the heart of the neonationalist movement from the beginning, only now carried much further than anything dreamt of by the *Miriskusniki* into "those basic matters of form, thematic content, harmony, polyphony, and sonority that are of lively current interest," to quote the Karatygin essay that furnished us with our point of departure. Moreover, although the novel partitions of the octatonic pitch field may have had their origin in his quest of a new "maximalistic" way of harmonizing folkloristic material, they remained a permanent stylistic resource for Stravinsky, carrying over into many works that had no overt connections with Russian musical traditions, whether "folk" or "art."

V

Stravinsky's innovations, though rooted firmly in neonationalism, went much further than their antecedents in their radicalism. Were there no painters who, as it were, kept up with him in his radical transformation of the folk heritage? Of course there were, and two in particular stand out as uncannily kindred spirits: Mikhail Larionov and his wife Natalia Goncharova, both born in 1881 and therefore Stravinsky's practically exact contemporaries.

Between them they constituted a recognized "school" dating from their triumph at the third exhibit organized by the journal *The Golden Fleece* in December 1909 and lasting until they left Russia, at Diaghilev's invitation, in 1914. This school, almost too neatly for comfort, was called neoprimitivist. Like the Stravinsky of *The Rite* and beyond, the neoprimitives shared the ideals and the cultural allegiances of neonationalism but went much further toward an abstract realization. In Larionov especially, one can trace the progressive absorption of motifs from folk art, particularly the *lubok,* to the point where nothing of the subject remained visible, but where the stylistic influence—the color sense, the perspective, the painterly surface—was absolutely pervasive.[60] Their works "not only reach back in their brilliant color and formal motifs to the revival of folk art by the Abramtsevo artists, but forward to the futurist movement in painting, of which they were the pioneers."[61] The words used to describe the neoprimitivist paintings exhibited at the epochal Knave of Diamonds exhibit of 1912—"brilliant sated color, intense surface patterning (based on folk motifs), and a radical simplification of form"—also describe *The Rite* to perfection.[62]

Stravinsky was extremely close to Larionov and Goncharova; they were among the very few with whom he used the familiar mode of address.[63] He dedicated the *Cat's Cradle Songs* [Berceuses du chat] to them. They designed the productions of some of his most characteristic neoprimitivist work (if for the moment we may borrow the term for him)—Larionov did *Renard* in 1922, and *Les Noces* the next year was Goncharova's. The latter, of course, had been in the works for years—since 1915, in fact, when Diaghilev, recognizing the extraordinary kinship between Goncharova and Stravinsky, commissioned from them a ballet to be entitled *Liturgiia,* whose original inspiration was a series of costume designs by Goncharova incorporating motifs from medieval icons. And repeatedly though he may later have denied it, Stravinsky did in fact embark upon this composition.[64]

Yet there is no known documentation of any contact between Stravinsky and these future friends until they had all left Russia for good. That they were unacquainted in their native country seems likely, in fact, because Larionov and Goncharova lived and exhibited in Moscow. But Diaghilev, who shuttled regularly between the two capitals, knew Larionov as early as 1906.[65] Stravinsky, through his friend and mentor, might well have known and taken inspiration from the work of these neoprimitivists, whose period of greatest prominence in Russia co-

60. Bowlt, *Russian Art,* p. 98.

61. Gray, *The Russian Experiment,* p. 56.

62. Ibid., p. 123.

63. Vera Stravinsky and Robert Craft, *Stravinsky in Pictures and Documents* (New York, 1978), p. 603.

64. The proof of this is in an article contemporaneous with the project, written by a Clarens neighbor of Stravinsky named C. Stanley Wise, "Impressions of Igor Strawinsky," *Musical Quarterly* 2 (April 1916): 256. "The other important composition, to which he was giving much thought during this winter of 1915–1916, is of a religious character *(Liturgie),* but it is not yet sufficiently advanced to be here discussed." My guess is that whatever was composed for *Liturgiia* at this time eventually wound up in *Les Noces.*

65. Arnold Haskell (with Walter Nouvel), *Diaghileff, His Artistic and Private Life* (New York, 1935), p. 269.

incided exactly with the two-year period from *The Firebird* to *The Rite*, into which it seemed at the time to Stravinsky, no less than it now seems to us, that twenty years of artistic growth were somehow crammed.[66] It would be extremely interesting to learn what role, if any, awareness and discussion of neoprimitivism played in this astonishingly accelerated stylistic development.

---

66. See his 7 March 1912 letter to Andrei Rimsky-Korsakov (D'iachkova and Yarustovsky, *I. F. Stravinskii*, p. 467).

3 Stravinsky and Prokofiev: Sizing Up the Competition

MALCOLM HAMRICK BROWN

IGOR STRAVINSKY looms so large from the perspective of the centennial year of his birth that it requires some effort to refocus on that period in the 1910s and 1920s when another Russian composer aspired if not to dominate then certainly to share the leadership of the musical vanguard. Sergei Prokofiev was nine years Stravinsky's junior and still a conservatory student when his thirty-one-year-old compatriot stunned Paris with *The Rite of Spring*. But while Stravinsky dominated the talk in Paris, Prokofiev already commanded the attention of St. Petersburg and Moscow. Unlike Stravinsky, who had been a latebloomer, something of a dilettante up to his mid-twenties, Prokofiev had entered the St. Petersburg Conservatory at the age of thirteen, an acknowledged prodigy, and by the age of seventeen had claimed the epithet *enfant terrible* of Russian music by playing an audaciously original group of piano pieces at the important Evenings of Contemporary Music in St. Petersburg. Called a radical "futurist" in music, Prokofiev was soon being compared with the dominant figures in Russian musical modernism—Scriabin, the recognized leader, secure in his reputation, and Stravinsky, the homegrown prophet, honored in Paris and now gaining recognition in his own country.

By 1914, the year after *The Rite*, when Prokofiev completed his studies at the conservatory, a few spokesmen for the vanguard had already started to debate the relative merits of Stravinsky and Prokofiev as standard-bearers of the future, implicitly relegating Scriabin, despite his eminence, to the ranks of the old guard. Scriabin's untimely death in April of the following year fixed him permanently in that category. As for the two younger contenders, no one questioned that Stravinsky had proven himself in Paris on a scale that dwarfed Prokofiev's homespun successes, but Prokofiev was still a youngster whose potential appeared limitless. As one critic put it in 1914, "This composer's fantasy is boundless . . .

I would like to thank Marianna Tax Choldin, Ralph Fisher, Laurence Miller, and their associates at the Summer Research Laboratory of the Russian and East European Center and at the Slavic and East European Library of the University of Illinois for their support in my research for this paper, which was completed during my residence as an associate of the Summer Research Laboratory in 1982.

the limits of his imagination are not visible and . . . it is impossible even to guess what they will turn out to be."[1]

A fair assessment of what both Prokofiev's and Stravinsky's limits finally turned out to be requires some familiarity with the judgments and the expectations of those who from the first were "sizing up the competition" between these two composers. Our sampling here of what the critics were saying will be confined to the 1910s and 1920s, when the two composers themselves were most often conscious of the competition. Prokofiev never failed to pay close attention to what Stravinsky was doing. "For him, Stravinsky was still the great authority, the consummate master, who commanded all the secrets of the art."[2] He attended performances of Stravinsky's music whenever he could, and we learn from his letters that he often spent time studying the scores, occasionally even playing through prepublication proof copies that he had access to at the offices of the Editions Russes de Musique in Paris. His frank opinions, succinctly and pointedly put, are available to us from the letters he wrote to two of his closest musical friends in Russia—composer and sometime critic Nikolai Miaskovsky and musicologist-critic and sometime composer Boris Asafiev. (The latter's important *A Book About Stravinsky* has finally been published in English in the United States.)[3]

Stravinsky must certainly have been interested in what Prokofiev was doing, and he surely indulged in some sizing up of the competition from time to time, especially during the 1920s. He was often present at performances of Prokofiev's music and doubtless formed strong opinions, but those available have come mostly from Stravinsky's conversations with Robert Craft and are therefore retrospective, filtered through time and memory, and lack the immediacy and specificity of Prokofiev's letters. But the two composers' sizing up of each other makes for entertaining reading and provides insights pertinent to our retrieval and understanding of the past.

The first public performances of music by both Stravinsky and Prokofiev took place in 1908. Stravinsky was then twenty-six; Prokofiev was seventeen. But substantive reviews of their compositions started to appear only later. Reading through those that date from the teens, one soon becomes conscious of the strikingly different way in which Russian critics characterized the two composers. Stravinsky was almost invariably spoken of as representing the Russian nationalist tradition, as the heir of Rimsky-Korsakov and the so-called "new Russian school." Prokofiev was never associated with an established school or move-

1. Igor Glebov [Boris Asafiev], "The Petrograd Concert Season," *Muzyka*, no. 203 (27 December 1914): 634.

2. Israel Vladimirovich Nestiev, *Zhizn' Sergeia Prokofieva* [The life of Sergei Prokofiev], 2d ed., rev., and enl. (Moscow, 1973), pp. 241–42.

3. Boris Asafiev, *A Book About Stravinsky*, Russian Music Studies No. 5, trans. Richard F. French, with an introduction by Robert Craft (Ann Arbor, 1982).

ment, despite the fact that he, too, had studied with Rimsky-Korsakov and might well have been expected to reveal a nationalist sensibility in his music. His apparent break with any immediate tradition, nationalist or not, was what attracted critical acclaim. This review from 1911, typical of what the leading Russian critics were saying, emphasizes Stravinsky's ties with the nationalist past:

> Igor Stravinsky is an interesting and well-nigh the most striking presence among the young Petersburg composers. Trained in the achievements of the "new Russian school" by his late father, that superb artist of the Russian operatic stage, and by Rimsky-Korsakov, and having lent an avid ear to the revelations of the young Frenchmen, Stravinsky may well turn out to be the most brilliant spokesman for the evolution of the principles of the national Russian school. After all of these flaccid imitators of the "Russian style"—who compose by ready-made clichés and who completely deserve the appellation coined by an idle Muscovite, "manufacturers from the St. Petersburg assembly lines"—one pauses before the works of Stravinsky with expectation and hope.[4]

This theme of Stravinsky as the "most brilliant spokesman of the national Russian school" recurs repeatedly in one form or another in the critiques and newspaper reports of the period. A sampling from several reviews by Nikolai Miaskovsky, Prokofiev's friend and a critic for the influential journal *Muzyka*, proves the point and demonstrates how centrally it was fixed in Russian musical consciousness at the time. Summing up his opinion about *The Firebird*, Miaskovsky writes: "That acuity, heartiness, and optimism . . . which distinguish Stravinsky from the ranks of his highly talented contemporaries, give him the right to be regarded as the direct descendant of Nikolai Rimsky-Korsakov."[5] The nationalist issue is brought even more sharply into focus in Miaskovsky's comments about the *Two Poems of Balmont:*

> Every new line of Stravinsky's testifies to the flowering of his miraculous, bright, purely Russian talent. . . . What is especially attractive and important in these pieces under examination is the unusually harmonious combination of French grace and subtlety with a genuinely Slavic sincerity and profound tenderness; in the latter qualities, the threads that connect Stravinsky with Rimsky-Korsakov and, moreover, with Musorgsky are quite clearly revealed.[6]

---

4. Vladimir Vladimirovich Derzhanovsky, reviews of Stravinsky's "Two Songs to Words by S. Gorodetsky," Opus 6, and "Pastorale" for voice and piano, *Muzyka*, no. 9 (29 January 1911): 211.

5. N. M. [Nikolai Miaskovsky], review of the piano, two-hand reduction of Stravinsky's *The Firebird*, *Muzyka*, no. 45 (8 October 1911): 972.

6. N. M., review of Stravinsky's "Two Poems of K. Balmont," *Muzyka*, no. 91 (22 August 1912): 705.

When some of the Russian critics haughtily disdained *Petrushka,* Miaskovsky roused up an almost biblical effusion in its defense:

> I believe that if that exceptional aristocrat of the kingdom of sound, Rimsky-Korsakov, were alive, he would stand without a moment's hesitation on the side of this work: I believe that Stravinsky's exceptional, radiant talent is flesh of his flesh and blood of his blood.[7]

Not long after Miaskovsky's impassioned declaration about *Petrushka* appeared in print, Prokofiev wrote him to share his own firsthand impressions of the work:

> I was in Paris at the Diaghilev ballets, and here's what I think. *Petrushka* is to the nth degree entertaining, alive, merry, witty, and interesting. The music—with lots of hustle and bustle—wonderfully illustrates the smallest detail on stage (just as on stage they very cleverly illustrate the most minute orchestral phrase). The orchestration is wonderful and, when it's needed, very witty. But now to the main thing: is there music in the ballet or not? Well, I can't say yes and I can't say no. . . . At the most interesting places, the liveliest moments on stage, he doesn't write *music,* but something to illustrate the moment brilliantly. That "something" is nothing more than *remplissage.* But if he can't compose music for the most crucial moments, only stuffs them with whatever's at hand, then he's musically bankrupt. If one can agree that Stravinsky is blazing a new trail, then he's doing it with a sharp little knife of the very latest design, but not with a big axe, which might grant him the right to the title of titan.[8]

The twenty-two-year-old Prokofiev obviously possessed plenty of self-confidence—a self-confidence consonant with the character of his music, which was already evoking accolades such as these from the Russian critics:

> Here are works from which gust a primitive strength and freshness. What a pleasure and surprise to come upon this vibrant and healthy presence amid today's widespread effeteness, enervation, and anemia. . . . Only the born blind or those blinded by prejudice can fail to recognize a powerful and original talent pregnant with still richer possibilities.[9]

Other reviewers sympathetic to musical modernism agreed, and the tributes to Prokofiev's talent mounted. Asafiev, for one, rhapsodized over those qualities he found most arresting in young Prokofiev:

---

7. N. M., "Igor Stravinsky's Ballet *Petrushka,*" *Muzyka,* no. 59 (14 January 1912): 75.

8. Prokofiev to Miaskovsky, 11/24 June 1913, in *S. S. Prokofiev i N. Ya. Miaskovsky: Perepiska* [Prokofiev and Miaskovsky: Correspondence], comp. and ed. M. G. Koslova and N. R. Yatsenko (Moscow, 1977): 107. Hereafter SP-NYa.

9. M. [Miaskovsky], review of Prokofiev's Four Etudes, Opus 2, for piano, *Muzyka,* no. 94 (8 September 1912): 772.

> . . . the colossal strength of the creative impulse, the intensity and expressiveness of the musical language, the mighty flights of fantasy, the inexhaustible wealth of themes, their individuality and their rhythmic and harmonic inventiveness, in a word, all of those things so difficult to come to terms with for the people who judge music from the viewpoint of its proximity to one or another school, circle, or tendency.[10]

This sampling of the vanguard critics' comments on Stravinsky and Prokofiev establishes the relative positions of the two within Russian musical modernism on the eve of the Great War. Prokofiev was seen as the intrepid independent, nonnationalist and nontraditionalist; Stravinsky was acknowledged as the heir apparent to the nationalist mantle of Rimsky-Korsakov. Even *The Rite,* with its radically transmogrified folklorism, was recognized as belonging to the canon and proclaimed to be, in the words of a St. Petersburg critic writing in 1914, "an event of enormous historical significance, an event in the life of Russian art."[11] And Miaskovsky, who had repeatedly emphasized Stravinsky's neonationalist tendency, declared *The Rite* "to be a work that synthesizes the entire path traversed by Stravinsky before it," thereby firmly aligning it with the Russianism of *Petrushka* and *The Firebird.*[12]

This idea, so often voiced by the vanguard Russian critics before World War I—of Stravinsky as bound to the past, a synthesizer of tradition, and Prokofiev as looking to the future, free to innovate—was given a decisive formulation by Boris Asafiev in the issue of *Muzyka* for 27 December 1914 (Old Style). I wonder if Stravinsky ever read the piece and what his reaction might have been. His correspondence with the editor of *Muzyka,* Vladimir Derzhanovsky, seems to have ended in May 1914, if their entire exchange is included in volume I of Stravinsky's *Selected Correspondence.*[13] This suggests the possibility that wartime communication became too difficult for contact to be maintained and that, as a consequence, Stravinsky never read the article. Although I have no direct confirmation, Prokofiev probably would have seen it, given his residence in Russia and his close association with Asafiev. Here are Asafiev's thoughts in 1914 about Russia's two most gifted young composers:

> Stravinsky is the last representative of an ultrarefined, yet fatigued and surfeited culture. The beauty of his tonal musings is a genuine beauty, but virtually devoid of insight into the future. There is no movement forward in Stravinsky's work, only an ultrarefined synthesis of previous achievements. Stravinsky remains wholly in the past. Despite his wondrous harmonic

10. Igor Glebov, "The Petrograd Gazette," *Muzyka,* no. 208 (31 January 1915): 72.

11. Viacheslav Karatygin, review of Stravinsky's *The Rite of Spring, Rech',* no. 64 (16 February 1914), rpt. in *Muzyka,* no. 171 (1 March 1914): 197.

12. Nikolai Miaskovsky, "About Stravinsky's *The Rite of Spring,*" *Muzyka,* no. 164 (1 February 1914): 111.

13. Robert Craft, ed., *Stravinsky: Selected Correspondence,* vol. 1 (New York, 1982).

> fancies, one feels that his strength lies in his weakness, that is, in his ability to grasp with an intuitive perspicacity the spirit and sense of any preceding epoch and to stylize it by means of the most ingenious techniques at his disposal today. Yet in every case he will be sincere, because he remains his own man in all traditions—they've all left traces in his brain. When one listens to Stravinsky's music, it seems that his word is final, that everything has been said, that it would be useless to go further, because there's nowhere left to go. And indeed, it would be useless to go Stravinsky's way, the way of synthesizing the ultrarefined techniques and the toxic yet attractive ideas of modernism. But then, Prokofiev's works appear, and the air is filled with freshness, good spirits, the self-assured tone of a man who knows his own strength. And above all, an immense creative will and an irrepressible creative impulse make themselves felt!. . . One hears nothing that is labored, amorphous; on the contrary, one gets the impression that he is almost joking, playing with the sonorous images that inhabit his soul, that beyond them much still remains unexpressed. . . . It would be a distortion to force Prokofiev's creativity into any framework for now, to measure it by any standard, because his work belongs to the future, and it ought to be judged by its own rules. Today, one cannot but believe . . . that before us stands true, genuine beauty—perhaps severe and astringent for our delicate taste, but not less acceptable on account of that than the ultrarefined, toxic beauty of Stravinsky's sonorous charms.[14]

Seventy years later we can easily criticize Asafiev on a number of counts, but I am still astonished by the prescience of his recognizing so early Stravinsky's "ability to grasp with an intuitive perspicacity the spirit and sense of any preceding epoch and to stylize it by means of the most ingenious techniques at his disposal today." This interpretation by Asafiev of the significance of Stravinsky's and Prokofiev's music in 1914 unquestionably represents the most comprehensive sizing up of the competition one could hope to find from that period. Most important, it provides a Russian perspective either ignored by or simply unknown to many Westerners involved in Stravinsky research. That such a review as this would encourage Prokofiev's aspiration to leadership of the musical vanguard can be easily understood.

When Asafiev's article appeared, Stravinsky and Prokofiev still barely knew each other personally. They became friendly, "both in shared compositional sympathies and otherwise" (according to Prokofiev), only in 1915, when Prokofiev went to Italy to consult with Diaghilev about a commissioned work-in-progress for the Ballets Russes.[15] Prokofiev's still unfinished score greatly disap-

14. Glebov, "The Petrograd Concert Season," pp. 634–35.

15. Some fifty years later, Stravinsky would declare that he had met Prokofiev during the winter of 1906–1907 at one of the Petersburg Evenings of Contemporary Music (Igor Stravinsky and Robert Craft, *Memories and Commentaries* [Berkeley and Los Angeles, 1981], p. 66), but Prokofiev played the first time for the Evenings only on 18 December 1908 (Old Style). Israel Nestiev writes

pointed Diaghilev, partly, the latter confided to Stravinsky, because "the music . . . does not look for Russianism; it is just music."[16] Diaghilev demanded that Prokofiev start over with a completely new ballet, "Only write the kind of music that will turn out to be Russian," he insisted, adding, "You there in your rotten Petersburg have forgotten how to compose in Russian."[17] Stravinsky, still the committed neonationalist and heir to Rimsky-Korsakov, joined Diaghilev in trying to change Prokofiev's orientation, and evidence that the two of them made some impression on him is found in one of Prokofiev's letters to Miaskovsky, written on the heels of the former's encounter with his fellow countrymen:

> This is now the most *avant-garde* position, which both Stravinsky and Diaghilev advocate: down with sentimentalism, down with pathos, down with internationalism! They're turning me into the most Russian composer there is.[18]

Several weeks later Prokofiev wrote directly to Stravinsky, assuring him that work was going well on the new ballet and confessing the usefulness of one particular Stravinsky suggestion: "Thumbing through Russian folk songs showed me lots of interesting possibilities," he acknowledged gratefully.[19]

Prokofiev's new ballet, *The Buffoon,* based on Russian folktales and incorporating folk song intonations in the thematic material, represented a truly radical departure from the anethnographic character of Prokofiev's earlier music. There is no little irony in the fact that the Stravinsky of *An Autobiography,* who was by then thoroughly antinationalist, would call this particular ballet "Prokofiev's masterpiece" or that the confirmed folklore-phobe of the 1950s would admit to Robert Craft, "Of Prokofiev's Diaghilev ballets I preferred *Chout* [The buffoon]."[20]

---

in his biography of Prokofiev (see n. 2), "At one of the public gatherings of the Evenings in 1910, Prokofiev became acquainted with Igor Stravinsky, who was already famous; Stravinsky played the music which he had just finished composing for *The Firebird* ballet. Prokofiev did not like it, and his slighting opinion offended the proud Stravinsky" (p. 64). Prokofiev's account of his first meeting with Stravinsky sheds little light on the year but clarifies the circumstances. Writing about a later meeting with his famous fellow countryman in 1915, he says, "I had already met Stravinsky earlier, a couple of years before in Petersburg. He had played the Introduction to *The Firebird* on the piano, which lost a lot without the orchestra. I told him that there was not any music in the Introduction, and if there was, it was out of [Rimsky-Korsakov's] *Sadko.* Stravinsky was offended." (Sergei Prokofiev, "After Finishing the Conservatory," in S. S. Prokofiev, *Materialy, Dokumenty, Vospominaniia* [Materials, documents, reminiscences], 2d ed., with an introduction by S. I. Schlifstein [Moscow, 1961], p. 151). Prokofiev to Miaskovsky, 21 March/3 April 1915, SP-NYa, p. 132.

16. Diaghilev to Stravinsky, 8 March 1915, in Stravinsky and Craft, *Memories and Commentaries,* p. 68.

17. Quoted by Prokofiev in "After Finishing the Conservatory," p. 151.

18. Prokofiev to Miaskovsky, 10 April 1915 (Old Style), SP-NYa, p. 133.

19. Prokofiev to Stravinsky, 3 June 1915 (Old Style), Xerox copy of the original kindly provided by Robert Craft. Translated by Natalia Rodriquez and Malcolm Brown.

20. Igor Stravinsky, *An Autobiography* (1936; rpt. New York, 1962), p. 94, Stravinsky and Craft, *Memories and Commentaries,* p. 69.

Prokofiev, the nonnationalist, would one day declare that Stravinsky's neoclassical works seemed "less important" to him than *Les Noces* or *The Rite*.[21] Nevertheless, his own temporary excursion into self-conscious ethnography for *Buffoon* produced no profound changes in either his basic aesthetic attitude or his characteristic musical style.

"Down with internationalism," Stravinsky and Diaghilev had preached to Prokofiev in 1915; but war and revolution soon turned life around for Stravinsky the zealous Russian and neonationalist, and along with it, the aesthetic position he had espoused so ardently. Now exiled in Paris, embarrassed and angered by the politics of Bolshevist Russia, sensitive to Diaghilev's assessment of the exigencies of contemporary professional life, and no doubt responsive to artistic motivations of his own, Stravinsky was soon advocating both a musical style and an aesthetic doctrine if not precisely "internationalist" in tone, then certainly "cosmopolitan."

Prokofiev's exile seems to have aroused in him a deeper personal sense of his Russianness, although it engendered no immediate or readily apparent change in his aesthetic position. Undoubtedly, Paris deflected the creative course he had taken earlier in St. Petersburg, but the new direction affected more the surface than the substance of his music. The wider implications of Stravinsky's retreat from the neonationalist position did not appear to concern Prokofiev very much; but the musical consequences of that retreat left him deeply puzzled. Prokofiev, after all, had long before tried his hand at gavottes and allemandes, rigadoons and minuets—even a "classical" symphony. But for him, such "classicism" had never been anything more than a momentary highlighting of an integral, normally more generalized component of his total musical personality. Now he was dismayed by what he perceived as Stravinsky's "scribbled-over Bach."[22] "I love Bach and think it's not so bad to compose according to his principles," he asserted, "[but] one ought not to stylize him."[23] Stravinsky, of course, continued along his new path with what seems to have been absolute conviction, telling Prokofiev, whom he often met socially, that everyone "ought only to be writing in this way."[24]

Although Stravinsky's newest music disappointed some of his vanguard supporters along with a substantial segment of the general audience and often aroused the ire of critics, when it came to sizing up the competition, the influential critics more often than not still handed the laurel to Stravinsky. Here's a

21. Prokofiev to Asafiev, 8 February 1925, in "The Letters of S. S. Prokofiev to B. V. Asafiev (1920–1944)," prepared for publication and with commentary by M. Kozlova, in *Iz proshlogo sovetskoi muzykal'noi kul'tury* [From the past of Soviet musical culture], part 2, ed. T. N. Livanova (Moscow, 1976), p. 9. Hereafter IPSMK-2.

22. Prokofiev to Miaskovsky, I June 1924, SP-NYa, p. 195.

23. Prokofiev to Asafiev, 8 February 1925, IPSMK-2, p. 8.

24. Prokofiev to Miaskovsky, 5 March 1925, SP-NYa, p. 211.

sample from a review written soon after Stravinsky turned to neoclassicism. The critic is composer Georges Auric, here speaking about the first performance of two major works, one each by Prokofiev and Stravinsky, that were played on the same program in Paris on 18 October 1923:

> The second of four concerts which Mr. Koussevitzky is now giving at the Opéra allowed us to hear, along with Sergei Prokofiev's [First Violin] Concerto, the Octet for wind instruments by Igor Stravinsky. Composed after the comic opera *Mavra*, the Octet continues its direction, but this time in the symphonic style. . . . It is a fact that an ensemble of wind instruments by themselves provokes astonishment and smiles. Old superstitions still accompany the bassoon and trombone! Uncomplimentary adjectives always abound in reference to them, while the actual music that they play (including this Octet) engenders very little comment. . . . But in the last analysis, one either appreciates or does not appreciate this Octet, and, quite naturally, the critics did not fail to dish up some commonplaces about it. It would appear that we are dealing here with a work devoid of "thought" and "distinction," whose themes are not very original. . . . We heard the Octet before a concerto for violin by Prokofiev, a witty, prolific, and agreeable musician. His ballet *The Buffoon* and the "Scythian" Suite contain pages of absolutely first-rate music. What reassures me about Stravinsky's Octet is that I see that the critics find the Concerto's ideas very original, very new, and brilliantly developed. Now then, Prokofiev will forgive me today, I am sure, if I don't care much for his new work. I find it, on account of its ideas, rather annoyingly Mendelssohnian, on account of its development, a little too much the rich uncle of the unfortunate Grieg, and drowned, in a word, by an orchestral picturesqueness that is quite artificial. Mr. Darrieux, moreover, played it admirably. . . . That is why I am scarcely astonished that the kinds of musicians who would love this concerto for dilettantes would not understand Stravinsky's fine work.[25]

(Stravinsky himself, interesting to note, liked this "concerto for dilettantes," we learn from Robert Craft.[26])

After such a review as Auric's, and Prokofiev got many in a similar vein during the 1920s, one should not be surprised that he envied Stravinsky's superior reputation. His letters from this period contain frequent gibes at his competitor's new works, often side by side with professional praise:

> Stravinsky has written himself a horrifying piano sonata that he himself performs, not without a certain *chic*. But its music is some sort of pockmarked Bach.
>
> Stravinsky has been delivered of *Oedipus Rex*, a scenically static opera-oratorio in 2 acts. . . . The librettist is a Frenchman, the

25. Georges Auric, "La Musique," *Les Nouvelles Littéraires* (27 October 1923): 5.

26. Robert Craft, *Stravinsky: Chronicle of a Friendship, 1948–1971* (New York, 1972), p. 394.

> text is Latin, the subject Greek, the music Anglo-German (after Handel), it will be produced by a Monegasquan enterprise and on American money—the height of internationalism.
>
> The material [in *Apollon*] is absolutely pathetic, and besides, picked from the most deplorable pockets: Gounod, Delibes, Wagner, and even Minkus. All of this is treated with the greatest cleverness and mastery, which would settle the question if Stravinsky hadn't overlooked the most important thing—the most awful boredom.
>
> I saw the proofs of Stravinsky's new *Symphony of Psalms:* severe, rather dry, technically interesting . . . closest of all to *Oedipus*, but thank god without the diminished sevenths.
>
> *The Fairy's Kiss* . . . in my opinion . . [is] more agreeable than *Apollon;* at least there's some material here, even if it was acquired by rental.[27]

Stravinsky was not privy to these quips and quibbles, although on at least one occasion a bit of Prokofiev's barbed humor got back to him. When Stravinsky launched his new career as piano soloist with the Concerto for Piano and Wind Instruments, Prokofiev admired his competitor's pluck and even cited him as an example for emulation to Miaskovsky, who could not overcome fear about conducting in public: "Just look at Stravinsky, who suddenly ups and becomes a pianist," Prokofiev wrote to Miaskovsky. "That's courage!" And going on in the same vein:

> [Nikolai] Tcherepnin has dreamed all of his life about playing his concerto, but up until now he's never gotten up the nerve; but Stravinsky sticks with his exercises for a year and a half, then suddenly makes his appearance. Now he's got more engagements than I have.[28]

But Stravinsky's success may have piqued Prokofiev's pride at least a little and set the stage for some joking by Prokofiev that Stravinsky found less than humorous. Once, handed an autograph book after a concert, Prokofiev found in it an outline drawing of Stravinsky's left hand, inside of which appeared, "Igor Stravinsky, pianist." Prokofiev studied the page a moment, then remarked flippantly, "If that's all it takes, I think I'll draw a picture of my lungs and sign it, 'Sergei Prokofiev, singer!' "[29] Some time later, the incident was reported to the papers, and Prokofiev received the following letter from Stravinsky (which is reproduced in full in the fascinating *Stravinsky in Pictures and Documents):*

---

27. Prokofiev to Miaskovsky, 4 August 1925, SP-NYa, pp. 217–18, 13 May 1927, SP-NYa, p. 257, 9 July 1928, SP-NYa, p. 281, 9 November 1930, SP-NYa, p. 347, 21 January 1929, SP-NYa, p. 291.

28. Prokofiev to Miaskovsky, 9 November 1924, SP-NYa, p. 206.

29. As recounted to me by Gabriel Paitchadze, former editor of the Editions Russes de Musique, during an interview in 1962.

> Dear Seriozha: . . . I suppose that your interpretation of your joke . . . had another character than the one given to it by these unknown-to-me slanderers in the newspapers. Surely it cannot have been your intention to laugh at me as a pianist—for, after all, I play only my own compositions . . . and not so shamefully, I think, that people might make stupid and nasty fun of me.[30]

The very next day Prokofiev answered Stravinsky:

> Dear Igor Fyodorovich, I very much appreciate the spirit of friendly indulgence with which you've taken this press notice, the appearance of which caused me no little grief. It's high time to forget the period to which it relates—what you said then about my music and what I wrote in ladies' albums. The news-hack who dug up and paraphrased this misconceived witticism has done no great service, for that any shadow should fall between us would be the purest indecency.[31]

This exchange of letters seems to have dispelled the shadow that Prokofiev feared might fall between the two composers on the personal level, but it could not dispel the larger shadow under which Prokofiev lived as long as he was competing with Stravinsky in the Western musical arena—the shadow of Stravinsky's professional preeminence. If, in sizing up the competition under such circumstances, one continually finds oneself the loser in the rulings of the local referees, one may well consider trying one's luck in another arena. It would be simplistic to suggest this as the only reason for Prokofiev's decision to resettle in his homeland, but as a direct consequence of that resettling, he escaped Stravinsky's shadow completely. Stravinsky's name was anathema in the Soviet Union during the Stalinist period, and although Prokofiev all too soon came to regret his move back home, he nevertheless enjoyed a prestige, with all its perquisites, such as he had never known in the West. But the vicissitudes of life under Stalin cost Prokofiev his health. Stravinsky outlived his younger colleague by eighteen years and therefore had an appropriate opportunity to make public his private assessment of Prokofiev the composer. He did so, acknowledging that the two of them "were not really in accord musically," thus confessing the subjectivity of his judgment.[32] Summing up his estimate, Stravinsky told Robert Craft, "Prokofiev *had*

---

30. Stravinsky to Prokofiev, 20 December 1933, rpt. in Vera Stravinsky and Robert Craft, *Stravinsky in Pictures and Documents* (New York, 1978), p. 311. The whereabouts of the original letter received by Prokofiev is unknown. Contrary to his usual practice, Stravinsky kept a draft copy of this letter in his personal files, and the draft served as the basis for the translation quoted here. Stravinsky's draft copy is among the composer's personal archives now owned by the Paul Sacher Foundation of Basel, Switzerland; the translation quoted here is reprinted by permission of the Paul Sacher Foundation.

31. Prokofiev to Stravinsky, 21 December 1933. Xerox copy of the original kindly provided by Robert Craft. Translated by Natalia Rodriquez and Malcolm Brown.

32. Stravinsky and Craft, *Memories and Commentaries*, p. 68.

merits, and that rare thing, the instant imprint of personality. Nor was he cheap—facility is not the same thing as cheapness."[33]

Prokofiev left us no such succinct, personal estimate of Stravinsky, but that he never ceased to size up the competition, even after his return to Russia, cannot be doubted. On hearing the first performance of Stravinsky's Concerto in D for Violin and Orchestra, Prokofiev declared, "as with everything of Stravinsky's, there was plenty of interest in it"—a statement that can be taken as representative of Prokofiev's general and enduring attitude toward Stravinsky's music.[34] Perhaps an even better gauge of the level of Prokofiev's professional respect can be found in an admission he made in the privacy of a letter to Asafiev: "I'm wary of criticizing Stravinsky, because he has often fooled us, and the unattractive at first glance has turned out in time to be intriguing."[35] Let this admission stand as Prokofiev's epitaph to his great compatriot and competitor. As for sizing up the competition, that says it all!

---

33. Ibid., p. 69.

34. Prokofiev to Miaskovsky, 19 December 1931, SP-NYa, p. 369.

35. Prokofiev to Asafiev, 9 August 1926, IPSMK-2, p. 19.

Dance, Theater, and Collaboration

4 Music and Spectacle in *Petrushka* and *The Rite of Spring*

JANN PASLER

EVEN THE MOST admiring of Stravinsky's friends in 1913, such as the composer Florent Schmitt and the critic Jean Marnold, found the force and speed of his evolution from *Petrushka* (1911) to *The Rite of Spring* (1913) to be "disconcerting" and "brusque."[1] Only two years earlier his *Firebird* and *Petrushka* had been hailed as "feasts for the senses" and praised for their "extraordinarily fascinating orchestration." Henri Ghéon went so far as to call them not only a new kind of ballet but also a new kind of theater, the realization of "Mallarmé's dream"—ballet as poetry in its ultimate theatrical form.[2] Parisian audiences could not comprehend why the composer would turn from the fantastic imagery of these ballets to the ugly primitivism of *The Rite* or, as Jacques Rivière put it, from "poetry" to "prose."[3] Some, less sympathetic, christened the latter ballet "Le Massacre du printemps," referring as much to the riot it caused on opening night as to the strange way the work celebrated spring with Nijinsky's "epileptic convulsions" and Stravinsky's "painfully dissonant" music.[4]

Stravinsky's rapid stylistic and aesthetic transformation between 1911 and 1913 remains puzzling even today. Music scholars have concentrated on the harmonic, melodic, and rhythmic complexities of Stravinsky's early ballets, the role

---

1. Florent Schmitt, "*Les Sacres du printemps*," *La France* (4 June 1913); Jean Marnold, "Ballets Russes: *Le Sacre du Printemps*," *Mercure de France* (1 October 1913). Both articles are reproduced in *Igor Stravinsky. Le Sacre du printemps. Press-Book*, ed. François Lesure (Geneva, 1980), pp. 23–25, 35–38. All translations from this volume are by the author.

2. In his "Propos divers sur le Ballet Russe," *Nouvelle Revue Française* (1910): 210, Henri Ghéon wrote, "Art ballet, art fantasy, Mallarmé's dream, our dream is being realized—and not by us." Mallarmé explains why he finds ballet "la forme théâtrale de poésie par excellence" in his essays, "Crayonné au théâtre," from *Divagations* (Paris, 1976). Ghéon was in a position to understand Mallarmé's statement as he himself was a writer and leading drama critic for the symbolist journal *L'Ermitage*. In 1902, he did a five-part series called "Renaissance dramatique," including an important review of Debussy's *Pelléas et Mélisande*.

3. Jacques Rivière, "Le Sacre du printemps," *Nouvelle Revue Française* 5 (1 November 1913): 706–30.

4. See G. de Pawlowski, "Le Sacre du printemps," *Comoedia* (31 May 1913), and L. Vallas, "Le Sacre du printemps," *Revue française de musique* (June–July 1913), rpt. in Lesure, *Igor Stravinsky*, pp. 18–20, 27–30.

of folk tunes, and the numerous revisions made by the composer.[5] Dance historians have reported descriptive accounts from the period and appreciations of the performances.[6] But both have largely ignored what was of significant concern to their creators and to the first critics—the ballets as spectacles, works of total theater. Yet the notion of *Gesamtkunstwerk* [total artwork] was central to the Ballets Russes; the cofounder of the troupe, Alexandre Benois, claimed their circle "was ready to give its soul" for this idea.[7] Memoirs by Ballets Russes members testify to the fact that they believed their power to communicate would be enhanced to the extent that they coordinated the individual effects of each art to the benefit of the whole.[8]

The initial critical reception of the ballets offers a perspective worth reconsidering, especially because it points to the extent to which a particular aspect of the spectacle, the "correspondences" or "agreement" between the arts, impressed the works' first audiences. In 1910, Ghéon called the collaboration between choreography, music, and design in *The Firebird* "the most exquisite miracle imaginable of the harmony of sound and form and movement." He observed, "When the bird passes, it is truly the music that bears it aloft. Stravinsky, Fokine, Golovin, in my eyes, are but one name."[9] Later, in describing *The Rite*, Marnold wrote: "One can hardly imagine that the collaboration between choreographer and composer could have been successive, that their results don't come from an ever-simultaneous invention and realization, because what one sees on stage appears so spontaneously appropriate to what is evoked in the music."[10] By 1913, Pierre Lalo complained that the spectacle was subordinating everything to it, including the music.[11] The value of these correspondences between the arts became

5. See the Forte, van den Toorn, and Cyr essays in this collection for these insights and further bibliography. See also Pierre Boulez, "Stravinsky demeure," in *Musique Russe*, vol. 1, ed. Pierre Souvtchinsky (Paris, 1953), pp. 151–224; Roger Smalley, "The Sketchbook of *The Rite of Spring*," *Tempo* 91 (Winter 1969–1970): 2–13; Robert Craft, " 'Le Sacre du Printemps,' The Revisions," *Tempo* (September 1977): 2–8, and "*Le Sacre du printemps:* A Chronology of the Revisions," in *Stravinsky: Selected Correspondence*, vol. 1, ed. Robert Craft (New York, 1982), pp. 398–408; Lawrence Morton, "Footnotes to Stravinsky Studies: 'Le Sacre du Printemps,' " *Tempo* 128 (March 1979): 9–16; and Richard Taruskin, "Russian Folk Melodies in *The Rite of Spring*," *Journal of the American Musicological Society* 23 (Fall 1980): 501–43.

6. Richard Buckle, *Nijinsky* (New York, 1975), and *Diaghilev* (New York, 1979); Arnold Haskell, *Diaghileff* (New York, 1935), and *Ballet Russe* (London, 1968); Lincoln Kirstein, *Movement and Metaphor* (New York, 1970); Boris Kochno, *Diaghilev and the Ballets Russes* (New York, 1970); Prince Peter Lieven, *The Birth of the Ballets-Russes* (London, 1936); Serge Lifar, *Serge Diaghilev* (New York, 1940); Nesta Macdonald, *Diaghilev Observed* (New York, 1975), as well as numerous published memoirs from the period.

7. Alexandre Benois, *Reminiscences of the Russian Ballet* (1947; rpt. New York, 1977), pp. 370–71.

8. For a lengthy discussion of this idea, see Jann Pasler, "Debussy, Stravinsky, and the Ballets Russes: The Emergence of a New Musical Logic," Ph.D. dissertation, University of Chicago, 1981.

9. Ghéon, "Propos divers," 210–11.

10. Marnold, "Ballets Russes," p. 35.

11. Pierre Lalo, "Considérations sur le 'Sacre du printemps,' " *Le Temps* (5 August 1913), rpt. in Lesure, *Igor Stravinsky*, p. 33.

the subject of critical debate. Some felt that collaboration with Nijinsky had corrupted Stravinsky. Henri Quittard asked, "How could such a musician let himself be contaminated by transposing the dancer's aesthetic into his art?" Others, such as Pawlowski, found that "through the agreement of gestures and music, a strange new type of stylization" was born—"a style of reflex movements, of automatism."[12] Among the most intriguing commentaries on *The Rite*, written after the work's English premiere in 1913, was one by H. Colles:

> The functions of the composer and the producer are so balanced that it is possible to see every movement on the stage and at the same time to hear every note of the music. But the fusion goes deeper than this. The combination of the two elements of music and dancing does actually produce a new compound result, expressible in terms of rhythm—much as the combination of oxygen and hydrogen produces a totally different compound, water.[13]

These are the perceptions of critics who saw the original productions and wrote at a time when symbolist ideas of correspondences among the arts and synesthesia, or the synchronization of senses resulting from these correspondences, were live topics of discussion—hardly the case today. Yet in 1967, Stravinsky himself pointed to the importance of the "synchronization of music and choreography" in *The Rite* and suggested that someone study his choreographic notations for the ballet because of the "unusual analysis of the rhythmic structure" contained in them.[14] Clearly, musical analysis alone cannot tell the whole story.

In this chapter I analyze the ballets as works of total theater. First, to understand to what extent these ballets can be interpreted as literally "collective" achievements, we must examine the collaboration between Stravinsky, the choreographers, and the set designers that led to their creation. With this in mind, I posit that the artists, knowingly or not, became increasingly aware of each other's means of expression as they worked to communicate the same message—the story or central idea underlying each ballet—and that their arts can be seen functioning as signs that offer the audience an understanding of that story through sensual means. The cooperative nature of this communication by all the arts resulted in the correspondences to which the early critics responded.

My story will go further than that of the early critics, however, and not only by demonstrating what some of these specific correspondences were. I show that the correspondences helped motivate some of the artists' most radical innova-

---

12. Henri Quittard, "Le Sacre du printemps," *Le Figaro* (31 May 1913), rpt. in Lesure, *Igor Stravinsky*, p. 17; Pawlowski, "Le Sacre," p. 19.

13. H. Colles (unsigned), "The Fusion of Music and Dancing. 'Le Sacre du printemps,' " *The Times* (12 July 1913), rpt. in Lesure, *Igor Stravinsky*, p. 63.

14. Stravinsky's statement dates from 1967 and is published in "The Choreography Stravinsky-Nijinsky," the appendix to Igor Stravinsky, *The Rite of Spring Sketches 1911–1913* (London, 1969).

tions. Distinctive stylistic characteristics of Stravinsky's music such as prolonged ostinati, systematic presentation of ideas first as fragments, abrupt juxtapositions, and implausible superimpositions can be understood as results of attempts to create an intimate correspondence between the music and the events on stage. Moreover, I suggest a change in the *nature* of the correspondences from one ballet to the next and discuss how this change can be interpreted as central to the musical developments from *Petrushka* to *The Rite.*

Collaboration

A new type of collaboration generated these ballets. In his review of the premiere of *The Rite* in 1913, Rivière goes further than Ghéon in his review of *The Firebird* by suggesting an important distinction between the working methods of Western Europeans and Russians:

> Who is the author of *The Rite?* Nijinsky, Stravinsky, Roerich? This preliminary question that we cannot elude, however, does not make sense to us Westerners. For us, everything is individual; a strong and characteristic work always carries the mark of only one mind. This is not the case for the Russians. If it seems impossible for them to communicate with us, while they are among themselves, they have an extraordinary ability to feel and think the same thing at once.[15]

Rivière was right: both *Petrushka* and *The Rite of Spring* developed from the composer, the set designer, and the choreographer working as equals. Unlike traditional nineteenth-century Russian ballets, such as those of Petipa (who both worked out the entire plan of his ballet before consulting the composer and gave strict orders as to detail), these two ballets were not dominated by the will of one overriding genius. The collective conception of both extended even to the smallest details.

Petruskha was not originally conceived as a ballet. Stravinsky at first thought in terms of a piano concerto and composed without any scenario in mind, only with certain guiding images. He initially imagined a Romantic poet rolling two objects on the black and white keys of the piano; later he dreamt of the traditional clown, the "immortal and unhappy hero" of "every fair in all countries."[16] Diaghilev heard the initial sketches in late summer 1910 and urged Stravinsky to develop the theme of the puppet's sufferings into a whole ballet. While he was in

15. Jacques Rivière, "Le Sacre du Printemps," *Nouvelle Revue Française* 5 (1 August 1913): 309.

16. Vera Stravinsky and Robert Craft, *Stravinsky in Pictures and Documents* (New York, 1978), p. 66. In his *Strawinsky* (Paris, 1931), André Schaeffner postulates that the piece actually began with the Petrushka chord itself (pp. 23–25).

Switzerland, Stravinsky relates in his *Autobiography,* they "worked out together the general lines of the subject and the plot . . . the fair, with its crowd . . . the coming to life of the dolls . . . and their love tragedy."[17]

This reminiscence acknowledges only that Benois, whose love of Russian puppet theater was well known, was chosen to do the scenery and costumes "by mutual agreement." However, Benois's memoirs and the recently published correspondence between him and Stravinsky reveal quite another picture.[18] Evidently, Benois was responsible for many details of the story, including—he claims—the addition of the Moor and several of the characters at the fair. Having tried to arrange a similar Petrushka performance the year before in St. Petersburg, he was full of ideas about a modern version of the traditional Punch and Judy shows that he had treasured since his childhood. The composer collaborated with Benois in writing the scenario to ensure that all parts of the production, in Stravinsky's own words, "be completely coordinated with the music."[19] He went so far as to dedicate the work to Benois. Admitting that Benois had also "played an important role in advising Fokine on the staging and choreography," Stravinsky actually named him coauthor, a point over which the two later squabbled because of the royalties involved.[20]

The genesis of *The Rite* was also collective, although in the beginning it did not involve Diaghilev or a commission for the Ballets Russes. Again, contemporary correspondence paints a somewhat different picture than that offered by Stravinsky in his *Autobiography.* Like *Petrushka,* the ballet began with a vision, "a solemn pagan rite: sage elders, seated in a circle, watched a young girl dance herself to death."[21] This idea came to Stravinsky while he was finishing *The Firebird* in early spring 1910, even before conceiving *Petrushka* in August of that same year. The composer says he described his vision immediately to Roerich, who thereupon became his collaborator. When discussing the conception of the work with N. F. Findeizen, the editor of the *Russian Music Gazette,* in 1912, Stravinsky confided that he "wanted to compose the libretto with Roerich, because who else could help, who else knows the secret of our ancestors' close feeling for the earth?"[22] Benois further claimed that "the original idea (for the libretto) was prob-

17. Igor Stravinsky, *An Autobiography* (New York, 1936), p. 32.

18. Benois, *Reminiscences,* and L. S. D'iachkova and Boris Yarustovsky, eds., *I. F. Stravinsky: Stat'i i Materiali* [I. F. Stravinsky: Essays and documents] (Moscow, 1973), pp. 449–56. Letters 13, 17, 19, 20, and 21 have been translated in Stravinsky and Craft, *Pictures and Documents,* pp. 68–70, but with errors that include putting a musical example in letter 17 that belongs in letter 21 and omitting the one that accompanies letter 17.

19. Stravinsky letter 21 to Benois in D'iachkova and Yarustovsky, *I. F. Stravinsky,* pp. 455, 456.

20. Stravinsky and Craft, *Pictures and Documents,* p. 71.

21. Stravinsky, *An Autobiography,* p. 31.

22. Stravinsky, letter of 15 December 1912 to Findeizen, quoted in French in Stravinsky, *The Rite of Spring Sketches,* pp. 33–34, and, in part, in English in Stravinsky and Craft, *Pictures and Documents,* p. 92.

ably Roerich's; if, in fact, it came to Stravinsky, it must have been due to the influence of his painter friend."[23]

Stravinsky's *Autobiography* reveals neither the important role Roerich must have played in the work's conception nor the initial secrecy in which *The Rite* was first veiled. By 2 July 1910, plans had advanced enough for Stravinsky to write to Roerich, "naturally the success of *The Firebird* has encouraged Diaghilev for future projects and sooner or later we will have to tell him about 'The Great Sacrifice.' "[24] On 9 August, he announced that work had begun, but even then Diaghilev's role remained ambiguous. Although Stravinsky must have told Diaghilev about the ballet over the summer, the composer wrote to Benois on 3 November, "Have Diaghilev and Fokine made up. . . .? This is very important to me, for if they have, then 'The Great Sacrifice' will be Diaghilev's, if not, then Telyakovsky's [the director of the Imperial Russian Theater], which is hardly good news." In July 1911, Stravinsky traveled at Roerich's invitation from Switzerland to Russia to see the set designer at the folk art colony, Talashkino. There the two settled on a plan of action for the ballet as well as on the titles of the individual dances. The actual commission from Diaghilev did not come until after this meeting, in August 1911, and Nijinsky apparently did not become actively involved until a year later. The composer's 14 December 1912 letter to Roerich says that Nijinsky "started his staging of 'The Spring' only yesterday" and that Stravinsky, at Nijinsky's request, was providing substantial help to the choreographer. Stravinsky's and Nijinsky's choreographic notations for *The Rite* document the extent to which composer and choreographer worked together at this final stage.[25]

Although the two ballets were nearly contemporaneous and involved a similar collaborative process, the choice of collaborators assured that very different kinds of spectacles would result. As was generally the case in the Ballets Russes, according to Benois, the set designers played a significant role in writing the scenarios.[26] Chosen for their knowledge of the ballets' subjects, both Alexandre Benois and Nikolai Roerich used the ballets as pretexts for dramatizing their images of earlier times. With his pre-Easter carnival, set in early nineteenth-century St. Petersburg, Benois expressed his fascination with eighteenth- and nineteenth-century popular culture. By contrast, Roerich, an amateur archaeologist, was able to draw upon the knowledge of primitive rituals he had gained from numerous archaeological expeditions.

The choreographers Mikhail Fokine and Vaslav Nijinsky also brought different perspectives to the two ballets. Fokine, at the turn of the century, was respon-

---

23. Benois, *Reminiscences,* p. 347.

24. All correspondence with Roerich and Benois cited in this paragraph comes from Stravinsky and Craft, *Pictures and Documents,* pp. 77–83, 92.

25. These are published in the Appendix to *The Rite of Spring Sketches.*

26. In his *Reminiscences,* Benois writes, "The part played by the painters was a great one. . . . It was the painters who helped arrange the main lines of the ballet and the whole production." (Cited in Serge Lifar, *A History of the Russian Ballet* [New York, 1954], p. 207.)

sible for liberating the dance from its narrow set of gestures and costumes, replacing pure virtuosity with a new vocabulary of expressive gestures inspired in part by Isadora Duncan. The story of *Petrushka* interested him precisely because it demanded new gestures, semantic in nature yet different from those of traditional pantomine. Nijinsky, then a young dancer, had only begun choreographing in 1912. As we shall see, *The Rite* provided him with an ideal opportunity to experiment with Dalcroze's eurhythmic techniques.

Correspondences

Even more crucial distinctions than those arising from the different collaborators' varying inputs can be found in the correspondences between the arts in *Petrushka* and *The Rite*. In Baudelaire's poem "Les Correspondences," one finds references to two types of correspondences and the synesthesia they effect. "Vertical" correspondences work between the material world of sense impressions and the spiritual world of ideas; "horizontal" correspondences work between the senses themselves in such a way that a stimulus upon one creates an impression upon another. In *The Firebird* and *Petrushka,* vertical correspondences result when the arts embody or create aesthetic "equivalents" (to use a symbolist term) for some aspect of the story. To the extent that the sounds, gestures, and colors are similar in quality, they reinforce one another and enhance one's understanding of the story.

Most scholars and critics agree as to the narrative or cinematographic nature of these earlier ballets; however, they cannot explain what is different about *The Rite*. Among the early critics, the Englishman H. Colles raised perhaps the most intriguing point in this regard. *The Firebird* and *Petrushka* were for him "the first heralds of a new order of things"—they "began to liberate music and to make it more definite and more directly illustrative of the stage." But he saw *The Rite* as "a step nearer to a real fusion of music and dancing."[27] The same year, in an article whose actual authorship has been much debated, Stravinsky admitted that *The Rite* "no longer calls to mind fairy tales nor human misery or joy," but that in it he "pushes himself toward a little more vast abstraction."[28]

27. Colles, "The Fusion of Music and Dancing," p. 63.

28. The debate concerning the authorship of this article, published as "Ce que j'ai voulu exprimer dans Le Sacre du printemps" in *Montjoie* (29 May 1913) has continued until recently. In *An Autobiography,* Stravinsky stated that the article was actually the result of an interview made by R. Canudo and that he "could not recognize" himself in it (p. 49). Craft devotes an entire appendix to the issue in *Pictures and Documents* (pp. 522–26). However, the corrections that Stravinsky gave in 1913 to a version of the article published in Russia (now available in Craft, *Stravinsky: Selected Correspondence,* vol. 1, p. 54) are so minor as to suggest that the original wording was not that far from Stravinsky's own.

But more can be said. By examining the nature of the narrative in each ballet and the relationships between the narrative and the arts and finally among the arts themselves, one can locate and define a change in the type of correspondences, and specifically an increasing interest in the horizontal correspondences posited by Baudelaire. As we will see, this can best be summarized as a change from the mutual replication of a story by each of the arts to the mutual replication of certain formal relationships. This transformation from correspondences that depend on a narrative to those based on similar structure in each of the arts signals a major shift in what is considered necessary for a work's coherence. In tracing this development from the middle tableaux of *Petrushka* to *The Rite of Spring*, I shall show how the correspondences created in the outer tableaux of *Petrushka* served as an important transition. I shall also suggest some long-lasting consequences of these correspondences in Stravinsky's stylistic evolution.

Petrushka, Tableaux Two and Three

In 1911, what seemed most unusual about *Petrushka* were its two middle tableaux. Like *The Firebird,* these two tableaux tell a story—the conflict between Petrushka and the Moor to win the ballerina. However, the novelty in both these ballets lies not in the use of a story, but rather in the kind of story used, one that was more imaginary than realistic. Such fantasies depend for their elaboration not on the psychological development of a series of motives, but on the direct communication of images that can be understood through many of the senses at once.

The action of the second and third tableaux takes place within the puppets' private cells, like a play within the play. In the first tableau, the puppets appear to be strictly mechanical, controlled by the magician and brought out to entertain the crowd. But in the second and third scenes, they reveal their hidden passions and act out their own drama. The story proceeds primarily by linear narrative, with a clear presentation of the conflict, the struggle between the two puppets, and the denouement.

Each of the arts assists the public in its perception of the story by creating aesthetic equivalents of the characters' states of mind and the action.[29] For example, to remind the viewer constantly of Petrushka's existential state, set designer Benois hung in his cell a portrait of the puppet's master, the magician. Stravinsky created a musical means of communicating the irreconcilable conflict between Pe-

29. "Equivalent" is a term Maurice Denis and other symbolist theorists use to describe the work of art not as the reproduction of reality but the translation of it in artistic terms. My use of the word also incorporates the notion of sign, meaning that the artwork not only translates the artist's inspiration into sensual expression but also communicates something to the perceiver. In referring to a story through some resemblance to it, the arts in the middle tableaux function as what Charles Peirce would call "icons." See his discussion of icons in his "Logic as Semiotic: The Theory of Signs," in *Philosophical Papers of Charles Peirce,* ed. Justus Buchler (New York, 1955).

truskha's mechanical body and the human emotions trapped in it by juxtaposing two sharply clashing triads a tritone apart, F♯ major and C major. (He links certain motivic material and instrumentation to each puppet throughout the ballet and creates between them musical interactions that mirror those of the scenario.) When Petrushka curses his condition and the man in the portrait, Fokine has him hitting his head against the wall to the rhythm of the alternating F♯-major and C-major arpeggios.

The real challenge of the tableau, according to Benois, was to express Petrushka's "pitiful oppression and his hopeless efforts to achieve personal dignity without ceasing to be a puppet." To do this, he notes, "both music and libretto are spasmodically interrupted by outbursts of illusive joy and frenzied despair."[30] The entrance of the ballerina into Petrushka's cell best exemplifies this. Particularly in this scene, Fokine found that "the rapidity and abruptness of [Petrushka's] ever-changing emotions" provided a perfect opportunity to experiment with unusual expressive gestures.[31] When the ballerina enters at rehearsal number **56,** he has Petrushka jump in delight in the middle of each of the 2/4 measures, extending his arms and legs outward in the shape of a large X (see Figures 4.1 and 4.2). When she leaves, he falls on the ground (**58**), resumes his curses (**58–60**), and finally crashes through the wall (**61**). To reflect Petrushka's changing emotions in this scene musically, Stravinsky experiments with frequently changing tempi and meters—there are nine tempo indications and many sudden stops and starts. By shifting from predominantly duple meter and two-measure groups to prolonged sections in triple meter and three-measure groups in **56** and **57,** the composer signals a turning point in Petrushka, a shift from dwelling on his loneliness to momentarily believing that he has succeeded in winning the ballerina.[32]

These correspondences may seem somewhat conventional, regardless of the startling innovations inspired by such a story. The relationship between the arts and the story is indeed representational, but I suspect that their significance goes beyond the creation of aesthetic equivalents. Because of the importance all the artists gave to the story, Stravinsky, Fokine, and Benois must have been drawn into a heightened awareness of one another's tasks, even their means of expression. Perhaps without the close coordination among the arts achieved in these two tableaux, the artists would not have been led to create the far more daring kind of coordination and correspondences among the arts characteristic of the outer tableaux.

---

30. Benois, *Reminiscences,* p. 338. One can study this choreography by examining the films made of the ballet found at the dance collection of the New York Public Library, New York City.

31. Mikhail Fokine, *Memoires of a Ballet Master,* ed. Anatole Chujoy (London, 1961), p. 186.

32. In his "The Music of the Ballet," in *Petrushka* (New York, 1967), pp. 173–84, Charles Hamm traces other narrative aspects of Stravinsky's music for these tableaux.

Figure 4.1 Premiere of *Petrushka* (1911). Sketch of Nijinsky as Petrushka in the second tableau of the ballet, expressing "outbursts of joy and frenzied despair," perhaps at rehearsal number **56.** Drawing made in 1911 by Valentine Hugo (née Gross). Courtesy of the Theater Collection, Victoria and Albert Museum, London.

Petrushka, Tableaux One and Four

The fair scenes of the first and fourth tableaux posed a different compositional problem for Stravinsky, Benois, and Fokine because they contain little story or characterization to be communicated or commented on. What Benois calls the "illusion of life" projected by these tableaux comes not from any narrative, but from the sheer multiplicity of characters and events on stage.[33] In order to create any

33. Benois, *Reminiscences,* p. 336.

Figure 4.2 Sketch illustrating Petrushka's antics after the ballerina enters, second tableau of *Petrushka*, at **56.** Drawing made in 1911 by Valentine Hugo. Courtesy of the Theater Collection, Victoria and Albert Museum, London.

relationship between their arts and what was happening on stage, the artists had to work with this multiplicity and find some way of coordinating a sequence of artistic ideas with the rapid succession of seemingly unrelated stage events. As a result, there develops a new kind of correspondence both between the arts and the stage in these tableaux and between the audience's various sensual perceptions that does not depend on a story. This increased attention to the actual stage action had profound consequences for Stravinsky.

Because of the sheer number of characters on stage and the diversity of movements and interactions within these tableaux, the tableaux open with crowd scenes for which each of the artists created equivalents, as in the middle tableaux. Benois filled the stage with flags, painted signs, a yellow balcony, a little blue theater, a merry-go-round, and people of all sorts "to reproduce the picture of our

St. Petersburg Butter Week fair in full detail."[34] Fokine had the people mill around in this setting as if at a carnival. To suggest the huge indistinguishable mass of people at the fair in the opening measures of both tableaux, Stravinsky used multiple planes of sound, with their own ostinati or tremoli. Each time the crowd swarms, swallowing any individuals who might have stepped out from it, the merry-go-round turns and Stravinsky increases the musical chaos by adding more ostinati to the thick, blurred texture.

Unable to focus on the feelings, personalities, or specific actions of the crowd's individual members, Stravinsky, Fokine, and Benois had to invent something else to accompany the various characters who take turns entertaining the crowd: the merrymakers, the showman, the organ-grinder, the street dancers, the magician with his puppets, the nursemaids, the peasant with his bear, the merchant with his gypsies, the coachman and stable boys, and the mummers and maskers. The problem posed by such variety is not only how to differentiate the groups but also how to direct the audience's attention from one to the next.

The collaborators resolved this issue for the most part traditionally enough—by giving each group of characters its own tune, its own way of dancing, and its own traditional garb that differentiate them from one another. Although these tunes, dances, and costumes suggest those of a carnival, the relationship between them and the characters with which they are associated, however, is relatively arbitrary. As many scholars have shown, most of the melodies are folk tunes or derivatives of folk tunes. By their very nature, such tunes are abstract melodies determined by the sequence of syllables in their original text and meant to serve several occasions. In these tableaux, the connection between a certain melody, dance step, or costume and a certain character on stage does not depend on any specific resemblance of artistic means to subject. Rather, it is simply the consistent coordination between each character's appearance and specific artistic ideas that creates an automatic association between the two in the perceiver's mind.[35]

The first tune in the ballet sets up this kind of connection immediately. At first, one hears only a three-measure fragment in the bass instruments at **2.** Then the fragment stretches to eight measures at **3,** though innumerable ostinati continue to hide it among a mass of indistinct sounds. From **3** to **5,** flutes and oboes superimpose rhythmic variants of the fragment. This fragmentation creates not only musical tension but also dramatic suspense before the rise of the curtain at **4.** Resolution of this tension is realized at **5** with the first appearance of the tune in its entirety and with full orchestra. Simultaneously, the scenario indicates that "a small group of tipsy merrymakers, prancing, passes by." The coincidence of the

34. Ibid.

35. Because the arts in this case refer to something on stage not by some similar trait but by automatic association, they function as what Peirce would call "indices." See his discussion of indexical signs in his "Logic as Semiotic."

entire tune with the merrymakers' presence before the crowd at **5** suggests an association of the tune fragments from **2** to **5** with some previous activity of the group, even before the curtain goes up (perhaps attempts to break through the crowd and gain its attention). The explicit return of the merrymakers when the tune recurs at **20** supports this hypothesis. Presenting only fragments of a melody as a certain group moves in front of the crowd, before the group has seized the audience's attention, Stravinsky gradually builds a direct association between his music and the different characters on stage. The composer may even have developed this highly characteristic technique to facilitate the creation of such correspondences.

This type of association between music and characters recurs throughout the tableau. After the merrymakers, the organ-grinder steps forward momentarily. Again one hears only a fragment of the melody with which he will entertain them thirteen measures later. Similarly, the nursemaids who appear in **90** of the fourth tableau are announced by two fragments of a tune still enmeshed in the whirling orchestral tremoli and ostinati that were associated with the crowd music from the opening of the scene. As with the ideas in the first tableau, the nursemaids' entire melody does not unfold until **92**, after its fragmentation. Like the merrymakers' motive, this melody returns when the nursemaids dance with the coachmen and stable boys later in the scene at **112**.

Such melodies in the first and fourth tableaux function as signals or instructions that, through repeated association, direct the audience's attention to the character they accompany. In other words, the melodic fragments associated with the characters not only create tension, direction, and drive in the music; they also condition the audience to *look* for the character whose music it *hears*. Stravinsky's music thus elicits a visual as well as an aural response. In this way, the composer builds horizontal correspondences between his audience's aural and visual perceptions. Rather than depending upon a scenario, this kind of correspondence among the arts produces a synchronicity in the public's aural, visual, and kinesthetic perceptions of stage events.

Two of Stravinsky's most significant techniques in *Petrushka,* which have often been discussed in strictly musical, formalist terms,[36] actually mirror this attention to a close coordination between the musical and visual aspects of the ballet. These techniques are vertical and horizontal juxtaposition. Abrupt vertical juxtapositions of contrasting musical ideas accompany the sudden emergence of each new character before the crowd. After the instantaneous switch from the different ostinati associated with the crowd to a tutti statement of the merrymakers' tune at **5**, the next major juxtaposition comes at **7**. The sudden change of tempo, meter, and style from the folk tune to the repeated staccato E's in the strings signals an interruption of their dance by the showman, who, according to the sce-

36. Edward T. Cone, "Stravinsky: The Progress of a Method," *Perspectives of New Music* 1 (Fall 1962): 18–26.

nario, "entertains the crowd from the height of his booth." This same music returns to interrupt the organ-grinder and the consistent 3/4 meter at **17** when "the barrel organ and the music box stop playing" and the "showman again attracts the attention of the crowd." It also breaks in on the merrymakers' tune at **22** and intervenes between two statements of the crowd music at **24–25**. These frequent changes from forte to piano, from one set of instruments to another, from one meter to another, as well as from one motive and accompaniment to others—all without transition—underscore Stravinsky's desire to embody in music the "visual blinks" called for in the scenario. Responding to these musical stimuli, a prime example of Baudelaire's horizontal correspondences, the audience suddenly shifts its concentration from one character to another.

The simultaneity of numerous stage events further motivates horizontal juxtapositions or the superimposition of musical ideas. In the first tableau, one finds the merrymaker's motive within the crowd music from **2** to **4** and together with the organ-grinder's tune and crowd motive at the end of **16**. In the fourth tableau, the rising-fourth motive from the opening of the first tableau appears with the nursemaids' tune at **92**. Also in this tableau, two motives, one in the horns and the other in the strings, simultaneously accompany the nursemaids at **98**. These simultaneities, inspired by the visual multiplicity on stage, resulted in a polyphony of quite independent ideas and consequently allowed Stravinsky to experiment with pluridirectional rather than unidirectional processes in music.

With rhythmic means borrowed from the dance, Stravinsky was able to integrate these vertical and horizontal juxtapositions. A constant eighth-note or quarter-note often provides continuity when the meter is changing frequently, such as during the showman's appearances at **7, 17, 22,** and **24–25** or in the rhythmic transformation of the merrymaker's motive by the flutes and oboes in **4** and **19**. Proportioned measure grouping—even periodic four- and eight-bar phrases, as in the Russian dance of the puppets—supply balance to sections brimming with juxtaposed textures; this is especially true in the many dances built upon an interaction between two tunes or motives. The ordering of events and the building of proportional relationships among them replace traditional development as a means of creating form.

By trying both to follow the rapid succession of events in these tableaux, rather than any story, and to create a close coordination between his music and those events, Stravinsky was led to explore discontinuity in music. Ideas first presented as fragments, abrupt juxtapositions, and implausible simultaneities reveal the composer's fascination with the unexpected and his desire to capture an element of surprise. But the music is not without its continuity. In the place of any story, the stage action itself provides the audience with conceptual coherence, a way of understanding relationships between perceptually discontinuous musical sections. The music's rhythmic organization also creates continuity in the work, but one that is relational rather than directional. Through its novel approach to discontinuity and continuity, Stravinsky's music makes *how* we hear as important as *what* we hear. Such techniques were expanded upon in *The Rite* and soon became hallmarks of the composer's style.

The Rite of Spring

If aspects of the music, dance, and costumes in a ballet could be made to refer almost automatically to stage events, then there was no longer need for a story in order to build correspondences. And if, in their simultaneous occurrences, music, gesture, and action could become directly associated with one another, then a new kind of artistic synthesis was possible, one based on horizontal correspondences between the arts rather than on vertical correspondences with some story.

In *The Rite of Spring*, whatever story there is serves principally as a pretext to bring the artists together. Both Grigoriev, the stage director, and Stravinsky spoke in 1913 of a lack of plot in the ballet and referred to the organizing principle of the work instead as choreographic "succession." Later, in his *Autobiography*, Stravinsky clarified this:

> Although I had conceived the subject of the *Sacre du printemps* without any plot, some plan of action had to be designed for the sacrificial action. For this, it was necessary that I should see Roerich . . . we settled on the visual embodiment of the *Sacre* and the definite sequence of its different episodes.[37]

There is, of course, some narrative in the ballet: a primitive people celebrates the onset of spring with a series of dances, chooses a virgin, and sacrifices her. But such a "plan of action" does not require linear connection between its distinct parts. The action is ritualistic; it consists of a succession of structures. This kind of action allowed Stravinsky full latitude within which to develop further his new ideas about musical continuity.

In a letter to N. F. Findeizen, Stravinsky describes the individual parts of the ballet as *"jeux"* or games:

> First part. Contains ancient slave games . . . ritual dance games in a circle . . . the game of abduction . . . the dance games between two villages. Second part. The secret night games of the girls on the sacred hill.[38]

This idea of games points to the real subject matter of the ballet—the creative act itself. Whether in sound, movement, or color, abstract play characterizes artistic creation. Prehistory, spring, and adolescence are metaphors for creation—moments when society, nature, and people emerge from their embryonic states.

---

37. Stravinsky, *An Autobiography*, pp. 35, 36.

38. See n. 22.

Such metaphors in turn encouraged the artists to focus on their own creative activities as well as those of their partners.

CENTRAL CONCERNS

Roerich, Stravinsky, and Nijinsky shared three concerns. Each was interested in suggesting a relationship between the idea of prehistory, spring, and adolescence; each saw primitive times as an opportunity to search for the primordial roots of his art, even to grope toward an abstract language of form and movement; and each was interested in group rather than individual effects, doing away with local devices in favor of the global instantaneous effect of the whole. By their nature, these preoccupations with creating a language of form and movement and with the effect of the whole cut across differences in artistic genre and set the stage for the artists' discovery of still closer correspondences between the arts.

Roerich believed that "the man who didn't understand the past could not think of the future."[39] Indeed, his interest in exploring man's relationship to his ancestors and the cosmos came from his desire to connect "our earthly existence with a Supreme."[40] In his studies, Roerich found rhythm to be the "sacred symbol" of ancient peoples. For him, artistic creation, or "the rhythm of human striving and the victory of the spirit," was a spiritual activity; it provided a key to understanding the Supreme Creator.

In seeking to recall both earliest times and the first days of spring, Roerich turned to the purest forms of nature. In his set design for the first scene of *The Rite*, "The Adoration of the Earth," he painted only a simple rounded hill, placed a boulder in front of it, and placed trees, rocks, smaller hills, and part of a lake around it. The second scene brings one to the top of a "sacred hill, amid enchanted rocks." Roerich's colors, applied in strong, heavy layers, reinforce the starkness of these timeless images. According to Benois, Roerich used them to "call forth a familiar echo in our hearts."[41]

Roerich also had another idea in designing *The Rite:* he wanted to suggest unity rather than diversity among peoples. With this in mind, he designed costumes of uniform shape—a one- or two-part tunic—and covered their borders with abstract patterns, circles, triangles, and other geometric images. That the

39. Edgar Lansbury, "The Art of Nicholas Roerich," *Nicholas Roerich 1874–1974* (New York, 1974), p. 5.

40. Nicholas Roerich, "Sacre," Address at the Wanamaker Auditorium under the auspices of the League of Composers, 1930. Communicated to the author by the Roerich Museum in New York. All following quotes in this paragraph also come from this speech.

41. "Alexander Benois writes about Roerich," *Nicolas Roerich*, p. 24. Another set designer for the Ballets Russes and one of the troupe's founders, Léon Bakst, had a similar notion. In his "Ways of Classicism in Art," *Apollon*, nos. 2, 3 (1909), Bakst wrote, "The painting of the future calls for a lapidary style, because the new arts cannot tolerate affection and effeminacy . . . the elements of painting are man and stone" (trans. Susan Summer).

two chosen ones honored by the tribe, the "oldest and wisest" in the first scene and the young virgin in the last one, have costumes like those of the others draws attention to the fact that they represent the collective spirit of their tribe.

According to Benois, "Stravinsky was attracted by the idea of 'reconstructing the mysterious past' " chiefly because it left him "free from all constraints and all rules" in "his search for unusual rhythms and sounds."[42] However, in his letter to Findeizen of 15 December 1912, Stravinsky expressed the same preoccupation as Roerich:

> I wanted the whole of the composition to give the feeling of the closeness between man and earth, the community of their lives with the earth, and I sought to do this with lapidary rhythms. The whole thing must be put on in dance from beginning to end. I give not one measure for pantomime.[43]

For Stravinsky, as for Roerich, the link between man and nature was rhythm.

In his sketchbook for *The Rite,* Stravinsky wrote himself this memorandum: "Music exists if there is rhythm, as life exists if there is a pulse."[44] He took as the subject matter of his composition the rhythm of nature, or what he calls in his own libretto "the sublime growth of nature which renews itself, the total panic ascent of the universal sap."[45] By its very nature, *The Rite* project offered Stravinsky an ideal opportunity in which to experiment with rhythm as his primary musical element.

To attract the audience's attention to the interaction of similar and contrasting rhythms, Stravinsky, like Roerich, preferred mass movements to individual articulations. In his *Autobiography,* he states, "In composing the *Sacre,* I had imagined the spectacular part of the performance as a series of rhythmic mass movements of the greatest simplicity which would have an instantaneous effect on the audience."[46] In these words lie the seeds of a return to thinking about music in purely abstract rather than programmatic terms.

In a 1913 interview given while he was choreographing *The Rite,* Nijinsky also expressed an interest in exploring man's relationship to nature, the primordial elements of his art, and man's community with his fellow men. His is perhaps the most radical expression of the shared artistic ideal:

> The *Sacre du printemps* . . . is really the soul of nature expressed by movement to music. It is the life of the stones and the trees. There are no human beings in it. It is only the incarnation of

42. Benois, *Reminiscences,* p. 347.

43. See n. 22.

44. Stravinsky, *The Rite of Spring Sketches,* p. 36.

45. Stravinsky-Canudo, "Ce que j'ai voulu exprimer."

46. Stravinsky, *An Autobiography,* p. 48.

> Nature . . . and of human nature. It will be danced only by the corps de ballet, for it is a thing of concrete masses, not of individual effects.[47]

For Nijinsky, pure movement was the best expression of both nature and man. "Away with anecdotes, away with action encumbered by pantomime and more or less ingenious twists in the plot; let us exalt solely the plasticity of movement for its own sake," he exclaimed.[48] This aesthetic inclination reflects, at least in part, Nijinsky's enthusiasm for Dalcrozian eurhythmics with which he had first come into contact in 1911, when Emile Jacques-Dalcroze came to St. Petersburg. He again encountered it in 1912, when he and Diaghilev visited Dalcroze's school in Hellerau several times. The two became so interested in eurhythmics that, at the end of 1912, they engaged a student of the school, Marie Rambert, to give eurhythmics courses for the troupe's dancers. Applying eurhythmic techniques, which taught that there can be a direct association between rhythms in time and rhythms in space and between the duration of a sound and the correlative gesture accompanying it, Nijinsky created a new type of dancing, "stylized gesture." This dancing was based on the physical embodiment of rhythms contained in the music.

Like Stravinsky and Roerich, Nijinsky knew that, in order to draw attention to the rhythmic invention of his choreography, he had to abolish individual articulations. For the most part, his choreography presents "only a succession of rhythmically moving groups."[49] (See Plates 4.1, 4.2, 4.3, 4.4.) By concentrating almost entirely on rhythmical movement, cynically referred to by some of the dancers as "rhythmical stamping without any other movement," Nijinsky returned to what he felt to be the most basic aspect of the dance.[50]

At the center of *The Rite of Spring*, then, lies a concept rather than a story. This concept, "the rhythm of human striving and the victory of the spirit," as Roerich put it, not only links people with their ancestors and the cosmos; it also links the arts with one another. One can detect in the three artists' work a fascination with elements they shared and, even more, with elements that were unique to their partners' art forms and therefore alien to their own. As a result, one can show two important developments in *The Rite*. First, the arts become imitative of one another's artistic processes—not just associated with one another when certain stage events recur, as in the outer tableaux of *Petrushka*. Second, this imitation of one another's means of expression led to the incorporation of formal relationships previously unknown in each art and resulted in new kinds of horizontal

---

47. Interview in the *Pall Mall Gazette*, 15 February 1913, cited in Macdonald, *Diaghilev Observed*, p. 90.

48. S. M., "Nijinsky chorégraphe," *Comoedia* 11/2053 (16 May 1913).

49. S. L. Grigoriev, *The Diaghilev Ballet, 1909–1929* (London, 1960), p. 89.

50. Ibid., p. 90; see also Lydia Sokolova, *Dancing for Diaghilev*, ed. Richard Buckle (London, 1960), p. 42.

correspondences between the arts. As composer, choreographer, and set designer struggled to achieve the same structural design, radically new types of construction arose. The resulting synthesis was an unprecedented achievement in the history of the theater.

VISUAL DESIGN AND MUSIC

The most difficult part of the challenge—and perhaps the most important—was a coordination between the temporal and spatial aspects of the ballet. In 1888, Gauguin defined the two primary characteristics of visual perception, instantaneity and simultaneity:

> In [painting], all sensations are condensed; contemplating it, everyone can . . .—with a single glance—have his soul invaded . . . everything is summed up in an instant. . . . The hearing can only grasp a single sound at a time, whereas the sight takes in everything and simultaneously simplifies it at will.[51]

Roerich's hard, clear colors and rough, primitive forms exaggerate the instantaneous effect on the viewer as described by Gauguin; they do away with any chiaroscuro veiling in order to address him directly. The strong, heavy lines and distinct layers underscore the simultaneous interaction of the various elements—the rocks, hills, trees, and the universe.

In order that his art form corroborate the visual effect of the ballet, Stravinsky attempted to create musical equivalents for the instantaneity and simultaneity projected by the set design. For example, thirty-two percussive repetitions of one chord (a combination of the dominant seventh on E♭ major over an F♭-major chord in the bass) accompany the first visual moment, the rising of the curtain in part 1. This passage affects the public with the same immediacy and stasis as the backdrop being revealed for the first time. The sound forms a block with the massive power of the boulders in the set design. Stravinsky even once described this ballet as an immense and heavy "stone sculpture"—quite different from the airiness sought by traditional ballet.[52]

Stravinsky also wrote in easily recognizable patterns that contrasted markedly with those around them, creating a direct and instantaneous association of specific music with specific visual phenomena. The effect of such contrasts recalls the visual relationship wherein a figure, because of its dynamic shape and inner coherence, stands out from the more uniform and static background. Because the two do not necessarily integrate or respond to each other, this is a somewhat different relationship than the musical one between a melody and accompaniment.

---

51. Paul Gauguin, "Notes synthétiques, 1888," in *Theories of Modern Art* ed. Hershel Chipp (Berkeley and Los Angeles, 1968), p. 61.

52. Cited in André Schaeffner, *Strawinsky* (Paris, 1931), p. 37.

An example comes after the curtain rises in part 1. In composing this scene, Stravinsky imagined a visual figure/ground relationship between the first person to step from the crowd (the old woman who prepares to predict the future) and the mass of people on stage. In September 1911, he wrote to Roerich:

> The image of the old woman in a squirrel fur sticks in my mind. She is constantly before my eyes as I compose the "Divination with Twigs." I see her running in front of the group, stopping it, and interrupting the rhythmic flow.[53]

Using a short succession of grace notes followed by triplets in the winds at **15**, Stravinsky focuses attention on the old woman with a motive that stands out, by its rhythmic and melodic shape, dynamic intensity, and contrasting timbre, from the repeating chord in the strings and horns. As in the first and fourth tableaux of *Petrushka,* this motive signals the audience to look for the old woman throughout the scene (compare **19, 21,** and **26**); but unlike in *Petrushka,* here the presence of a figure/ground relationship both on stage and in the music creates a horizontal correspondence between them that involves a similarity of structure, not just an automatic association.

Stravinsky amplifies the immediacy of his statements by regularly and deliberately breaking the momentum, by abruptly switching without transition from one idea to the next. His orchestration reinforces these discontinuities with crisp, dry articulations that stand apart like the flat colors and distinct lines of Roerich's backdrop. As in *Petrushka,* contrasting musical ideas are often associated with different characters on stage. But in *The Rite,* he goes further, building horizontal correspondences between the motivic structures of the two arts. In the "Games of the Rival Tribes," for example, Stravinsky juxtaposes two different sets of instruments, two motives, and two rhythmic patterns to mirror the visual confrontation. The sudden collision of the trumpets, trombones, and tubas backed up by wind trills with the horns, bassoon, and celli characterizes the entire dance. Such music reflects the struggle between the two groups of dancers on stage. From **60** to **65**, two motives constantly alternate, with the loud marcato motive characterizing the beginning of their dance from **57** to **60** and the soft, more lyrical one dominating the end from **64** to **65.** Instrumental and motivic forms of juxtaposition *implicitly* refer to the contending tribes, but in his choreographic notes, Stravinsky *explicitly* links a third form of musical juxtaposition with the visual juxtaposition of the different groups on stage—that between two rhythmic patterns. At **60,** Stravinsky notes that the women should dance in 4/4 to the new motive in the oboes and clarinets while the men dance in 2/4 to the counterrhythm in the English horns—an indication that Stravinsky specifically intended the visual counterpoint of the dancers to underline the musical counterpoint of the two rhythms.

Contrasting instrumentations, motives, and rhythmic patterns thus reflect

53. Letter of 16 September 1911, cited in Stravinsky and Craft, *Pictures and Documents,* p. 83.

Stravinsky's sensitivity to the visual aspect of the ballet. As in *Petrushka*, these interruptions to the musical flow jar listeners into looking from one character to another while accustoming them to hearing the elements of Stravinsky's sharply differentiated musical design. Watching characters interact on stage while listening to the music, then, not only makes these sudden juxtapositions plausible; it also introduces a new way of listening, one that allows for frequent discontinuities.

In *The Rite*, Stravinsky also extended his technique of superimposing independent ideas beyond the point represented by *Petrushka*. Here they reflect the visual multiplicity on stage and suggest the simultaneity of unrelated actions. Jacques Rivière called this the "active ubiquity" of his music that "permits him to proceed in several directions at the same time."[54] The most striking example of such superimposition occurs when the sage enters while the rival tribes, taking no notice, continue their games. (See Plates 4.2 and 4.3.) For this occasion, Stravinsky repeated two motives, one in the strings and winds (associated with the tribes, as mentioned previously) and one in the tubas (representing the sage), each to be played forte. Both are figures; both refuse to respond to each other just as the characters on stage do. Completely independent of each other, like the old man and the fighting tribes, these motives compete throughout ten measures for the audience's attention. By superimposing two contrasting ideas, Stravinsky not only makes his audience hear in the way they saw—unrelated events occurring simultaneously—but also makes plausible the unusual sounds resulting from their clash. This technique of superimposing autonomous, even irreconcilable ideas replaces the traditional notion of transition in music. As a way of bridging a shift in thought, it acknowledges the independence of the two ideas while allowing the audience to transfer its attention gradually from one to the next.

Used to synchronize the audience's visual and aural perception of the ballet, the techniques of contrast, juxtaposition, and superimposition help explain why the reviewers of the first performances were struck by the correspondences between the arts and wrote that it was "possible to see every movement on stage and at the same time to hear every note of the music."[55] Although Stravinsky experimented with these techniques in parts of *Petrushka*, he used them so systematically in *The Rite* that they soon came to characterize his style.

VISUAL DESIGN AND DANCE

Like Stravinsky, Nijinsky kept in mind the visual design of a ballet when creating his choreography. One can find in his work a special relationship between the painted backdrop (the only set) and the dancer's movements that echo the flat, static, and multiple effects of the set design. In working on *Afternoon of a Faun*

54. Rivière, "Le Sacre," *Nouvelle Revue Française* 5 (1 November 1913): 709.

55. See quotation from Colles, "The Fusion of Music and Dancing," in this chapter.

(1912) with the painter Léon Bakst, Nijinsky had learned how to produce the effect of an archaic Greek bas-relief by making the dancers "move with bent knees and feet placed flat on the ground, heel first (thereby reversing the classical rule)."[56] He achieved a two-dimensionality comparable to that of the backdrop by having the dancers move only in profile and across the stage rather than forward or backward. In order to imitate Greek vase paintings for this Greek pastoral, Nijinsky had the dancers actually pause after each change of position, as if they were characters in a series of paintings, one viewed after another. In *Jeux* (1913), also designed by Bakst, Nijinsky used the same technique, but this time modeled his poses on Gauguin reproductions, also notable for their two-dimensionality. Whether the idea of ballet as continuously moving painting originated with Bakst, Nijinsky, or Diaghilev, it had a profound effect on the history of the dance.[57]

For *The Rite,* Nijinsky reportedly took inspiration from "archaeological documents, primitive slave paintings gathered by Roerich, in which people are contorted, their knees turned in and their arms twisted outward."[58] With such awkward positions, he aimed to suggest primitive people at the mercy of the elements and their own superstition. In keeping with Roerich's stark, primitive forms and heavy lines, Nijinsky based his choreography on the "pull of the earth and the dead weight of the body" instead of aiming for the weightlessness that characterizes traditional ballets.[59] One of Valentine Gross's drawings of the original production shows the adolescents in the opening scene huddled in groups that resemble closely the boulders painted on the backdrop (see Figure 4.3).

As in *Afternoon of a Faun,* the instantaneous and simultaneous effect of the set on the audience inspired deliberate interruptions in the movement. However, the effect of the broken movement in this ballet is not just that of a juxtaposed series of static poses, each interesting in its own right. For Rivière, writing of the first performance, this technique suggested the "thousand latent directions" of the body at rest, the multiplicity in the body's potential for motion. "Because [the dancer] cannot follow all [the directions in the body] at the same time, the moment he has followed one of them for an instant, he leaves it abruptly; he breaks from it and returns to pursue another." Such a choreography, he said, implies the same "ubiquity" as Stravinsky's music.[60] Both result from attempts to delineate

56. Grigoriev, *Diaghilev Ballet,* p. 77.

57. In his commentary to the exhibition catalogue *Bakst 1876–1976* (London: 1976), p. 30, Charles S. Mayer points to the conflicting arguments over who first suggested that Nijinsky imitate the angular movements of Greek sculpture: Stravinsky acknowledges Bakst's role in instructing Nijinsky; Lifar claims the idea was Diaghilev's; W. A. Propert insists it was Nijinsky's own invention.

58. Henri Prunières, "Conclusion," *La Revue Musicale,* no. spéciale (December 1930): 103.

59. Arnold Haskell, *Ballet Russe* (London, 1968), p. 81.

60. Rivière, "Le Sacre," 719.

Figure 4.3 Premiere of *The Rite of Spring* (1913). In a letter of 1 December 1970 to Richard Buckle, Lydia Sokolova, who danced in the first performance, describes this sketch as "groups seated whilst [the] solo dances," perhaps from the "Augurs of Spring, Dances of the Young Girls." It illustrates how *The Rite*'s choreography achieved remarkable correspondences with Roerich's set design. Here the dancers look to be an extension of the series of boulders painted on the backdrop. Drawing made during rehearsals for the work in 1913 by Valentine Hugo. Courtesy of the Theater Collection, Victoria and Albert Museum, London.

several ideas or several movements at once by moving abruptly from one to the next.

MUSIC, SET DESIGN, AND CHOREOGRAPHY

Just as the visual aspects of the ballet exercised profound influence on the music and the dance, so fundamental characteristics of Stravinsky's music became important components in the conception of the work's set design and choreography. The music energizes the space that Roerich created and transforms the simultaneity of elements in the set design and the characters on stage into a tension of contrasting forces. It breathes the pulse of life into the artwork. The balance between these contrasting forces, achieved through the music's temporal process, complements that of the spatial dimension.

With the essential element of rhythm in common, the music for *The Rite* had its greatest impact on the choreography of the ballet. At the time, Stravinsky considered the choreography to be "of the utmost importance," even going so far as to label the ballet a "musical-choreographic work."[61] The choreography was capable of making his music visual and seemed crucial to the audience's understanding. Whereas the extraordinary music of *The Firebird* "led Fokine to the invention of original steps,"[62] the music of *The Rite* demanded an entirely new approach to the dance. "Filled with misgiving" about collaborating with Nijinsky because of what the composer considered "his ignorance of the most elementary notions of music," Stravinsky "did not want to leave him to his own devices" and so took an active role in the composition of the choreography.[63] Stravinsky even "traveled a great deal so as to attend the rehearsals of the company," and Grigoriev goes so far as to say that Nijinsky "relied entirely on suggestions from Diaghilev and Stravinsky."[64]

The choreographic notations published as an appendix to the sketches for *The Rite* contain detailed indications concerning the coordination Stravinsky intended between music and dance. Some of the indications specify what type of movement the dancers should make, whether clapping, stomping, or leaping. For example, in the final dance, the chosen one is instructed to move her arms and head alternately to the left and to the right from **186** to **192** as the music alternates between the chords in the basses, bassoons, trombones, and tubas and the sixteenth note pattern, the 2/8 measures, in the strings (see Figure 4.4). At **199**, she must turn three times, fall at the third measure of **200**, and fall again (see Figure 4.5).

For the most part, however, these notations reveal that Stravinsky wanted the dance to reflect the music's alternation between mobility and immobility, its patterned movement, and its organization of time. The pulse of springtime, sometimes frantic and sometimes slowly gathering its forces for a new explosion,

---

61. Stravinsky letter to Florent Schmitt, June 1912, cited in Stravinsky and Craft, *Pictures and Documents*, p. 87; Ibid. p. 75.

62. Grigoriev, *Diaghilev Ballet*, p. 43.

63. Stravinsky, *An Autobiography*, pp. 40–41. To be fair to Nijinsky, though, one should take note of the fact that he recorded an entire score of *Afternoon of a Faun* in Stepanov notation, a choreographic shorthand that requires knowledge of the rudiments of music because it uses musical notes and rhythms to indicate durations of gestures. This manuscript, now in the British Library, reveals a very clear understanding of the structure of Debussy's music. Nijinska's memoirs reveal Nijinsky's point of view and his exasperation at having been treated "as though [he] had never studied music at all"—"so much time is wasted as Stravinsky thinks he is the only one who knows anything about music . . . he even teaches Steinman how to read notes when they play together on the piano, and Steinman is not only a pianist but also a conductor" (*Bronislava Nijinska: Early Memoirs*, trans. and ed. Irina Nijinska and Jean Rawlinson [New York: 1981], p. 458).

64. Grigoriev, *Diaghilev Ballet*, p. 87.

Plate 4.1 Plates 4.1–4.4 of the premiere of *The Rite of Spring* (1913) reveal the extent to which the choreography was conceived in terms of rhythmic mass movements. With "girls bent, stamping rhythms on left front, right" and the "elders standing close, trembling," this pastel was probably made of the "Ritual of Abduction." The choreographic notations for the ballet indicate that, from **43** through **44** of this dance, the women dancers are instructed to "stomp each eighth note" and to give up trying to count the measures. Quotations from a letter of 1 December 1970 by Lydia Sokolova, who danced in the premiere performance. Pastel by Valentine Hugo (née Gross). Courtesy of the Theater Collection, Victoria and Albert Collection, London.

Plate 4.2 Most likely the transition from the "fighting men" in the "Games of the Rival Tribes" to the entrance of the elders with bear skins on their backs in the "Procession of the Sage" of *The Rite of Spring* (1913). Note that the groups are again portrayed in masses that look to be boulders. Pastel by Valentine Hugo. Courtesy of the Theater Collection, Victoria and Albert Collection, London.

Plate 4.3 Group scene, possibly following that depicted in Plate 4.2. Premiere of *The Rite of Spring* (1913). Pastel by Valentine Hugo. Courtesy of the Theater Collection, Victoria and Albert Collection, London.

Plate 4.4 "Could be any girls in the second act opening" [as in the "Mystic Circles of the Young Girls" or a little later in the "Glorification of the Chosen One," after one virgin has been chosen and stands motionless among the others from that point on]. "These were the movements we did. Also wore white bandeau on our heads figured with designs." From 1 December 1970 letter of Lydia Sokolova. Pastel by Valentine Hugo. Courtesy of the Theater Collection, Victoria and Albert Collection, London.

Figure 4.4 Maria Piltz in the final scene of *The Rite*. The top of this drawing shows how Piltz realized the choreographic instruction, beginning at **186,** that she move her arms and head back and forth from left to right. The drawing also illustrates how she turned and leapt, as Stravinsky indicated throughout the last part of the ballet. Drawing made during rehearsals for the work in 1913 by Valentine Hugo. Courtesy of the Theater Collection, Victoria and Albert Museum, London.

Figure 4.5 The last gesture of the ballet, the moment when "Piltz [is] carried off, held high at arms length by 6 or 8 men"—more likely "8," according to Lydia Sokolova. Drawing made during rehearsals for the work in 1913 by Valentine Hugo. Courtesy of the Theater Collection, Victoria and Albert Museum, London.

inspired the first of these—a constant alternation between movement and stillness in the music. Stravinsky's notes confirm his desire for direct and exact correspondences between, on the one hand, the alternation of momentum and arrest in the music and, on the other, the alternation of gesture and paralysis on stage. At **22**, for example, after the extended passage of the repeated chords reduces to trills and an oscillating figure, Stravinsky demands that "no one budge"; the crowd must anticipate the arrival of the adolescents at **27** while hearing the same music that the audience did as they waited for the curtain to rise at **12.** Another momentary arrest is called for in the midst of the ferocious struggle between the juxtaposed orchestral groups, motives, rhythmic patterns, and visual forces in the "Games of the Rival Tribes." As the musical confrontation pauses on an extended chord for four measures before **59**, Stravinsky instructs the dancers to "cease" their struggle; then at **59**, as the characteristic motive returns, "the struggle between the rival tribes begins again." The most striking interruptions of all take place at **71**, just before the sage kisses the earth, and one measure before both **101** and **102**, where "one of the girls is chosen by lot to fulfill the sacrifice." (See

Plate 4.4.) Here the suspensions of the movement in the music and the dance suggest moments of mysticism and enchantment, the otherworldliness of another temporal dimension. Such arrests in the flow of time help differentiate musical ideas and sections. Perhaps more important, they also delineate moments of major significance in the ballet, moments in which the temporal structures of the music and the dance are in perfect correspondence.

Throughout *The Rite,* Stravinsky expected the dancers to articulate the musical phrases and to help the audience grasp their contrasting rhythms. In "Spring Rounds," for example, he indicates that one group of dancers should bring out the syncopated beats of the "first rhythm" (beginning in the first three measures of **49**) while another group should accent the downbeats of the "second rhythm" (the first four measures of **50**). In the "Mystic Circles of the Young Girls," Stravinsky directed the dancers to articulate the different meters in which the contrasting phrases of the music were conceived. One group of dancers should "count in 5/4" to accompany the flute solo in **93;** a second one should "count in 2/4" along with the duple patterns in the clarinets throughout **94;** and a third one should "count in 5/4, like the first group," to reinforce the third phrase of **95.** If they followed these instructions, the dancers would clarify the musical relationships between three motives that exhibit similar pitch structures but are either prolonged or altered internally.

Stravinsky often wanted entire sections of the dance to be structured like the music. After the exposition of the two motives in "Spring Rounds," for which Stravinsky envisaged two groups of dancers as previously described, he notes three choreographic "phrases," which coincide with **52, 53,** and **54.** The first one is identical to the opening of the dance, with two rhythmic ideas superimposed and two choreographic groups articulating them. As the music shifts to an orchestral tutti and a fortissimo at **53,** the second "phrase" of the dance calls for a similar increase in texture and intensity by the addition of three, four, and then five different choreographic groups, many of them dancing independent of the musical meter. The change of tempo, motive, and texture at **54** signals the "third phrase" of the dance, which begins as "the men go behind the women" at **54** and finishes when "the tribe is established" at **56.** Stravinsky also notes three "phrases" of the dance at the end of the "Games of the Rival Tribes." This organization of the dance again highlights three musical divisions, the first a dialogue between the trumpets and horns at the beginning of **63,** the second an extended answer by the horns, and the third an orchestral tutti at the end of **63.**[65]

With the help of eurhythmic theories, Nijinsky was able to ignore the con-

65. Not all of Stravinsky's choreographic notations aim to ensure a synchrony between the music and the dance. Sometimes his indications of what meter the dancers should be moving in and what beats they should be accenting bear little relation to the musical context; the dance then functions as an autonomous musical dimension. In the "Dance of the Earth," for example, while the music unfolds entirely in 3/4, Stravinsky instructs all the dancers to count first in 5/4 at **75,** accenting their first beats, and then to count in 2/4 at **78.**

ventions of the dance and to follow the construction of Stravinsky's music. In a 1913 interview he said:

> One must score the living music of costume and flesh. The essence of the dance lies here and not in the puerile choreographic story-telling. . . . It is through the interpretation of resolutely modern plastic harmonies that decisive progress will be made.[66]

Accustomed to periodic rhythms of great regularity, dancers were not used to providing visible shape for such unpredictable patterns. *The Rite* introduced dance to plastic polyrhythms and asymmetrical groupings on a large scale. While one critic called "the absolute asymmetry . . . the very essence of the work," another wrote that "what is really of chief interest in the dancing is the employment of rhythmical counterpoint in the choral movements."[67] Through his efforts at creating structural correspondences with the music, Nijinsky liberated the dance from its classical conventions and from a dependence on narrative—he restored it to its pure original state of abstract movement.[68] Although Stravinsky later took another point of view,[69] he praised Nijinsky for having accomplished what he wanted in a letter written to Steinberg just after the 1913 premiere.

> Nijinsky's choreography is incomparable and, with a few exceptions, everything was as I wanted it. But we must wait for a long time before the public becomes accustomed to our language—of the value of what we have done I am certain.[70]

Probably because Nijinsky was the least active of the collaborators and the last to be involved in the composition of the work, the dance had the least direct impact upon the other arts. Yet it does provide a significant complement to the

---

66. S. M., "Nijinsky chorégraphe."

67. Rivière, "Le Sacre," translated in Richard Buckle, *Nijinsky* (New York, 1971), pp. 297–99; Colles, "The Fusion of Music and Dancing."

68. In his commentary to the exhibition catalogue, *The Diaghilev Ballet in England* (London: 1979), pp. 17–18, Richard Buckle cites two critics who were immediately aware of Nijinsky's turn to abstraction. In the *New Weekly* (May 1914), O. Raymond Drey speaks of Nijinsky's "use of the human body to realize arbitrary conceptions of movement, to devise a scale of gesture just as abstract as a scale of musical notes" and draws an analogy between this and contemporary trends in nonrepresentational painting. Geoffrey Whitworth also points to this abstract quality of the choreography in his *Art of Nijinsky* (1913).

69. In the famous interview with Georges-Michel, "Les deux Sacre du printemps," *Comoedia* (14 December 1920) in which the composer praises Massine's new choreography for his ballet, Stravinsky not only says that his work should be viewed as "architectonic and not anecdotal" (which does not actually show displeasure at the first choreography) but that the error in Nijinsky's choreography was that it followed the music too closely, note by note. The beauty of Massine's choreography is said to come from its alliance with larger periods of the music rather than with individual notes or even measures.

70. Letter of 3 July 1913, cited in Stravinsky and Craft, *Pictures and Documents*, p. 102. Stravinsky also apparently stated this opinion to Yuri Grigorovich in 1967, according to Nijinska, *Early Memoirs*, p. 471.

decoration, imparting living shape to Roerich's atemporal designs and simple costumes. The presence of the dance balances the timelessness of these designs while signifying a physical connection between the past and the future. The spatial patterns and the turning in place of the dance also fulfilled an important function for Stravinsky, who preferred to think in formal rather than expressive terms. Because he sought to work in a way that resembled the "routine of ballet," Stravinsky provided his music with a clearly defined pulse.[71] This enabled him to ask dancers to "count the beats rather than the measures," freeing him to vary the meter and to concentrate on unusual rhythmic groups. Because of the steady pulse on which each is based, the interplay among the groups and their proportional relationships are clear to the listener.

Stravinsky, Roerich, and Nijinsky clearly achieved a fusion of the arts in *The Rite of Spring,* one whose consequences were much more profound than that achieved in either the middle or the outer tableaux of *Petrushka.* Although the use of spectacle as an object of imitation injected immense creative energy into the arts in both *Petrushka* and *The Rite,* the focus in the latter ballet on abstract relationships rather than a story brought with it the seeds of a new formalism. The change from vertical correspondences to a story in *Petrushka* to horizontal correspondences between the actual motivic and temporal structures of each art in *The Rite* is one example of how the modernist aesthetic favoring structure over narrative as a work's organizing principle began to shape the development of music in the early twentieth century. Stravinsky's own turn from the programmatic to the abstract set the stage for his neoclassicism in the 1920s.

71. Stravinsky, "The Choreography Stravinsky-Nijinsky."

5 The Devil's Dance: Stravinsky's Corporal Imagination

ROGER SHATTUCK

Roger Shattuck's contribution to the symposium consisted of a witty exchange of imaginary letters between Patrick Cartnell, "an aging, part-time graduate student" and Lydia Glaser, a musicology professor at another university. In the correspondence, the former takes limited issue with and expands upon an article by the latter. The article in question bears a striking resemblance to Jann Pasler, "Stravinsky's Visualization of Music: The Choreography for The Rite of Spring,*" which appeared in* Dance Magazine *55 (1981): 66–69. Because Mr. Shattuck's epistolary framework for his striking ideas about Stravinsky's physical relation to music seemed a little lighthearted for publication in this book, he has allowed us to extract several passages from Patrick Cartnell's letters and one from Lydia Glaser's. [Editor's note]*

PATRICK CARTNELL

. . . You find something all Stravinsky scholars know perfectly well but have neglected, and you make it obvious. The quotes cannot be dismissed. In the *Poetics of Music,* Stravinsky says it is "not enough to hear music . . . it must also be seen" (p. 128). I had forgotten the "fleeting vision" and all the visual imagery that Stravinsky tells us inspired the composition of *The Rite of Spring.* It's wonderful the way you demonstrate how Stravinsky participated actively with Nijinsky to work out the original choreography for *The Rite* along with the music. What you say about Stravinsky's insisting on placing the musicians on stage for *Histoire du soldat* and *Les Noces* could be developed a lot more. That's the aspect that caught my attention in connection with performance arts. Perhaps you didn't have space. How could you leave out this wonderful quote from the *Autobiography:* "I wanted all my instrumental apparatus to be visible side by side with the actors or dancers, making it, so to speak, a participant in the whole theatrical action" (p. 106)? And there's the "eye music" passage from *Themes and Episodes* that you must know. "To see Balanchine's choreography of the *Movements* is to hear the music with one's eyes; and this visual hearing has been a greater revelation to me, I think, than to anyone else" (p. 24). I even have two more examples for you—the importance of two-dimensional Japanese prints for the conception of the *Three Japanese Lyrics* of 1912–1913 and S. noting choreographic ideas in the manuscript score while composing *Agon.* The visual inspiration was often there, and you make us sit up and take notice of it.

Of course, someone could question what the role of the visual was—is—in vocal works like *Pribaoutki, Renard, Symphony of Psalms,* Cantata. And there's something constricting, incomplete, in any attempt to concentrate the appeal of stage works on the visual. The visual image distances and locates our experience in space outside us; whereas the auditory distributes it throughout space and carries it deep into our listening mind. Do I make myself clear? Still, Stravinsky must have had an alert eye, maybe a compulsive eye. Now I'm going to try to go beyond you, thanks in great part to what you've shown me.

One of my sources is Vera Stravinsky's and Robert Craft's *Stravinsky in Pictures and Documents (SPD),* that wonderful, undigested mishmash of information on the man and his music. I finally had to buy a copy. After this free-form performance, I'll wager Craft never tries a sit-down biography. He doesn't have to. But I'm getting off the subject.

I'll begin *ad hominem.* Look at the descriptions of S. playing the piano, not in concert but in rehearsal or in private. The written record goes back at least to *The Firebird.* In her little memoir on Stravinsky, Karsavina recalls how he played her part for her over and over before rehearsals. "His body seemed to vibrate with his own rhythm; punctuating staccatos with his head, he made the pattern of his music forcibly clear to me, more so than the counting of bars would have done. Rhythm lived in, at times took possession of his body. . . ." He played a two-hand reduction of *The Rite* for Diaghilev and Monteux in 1912, a session that Monteux later described. "Before he got very far, I was convinced he was raving mad. . . . The very walls resounded as Stravinsky pounded away, occasionally stamping his feet and jumping up and down. . . ." (*SPD,* p. 87) He played with equal vehemence at early rehearsals, according to Marie Rambert (*SPD,* p. 90): "Hearing the way his music was being played, Stravinsky blazed up, pushed aside the fat German pianist . . . and proceeded to play twice as fast as we had been doing and twice as fast as we could possibly dance. He stamped his feet on the floor and banged his fist on the piano and sang and shouted. . . ." In 1914, Diaghilev took the composer to a meeting in Milan of futurist and bruitist musicians. According to the sculptor Cangiullo, S. felt far from left out. He "leaped from the divan like an exploding bedspring, with a whistle of overjoyed excitement. At the same time, a rustler rustled. . . . The frenetic composer hurled himself on the piano in an attempt to find that . . . sound" (*SPD,* p. 657). Elliott Carter's version of S.'s "electricity-filled piano playing" in the thirties catches the same effects barely tempered by twenty years. Carter speaks of "the very telling quality of attack he gave to piano notes," of "intensity" and "extraordinary dynamism" even in the soft passages (*SPD,* p. 215). There must be scores of such descriptions.

Stravinsky was a man of enormous physical energy. Do you know the 1924 photograph of him (*SPD,* p. 298) doing his daily set of Swedish-German gymnastics? A musical psychoarchaeologist could reconstruct all his music from that one image. He was always in training, acutely aware of his physical condition. It may be the natural attitude toward life of a midget who had become a conductor and a star. Ansermet says somewhere that S.'s morning calisthenics could become highly competitive and relates how the tiny composer tried to wrestle him to the floor when they went on tour together. Ansermet was a big man.

I find it much harder to locate believable accounts of S.'s physical behavior while conducting. Apparently in public performance his movements were fairly restrained and concentrated. Some observers considered him mechanical. According to Eric Walter White in *Stravinsky: The Composer and His Works,* Toscanini was shocked to hear him counting aloud (p. 518). But the best firsthand accounts of his rehearsals—by Paul Rosenfeld (*SPD,* p. 255), a Vienna journalist (*SPD,* p. 302), Emile Vuillermoz (*SPD,* p. 310), and a Belgian critic in 1924 (*SPD,* p. 325)—all emphasize the nervous imperious dynamism of his movements. It's incredible. They all use exactly the same verb for him: *dance.* Rosenfeld's famous article-interview is still one of the best. "He commenced singing the words in Russian, even danced a little in his pink sweater up on the conductor's stand. . . . His arms at all times mimed the rhythmic starts and jerks, till one could actually perceive where his music came from" (*SPD,* p. 255). That says it all. S. once ridiculed an overly demonstrative conductor by comparing the performance to "a belly dance seen from behind" (*SPD,* p. 382). In his own case, I have a hunch he tried to make the physical postures of conducting recapitulate and even extend the process of composition. Here's a 1930 interview. "I have the impression that only in conducting his works does a composer feel the fullest blossoming of his temperament. To realize the composition that one has conceived gives an incomparable pleasure" (*SPD,* p. 629). Those are not the words of a man who conducted only for the fee and the glory. I believe his statement—above all for his own case.

You must see what I'm driving at. I find it even more obvious than your demonstration about the visual. S. composed with his whole body, not just with his enormous ears and his sharp eyes. (He even said ear and eye get in each other's way. Remember? [*SPD,* p. 347]) This son of a famous opera singer loved amateur theatricals before he loved the piano. In 1924, he improved on Ramuz's description of him from "born conductor" to "born performer" *(Interprète né)* (Letter 1051). I think it's essential to understand that S.'s music emanates from a whole dancing body, his own. Look at the dancing bear in *Petrushka.* In one performance, I saw the bear lead the whole ensemble. A metaphor for Stravinsky conducting.

Now, I haven't really parted company with you. You just didn't go far enough with your visual thesis. The corporal is right there in the same passages you quote, but you have to read on. From the *Autobiography,* you quote the section where Stravinsky speaks about the "vision" and the "picture" that seemed to provide the theme of *The Rite.* A few pages later he refers to deciding with Roerich on the "visual embodiment" of the episodes (p. 36). You underline *visual;* I underline *body.* He's correcting himself. And here's your key quotation. "I have always had a horror of listening to music with my eyes shut, with nothing for them to do"

(*Autobiography,* p. 72). But you stopped too soon. In the very next sentence, he corrects himself again. "The sight of the gestures and movements of the various parts of the body producing the music is fundamentally necessary if it is to be grasped in its fullness" (*Autobiography,* p. 72). Body again, and always, no? In the *Poetics,* where he talks about "seeing" music, he makes it clear that he is referring to the physical performance, the gestures of dancers and instrumentalists.

It's frustrating to discover that S. has said it all. He talked too much and too well for our own good. There's nothing left to do but collate. He wrote my conclusion, and you must know the passage as well as I do. A month after the *Petrushka* premiere, in mid-composition of *The Rite,* he already foresaw his whole career and described it in a letter to Rimsky-Korsakov's son. I consider this S.'s only true manifesto. Every word counts: "I believe that if some Michelangelo were alive today—so it occurred to me, looking at the frescoes in the Sistine Chapel—the only thing that his genius would admit and recognize is choreography . . . not until I had worked in choreography did I realize this, as well as the necessity and value of what I am doing."

In her response, Professor Glaser concurs about the corporal side of Stravinsky's imagination and adds that the point should be established in the music itself, and not exclusively from written sources by and about Stravinsky.

PATRICK CARTNELL

. . . I'll pick a piece I know well, *Histoire du soldat.* Let's forget what people have said about it—Stravinsky himself, Ramuz, Ansermet, and everyone else—even though the original conception based on itinerant theater is marvelous, as is the way the piece evolved from it. The first three measures say everything. A brisk cornet call to launch us on a regular walking pulse that will keep coming back. The phrasing and the instrumentation in those measures sound both military and circusy—like fairgrounds music. It involves a very odd sideslip into the key of G. How would you analyze it? I can't. Polyphony? I hear it as a physical summons to a performance, to start walking, to find some spring and verve in our bodies. Nothing visual here, rather two insistent and coherent lines directed more toward bodily movement than toward a tonal center. You must know the section in Adorno's *Philosophy of Modern Music* where he works himself up to assassinate "the schizoid dispersion of aesthetic functions" and the "hebephrenia" of *Histoire du soldat.* What does all that mean? But Adorno still had a sensibility behind his crass prejudices and talks about "passages in which the 'melody' is bypassed, in order that it might appear in the actual leading voice—in bodily movement on the page" (p. 175–176). That's far from stupid. Stravinsky composes music there to galvanize everyone into action.

Or take the music that forms a complete contrast in the same piece, the two chorales near the end. To my ear, it's the most successful counterpoint Stravinsky ever wrote, with fermatas held until you think it's all finished and it isn't. The slowly revolving harmonies won't allow the tension to drop. They create the feeling of plenitude, of life completely realized, of an almost superhuman condition. To me, it's a sustained instrumental gesture, yes, a chorale for all our voices rejoicing with arms outstretched and necks straining. Personal associations? Perhaps. But I don't think so. You cannot hear the "Great Chorale" without experiencing a vast expansion of physical space—visual perhaps, but above all corporal. Of course, he breaks it off with the devil's dance.

And there's the crux. Do you know about the ending? It's in Ramuz's letters. An actor and a dancer alternated in the devil's role. In rehearsal, neither one could begin to produce the wild, jerky, energetic movements Stravinsky and Ramuz wanted for the last "Triumphal March." Solution? Stravinsky would do it himself. Stravinsky on stage as devil dancing to his own music. Ramuz agreed enthusiastically, asked others to encourage the composer, and wrote Stravinsky urgently. "Dance that *last scene yourself;* you'll live it rhythmically and you'll save everything." Before conducting offered him an appropriate (and lucrative) outlet, Stravinsky showed signs of a Molière syndrome, the desire to write and direct performances in which he would perform himself. That little tidbit about S. almost dancing the devil's role in *Histoire du soldat* sums up his entire corporal genius.

Can you hear the *Octet* without sensing that S. was thinking not so much in terms of sounds as in terms of bodily movement suggested by, reached through those sounds? I haven't seen the Jerome Robbins choreography; I'm told it's wonderfully inventive and witty. After a while, I hear almost everything Stravinsky wrote that way—I don't mean foottapping or some kind of routine body language, such as ballet can become at its worst. S. composed to reveal the expressive resources of the body. Take the opening of *Symphonies of Wind Instruments.* A friend of mine calls it "eerie lyric." Yes. But I begin to hear it as another summons to action like *Histoire*—the torso twisted, legs slowly tensing and releasing, a contortion, but not painful. The end of *Les Noces* takes the opposite position. Those slow-flowing measures of silence punctuated by chimed beats spaced out to the limits of our capacity for time perception—Stravinsky wrote an extended, shimmering, precise, perpetual-motion device that leads us out finally onto a plateau of pure silence—what he would call "ontological time." The piece must be heard almost backwards, I think, as one prolonged convoluted cadence announced at rehearsal number **58** or at least by **80** and going on and on like a great amen. The insistent physicality of the music carries us to an ultimate repose, quietness and silence as forms of expression, calm after the storm.

LYDIA GLASER

. . . You're right of course. Stravinsky was a dance musician with a choreographic imagination. But not exclusively. You know about his near *ménage à trois* in the twenties and thirties. Musically he kept a *ménage à trente-six*, or maybe *à 1001*. Take *Histoire*. It's almost all dances, some of his most inventive. But what holds it together? The chorales. All the driving ragtime and tango and marching frame the near immobility of the "Great Chorale," which in turn frames and guards the secret place, the tabernacle of the composition that keeps its holy emblem. Have you heard the Oubradous recording with French actors reading the script? At **3** in the Chorale after that incredibly open and beautiful counterpoint and voice leading, the six instruments hold a fermata on a D chord with the seventh doubled; then Jean Marchat's unhurried, worldly wise voice says the words. They have to be in French.

> Il ne faut pas ajouter à ce qu'on a ce qu'on avait.
> On ne peut pas être à la fois qui on est et qui on était.
> Il faut savoir choisir.
> On n'a pas le droit de tout avoir. C'est défendu.
> Un bonheur c'est tout le bonheur, deux, c'est comme
> s'ils n'existaient plus.
>
> You cannot add to what you now have what you once had.
> You cannot be both what you are and what you were.
> You must know how to choose.
> No one has the right to have everything. That's forbidden.
> One happiness is all happiness. Two—that cancels every-
> thing out.

As I see it, hear it, Stravinsky wrote *Histoire* to house those words. They deserve it. He felt them deeply, personally. The "Great Chorale" corresponds to the pure time sequence at the end of *Les Noces*.

Still, neither of us can generalize from these examples. Stravinsky had no one overriding preoccupation. The quotations get confusing. "What survives every change of system is melody." Other times his chief concern seems to be note-against-note counterpoint. A critic would not be wrong to claim that no twentieth-century composer has been so single-mindedly devoted to extending the rhythmic resources of our musical language. Or that Stravinsky composed most consistently and brilliantly on syllables, words reduced to nonsense noises in five languages. You say the body and choreography. Yes—and more.

Lydia Glaser goes on to wonder if Patrick Cartnell's hypothesis doesn't apply primarily to Stravinsky's preserial music, thus slighting some of his greatest works after 1940.

PATRICK CARTNELL

. . . Yesterday I reread by "chance" Craft's journal notes for 31 March 1948 (*SPD*, p. 399). He contrasts a physically disheveled Auden little interested in his meal with the slightly dandified Stravinsky savoring his Chateaubriand and his glass of Chateau Margaux. Then this sentence. "While with Auden the senses seemed to be of negligible importance, with Stravinsky the affective faculties were virtual instruments of thought." May I rest my case? The contrast is too neat, probably. But it's another version of what I've been trying to say about the physicality, the corporal side of Stravinsky's music. For me, his preserial compositions—this will sound pretentious and literary, but here goes—his preserial compositions accomplish a reassociation of sensibility, favor the thinking body, the choreographic imagination, have the order and sense of limits that allow reason and feeling to fuse. T. S. Eliot kept talking about this fusion and our lack of it today. He deplored our "dissociation of sensibility." In poetry, we want all feeling, no conceptual thought. Hasn't the opposite happened in twentieth-century music? It's becoming more cerebral than corporal. Is that a prejudiced opinion? I know that there are neoprimitive composers around like Crumb and Berio. But even a popular composer like Glass, with all his endless repetitions and variations, strikes me as basically cerebral. He's working out a concept of music, an extended set of intellectual patterns, not giving us the discoveries of a wonderfully sensitive ear or body. Perhaps the quality of S.'s music that unifies the intellectual and the sensuous exists also in his later compositions, and I just don't hear it. I don't dislike those works. I just find them wanting or remote.

6 Set Designing for Stravinsky

DAVID HOCKNEY

David Hockney designed sets and costumes for the 1974–1975 Glyndebourne production of The Rake's Progress *and the 1981 New York Metropolitan Opera production of* The Rite of Spring, The Nightingale, *and* Oedipus Rex. *These remarks are excerpted from the talk, illustrated with slides, that he delivered at the International Stravinsky Symposium. Photographs appear by courtesy of the artist. [Editor's note]*

. . . What I liked about the program of *The Rite of Spring, The Nightingale,* and *Oedipus Rex* at the Metropolitan Opera was how you went from Stravinsky's most kinetic to his most static work for the stage—seemingly from birth and awareness to self-knowledge and death. We conceived it as one total piece of theater. Slowly the sets come toward you. When we get to *Oedipus,* the whole theater is the set. The obvious connection between the works was the circle we used, which was ritualistic. It appears in them all.

The Rite of Spring

The Rite (Plate 6.1) uses a disc that we lit up and whose color we could change. The color somehow seemed easy because the music suggests it almost straightaway. Having listened to the music over and over again, I was trying to find some color or visual equivalent for it. When I first began listening very hard to *The Rite,* the colors seemed strong—I kept thinking of oranges and strong contrasts. But the longer and longer I listened and the more I tried different things, I concluded that a great deal of the music is impressionistic in a way, very subtle. So I made about twenty-seven versions of that disc with different colors on them. I had a light box in London on a kind of remote control, and I would play the music over and over, changing bits of color with it for the different sections of the music. The music seemed to be about something changing visually, going from one thing to another, and about an awareness of the force that changes this landscape in front of your eyes.

The Nightingale

I think of *The Nightingale* (Plate 6.2) as a theater piece—it's magical and in concert would lose a great deal. I read the original Hans Christian Andersen piece, then listened to the music, which reminded me of glazes, transparencies, and porcelain—the way the Chinese would put their glazes on plates, with a watery look. So I went to the Victoria and Albert Museum in London and photographed two vases and created most of the design from these.

Plate 6.2 shows the Little Cook leading the chamberlain and bonze into the forest looking for the Nightingale. I drew the mountains from pictures I had seen on the Chinese vases. Yet when I'd finished the design but before we did it on the stage, I actually went to China on a visit with Stephen Spender and found that the Kui Lin Mountains looked exactly like that. It was a wonderful landscape that looked as though children had drawn it. The sets are just painted drops with blue light on them, which makes the color much more vivid. Everything is blue and white until the Japanese arrive.

The chorus had masks. In *The Rite,* there were masks all around the back of the disc, and in *The Nightingale,* there are masks still around. The chorus members carried masks above them, so you're really looking at the masks all the time. Everybody but the Fisherman, the Cook, and the Nightingale, who have painted faces, wears a mask. *Oedipus* is also about masks.

Oedipus Rex

Oedipus (Plate 6.3) begins in the same way, with a circle and the curtain going through the space on stage. This time the outside of the proscenium is used, which is why we had it photographed this way. The red was because of the theater itself. I thought of the Greek theater in which what you sat looking at looked the same as the place where you sat (you were sitting on stone). There's no real illusion. Because since you can't alter the Metropolitan Opera, you accept what is in the seats, the color of the carpets, the black, the gold, and simply extend it round and onto the stage. Suddenly, instead of ignoring the proscenium, you are forced to look at it or consider it, which gives you a different aspect of the theater.

In Plate 6.3, it is clear that we had raised the orchestra three or four feet, for I wanted the orchestra always to be visible. At the front, there is a glass panel so that even the people in the stalls could see the orchestra. We wanted it to be part of the actual picture you were looking at. With the chorus and the main characters in black ties, the orchestra as well in black, and the minks in the audience, it

Plate 6.1 The 1981 New York Metropolitan Opera production of *The Rite of Spring*. Design by David Hockney.

Plate 6.2 The 1981 New York Metropolitan Opera production of *The Nightingale*. Design by David Hockney.

Plate 6.3 The 1981 New York Metropolitan Opera production of *Oedipus Rex*. Design by David Hockney.

Plate 6.4 The 1975 Glyndebourne production of *The Rake's Progress*. Design by David Hockney.

meant that wherever you sat in the theater, in a sense the picture began with the person in front of you.

Originally, there were going to be lit masks above the heads of the chorus—just a simple version of the Greek tragic mask—but we had to take them out because the platform had to be lower. James Levine said he couldn't see the soloists unless they were right in front of that platform, and they didn't like walking up there—thought it was too high. So we had to take the masks away. This seemed to me to alter the design considerably.

Oedipus Rex was the simplest set of all. There was hardly anything there—I think it was the cheapest set the Met ever did. It's really just the middle column painted with the same bronze as the outside of the proscenium. We simply projected light onto them so that you'd get a brighter gold and a dull gold and connect the two. In this way, your sense of space in the theater would be altered and you would no longer ignore the sides and concentrate only on everything in the middle of the space. It was just making you aware of where you were. The illusion in *The Nightingale* has disappeared.

The Rake's Progress

My first set design for a Stravinsky work, the Glyndebourne production of *The Rake's Progress* (Plate 6.4), was only the second theater piece I'd ever done. Something I didn't know then was that lighting painted sets is very different from lighting anything three-dimensional. If you light something three-dimensional, you can create all the effects. For something at night, you simply dim the lights. If you are painting pictorial ideas on sets, you have to light them differently. You have to paint the shadows if you want shadows; you have to paint the night; you have to paint the day.

Theoretical Perspectives

7 Harmonic Syntax and Voice Leading in Stravinsky's Early Music

ALLEN FORTE

STRAVINSKY'S use of harmony in the works of 1908–1914, beginning with *The Nightingale* [Le rossignol], is still incompletely understood, both with respect to the individual works of the period (with the possible exception of *The Rite of Spring,* which has been studied extensively) and with respect to Stravinsky's subsequent compositions, notably the remarkable works of the immediate postwar period, of which *Symphonies of Wind Instruments* (1920) is a landmark and *Symphony of Psalms* (1930), an apex. Moreover, the traditional concept of voice leading, which undergoes significant metamorphosis in Stravinsky's music from 1908 onward, has not been fully explicated. In its most general form, voice leading is basic to the temporal succession of musical components, both as it pertains to vertical harmonies—narrowly conceived as "harmony" in the textbook sense—and also as it determines melodic configurations. In this chapter, I explore these notions with reference to a standard technical vocabulary (pitch-class set theory) and attempt to elucidate certain apparently unusual as well as specifically normative procedures in Stravinsky's early music.

Basic Definitions

The term "harmonic syntax" designates both the elements of the harmonic vocabulary that characterize Stravinsky's early music and the way those elements are combined to form musical configurations. "Voice leading" refers to the way the harmonic elements are connected, to how one component proceeds to the next, hence is close to the traditional meaning of that term.

Analytical Approach

Intersections with the writings of Arthur Berger, Pieter van den Toorn, and Joseph Straus are inevitable because theirs are major studies dealing with the subject of this chapter.[1] I will not attempt to document those intersections but merely state that I am familiar with Straus's excellent dissertation and have long been an admirer of van den Toorn's expert and insightful writings on Stravinsky. I count myself among the serious students of Stravinsky's music who are indebted to Berger's path-breaking article.

This chapter stems primarily from my own theoretical work and the analytical approach derived from it, which differ in several basic respects from the orientations of Berger and van den Toorn.[2] I take as basic analytical objects in Stravinsky's music its unordered pitch-class sets, but Berger and van den Toorn regard the ordered set as primary.

By often revealing significant relations that would otherwise be overlooked, the unordered set approach offers significant advantages to the analyst and solutions to passages that are often regarded as anomalous. As one example of this, the set underlying the so-called Petrushka chord also determines other pitch configurations throughout the ballet, not only in the scene in Petrushka's room as the famous ordered "bitonal" juxtaposition of "C major" and "F♯ major."[3]

Pitch-Class Set Names

An understanding of pitch-class set names (set names for short) and a few other basic matters will facilitate comprehension of the discussion that follows.[4] Every collection (set) of pitches that can be formed in the twelve-note system can be designated by a name that consists of a number that specifies the number of notes in the set, followed by a hyphen, followed by another number that specifies the position of that set on a master list.[5] If the positional number is preceded by the letter Z, the set has a twin with the same interval-content. In the case of hexachords, such twins are also complements of each other. Indeed, the complement relation is so important and so amply represented in Stravinsky's music that a

1. See Arthur Berger, "Problems of Pitch Organization in Stravinsky," *Perspectives of New Music* 2, no. 1 (1963): 11–42; Pieter van den Toorn, "Some Characteristics of Stravinsky's Diatonic Music," *Perspectives of New Music* 14, no. 1 (1975): 104–38; 15, no. 2 (1977): 58–95, and *The Music of Igor Stravinsky* (New Haven, 1983); and Joseph Straus, "A Theory of Harmony and Voice Leading in the Music of Igor Stravinsky," Ph.D. dissertation, Yale University, 1981.

2. Allen Forte, "A Theory of Set Complexes for Music," *Journal of Music Theory* 8, no. 2 (1964):136–83, *The Structure of Atonal Music* (New Haven, 1973), and *The Harmonic Organization of The Rite of Spring* (New Haven, 1978).

3. Nothing here is intended to suggest the composer himself was analytical or theoretical or would have subscribed to one or another point of view.

4. See Forte, *Structure of Atonal Music.*

5. Set names are preferable to prime form numerical notation because the name is general, applying to any pitch form of the set.

simple explanation is required here: the complement of a pitch-class set consists, in the literal sense, of all the notes remaining in the twelve-note chromatic that are not in that set. In addition, complements may be inverted or transposed so that they are not necessarily "literal" complements—a significant extension of the concept of complementation.[6]

Repertory to Be Discussed

The music to be discussed spans the period from 1908 through 1914, beginning with act 1 of *The Nightingale* and ending with the third of Three Pieces for String Quartet, a special composition in Stravinsky's oeuvre for a number of reasons. I pay particular attention to *The Firebird* because it has been somewhat neglected in the technical literature. However, I draw only two examples from *The Rite of Spring*, a work that has been studied extensively.

I do not include all the music in this period. For example, *Two Poems of Balmont* of 1911 and *Three Japanese Lyrics* of 1912–1913 are omitted. This music often does not relate to what became the main thrust of the music of the postwar period, the truly modern music, of which *Symphonies of Wind Instruments* is surely the prime exemplar. I chose to exclude the music composed before *The Nightingale*, act 1, in order to isolate a consistent and homogeneous repertory. Isolated passages in the earlier music, however, exhibit characteristics of the later repertory. For instance, rehearsal number **9** of *Fireworks*, Opus 4, has a passage based upon a regular succession of transpositionally related forms of set 7–32, a favored harmony later to return in *The Rite* and elsewhere. As a later example, **92** in *Les Noces* contains long strings of set 4–27. In both cases, the parallel voice leadings may be regarded as simple manifestations of a general idea that takes on great significance in Stravinsky's early music: the replication of pitch-class sets.

Master Octads

Before proceeding to the musical examples, one general observation on harmonic syntax in Stravinsky's music is required. In all the large works from 1908 onward, a small number of referential octads is operative. These master octads govern harmonic constellations that comprise pitch-class sets of seven, six, five, and four

6. Except for the Z-hexachords, the positional number in the set name is the same for both members of a complement-related pair. Thus, 4–28 is the complement of 8–28, 5–31 is the complement of 7–31, and so on.

elements. As will be evident in the musical examples, tetrachords are especially important in Stravinsky's music, and it is not accidental that some of the most prominent of these are complements of the master octads. Throughout this repertory are multiple occurrences of 4–12, 4–Z15 (and its twin, 4–Z29), 4–18, 4–23 (which is the complement of the master diatonic octad), 4–27, and finally, 4–28 (the complement of the so-called octatonic collection).[7] As but two instances of the large octads in Stravinsky's works, I cite the music at **98** + 2 in *Petrushka* (Petrushka's room), which is based upon set 8–Z15, and measure 42 of *Zvezdoliki* [The king of the stars], which presents 8–27. (See footnote 15.) Recognizing the occurrences of these master octads in Stravinsky's music is important because much of its harmonic syntax cannot be referred exclusively to the diatonic collection 8–23 or to the octatonic collection 8–28.

Key to Pitch-Class Sets in Musical Examples

Table 7.1 provides an overview of the harmonic constituents I shall discuss. The key is set up in columns, with the leftmost one giving the set name. To the right of each set name is the prime form (a basic referential form to which any manifestation of the set can be reduced), first in chromatic numerical notation, with 0 fixed on C, and then in ordinary letter-name notation. Most of the sets are provided with a comment or two. For example, set 4–17 is both diatonic (that is, within the orbit of 8–23) and octatonic (within the orbit of 8–28).[8] It is also symmetric: inversion does not produce a form of the set distinct from one of its unordered transpositions.

The key may be regarded as a partial list of the composer's harmonic vocabulary, one that contains many of the most prominent elements of his early music. For example, 5–31 and 5–32 are to be found throughout *The Rite*, while the hexachords listed in the key include five of the six hexachords of the octatonic set 8–28.

The Musical Evidence

We now proceed to a consideration of major aspects of harmonic syntax and voice leading in Stravinsky's early works as they appear in representative segments of

7. See Forte, *Harmonic Organization*, examples 130–41 for displays of the intersections of set complexes with these master octads.

8. The term "diatonic" is not coextensive with "tonal." It is used informally, in the meaning ascribed to it by van den Toorn (see n. 1) to refer to diatonic collections, one instance of which is the scale of tonal music.

Table 7.1. Key to Pitch-Class Sets in Musical Examples

Set Name	Prime Form (numerals)	Prime Form (letters)	Comment
4–3	0 1 3 4	C C♯ D♯ E	Symmetric; octatonic
4–5	0 1 2 6	C C♯ D F♯	
4–7	0 1 4 5	C C♯ E F	Symmetric
4–8	0 1 5 6	C C♯ F F♯	Symmetric
4–10	0 2 3 5	C D E♭ F	Symmetric; octatonic
4–11	0 1 3 5	C D♭ E♭ F	Diatonic
4–12	0 2 3 6	C D E♭ F♯	Octatonic
4–13	0 1 3 6	C D♭ E♭ F♯	Diatonic; octatonic
4–Z15	0 1 4 6	C C♯ E F♯	Diatonic; octatonic
4–16	0 1 5 7	C C♯ F G	
4–17	0 3 4 7	C E♭ E G	Diatonic; octatonic; symmetric
4–18	0 1 4 7	C C♯ E G	Diatonic; octatonic
4–19	0 1 4 8	C C♯ E G♯	Classic atonal set
4–21	0 2 4 6	C D E F♯	Diatonic; whole tone; symmetric
4–22	0 2 4 7	C D E G	Diatonic
4–23	0 2 5 7	C D F G	Diatonic; symmetric
4–24	0 2 4 8	C D E G♯	Whole tone
4–25	0 2 6 8	C D F♯ G♯	Octatonic; whole tone; symmetric
4–26	0 3 5 8	C E♭ F A♭	Diatonic; octatonic; symmetric
4–27	0 2 5 8	C D F A♭	Diatonic; octatonic
4–28	0 3 6 9	C E♭ F♯ A	Octatonic; symmetric
4–Z29	0 1 3 7	C C♯ D♯ G	Diatonic; octatonic
5–16	0 1 3 4 7	C C♯ D♯ E G	Octatonic
5–Z18	0 1 4 5 7	C C♯ E F G	
5–22	0 1 4 7 8	C C♯ E G A♭	
5–31	0 1 3 6 9	C C♯ D♯ F♯ A	Octatonic
5–32	0 1 4 6 9	C C♯ E F♯ A	Diatonic; octatonic
6–Z13	0 1 3 4 6 7	C C♯ D♯ E F♯ G	Octatonic; symmetric
6–27	0 1 3 4 6 9	C C♯ D♯ E F♯ A	Octatonic
6–Z28	0 1 3 5 6 9	C C♯ D♯ F F♯ A	Complement of 6-Z49; symmetric
6–Z29	0 1 3 6 8 9	C C♯ D♯ F♯ G♯ A	Complement of 6–Z50; symmetric
6–30	0 1 3 6 7 9	C C♯ D♯ F♯ G A	Octatonic; "Petrushka"
6–33	0 2 3 5 7 9	C D E♭ F G A	Diatonic
6–34	0 1 3 5 7 9	C C♯ E♭ F G A	Scriabin's Mystic Chord
6–Z49	0 1 3 4 7 9	C C♯ D♯ E G A	Octatonic; symmetric
6–Z50	0 1 4 6 7 9	C C♯ E F♯ G A	Octatonic; symmetric
7–22	0 1 2 5 6 8 9	C C♯ D F F♯ G♯ A	
7–31	0 1 3 4 6 7 9	C C♯ D♯ E F♯ G A	Octatonic
8–23	0 1 2 3 5 7 8 10	C C♯ D D♯ F G G♯ B♭	Master diatonic set
8–28	0 1 3 4 6 7 9 10	C C♯ D♯ E F♯ G A B♭	Master octatonic set

music from that period. In order to gain a certain chronological perspective, let us first consider a segment of one of the masterworks of a later period.

The famous E-minor triad, the musical emblem of the *Symphony of Psalms*, is followed by arpeggiated forms of two sonorities of type 4–27 (shown at the right of Example 7.1, under letter a). However, there is more to the music here. As

Example 7.1. *Symphony of Psalms* (1930), "Introduction"

continued

Example 7.1. *continued*

Berger shows, the boundary pitches of the configuration form set 4–3, beamed in the example and displayed in close formation under letter b.[9] Craft described this set as among "eleven notations" in the sketches for the work.[10] An equally important component is the dyad D-F within the arpeggiation configuration. This is the stepwise continuation of the inner parts of the E-minor triad, with which it forms set 4–10, as shown at b. Subsequently, as shown at d, 4–10 becomes a primary feature of the upper voice melody, in counterpoint with 4–27. Thus, although it originates as a somewhat concealed structure of a voice-leading nature, set 4–10 later comes to the surface to play a major role.[11] Similarly, 4–3, embedded in the

9. Berger, "Problems of Pitch Organization," p. 33.

10. Vera Stravinsky and Robert Craft, *Stravinsky in Pictures and Documents* (New York, 1978), p. 296.

11. Pitch-class set 4–11, together with 4–10, is as ubiquitous in Stravinsky's music as are major and minor triads in the music of Mozart.

arpeggiations of set 4–27 in m. 2–3, surfaces in m. 26 to contribute to the ostinato figure shown at e. Notice that both 4–3 and 4–27 occur in two planes here: in the separate lines of the horizontal plane and as a result of the juxtaposed dyads in the vertical plane, bracketed in the example. The other component of the music here, the dyad E-F in the descant, refers directly to set 4–10, shown at b. And the entire segment of music expresses the octatonic heptad 7–31, which was also manifested in the very opening music shown at a and b.

From this highly organized music of a later period we can conclude that (1) melodic structure is closely associated with voice leading and (2) significant harmonic components (pitch-class sets) may exist just below the more obvious surface features of the music.

Still another small example, this time from *The Rite,* supports the latter point concerning voice leading and melodic structure. The music at **86** (Example 7.2) appears in the sketchbook in the form shown in Example 7.3: as a single melodic line.[12] Thus, the biplanar voice-leading pattern of the final music (Example 7.2) originated in what appears to be a single musical dimension.

Also of relevance to the topic at hand is the "passing note" G in the letter-name graph below Example 7.2, circled to elicit special attention. This melodic note completes the fundamental tetrachord 4–3 in the lower voice while it forms an additional 4–3 shape with the upper voice. At c is displayed the voice-leading succession of chords 4–13 and 4–24 formed by the stepwise ascent C♭–C in the descant against the stepwise descent F–F♭ in the lower voice, while the dyad A♭–B♭ remains fixed as a fulcrum. In terms of harmonic syntax, then, the passage is based upon 4–13 and 4–24, shown at c, while a secondary dimension is created by the two intersecting forms of 4–3, shown at b.

Example 7.2. *The Rite of Spring* (1911–1913), Part 2, "Introduction": **86**

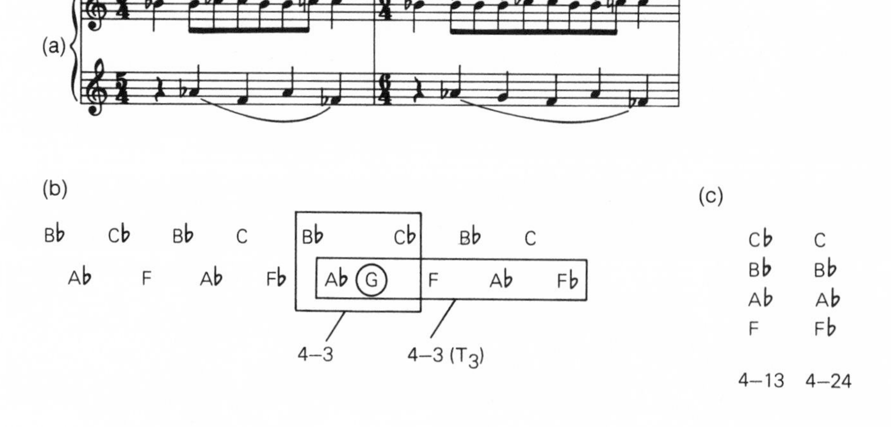

12. Igor Stravinsky, *The Rite of Spring: Sketches 1911–1913* (London, 1969), p. 62.

Example 7.3. *The Rite of Spring Sketches: 1911–1913,* p. 62: Music at **86**

Consideration of these initial examples leads one to wonder where and when these highly refined and elegant structures originate. They first become a consistent part of Stravinsky's music around 1908, in the music to act 1 of *The Nightingale.*

The beginning of *The Nightingale* has been compared to the opening music of Debussy's *Nuages,* and there is, indeed, a resemblance. Just below the surface, however, the similarity vanishes. As in *Nuages,* the descant of *The Nightingale*'s opening is organized in tetrachords, the first of which is the diatonic tetrachord 4–11 (as in *Nuages*), followed by 4–13. These are shown in the letter-name graph below Example 7.4, which here and in all the musical illustrations corresponds to the music notation at the top of the example. An "unordered" inversion of 4–11 then unfolds in the descant of m. 5–6, answering the form of that same set at the opening.

More interesting is the harmonic succession created by the pairs of eighth-notes in both voices. This is indicated by the set names attached to the brackets below the letter-name graph. Set 4–22 is repeated, as is set 4–19. However, unlike set 4–22, 4–19 is not repeated in the same plane. The first form of 4–19 combines dyads in upper and lower voices; the second is the "melodic" configuration A♭–C–G–C–E, bracketed and labeled in the example. Set 4–7 is also repeated, but in the second phrase, which begins in m. 5, where it interlocks with 4–3 as well as with another form of itself. Syntactic structures of this type are voluminously represented in Stravinsky's music of this period.

Still another aspect of the structure of this opening music of *The Nightingale* is depicted in the small figure in letter-name notation at the lower right of Example 7.4. There the repeated dyad C–F forms a separate stratum, allowing the counterpoint of 4–12 and 4–10 to shine through, as indicated by the circled and beamed notes. In this way, the voice-leading pattern creates new and significant melodic structures, again suggesting the strong connection between voice leading and melody.

Pitch-Class Set Leitmotivs

A far less intricate musical situation, yet one that has far-reaching implications for understanding Stravinsky's early music, exists at the beginning of *The Firebird.* Example 7.5 illustrates.

Example 7.4. *The Nightingale* (1908–1914). "Introduction"

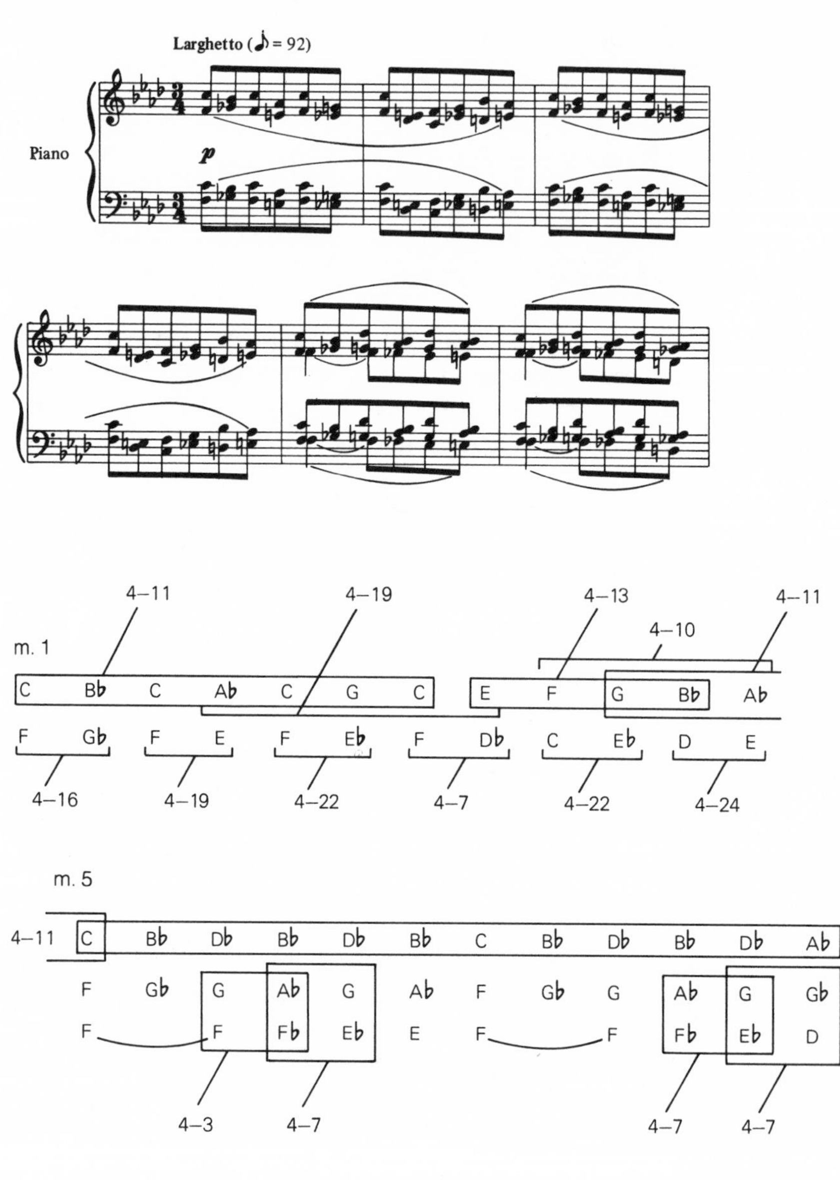

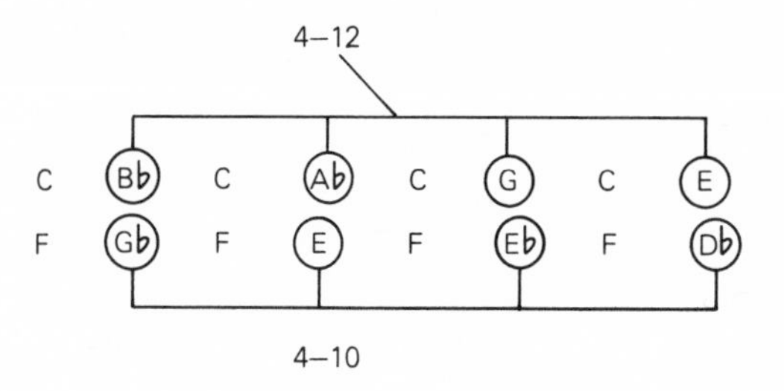

Example 7.5. *The Firebird* (1910), "Introduction": m. 1

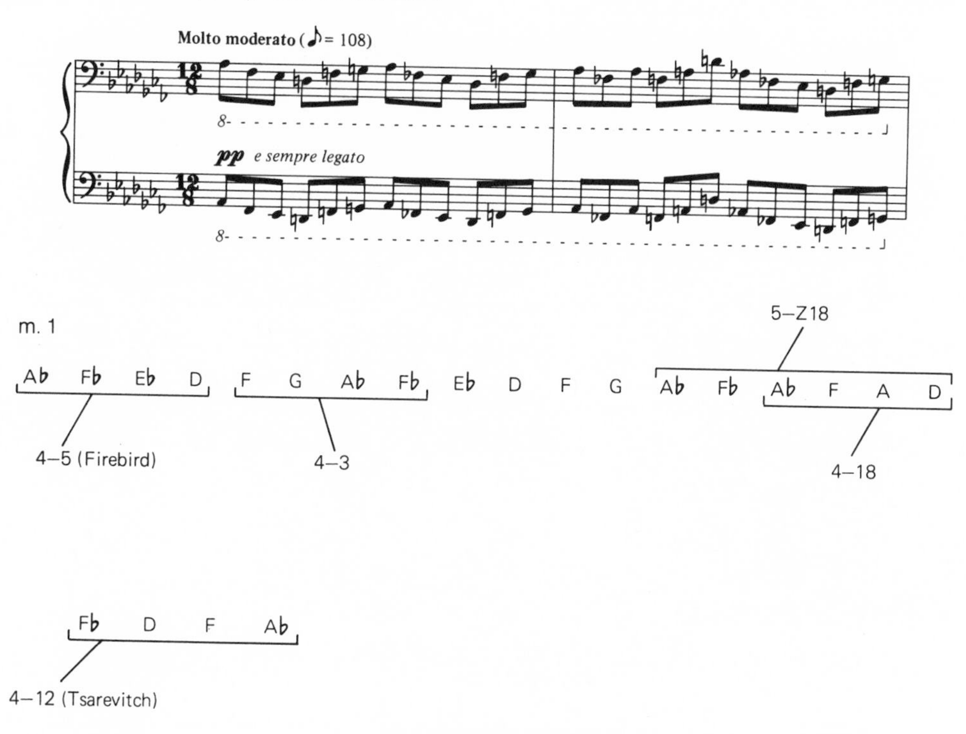

In *The Firebird,* as well as in the other ballets of the period, one must recognize the existence and operation of pitch-class set leitmotivs: pitch-class sets that have fixed associations with personae in the artwork. One of the main leitmotivs in this composition is given right at the outset, the pitch-class set 4–5, which is associated throughout the work with the Firebird. Other sets of importance to the music are also incorporated in the opening passage and marked in Example 7.5: sets 4–3, 4–18, and 5–Z18. Concealed by distribution among noncontiguous notes is set 4–12, which is very prominent in *The Firebird* and is the pitch-class set leitmotiv of Ivan Tsarevitch, the protagonist of the ballet.

In the music that begins at m. 10 (Example 7.6), the set 4–12, embedded in the opening music, emerges to become the main component of the canonic passage.[13]

Inversionally related forms of 4–12 create the basic syntax of the passage, with 4–25 recurring regularly as a vertical. The latter set is the main leitmotiv of Kastchei, the Immortal. Presented in the linear dimension is set 4–23, also associated with that persona. Thus, the music unfolds in distinct but interacting

13. A traditional double canon: descant-bass, alto-tenor.

Example 7.6. *The Firebird* (1910), "Introduction": m. 10

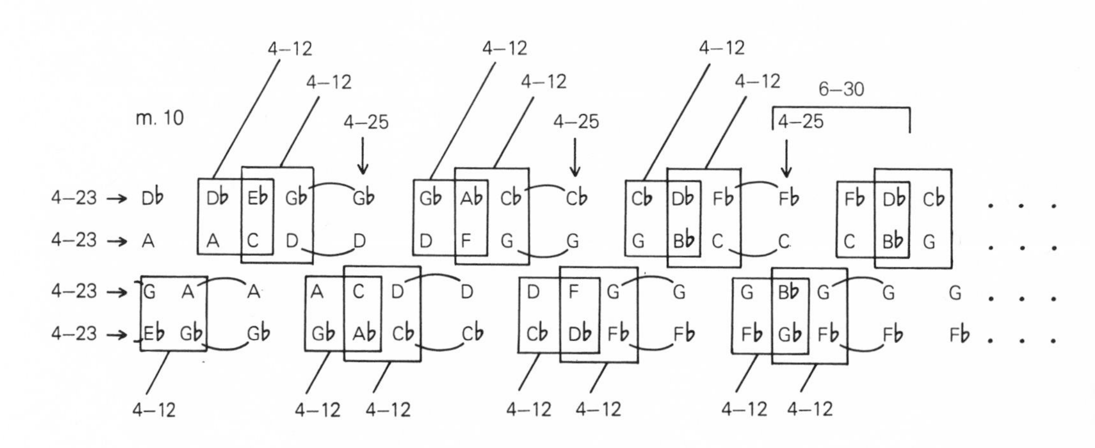

planes: the interlocking 4–12 formations (which may be called "lateral" sets), the forms of 4–25, which punctuate the progression at regular intervals, and the linear formations, which express the diatonic tetrachord 4–23. Each set has a leitmotivic function in *The Firebird*, and voice leading here may be understood as the medium through which these distinct musical elements interact coherently and cohesively by creating multiple replicas of the same set types. Ramifications of this idea will be pursued in connection with the examples that follow.

Multiple interlocking forms of the same set may also occur in a single dimension, as indicated in the analysis below Example 7.7. There "prime" and "inverted" forms of the Firebird leitmotiv 4–5 interlock, with the common pitch classes between each pair, B♭♭ (A) and E♭, forming a dyadic axis over the span of the entire passage. Thus, the choice of transposition level (with or without inversion) seems to be motivated by a concern for preserving a specific pitch-class axis interval, the tritone A–E♭. What this means in terms of the entire work cannot be discussed here; suffice it to say that many passages exhibit these axial characteristics.

Example 7.7. *The Firebird* (1910), "Capture of the Firebird": **22** + 3

Example 7.8 provides an opportunity to deal with certain notational matters in Stravinsky's music as they relate to structure. In particular, the moving upper parts (above the pedal E♭) consist of major triads from **91** to **92.** However, these components are merely subcomponents of larger pitch-class sets that are more important to the syntax here. A correct parsing shows that the "triads" group in pairs or quadruples to form the sets indicated on the letter-name graph: 6–30, 6–33, 8–Z29, 6–30 again, and 6–27. Here both 6–33 and 6–30 refer to the master octad 8–Z29. This set, which consists of the third and fourth pairs of "triads," has the same pitch-class content as the entire upper voice from **91** to **92.** The final chord, 6–27, is one of the six hexachords of 8–28, and its occurrence here represents a referential shift to that octad.

Example 7.8. *The Firebird* (1910), "Sunrise": **91**

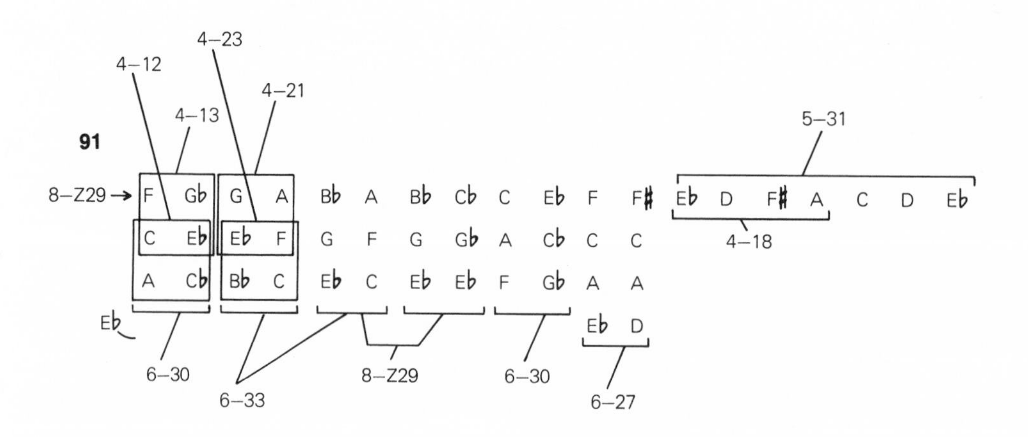

Example 7.8. *continued*

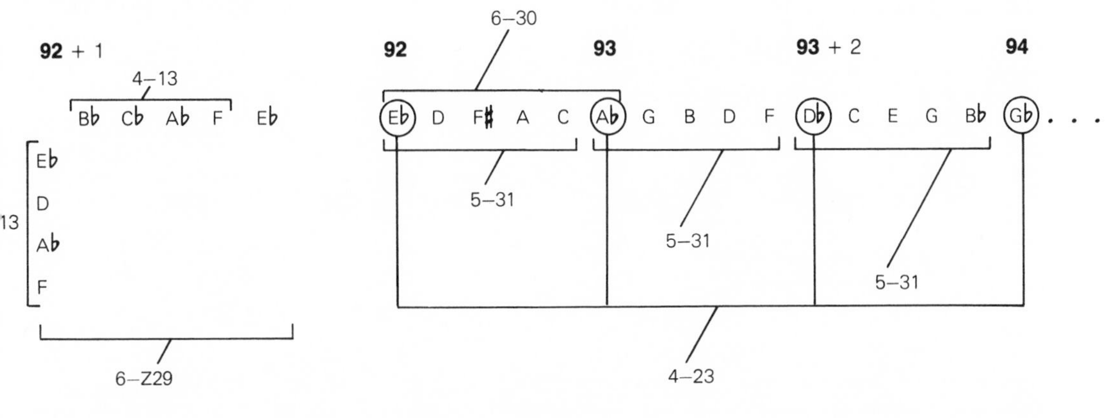

Such shifts are an important part of the harmonic syntax of Stravinsky's early music. For instance, at important junctures in the music, there often occurs a shift from the octatonic or other master octad to the diatonic octad 8–23. This may coincide with a major articulation in form. An example is the final motion of *Symphonies of Wind Instruments,* which, in its diatonicism, offers a marked contrast to the preceding octatonic music of the chorale. Still another instance is the music at **37** in the first movement of *Symphony of Psalms,* the oboe solo, which presents a complete statement of set 8–23.

At **92** in Example 7.8, the tetrachord 4–18 from the opening music (recall Example 7.5) unfolds within set 5–31, which is octatonic. In the next measure (**92** + 2), the upper voice configuration expresses 4–13, another prominent tetrachord in *The Firebird,* and is accompanied by a different form of the same set, to which it relates as an inversion. As indicated in the example, the two forms of 4–13 sum to hexachord 6–Z29. To understand the syntax here, one must know that 6–Z29 is the complement of 6–Z50, which occurs just before **92** and references the octatonic set, 8–28. Set 6–Z29 and other complements of subsets of 8–28 not in 8–28 may be termed octatonic by complement-extension.

Beginning at **92** (lower right part of the analysis in Example 7.8), the melodic figures express a beautiful linking of octatonic and diatonic structures: the individual figures form 5–31 (octatonic), as indicated on the letter-name graph, while the headnotes that are created by the fifth-transpositions form 4–23 (diatonic).

Finally, in connection with Example 7.8, the tetrachordal components are leitmotivic, as marked at **91** on the upper right portion of the letter-name graph. Sets 4–12 and 4–13 are associated with Tsarevitch; 4–23 and 4–21 refer to Kastchei. Thus, the passage is a musical depiction of the opposing forces in the ballet.

Analysis of the music at **98** + 1 shows how the composer creates new music in the most elegant way from pitch-class set leitmotivs. Pitch-class set 4–5, the Firebird motiv, may be viewed as a combination of a chromatic trichord and a dyad that forms a "major third." Here Stravinsky uses the chromatic trichord of

Example 7.9. *The Firebird* (1910), "Fairy Carillon," "Appearance of the Monster-Guardians of Kastchei," "Capture of Ivan Tsarevitch": **98** + 1

98 + 1

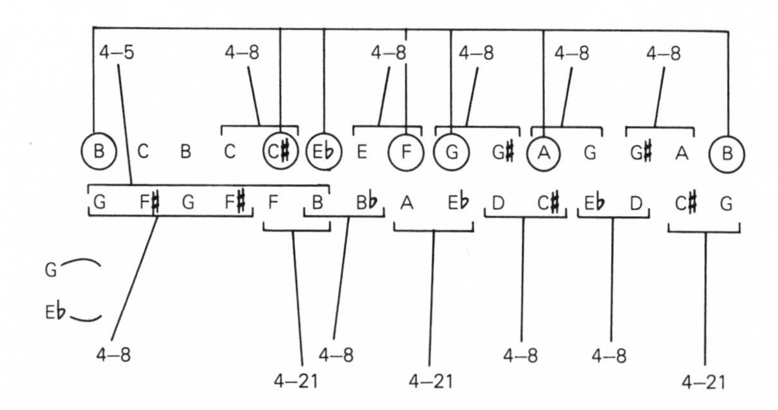

4–5 to create a new set, 4–8, as shown in the analysis below Example 7.9. In this way, set 4–8, which becomes the leitmotiv of the Monster-Guardians, is derived from the music of the Firebird, one of several transformations that unify the music of the ballet.

Set 4–5, the Firebird motiv, is also present, however, in the lower strand of the voice leading: G–F♯–F–B; B–B♭–A–E♭; A–E♭–D–C♯; and E♭–D–C♯–G—a succession of ordered forms of the set.

Example 7.10. *The Firebird* (1910), "Fairy Carillon": **101**

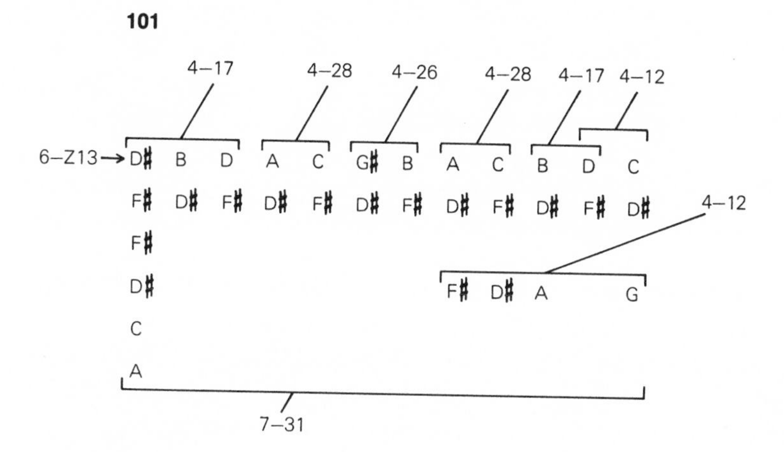

The other leitmotivic constituent of the passage is 4–21 (marked on the letter-name analysis), a set of whole-tone nature that is associated with Kastchei in the ballet. This set also occurs in the upper part, as indicated by the circled letter names.

Because the upper voice of the carillon shown in Example 7.10 is hexachord 6–Z13, one of the six hexachords of the octatonic 8–28, one might suspect that the entire passage is octatonic. That is indeed the case, for its pitch content sums to 7–31, as shown, and 7–31 is the only seven-note subset of 8–28.

Within 7–31, the leitmotivic set 4–12 (Tsarevitch) appears, with the indication ben marcato and in an ordering that emphasizes its connection with the diminished-seventh sonority characteristic of 8–28.

The voice leading of the passage forms the symmetric succession 4–17 / 4–28 / 4–26 / 4–28 / 4–17. However, the symmetry is broken at the very end by the appearance of the leitmotivic set 4–12, an inversion of the ben marcato form in the lower register, with which it shares two pitches: F♯ and D♯.

In sum, this excerpt illustrates the role of leitmotivic sets in Stravinsky's music as well as the role of voice leading in creating regular progressions of pitch-class sets. Although the tetrachords of this section will naturally be related because of the presence of the controlling octatonic set 7–31, the symmetric arrangement is not automatic and must have been carefully planned by the composer.

Perhaps the most remarkable feature of the well-known music shown in Example 7.11 is its derivation from the introductory music of the ballet—a concealed relationship. Specifically, pitch-class set 5–Z18 at the beginning of m. 2 in Example 7.5, when transposed and reordered, becomes the subject of the "Infernal Dance." However, a common segment is preserved between the two forms of 5–Z18, albeit an unordered segment, namely, the subset 4–18, which occurs as the last four notes in each configuration.

The consequent phrase at two measures before **135** in Example 7.11 begins with 4–18, which occurs at the end of the subject but then introduces other tetrachords, as shown on the letter-name graph of the example. These two measures are clearly within the octatonic orbit, represented by the octatonic hexachord 6–27 and, within it, by the octatonic pentad, 5–31.

At **135,** the upper voice resumes the melodic contour and rhythm of the subject, but introduces new sets. In particular, 5–16 now becomes surrogate for 5–Z18, bringing this new phrase within the octatonic orbit as well. Remarkably, however, this new set, 5–16, has as its last four notes the set 4–18, which, as noted earlier, also comprises the last four notes of the subjects 5–Z18. (The unordered transposition is by minor third.)

A similar substitution occurs in the consequent phrase of this new form of the subject at **135** + 2, at the very end of Example 7.11. As indicated on the letter-name graph, the consequent phrase now lies within 6-Z28, not within 6–27, the octatonic hexad, as before. Here we have another instance of complement-extension, for although 6-Z28 is not octatonic, its complement, 6–Z49, is.

In addition to the new set 4–19, which also has leitmotivic significance in *The Firebird,* the leitmotivic sets 4–12 (Tsarevitch) and 4–24 (Kastchei) are embedded and combined in this new configuration, an extraordinary transformation similar to the one shown in Example 7.6.

The composer again preserves a specific connection between the first consequent phrase (two bars before **135**) and the new consequent phrase (two bars after **135**): the last five notes in each comprise a form of 5–31. (The second 5–31 is an unordered transposed inversion of the first.)

However, the music in the last two measures of Example 7.11 is not octatonic because the entire passage is based upon the heptad 7–32, which is not a subset of 8–28. Yet the relations between this structure and the octatonic octad are multiple. For instance, 8–28 contains the complement of 7–32, 5–32. But the most interesting connection here, and one mentioned earlier, is that between the final hexachords in the two versions of the consequent phrase. Set 6–27 in the first ver-

Example 7.11. *The Firebird* (1910), "Infernal Dance of All the Subjects of Kastchei": **134** + 4

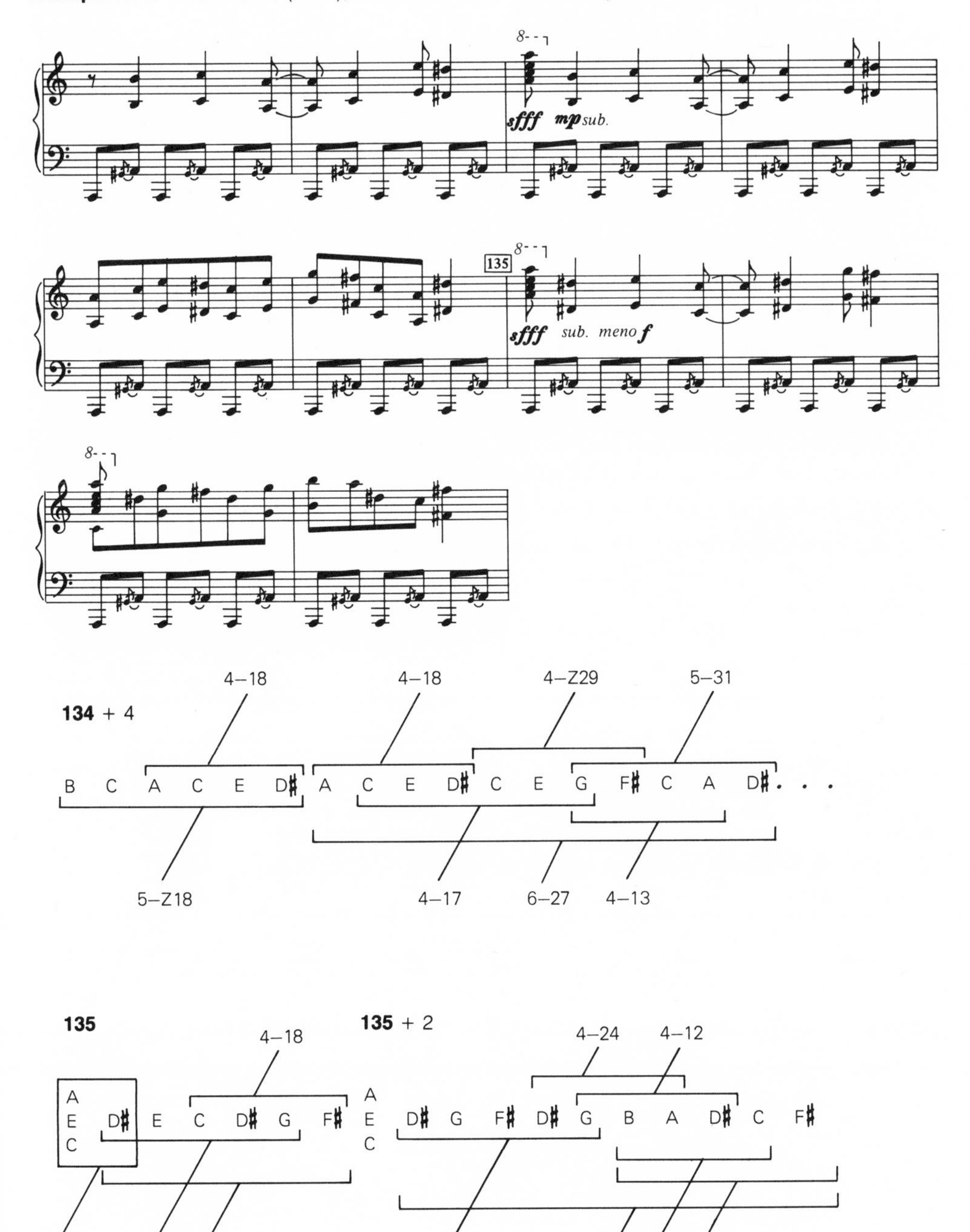

sion is octatonic; 6–Z28 in the second version is octatonic by complement-extension.

Still another transformation of the subject of the "Infernal Dance" is shown in Example 7.12. Here we find two interlocking forms of 4–12, a linear expression of the interlocking voice-leading pattern illustrated in Example 7.6. This provides yet another demonstration of the basic similarity between voice leading and melodic configuration in Stravinsky's music, specifically, with respect to pitch-class set replication.

Also prominent in this new transformation of the subject are the chromatic dyads at the ends of each figure. These refer to 4–5, the Firebird leitmotiv, and together form 4–8, recalling the passage shown in Example 7.9. In addition, the tritone formed by the middle notes is a leitmotivic reference to Kastchei (set 4–24) as well as to Kastchei's nemesis, the Firebird (set 4–5).

Finally, each complete thematic figure presents the hexachord 6–Z28, an unordered transposition of that set in the music at **135** + 2 (Example 7.11). In Example 7.12, the two forms of 6–Z28 are related (obviously) by ordered transposition at the tritone, which retains 4–28 as a common subset between them, providing a direct reference to the octatonic octad, 8–28.

Example 7.12. *The Firebird* (1910), "Infernal Dance": **141**

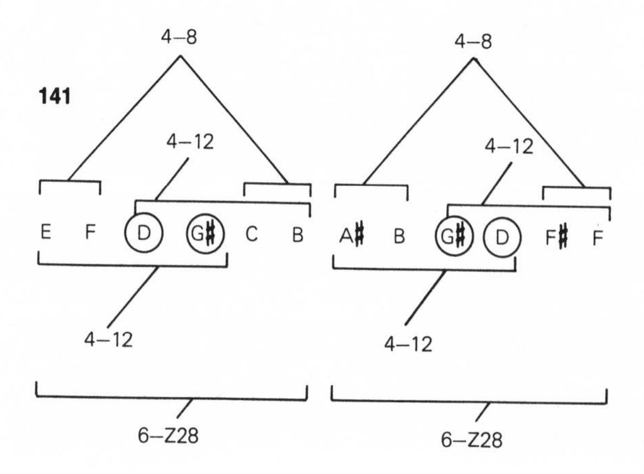

As in Example 7.8, the passage in Example 7.13 presents a series of vertical triads. Again, analysis reveals that these are secondary formations; the correct harmonic syntax of the passage is displayed on the letter-name graph below Example 7.13.

Example 7.13. *The Firebird* (1910), "Disappearance of the Palace": **195**

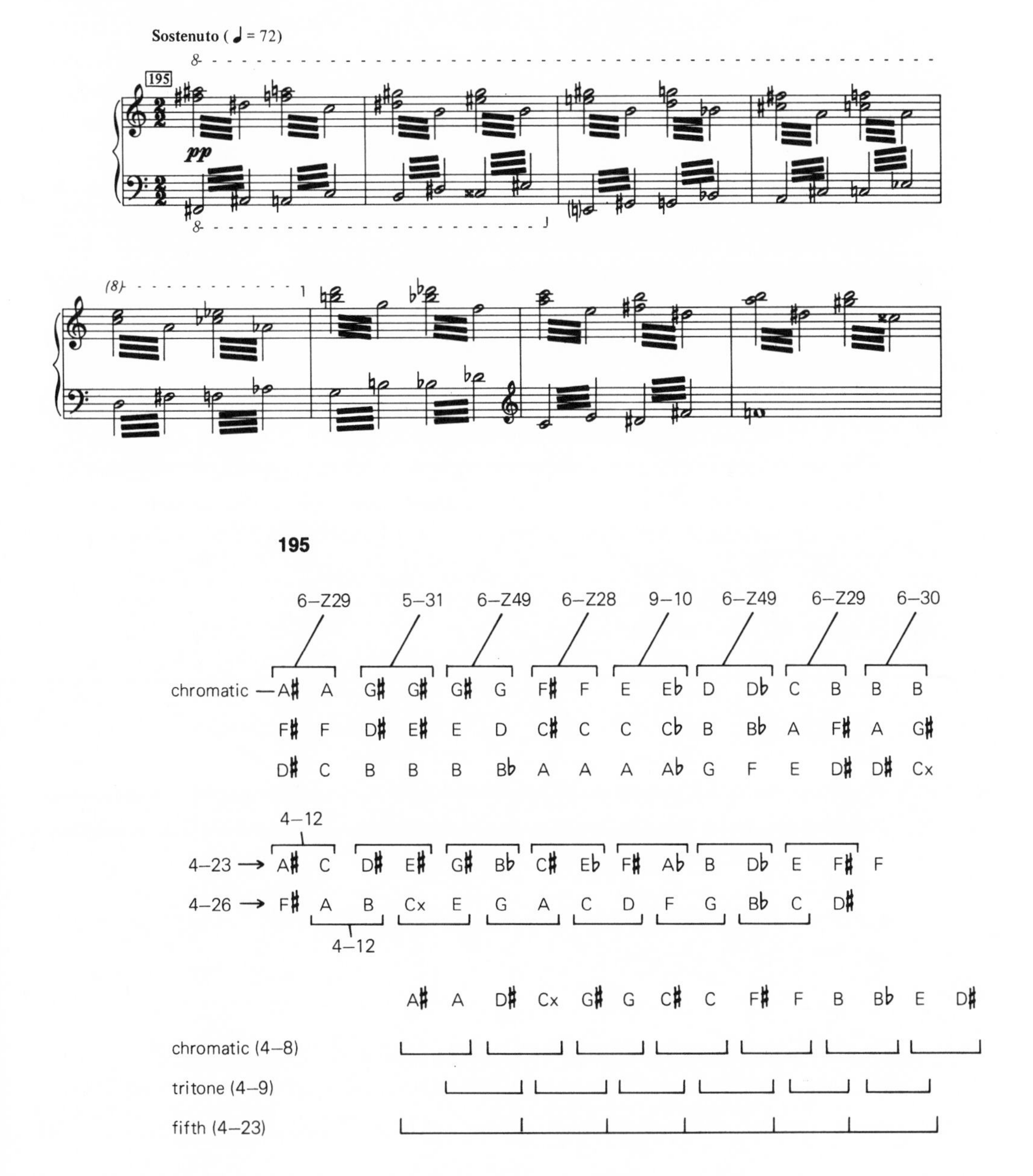

Were it not for the presence of 6–Z28 and 6–Z29, the passage would fall neatly into the octatonic species, for all the other sets are subsets of 8–28. However, here again the anomaly is only apparent, for, as noted earlier, 6–Z28 complements the octatonic hexachord 6–Z49, and 6–Z29 complements the octatonic hexachord 6–Z50. Thus, the two presumably anomalous hexachords relate to the octatonic sphere by complement-extension.

The lower two voices here form a separate plane, by virtue of projecting set 4–12 both in disjunct and overlapping fashion, as indicated by brackets above and below the lower letter-name graph. That is, every adjacent pair of voices forms 4–12. The disjunct pairs are related by fifth-transposition, so forms of 4–23 are projected by the head notes of each 4–12. The overlapping forms are related by inversion, and the head notes form regular patterns of 4–8 and 4–9. A more cogent demonstration of the central roles of transposition and inversion in voice leading or a more coherent display of the primary significance of set replication in the voice leading and harmonic syntax of Stravinsky's early music would be difficult to find.

In addition to the sets formed laterally in Example 7.13, three of the lines offer regular patterns in themselves. The descant presents a descending chromatic set, which refers to the leitmotivic set 4–5, and the lower lines of the bottom stratum unfold 4–23 and 4–26, as marked.

The original music for *Petrushka* is shown in Example 7.14. Except for the chromatic motion in the upper voice from m. 3, it is totally octatonic in orientation, with the first eight measures bounded by inversionally related forms of the octatonic pentad 5–16.[14] The remaining components are primarily tetrachords. Notice, in particular, the penultimate sonority of the first eight measures, 4–Z29. This contains the same pitches as the opening tetrachord, C–E–F♯–G, and foreshadows the Petrushka chord, 6–30, at the beginning of the second section of the music here.

All the tetrachords displayed in Example 7.14 are leitmotivic. In particular, 4–21, which enters with the dyad G♯–F♯ in the next-to-last measure, is associated with the Moor. As in *The Firebird,* the sinister persona is expressed musically through a whole-tone figure.

The Petrushka chord, 6–30, breaks down into three overlapping leitmotivic tetrachords, 4–12, 4–13 (the final tetrachord in the ballet), and 4–Z15. The latter set, which has the same interval content as 4–Z29, its twin in m. 6, is closely associated with Petrushka in the ballet. In sum, the substructure and detailed voice leading of the Petrushka chord express basic leitmotivic components of the work and are not at all arbitrary.[15]

---

14. This pentad occurs eight times in 8–28, as do each of the other six pentads.

15. At **98** + 2 in *Petrushka*, harmonies 6–Z19 and 6–30 alternate, summing to 8–Z15, which is the complement of the Petrushka tetrachord, 4–Z15. The noncommon tones of these two sonorities, B–C–D–E, form tetrachord 4–11, which occurs throughout *Petrushka* in a variety of roles.

Example 7.14. *Petrushka* (1911), "Second Tableau": **48**

48

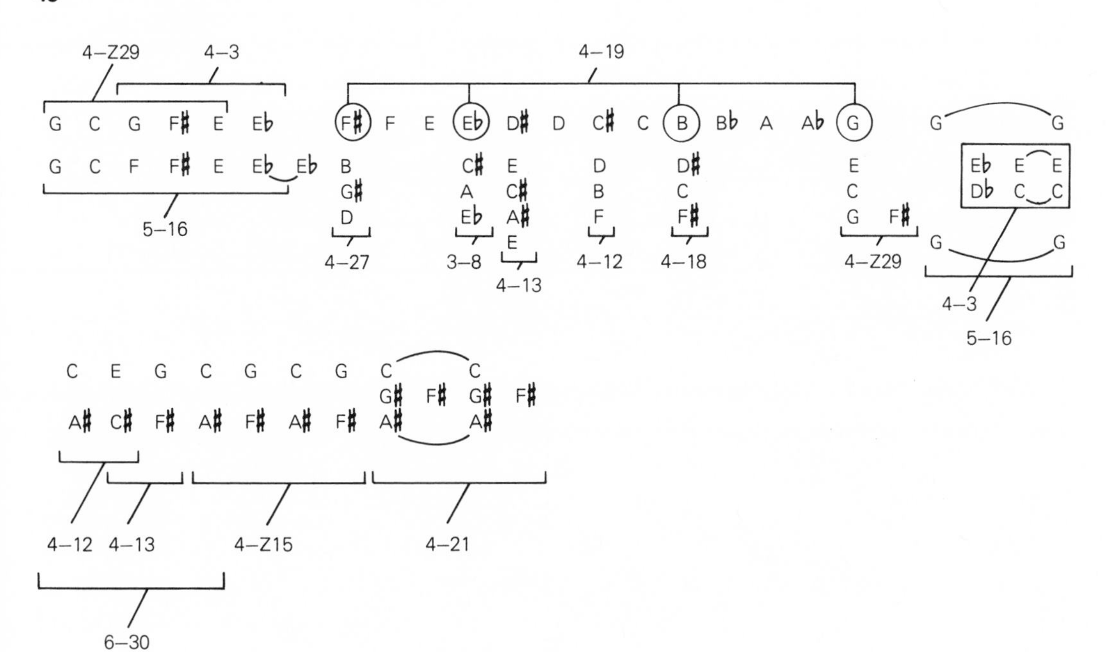

Example 7.15 presents a portion of the Mummers scene from *Petrushka*. The letter-name graph below the musical score provides a close-up of a section of **117** + 4 bracketed on the music. Here we see how refined voice leading has become in Stravinsky's music. The two successive forms of 7–31 differ by only one note: the first contains D♯, the second, D. All the rest are common notes between the two forms.

The half-step voice leading changes 4–12 to 4–10 in the lower plane, as indicated, while the lateral tetrachords consist of the succession 4–18 / 4–Z15 / 4–Z15 / 4–Z15, the latter set associated with Petrushka. Participating in this voice-leading pattern are the chromatic dyads in the upper voice, which combine to

Example 7.15. *Petrushka* (1911), "Fourth Tableau": **117** + 4

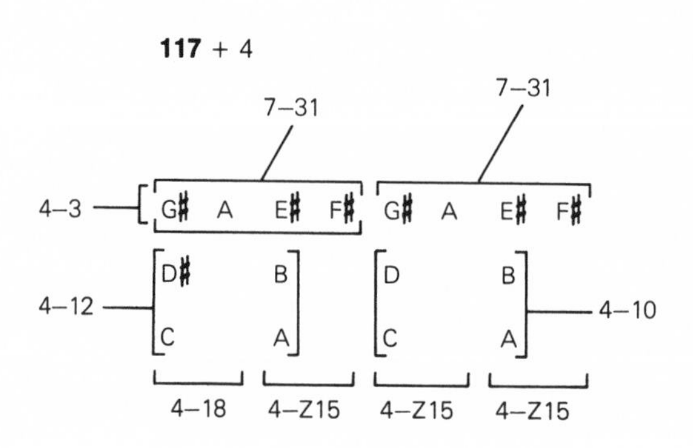

form set 4–3, a leitmotivic set in *Petrushka* that we also saw in m. 7 of Example 7.14. Thus, every detail of this microcosm contributes to the whole, and a basic feature of voice leading, set replication, is apparent on every plane of motion.

The letter-name graph of the music shown in Example 7.16 provides a condensed view of the passage. The music up to **120** is octatonic. Indeed, the pitch classes of the section sum to 8–28, as shown on the letter-name graph.

Against the repeated forms of 4–18 in the upper parts (associated with the appearance of the devil among the Mummers), two interlocking forms of 4–3 unfold in the bass. They are transpositionally related and share the middle notes, B♯ and B. Here we have an ordered segment of the octatonic scale, in "retrograde," yielding the hexachord 6–Z13. In sum, the entire passage consists of the interaction of 4–18, on its own plane, with the interlocking forms of 4–3, which form the hexad 6–Z13—all within the master octad 8–28.

At **120,** there is a radical harmonic shift with the appearance of 6–34. This hexad, one form of which is Scriabin's "mystic chord," is a favorite of Stravinsky. It almost always refers to the master octad 8–27, of which it is a subset.[16]

The choral-orchestral work, *Zvezdoliki,* from 1911–1912, is also characterized by the type of voice leading and harmonic syntax found in Stravinsky's other early music.[17] Example 7.17 presents one such passage, beginning with the section marked by a downward-pointing arrow on the score.

Although the master diatonic octad, 8–23, is not literally present here, it is represented by the array of tetrachords that makes up the harmonic succession. Note in particular the many recurrences of 4–Z29 and the grouping 4–16 / 4–22 / 4–26 / 4–14.

At b are shown a few of the sets in the vertical dimension repeated as linear and lateral configurations, an intricate example of set replication.

Details of voice leading are shown at c in Example 7.17. The passage begins with set 4–Z29. This is then transposed up two half-steps, but the transposition is not fully ordered. With the exception of tenor 1, the voices switch. Thus, the successor to E in tenor 2 is F♯ in bass 1, the successor to C in bass 1 is tenor 2's D, and G in bass 2 is continued by A in bass 1. To form the next vertical, three pitches are held in the bottom three voices while tenor 1 moves to E♭, changing 4–Z29 to 4–18. Then the top three voices are held fixed while bass 2 moves stepwise from F♯ to F, a voice leading that restores 4–Z29, now inversionally related to the two prior forms. This detailed illustration indicates the elegant ways in which the

16. This sonority, which is found in both Stravinsky's and Scriabin's music, is also prominent in Berg's music, the most famous instance being the *Wozzeck* hexachord.

17. This composition seems to have perplexed several authors. Jim Samson writes: "There is little in these early compositions which could have prepared Stravinsky's contemporaries for his next work, the Cantata" (*Music in Transition* [New York, 1977], p. 44). Study of the work, however, indicates it is wholly consistent with its predecessors as regards harmonic syntax and voice-leading procedures.

Example 7.16. *Petrushka* (1911), "Fourth Tableau": **118**

Example 7.16. *continued*

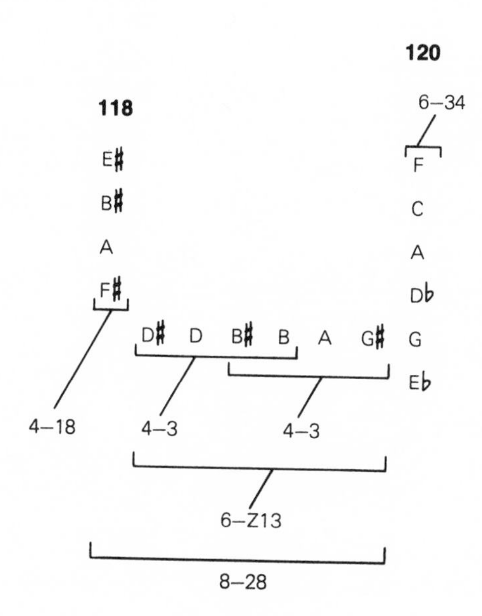

composer developed his art of voice leading, avoiding the parallel successions of his music before 1908, but achieving replication of sets through "unordered" inversion and transposition.

Act 3 of *The Nightingale* begins with a striking melodic figure that unfolds against a sustained diminished triad. Example 7.18 presents a detailed picture of this music. The upper voice is a form of the octatonic hexachord 6–Z50; the first and last verticals, which circumscribe the passage, are 4–18 and 4–13, respectively. Further examination of the passage reveals that it is based upon an elaborate intertwining of six tetrachords. As shown in the first letter-name graph below Example 7.18, set 4–18, the first tetrachord, is replicated successively by the other verticals as the descant moves against the sustained trichord. Each time D♭ occurs in the melody, it forms 4–18, in inversional relation to the initial vertical. When G♭ and F♭ occur, they form adjacent 4–12s and with B♭ create 4–27.

Overlapping tetrachords in the melody alone also include 4–18 and 4–27, as shown on the lower letter-name graph, but they introduce two types of sets that do not occur as verticals: tetrachords 4–10 and 4–Z15, which are so characteristic of this repertory.

Example 7.17. *Zvezdoliki* (1911–1912): m. 5

Example 7.17. *continued*

(a)

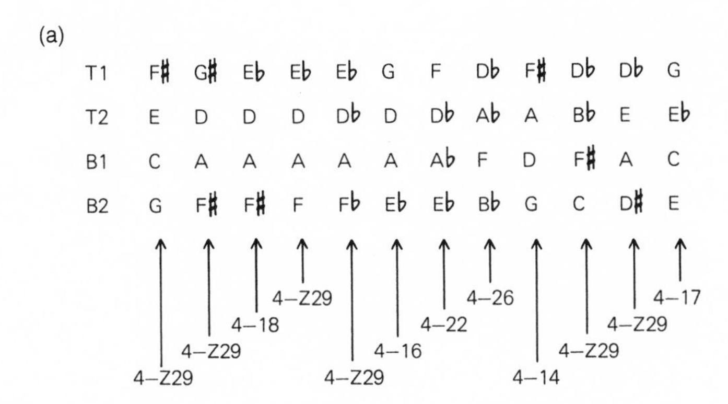

(b)

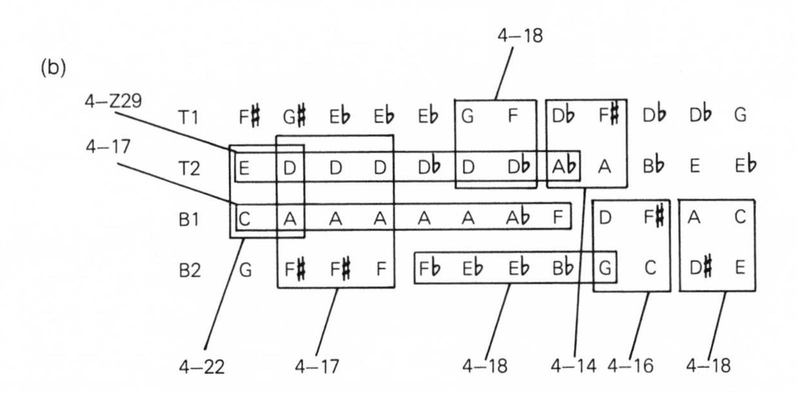

(c)

T_0(4–Z29) T_2(4–Z29) 4–18 T_0(4–Z29)

T1 F♯ → G♯ → E♭ E♭

T2 E D D D

B1 C A A A

B2 G F♯ F♯ → F

Example 7.18. *The Nightingale* (1908–1914), Act 3: **101**

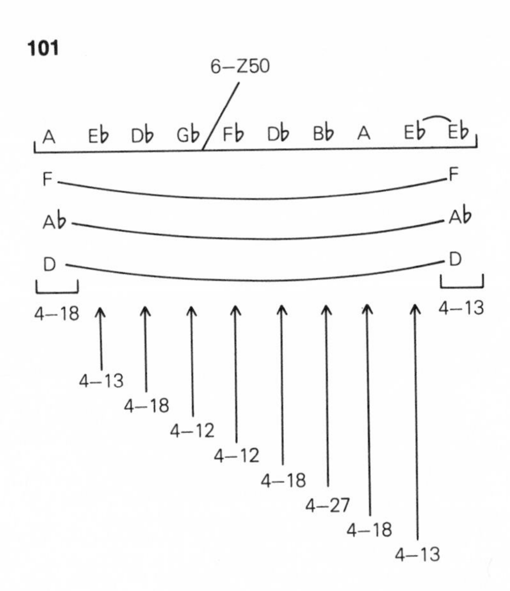

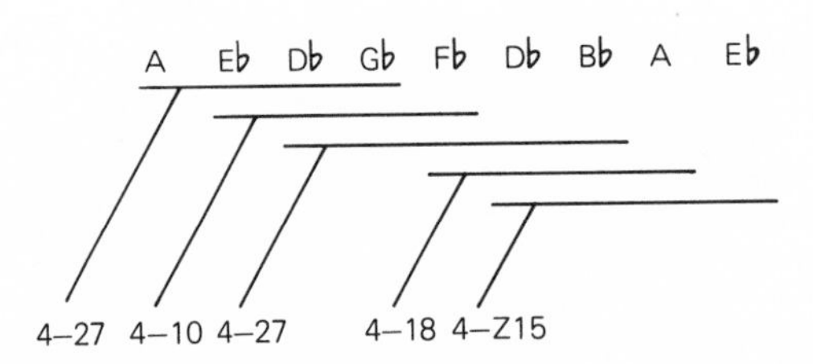

The remaining music of act 3 of *The Nightingale,* composed some five years after act 1 (overlapping with the last part of *The Rite),* also contains remarkable passages, similar to the one presented in Example 7.18. The letter-name graph of Example 7.19 shows a tetrachordal analysis of one of these.

A progression of four tetrachords occurs, with some variation, three times. In all three repetitions, the two upper parts remain the same; only the lower parts

Example 7.19. *The Nightingale* (1908–1914), Act 3: **107**

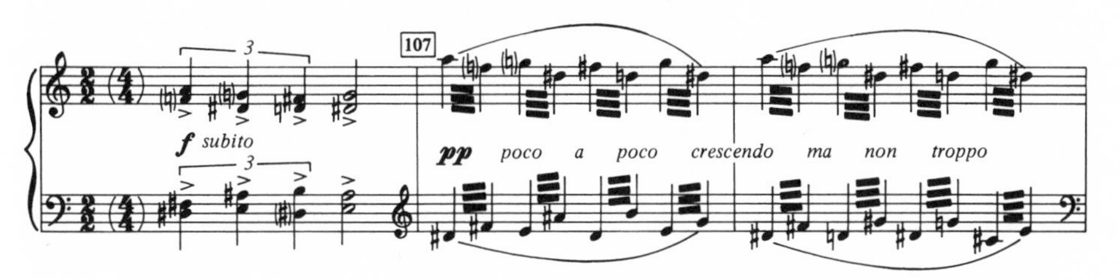

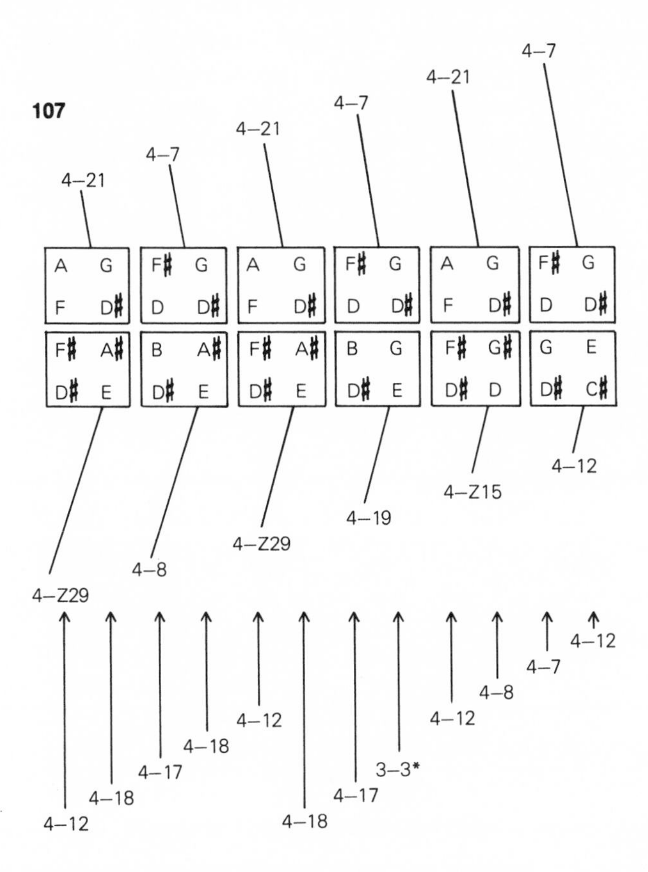

change. This differentiation is reflected in the analysis, which treats the two planes of voice leading separately. In the vertical dimension, shown at the bottom of the letter-name graph, the progression that begins one measure before **107** features 4–12 and 4–18, with the symmetric tetrachord 4–17 serving as a connector. At **107,** the progression is repeated, with a change occurring in the lower parts only at the end, where trichord 3–3 is formed. (Possibly there is a misprint here.)

The third progression begins at one measure after **107** with 4–12 and ends with a transposition of that set, framing the two symmetric tetrachords 4–7 and 4–8 in the middle. All these tetrachords are leitmotivs in *The Nightingale.*

As shown on the letter-name graph, the lateral tetrachords of the two upper parts exhibit complete regularity: an alternation of tetrachords 4–21 and 4–7, each with fixed pitch-class content. Although the succession of lower tetrachords is not quite so regular, it does make a consistent and coherent pattern. Tetrachords 4–Z15 and 4–Z29, the twin "all-interval" tetrachords, are its pillars. Tetrachord 4–8 anticipates the appearance of that set as a vertical in the third of the three progressions, and 4–12, the final lateral tetrachord in the lower parts, is an exact pitch-class replica of the vertical that ends the progression. Only tetrachord 4–19 seems out of place here. Nor is it represented anywhere else in the music. Possibly, as suggested earlier in connection with trichord 3–3, there is a misprint in the score at this point.

Example 7.20. *The Nightingale* (1908–1914), Act 3: **132** + 3

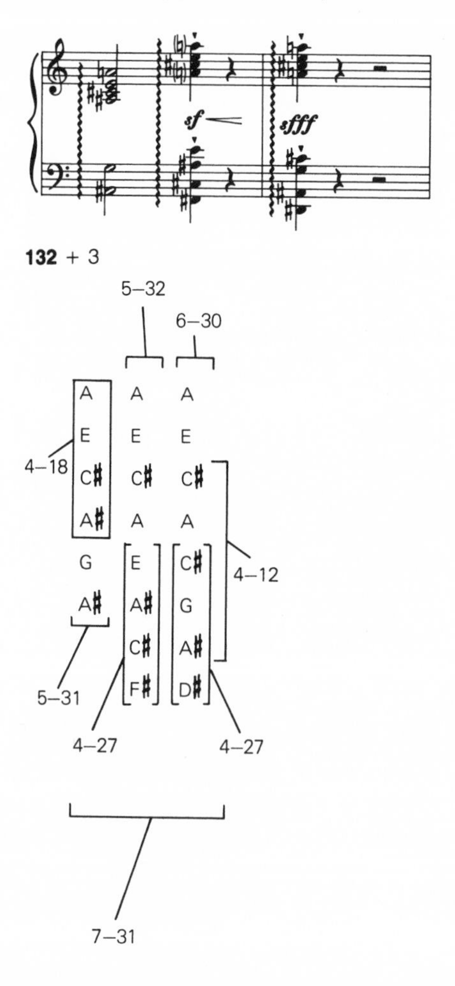

Example 7.20 offers another short passage from act 3 of *The Nightingale*, a special moment in the closing music. Here the referential octad is 8–28, which is represented by 7–31. Within 7–31 is its complement, 5–31, the first vertical; 5–31 contains, in turn, the leitmotivic set 4–18 as its upper tetrachord. When the lower tetrachord of the second vertical, 5–32, is replicated by an ordered transposition down three half-steps, the harmony changes to the octatonic hexad 6–30. The transposition also brings into play the leitmotivic sonority 4–12, as shown on the letter-name graph.

Example 7.21. Three Pieces for String Quartet (1914), Number Three

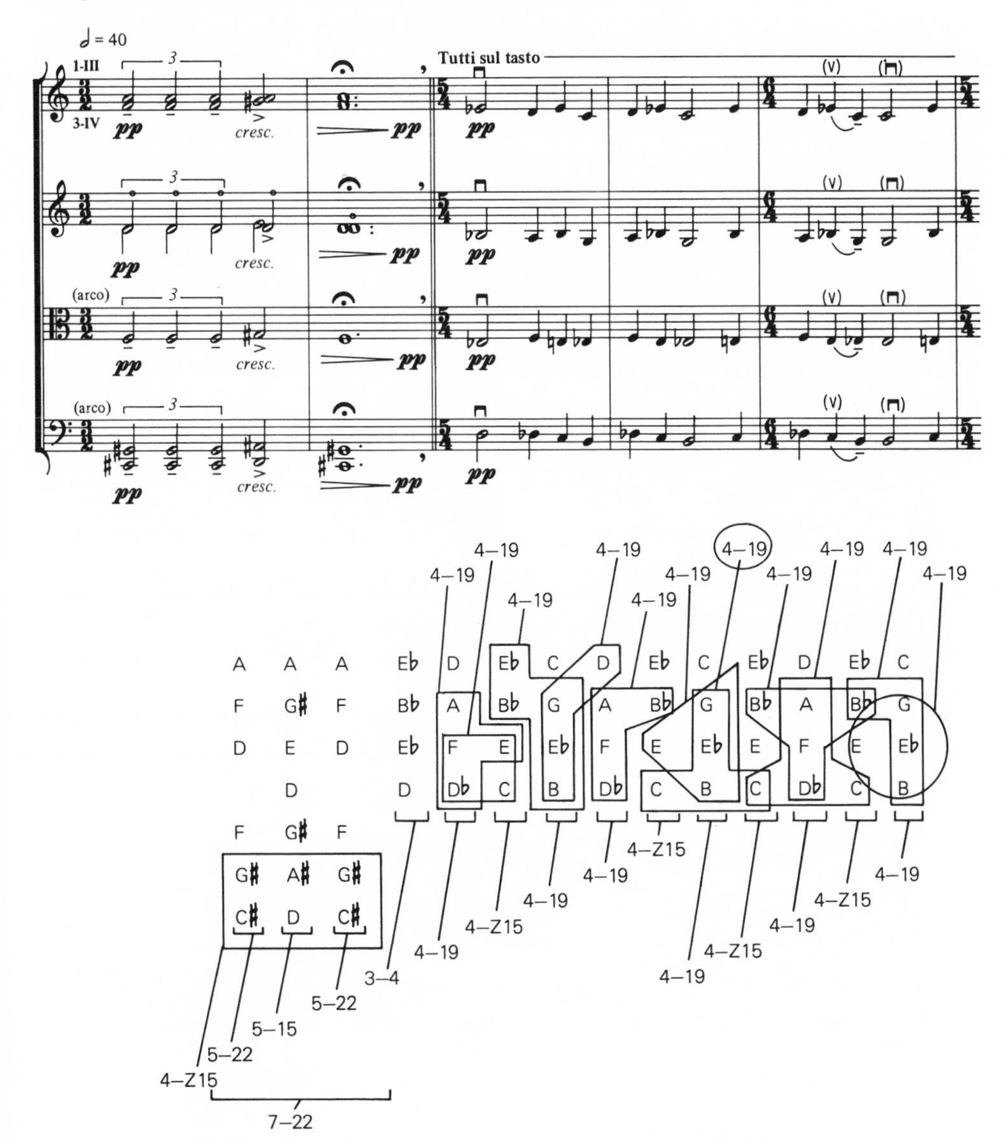

The third of Three Pieces for String Quartet serves as a final example of harmonic syntax and voice leading in an early work (Example 7.21). At the opening of the music, the verticals all lie within the heptad 7–22, as marked on the letter-name graph. Remarkably, the first and last verticals in this initial succession represent 5–22, the complement of the large heptad. However, the most extraordinary feature of the composition is its multiplanar organization, some of which is shown on the letter-name graph. For instance, the voice leading from 5–22 to 5–15 creates a lateral tetrachord that is of great significance throughout the first part of the work because its complement, 8–Z15, underlies the refrain in m. 8–9, 15–16, and 22–23. Other important sets are also brought into play in this introductory portion but are not shown on the graph in order to focus on one aspect of the music, namely, the replication of one of the verticals in other planes through voice leading. As indicated on the letter-name graph, tetrachords of only two types occur in the vertical dimension: 4–Z15 and 4–19. The analysis shows no fewer than eleven forms of 4–19 in other planes, a remarkable demonstration of Stravinsky's mastery of voice-leading procedures that he had begun to develop some six years earlier.[18]

Craft's comments on the genesis of this composition shed light on its harmonic syntax and extraordinary voice leading:

> The first notation in No. 3 is for the music that begins in the third measure . . . but the sketch is for violin and viola alone, playing in parallel fourths. . . . The next sketch, for the passage beginning twenty measures from the end, is substantially the same as in the finished version. In the third sketch, Stravinsky discovered the final versions of the melodic and harmonic progressions that begin in the third measure of the piece. The music of the opening measures, and of the refrain, was the last to be composed.[19]

From this we can deduce that Stravinsky composed a skeletal version of the voice leading (the parallel progression), then returned to elaborate this in the third sketch (which introduced the replications marked on Example 7.21), after having composed the closing music, in which there is an intricate intertwining of tetrachords. Only then did he compose the introductory measures, which also include "concealed" tetrachords, one of which, 4–Z15, is the complement of the master octad 8–Z15, the harmony of the refrain.

---

18. The orchestrated version of this movement, "Cantique," maintains the voice leading of the quartet version, even though the instruments shift about and do not follow the individual voices of the quartet. This suggests that the composer was not as concerned about the progression of individual voices (the traditional concept) as he was with preserving set and subset replication through voice leading.

19. Robert Craft, "Three Pieces for String Quartet: The Revisions," in *Stravinsky: Selected Correspondence*, vol. 1, ed. Robert Craft (New York, 1982), p. 408.

Conclusion

Why is Stravinsky's early music from 1908 to 1914 so cohesive, yet so rich and interesting? In large part, this is due to the fundamental harmonic syntax it represents and to certain regularities of set succession, particularly those involving leitmotivic collections. Harmonic syntax in this music is based upon referential sonorities, called master octads in this chapter. It is a syntax of subsets and supersets, related by transposition and/or inversion.

Harmonic syntax in Stravinsky's music cannot be considered apart from voice leading, however. Voice leading, in turn, is intimately connected with harmonic syntax, in the specific sense that voice leading is determined by the replication of pitch-class sets in more than one musical dimension—the multiplanar structures that have been explained and illustrated.

Finally, voice leading and harmonic syntax are also represented in the melodic dimension. Indeed, Stravinsky's concept of melody may be the ultimate origin of his complex voice-leading structures, of which the third of Three Pieces for String Quartet represents a zenith in this early period.

8 Octatonic Pitch Structure in Stravinsky

PIETER C. VAN DEN TOORN

SOME TIME AGO Arthur Berger, in a comprehensive survey of quite remarkable implications, drew attention to the role of the octatonic pitch collection as a cohesive frame of reference in Stravinsky's music.[1] It was Berger's contention that the bulk of Stravinsky's oeuvre, stretching from the "Russian" period to the early serial, did not readily submit to an analysis along tonal, atonal, or serial lines. And the difficulty seemed to rest not merely with Stravinsky's octatonic contexts, which could in fact often handily be dealt with, but equally with the still more numerous contexts of explicit diatonic intent. For quite apart from the diatonic reference itself, the central position of the triad (however novel in function and general appearance), together with an often unmistakable sense of pitch-class priority, seemed too conspicuously at odds with atonality (given the most generous interpretation of this ambiguous notion). At the same time, this diatonic articulation seemed often to implicate interval orderings other than those defined by the familiar major and minor scales of the tonal tradition. Indeed, even when, in neoclassical pieces, the major scale did impose itself, it often did so with the functional relations of this ordering (the familiar progressions, modulations, definitions of key and cadence) either absent or obscured by other forces of at least equal consequence.

These concerns led to a kind of threefold attack. There were contexts wholly referable to the octatonic collection (here defined as any collection of eight distinct pitch classes that, in scale formation, yields the symmetrical interval ordering of alternating ones and twos, half-steps and whole-steps). There were diatonic contexts in which, as indicated, the articulation might implicate orderings other than those of the major and minor scales. And there were octatonic-diatonic contexts that suggested a fusion or intermingling of these otherwise distinct collections of reference.

Now a considerable merit of this approach was that it allowed for a hearing and understanding of Stravinsky's music considered as a whole. It confronted that elusive sense of a distinctive musical presence (about which there has always

1. Arthur Berger, "Problems of Pitch Organization in Stravinsky," in *Perspectives on Schoenberg and Stravinsky*, ed. Benjamin Boretz and Edward T. Cone (New York, 1972), p. 123.

been such insistence on the part of enthusiasts) that transcends the three celebrated stylistic periods or orientation categories: "Russian," neoclassical, and serial. Thus, octatonic contexts are prevalent not only in early "Russian" pieces like the *Scherzo fantastique* (1907–1908), *The Rite of Spring* (1911–1913), and *Les Noces* (1914–1917, 1921–1923), but also in such neoclassical summits as the *Symphony of Psalms* (1930) and *Orpheus* (1947), and then later in partially serial compositions like *Canticum Sacrum* (1955) and *Agon* (1953–1957).

This is not to suggest that the collection is in itself unique to Stravinsky's music. Stravinsky's source was undoubtedly Rimsky-Korsakov, who used it as a colorful harmonic device to complement the magical element in operas like *Sadko*. The collection also figures prominently in the music of Scriabin, and then later in that of Messiaen (who codified it as the second among what he called "modes of limited transposition").[2] Moreover, a triadic grouping or partitioning of the octatonic collection is characteristic of both Rimsky-Korsakov and Stravinsky.[3] But beginning with the second tableau of *Petrushka* (1911), octatonic construction takes on a dimension that was to remain for some fifty years peculiarly Stravinsky's own. And when heard and understood in conjunction with techniques of triadic superimposition, oscillation, block juxtaposition, and fragmental repetition, it offers a framework from which a consistency in musical thought is revealingly gauged.

And so we shall briefly be documenting the mechanics of Stravinsky's octatonic routines, and how these routines interact with diatonic material or, more significantly, how certain octatonic routines, typical of the "Russian" period, are distinguished from others that are common to neoclassicism.[4] For while octatonic or octatonic-diatonic construction is fundamental to Stravinsky's oeuvre (excepting some of the later serial works), this fact in no way undermines the legitimacy of the three "stylistic" trends. On the contrary, focusing on the works as a whole allows clearer distinctions not only between these three general orientation categories, but also between the individual pieces themselves. Close attention will be paid to a handful of passages from *The Rite of Spring* (which is an ignition, a catalogue of resources on which the composer was persistently to draw in succeeding works), *Les Noces*, and the *Symphony of Psalms*.

Before continuing, however, it will be useful to consider a few elementary details. The octatonic scale (consisting of alternating ones and twos, half-steps and whole-steps) yields but two interval orderings, the first of these with its sec-

---

2. *Technique de mon langage musical* (Paris, 1944).

3. The term "partitioning" derives from a consciousness of the reference collection, in the sense that one interprets or conceives of intervals, themes, fragments, motives, chords, or simultaneities (a more general and noncommittal term than chord) as partitionings of the reference collection.

4. For more discussion of these issues, see Pieter C. van den Toorn, *The Music of Igor Stravinsky* (New Haven, 1983).

ond scale degree at the interval of one from its first (the 1–2, half-step–whole-step ordering), the second with its second scale degree at the interval of two from its first (the 2–1, whole-step–half-step ordering). These are shown in Example 8.1, with the 1–2 ordering on the left side, the reverse 2-1 ordering on the right. And the question as to which of these might actually pertain to a given context naturally hinges on questions of priority and articulation. For example, octatonic contexts that are tetrachordally oriented with a pitch numbering of (0 2 3 5) will tend to implicate the 2-1 ordering cited on the right side of Example 8.1 as the most favorable approach in scale formation.

Example 8.1. Octatonic Collections

Moreover, the octatonic collection is limited to three transpositions, that is, three collections of distinguishable pitch content. In Example 8.1, these are labeled I, II, and III. Thus, in regard to collection I, the 1–2 ordering on the left side: following the initial C♯, transposing beyond D (collection II) and E♭ (collection III) to E would merely yield the initial collection (collection I), only starting with the E rather than the C♯. Moreover, because this transposition to E defines the interval of 3 (the "minor third") with the initial C♯ (as pitch number 0), transpositions at 6 and 9 will entail similar duplications. And it follows that this (0, 3, 6, 9) partitioning is fundamental to the integrity of the single octatonic collection: given an octatonic fragment, transpositions at 3, 6, and 9 will remain confined to that collection.

Finally, note that the 1–2 ordering on the left side in Example 8.1 ascends, and the reverse 2–1 ordering on the right descends. Such a display allows representation of longer spans of material, which may be confined to a single collection but in articulation may implicate both orderings. In other words, in regard to collection I again, with the ascending 1–2 ordering at C♯ on the left side, were we to switch to the 2–1 ordering and yet remain committed to the customary ascending approach in scale representation, the resultant scale would no longer represent collection I, but rather collection III. However, by *descending* with the 2–1 ordering from C♯, not only do we remain confined to collection I, but the (0, 3, 6, 9) symmetrically defined partitioning elements in terms of (C♯, E, G, B♭) are the same.

Still, this ascending-descending formula is not wholly a question of analytical convenience. In many "Russian" pieces it is often an "upper" pitch element, along with an "upper" (0 2 3 5) tetrachord, that assumes, by means of persistence, doubling and metric accentuation, a certain priority in moving from one block or section to the next. And if the scalar ordering and pitch numbering are to reflect these conditions, the descending formula is the logical course. In the opening two blocks of *Les Noces,* for example, a punctuating E, along with an incomplete (E D [C♯] B) tetrachord with which this E identifies articulatively, assume priority. By descending from the E, with the (0 2 3 5) tetrachordal numbering synchronized with the principal (E D [C♯] B) unit, the priority of these units is properly represented: (0 2 3 5 6 8 9 11) in terms of (E D C♯ B B♭ A♭ G F), collection I. (To *ascend* from the E with the 2–1 ordering would, as indicated, have yielded a different octatonic collection.) The symmetrical discipline of these orderings naturally allows for options of this kind. Thus, the 2–1–2 ordering and consequent (0 2 3 5) pitch numbering remains the same, whether ascending or descending.

The Rite of Spring: Part 1

The vocabulary of *The Rite* consists in large part of 0–2 whole-step reiterations, (0 2 3 5) tetrachords, 0–11 or "major seventh" vertical interval spans, "minor" and "major" triads, and "dominant seventh" chords. (Conventional terminology is employed for purposes of identification, there being no intent to invoke major scale tonally functional relations.) Given the reputation of this piece as one of considerable complexity, this may seem a bit fanciful. But in fact, we can narrow the scheme somewhat. The (0 2 3 5) tetrachord is the principal melodic fragment of *The Rite,* as it is for the "Russian" period generally, surfacing by way of all manner of reiterating, folkish tunes. As such, it is invariably articulated in the tightest or closest arrangement possible, confined to the interval of 5, the fourth (without interval complementation, in other words). It may nonetheless be (0 2 5/0 3 5) incomplete (as with the previously noted (E D [C♯] B) unit in *Les Noces*), lacking either pitch number 2 or 3.

By contrast, the 0–11 interval span is rarely fragmental or linear in character, but defines "harmonically" or vertically the span between pitches of unmistakable priority among superimposed, reiterating fragments. Thus, in Example 8.2, from the "Ritual Action of the Ancestors" in part 2, a (C♯ B A♯ G♯) tetrachord is superimposed over a D-B♭ ostinato in the bass. The 0–11 span is therefore C♯–D,

Example 8.2. "Ritual Action of the Ancestors"

as defined between the C♯ of the "upper" (C♯ B A♯ G♯) tetrachord and the low D of the D–B♭ unit (*reading down*, with the [0 2 3 5] tetrachord implicating the descending 2-1 scale, as indicated already in connection with Example 8.1). Note the metric accentuation of the 0–11 span, a downbeating that, throughout *The Rite*, typifies its articulation and that, among other variables, renders it highly conspicuous in moving from one block or section to the next. The referential commitment here is to collection I.

The triads and "dominant sevenths" also assume a characteristic disposition: the tight or close arrangement as with the (0 2 3 5) tetrachord. Though not invariably the case, this is customary, especially in the treble registers. The typical "dominant seventh" placement is shown in Example 8.3: closed position, "first inversion." And as might be expected, all these fixed arrangements are of considerable consequence to a local or global reading of *The Rite*, to which we shall therefore be returning for further comment. For the moment, however, note how this tight articulation is linked to the fragmental repetition in *The Rite* and then to the rhythmic-metric implications of this repetition. Given the superimposed, layered

Example 8.3. Typical "dominant seventh" placements in *The Rite*

structure so typical of Stravinsky (a construction in which fragments, fixed registrally and instrumentally, repeat en masse or, with a steady meter, to periods that vary independent of one another), the tight or close arrangement, the limited fragmental compass, become something of a foregone conclusion.

And so these are the principal articulative units of *The Rite,* the common denominators, so to speak, often with dispositions of marked character. What may in turn be judged the referential glue of these components, what binds within and between blocks and sections, is often the octatonic pitch collection. Or, more precisely, the referential character of these parts is often determined by their confinement, for periods of significant duration, to one of the three collections of distinguishable content. This may be demonstrated in straightforward fashion by examining a few passages from the "Introduction," "Dances of the Young Girls," and the "Ritual of Abduction" in part 1.

In the first of these from the "Introduction," the (0 2 3 5) tetrachord in the English horn (0 [2] 3 5), incomplete in terms of (B♭ [A♭] G F), is the principal melodic fragment. In Example 8.4, it is traced from an initial appearance at rehearsal number **6,** through a condensed repeat at **7** + 3, to the climactic block at **10.** This (B♭ [A♭] G F) tetrachord is confined to a B♭–B vertical span, defined here between the tetrachord's high B♭ and, at **6,** the low B sustained in the bassoon. This B♭–B delineation persists at **7** + 3 (with the parts reshuffled somewhat), and then at **10**

Example 8.4. Part 1, "Introduction"

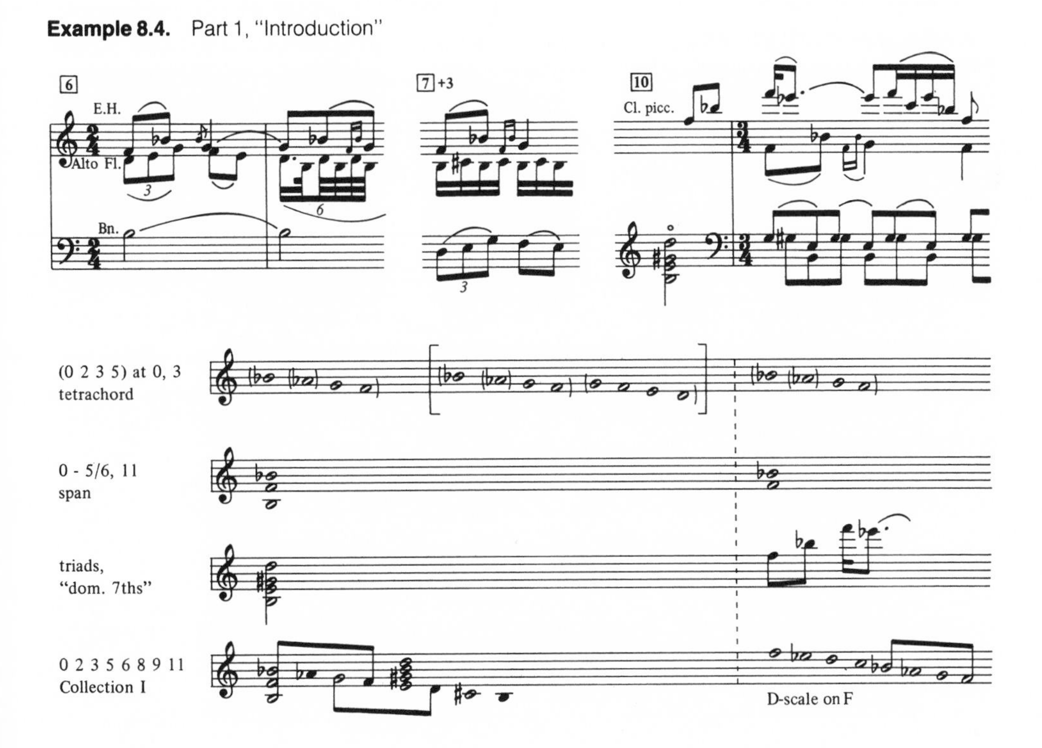

where the "dominant seventh" on E is significantly "second inversion," with B positioned in the bass. Note, too, the additional (G F E D) tetrachord in the alto flute at **6** and **7** + 3, which relates to (B♭ G F) by the interval of 3. This (0,3) relationship between superimposed fragments persists in the sections directly ahead.

In Example 8.5 from the "Dances of the Young Girls," the principal fragment is the D♭–B♭–E♭–B♭ ostinato in the English horn, an (0 2 [3] 5) incomplete tetrachord in terms of (E♭ D♭ [C] B♭). (Although not shown here, the ostinato is anticipated at **12** + 3 in the "Introduction," pizzicato in the first violins. In fact, its contour is foreshadowed by the "Introduction"'s opening bassoon melody: the C–(B)–A–D–A phrase of this melody identifies with D♭–B♭–E♭–B♭. The anticipation is made explicit by the transposed repetition of the melody at **12.**) The vertical interval span is E♭–E, with E♭ of the ostinato, or of the (E♭ D♭ B♭ G) "dominant seventh," positioned over a "lower" E.

Critical at **13** to **15** (Example 8.5), however, is the mixed (0 2 3 5) tetrachordal, triadic, and "dominant seventh" articulation. The rationale is as follows: the (E♭ D♭ B♭ G) "dominant seventh" preserves, in simultaneity, the ostinato's incomplete (E♭ D♭ [C] B♭) tetrachord. In other words, E♭, D♭, and B♭ become the root, seventh, and fifth, respectively, of (E♭ D♭ B♭ G). Hence the tight, "first inversion" articulation of the "dominant seventh": the disposition, registrally fixed at **13–15,** exposes the persistence of E♭, D♭, and B♭ as a tightly articulated (0 2 [3]

Example 8.5. "Dances of the Young Girls"

13 14 E.H. 15

(0 2 3 5) at 0, 3
tetrachord

0 - 5/6, 11
span

triads,
"dom. 7ths"

0 2 3 5 6 8 9 11
Collection III

5) tetrachord. Hence, too, the frequent (0 2 5) incomplete articulation of the (0 2 3 5) tetrachord: (0 2 5) becomes the connecting link between these tetrachordal and "dominant seventh" partitionings of the octatonic collection. Indeed, as shown in Example 8.5, pitch number 5 is added to the 0–11 vertical span, 0–5, 11 in terms here of E♭–B♭, E. Because numbers 0 and 5 persevere as root and fifth of the "dominant seventh" (and because the [0 2 3 5] tetrachord may be [0 3 5] as well as [0 2 5] incomplete), 0, 5, and 11 are the global constants. And we add an optional number 6 here to cover those fewer instances where it is the "lower" of the octatonic collection's (0,6) tritone-related (0 2 3 5) (6 8 9 11) tetrachords that prevail.

Finally, in Example 8.5, the "background" (0,3) relationship persists in terms of (E♭, C). This is realized tetrachordally in terms of the D♭–B♭–E♭–B♭ ostinato and (C B♭ A G) in the flutes at **15** and then triadically in terms of (E♭ D♭ B♭ G) and the (C E G) triad. And this latter (E♭ D♭ B♭ G) (C E G) relationship naturally preserves the E♭–E vertical span, with E as "major third" of (C E G). Hence the 0–5/6,11 octatonic presence is realized articulatively by means of an "upper" (0 2 3 5) tetrachord sustained over a "lower" pitch number 11 or by means of a "dominant seventh," closed position, "first inversion," superimposed over a (0,3)-related "major" triad, also closed position.

These groupings reappear at the outset of the "Ritual of Abduction" at **37**, shown in Example 8.6, and then further along in the climactic block at **42**, where

Example 8.6. "Ritual of Abduction"

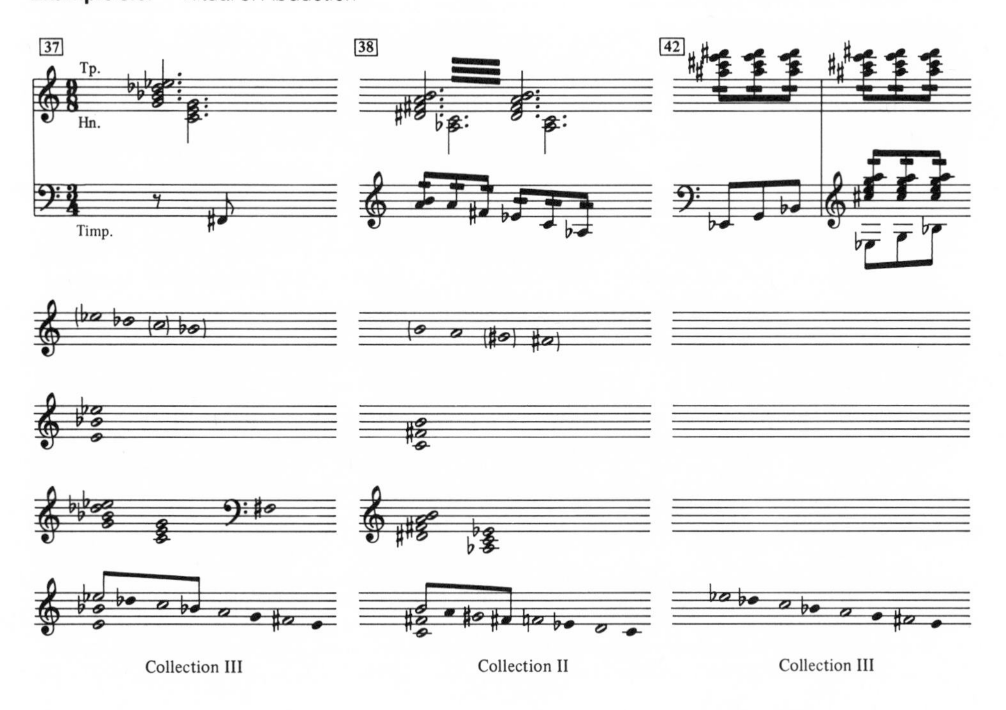

transpositions at 6 and 9, here A and F♯, complete a (0,3,6,9) symmetrically defined partitioning of collection III, with "major" triads and "dominant sevenths" at E♭, C, A, and F♯. The point of the concluding stretch at **44–46,** shown in Example 8.7, is the eventual juxtaposition of this octatonicism with a diatonic block at **46.**

For while *The Rite* is ostensibly octatonic in conception—perhaps the most thoroughly octatonic of all Stravinsky's works—there are nonetheless fragments, blocks, and even sections that are explicitly diatonic. In Example 8.7, collection III's "dominant sevenths" are transposed at **44** to within collection II, a block in turn followed by the unimpaired diatonicism at **46.** And in this moving from an octatonic to a diatonic framework, what is in turn shared by these two blocks of distinct referential character is the (0 2 3 5) tetrachord.

The presiding (F E♭ C A) "dominant seventh" at **44** preserves, in tight formation, the incomplete (F E♭[D] C) tetrachord; and as indicated by the brackets in Example 8.7, (F E♭ [D] C) is retained by the succeeding diatonic block. Moreover, the (0 2 3 5) articulation will implicate a D-scale or "Dorian" ordering of the diatonic collection, the D scale on F here.[5]

These equations pertain equally to blocks and passages of octatonic-diatonic interpenetration. At **10** in the "Introduction," shown earlier in Example 8.4, a diatonic fragment in the clarinet piccolo, first introduced within a contrasting diatonic setting at **9,** is superimposed over the orchestra's collection I network. In this octatonic-diatonic interaction, (B♭ A♭ G F) is shared by collection I and the D scale on F.

Indeed, the reverse is equally plausible. In marked contrast to *The Rite, Petrushka's* first tableau and certain portions of *Les Noces* are primarily diatonic. This in turn suggests moving from a prevailing diatonic framework (most often implicating, referentially, the D scale or the [0 2 3 5 7 9] hexachord thereof) to a variety of octatonic settings. The specifics of this reversal are shown in Example 8.8.

Thus, both the D scale and the octatonic scale, the 2–1 descending ordering, may be partitioned by means of two conjunct (0 2 3 5) tetrachords. (The octatonic scale actually contains four overlapping (0 2 3 5) tetrachords, but here we consider only the two adjoining ones.) However, the D scale's tetrachords are separated by the interval of 2, a whole step at pitch numbers 5-7, and are hence (0,7) or fifth-related. Those of the octatonic scale are separated by the interval of 1, a half-step at pitch numbers 5–6, and are hence (0,6) tritone-related. In moving from a diatonic to an octatonic or octatonic-diatonic framework (with the [0 2 3 5] tetrachord held in common), pitch numbers 6 and/or 11 often "intrude" to signal this shift. (See the arrows in Example 8.8.) And we apprehend within all these varied

5. As with the two orderings of the octatonic scale, the diatonic D–scale exhibits the same interval ordering and consequent pitch numbering, whether ascending or descending. The scale may therefore without complications descend in Examples 8.4, 8.7, and 8.8 in order to conform to the (0 2 3 5 6 8 9 11) octatonic arrangement.

Example 8.7. "Ritual of Abduction"

Example 8.8.

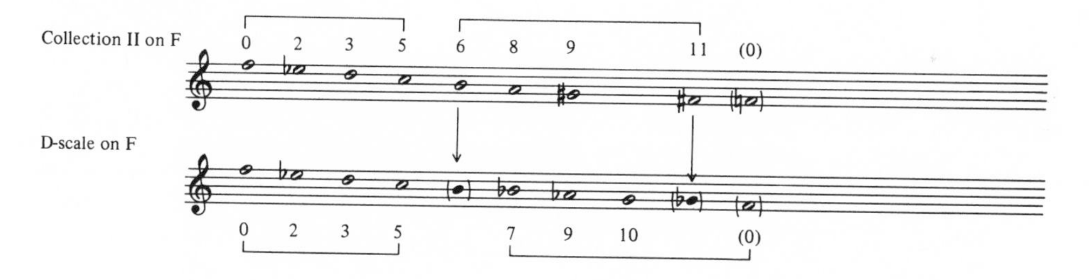

octatonic and octatonic-diatonic transactions one of the deepest "secrets" pervading Stravinsky's "Russian" musical thought: the (0 2 3 5) tetrachord, as the principal fragment of the "Russian" period, may in its referential implications be either octatonic or diatonic. It serves therefore as a pivot, as the principal connecting link between blocks of octatonic, diatonic, or octatonic-diatonic content. And when (0 2 [3] 5) is incomplete, it connects a (0 2 3 5) partitioning of the octatonic collection with a "dominant seventh" partitioning. Consequently, its very (0 2 [3] 5) incompleteness, even when inferred on a surface articulative level, as with the English horn's D♭–B♭–E♭–B♭ ostinato at **14** in *The Rite* or indeed as the "basic cell" of *Les Noces,* may be envisioned as embodying matters fundamental to the identity and distinction of "Russian" works.

In Example 8.9, the articulative units are assembled on five successive levels, a partitioning forwarded on behalf of each of the three octatonic collections. And

Example 8.9. Master Chart of Octatonicism in the "Russian" Works

Example 8.9. *continued*

while, in disposition, reference is here made to particulars that pertain peculiarly to *The Rite,* the format may nonetheless be applied, with a few generalizing adjustments, as a kind of master chart to the whole of the "Russian" period, to the octatonic and octatonic-diatonic sections of *Petrushka, Renard, Les Noces,* and even *Histoire du soldat* (1918).

The Rite of Spring: Part 2

Greater complexity is generally ascribed to the six sections constituting part 2 of *The Rite.* In the current view, this has principally to do with a more intimately paced relationship among the three transpositions of the octatonic collection. Contexts of transpositional purity (confined, that is, to a single collection) are naturally still to be found. The block at **134** in the "Ritual Action of the Ancestors" (shown earlier in Example 8.2, where collections I's [C♯ B A♯ G♯] [G F E D] tritone-related tetrachords are superimposed within a C♯–D vertical span), is as explicitly octatonic as any in this music. And the collection II bar at **106** + 1 in the "Glorification of the Chosen One" (Example 8.10), exposes the partitioning units of *The Rite* in a blunt, primitive fashion. Still, following subsequent repeats of this 7/4 bar (a separate block, really), there occurs the sequence of 0–5/6,11 verticals shown in Example 8.10. And because these verticals relate to one another not by

Example 8.10. "Glorification of the Chosen One"

the intervals of 3, 6, or 9 (as would be necessary if the succession were confined to a single octatonic collection, one transpositional level), but delineate a 2–2–2–1 succession (with set affiliations shown below in Example 8.10), referentially, the formulae pursued thus far clearly carry a flexibility beyond that encountered in part 1. It is as if the composer, having exposed an explicit octatonic hand in part 1, felt the necessity of venturing a bit further in part 2, upping the octatonic coherence stakes, as it were.

These implications are apparent in the opening measures of part 2's "Introduction" at **79** (Example 8.11). Here, two "minor" triads, (E♭ G♭ B♭) and (C♯ E G♯), move back and forth over a sustained (D F A) triad in the horns.[6] And like the verticals in Example 8.10, the relationship defined does not conform to the octatonically conceived (0,3,6,9) arrangement. They define a 1–1–1 relationship, which means that each triad will refer to a different octatonic collection. So these, too, are circumstances which do not lend themselves favorably to an octatonic interpretation.

Yet when the configuration at **79** is heard and understood in relation to what follows, there is no mistaking its octatonic purpose. The oscillating (E♭ G♭ B♭) (C♯ E G♯) triads in the upper parts define an alternation between collections III and I, the (E♭ G♭ B♭) triad referring to collection III, (C♯ E G♯) to collection 1. And

6. Stravinsky's notation for (E♭ G♭ B♭) at **79** is (D♯ F♯ A♯). However, because (E♭ G♭ B♭) conforms to collection III's format in Example 8.9 and Stravinsky himself switches to (E♭ G♭ B♭) later at **80,** I found it convenient to employ (E♭ G♭ B♭) from the start.

Example 8.11. Part 2, "Introduction"

it is to this collection III-collection I alternation that succeeding measures and blocks in this introductory section conspicuously refer.

Thus, in the 4/4 measure directly following **79,** collection III's (E♭ G♭ B♭) triad remains fixed on the beat while collection I's contribution expands beyond (C♯ E G♯) to include (B♭ D♭ F) and (E G B)—triads which are (0,3,6,9)—related to (C♯ E G♯), and so remain confined collection I. And this collection I expansion is underscored by the progression from the octave A to (B♭ D♭ F) in the strings and then by the (E G♯ B D) "dominant seventh" in the bass. Moreover, these collectional shifts are patterned rhythmic-metrically. Collection III's (E♭ G♭ B♭) triad assumes an on-the-beat or downbeat identity; collection I's expansion unfolds either off the beat or on the upbeat.

The scheme perseveres at **79** + 5 (again, see Example 8.11). The (E♭ G♭ B♭) triad remains fixed on the first and third quarter-note beats of the 4/4 measure while collection I's three "minor" triads at C♯, B♭, and E are sandwiched in between. Then, in the lengthy succession beginning at **82** + 1 (Example 8.12), the bass rises from a D to, ultimately, an A. The shifts are here stretched to 3/4 measures for each collection. The collection I (B♭ D♭ F) (E G B) "minor" triads at **82** + 2 are followed in the succeeding measure by collection III's (C E♭ G) (A C E)

Example 8.12. Part 2, "Introduction"

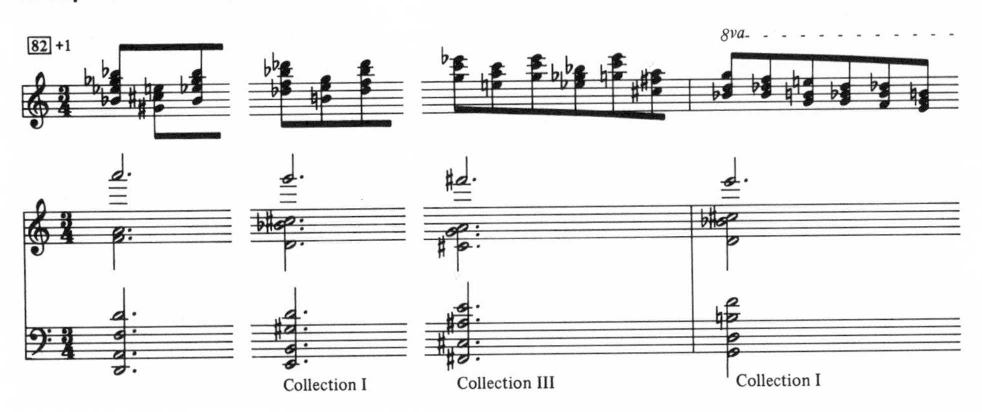

(F♯ A C♯) triads, which are in turn followed by the collection I triads at **82** + 4. And as earlier, at **79** + 5, the bass line reinforces these collection III—collection I shifts with "dominant sevenths" on E and G (for collection I) and on F♯ and A (for collection III).[7] Consequently, from an initial triadic configuration seemingly without octatonic qualifications, an octatonic cohesion is nonetheless brought to bear on the passage as a whole, and in the form here of a carefully patterned alternation between the four "minor" triads and "dominant sevenths" of collection III and those in turn of collection I.

Of course, the Khorovod tune of the "Introduction," for which the sustained A and the (D F A) triad are a preparation, has been overlooked. And the collection II implications of these components are occasionally evident. But with the appearance of the two trumpet fragments at **86** + 1 (Example 8.13), and then of the superimposition of these fragments over reiterating 0–5, 11 verticals in the

7. A passage similar to that at **82** + 1 in the "Introduction"—with the same contrary motion in the outer parts—occurs at **161** in the "Sacrificial Dance." According to Igor Stravinsky, *The Rite of Spring: Sketches 1911–1913* (London, 1969), both passages did in fact spring from the same source: a succession of seven verticals for the "Sacrificial Dance," p. 85 in *Sketches*, occurs in connection with the part 2 "Introduction" on p. 104. In *The Harmonic Organization of The Rite of Spring* (New Haven, 1978), p. 119, Allen Forte suggests "a predilection" for this succession on the part of Stravinsky, noting that it contains "many, if not all, of the basic harmonies of the work." Robert Craft, in "Craft on Forte," *Musical Quarterly* (October 1978): 529, cites a still earlier 1911 source among Stravinsky's sketches for a setting of a poem by Sergei Klychkov. Craft concludes that, in moving from the "Klychkov sketches," through the single sketch for *The Rite*, to the two final, expanded versions in the part 2 "Introduction" and the "Sacrificial Dance," "an evolution of the harmonic content" took place, with the composer steadily gravitating "toward the music's fundamental combinations" (p. 534). This is clear from an octatonic standpoint. For although five of the seven verticals are octatonic in the original sketch for *The Rite*, these refer to collections I, II, and III. But in the version at **82** + 1 in part 2's "Introduction," the succession is committed solely to collections I and III, with each 3/4 measure—or vertical—representing one of these two collections. This naturally adheres to the collection III–collection I emphasis of preceding measures in this section (Example 8.11), and of succeeding passages as well (Examples 8.13, 8.14, and 8.15).

Example 8.13. Part 2, "Introduction"

strings at **86** + 3 (Example 8.14), the collection III–collection I bond is further solidified. And here, as earlier in Example 8.11, with the specifics of the bond directly traceable to the initial triadic configuration at **79.**

As illustrated in Example 8.13, the left-hand side, the upper part of the configuration consists of a B♭–E tritone motion (which in fact refers to both collections III and I, although B♭ and E are not among the (0,3,6,9) symmetrically defined partitioning elements for collection III as they are for collection 1). Beginning with the unison B♭ at **86** + 1, the second trumpet completes this B♭–E interval by way of a (0 2 3 5) tetrachordal delineation in terms of (B♭ A♭ G F) and then by a conclusion on E, the entire B♭–A♭–G–F–E succession accountable to collection I. Moreover, the accompanying B♭–C♭ reiteration of the first trumpet, with C♭(B) as pitch number 11 in relation to B♭, also refers to collection I, the complete succession now B–B♭–A♭–G–F–E. Nevertheless, as these two fragments draw to a close, the terminating C in the first trumpet, together with the (C E G) triadic outline, refer not to collection I but to collection III. (In other words, the C upsets the 1–2–1–2–1 ordering in terms of B–B♭–A♭–G–F–E. C♯[D♭], instead of the C, would have ensured this ordering's continuance, and hence also continued confinement here to collection I.) Hence the shift at this point from collection I to collection III.

Example 8.14. Part 2, "Introduction"

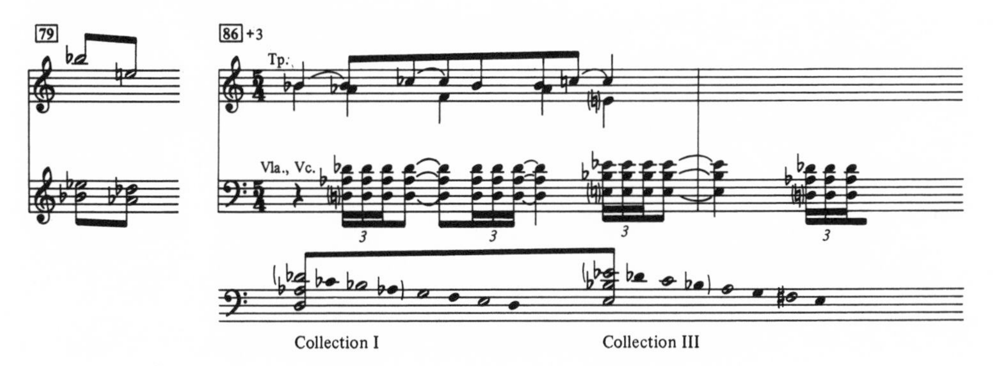

This shift is confirmed by the entrance of the reiterating 0–5,11 verticals at **86** + 3. As shown in Example 8.14, these verticals also derive in straightforward fashion from the initial configuration at **79.** For embedded in the configuration, below the B♭–E tritone motion in the upper parts, are the verticalized intervals of 5, two fourths, D♭/A♭ and E♭/B♭, which move back forth. And the D♭/A♭ fourth, being part of the initial (C♯ E G♯) triad, refers to collection I; E♭/B♭, being part of (E♭ G♭ B♭), refers to collection III. The collection I-collection III implications of these fourths are neatly synchronized with those of the two trumpet fragments: the D♭/A♭ fourth relates to the B–B♭–A♭–G–F–E succession respecting collection I. E♭/B♭ relates to C and the (C E G) triad respecting collection III. Furthermore, a pitch number 11 is added to both fourths, yielding the familiar 0–5, 11 vertical span in terms of D♭–A♭, D for collection I, and E♭–B♭, E for collection III. Finally, in the climactic block at **87** + 1 (Example 8.15), the (0,3) relationship between superimposed fragments, so prominent a feature in part 1, also surfaces: a "lower" (B♭ D

Example 8.15. Part 2, "Introduction"

87 + 1

9(3+6)

Fl.

9

Cl., Hn.

Strings

9

9

(0 2 3 5) tetrachord

0 - 5/6, 11 span

triads at 0, 3

Collection I

Collection III

F) triad is added to collection I's D♭–A♭, D span, while (C E G) accompanies E♭–B♭, E. The second trumpet's (B♭ A♭ G F) tetrachord is of course (0,3)-related to D♭–A♭, D. Hence, within this intimately paced alternation between collections I and III, stemming from the initial triadic configuration at **79,** the principal articulative units and their characteristic dispositions, as examined in part 1, are conspicuously brought to the fore.

Still, the collection I-collection III distinction, carefully patterned in the preparatory blocks at **86–87,** is eventually obscured at **87** + 1 (Example 8.15). This is principally a rhythmic-metric issue. The block at **87** + 1 exemplifies a most common construction with Stravinsky: the fragments, lines or parts, fixed registrally and instrumentally in repetition, repeat according to periods or cycles that vary independently of one another, effecting a vertical (or "harmonic") coincidence that is constantly changing. Given this independence and consequent overlapping in period-duration, the initial synchronization at **86** + 3 will not hold, and the collection I fragments will become interwoven with those of collection III. At **87** + 2, collection III's E♭–B♭, E span enters prior to the first trumpet's C; and collection III's (C E G) triad is a separate layer, superimposed over collection I's contribution. Moreover, a steady meter, which reflects the stable periods of one of the several superimposed, reiterating fragments, is generally applied in constructions of this type. But here at **87–89,** a steady 3/4 meter is not reached until **88,** with the shifting 5/4 and 4/4 bars prior to this apparently reflecting the successive entrances of the trumpet fragments. An outline of the scheme appears in Example 8.16.

Example 8.16. Part 2, "Introduction"

"Sacrificial Dance"

Turning to the opening passage of the "Sacrificial Dance" (Example 8.17), the very opposite may be found in rhythmic-metric construction.[8] Here the superimposed fragments, fixed registrally and instrumentally in repetition, do not repeat according to periods or cycles that vary independently of one another but share the same irregular periods as defined by the shifting meter. They are hence synchronized unvaryingly in vertical (or "harmonic") coincidence. And these constitute the two prototypes in Stravinsky's music, apparent as such from the earliest pieces of the "Russian" period to the serial works. Thus, with the first of these types, as examined at **87** + 1 in part 2's "Introduction" (examples 8.15 and 8.16), a sense of "development," of within-block movement or "progress" beyond static repetition, superimposition, and symmetrical confinement, will come by

Example 8.17. "Sacrificial Dance"

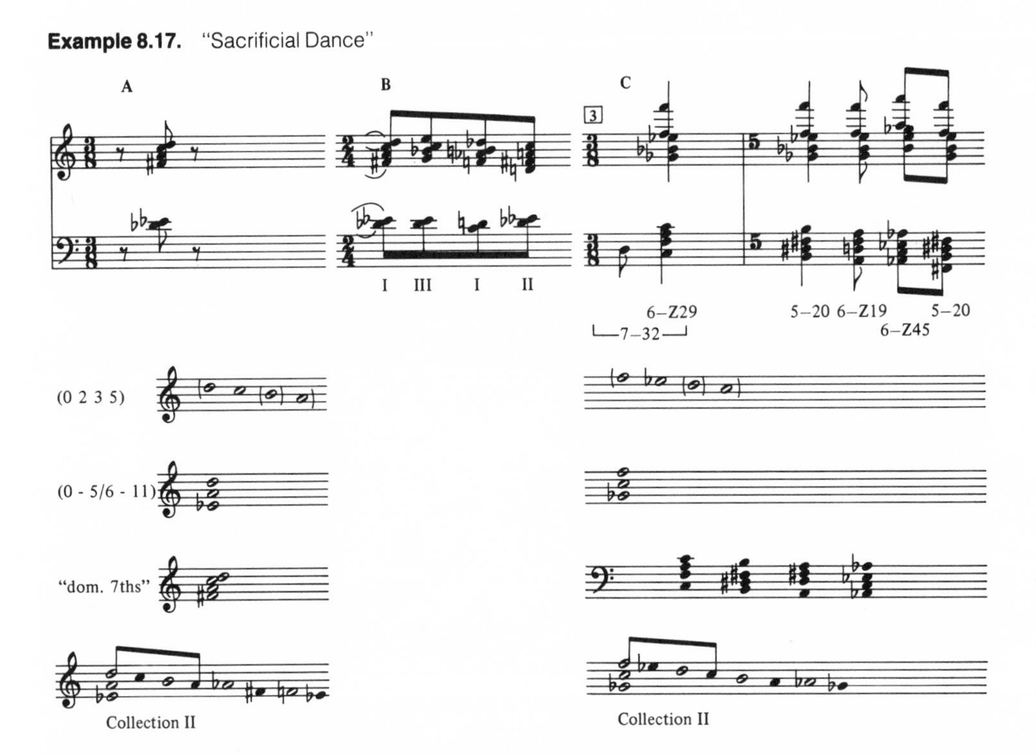

8. As can be seen from the rehearsal numbers, Examples 8.17, 8.18, 8.19, and 8.20 are derived from Stravinsky's 1943 revised version of the "Sacrificial Dance." Apart from the switch from sixteenth- to eighth-note beats, this edition encompasses a number of significant alterations. I shall presently discuss Allen Forte's extensive analysis, where reference is likewise made to this 1943 revision.

way of changes in vertical coincidence, changes in turn brought about by the conflicting rhythmic-metric periods as defined by the reiterating fragments. With the second type, as here in the "Sacrificial Dance" (Example 8.17), such "development" will stem from a lengthening or shortening of the jointly sustained periods upon successive repeats, which are in turn reinforced by the shifting meter. In this latter construction, the successive blocks, labeled A, B, and C in Example 8.17, are often of short duration, consisting at times of a single measure, and placed in a rapid and abrupt juxtaposition with one another.

But equally apparent in Example 8.17 is the adherence at the outset of the "Sacrificial Dance" to *The Rite*'s by now standard formulae. There is, first, the punctuating "dominant seventh" of block A, (D C A F♯) here, which refers to collection II, and with the familiar disposition of the unit, closed position, "first inversion," very much intact. This (D C A F♯) "dominant seventh" is superimposed, typically again, over a "lower" pitch number 11, yielding the 0–5,11 vertical span, in terms here of D–A, E♭. Moreover, the rapid collectional shifts characteristic of part 2 are apparent in block B, where the "dominant sevenths," enclosed within 0-11 spans, implicate first collection II, then collections III and I, and finally collection II again with (C A F♯ D), which thus frames the succession. Finally, in block C, the referential commitment to collection II is restored and enhanced. With an F–G♭ span fixed in the upper parts, collections II's "major" triads at F,B,D and A♭ unfold underneath. And in the final, extended repeat of this passage toward the end of the "Sacrificial Dance," the octatonic implications of this triadic succession are rendered even more explicit (with the succession transposed from collection II to collection III, however, as shown in Example 8.18): the material in the upper parts is omitted, the succession consisting now of "dominant sevenths" rather than "major" triads. (Note that the familiar disposition of the "dominant seventh" can apply only at C, A, and F♯, that is, only at those pitches in the C–B♭–A–G–F♯ succession that are among the [C,A,F♯,E♭] symmetrically defined partitioning elements of collection III, the "roots" of this collection's four triads and "dominant seventh" chords.)

Example 8.18. "Sacrificial Dance"

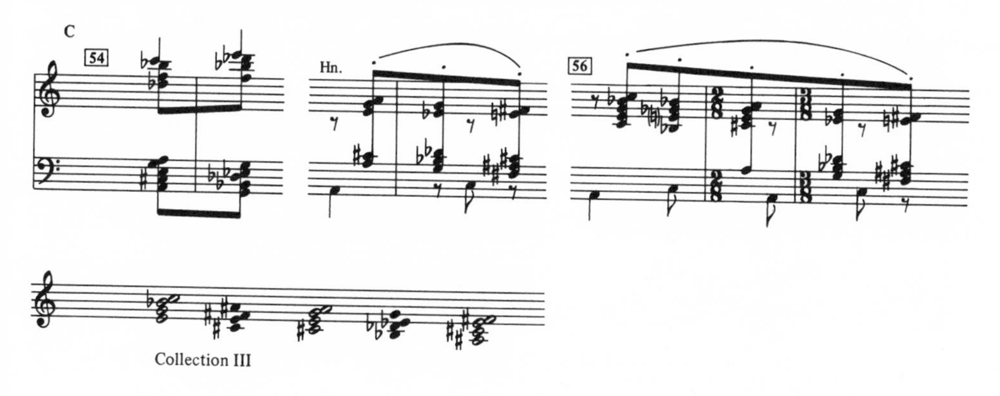

Indeed, even the nonoctatonic pitches in this opening stretch, the non–collection II D♭ in block A, for example, derive from intercollectional relations of significance in part 2. Thus, as shown in Example 8.19, the two 0–11 verticals embedded in the initial "cluster" simultaneity of block A, D/E♭ and C/D♭ are directly traceable to the oscillating E♭/E and D♭/D verticals at **87** + 1, the only difference being that while these two (0,2) whole-top-related verticals define a collectional shift in the "Introduction," they are wedded in the "Sacrificial Dance" as part of a single simultaneity. And in each case, the verticals jointly yield the "chromatic" (0 1 2 3) tetrachord (as shown by the brackets in Example 8.19), with pitch number 2 lying outside the octatonic ordering, the D♭ lying outside collection II in block A.

Of greater consequence in the "Sacrificial Dance," however, are the two "upper" and "lower" twos or whole-steps of this (0 1 2 3) tetrachord: that is, in block A, D/C and E♭/D♭. (See again the brackets in Example 8.19.) For instead of the two 0–11 verticals, these twos or whole-steps refer to the collectional shifts in subsequent passages of the "Sacrificial Dance." Thus, further along at **18** (Example 8.19), the two oscillating 0–5, 11 verticals in the strings, D–A, E♭ and C♯–G♯, D, define a shift from colleciton II to collection I. This shift is neatly synchronized with the octatonic implications of the (G♯ G F♯ F) tetrachord's two twos or whole-steps, G♯–F♯ and G–F in the trumpets: respecting collection II, G♯–(G)–F♯ is superimposed over D–A,E♭, respecting collection I, G–(F♯)–F is superimposed over C♯–G♯,D. By such means, seemingly nonoctatonic, "chromatic" elements in

Example 8.19. "Sacrificial Dance"

87 +1
1
18
(0, 2) whole steps
0 - 5/6, 11 span
Collection II
Collection II
Collection I

these passages derive from intercollectional shifts, and, in turn, the octatonicism here inferred acquires is special intricacy.

Still, questions may linger about the completeness of the octatonic record here in part 2, about these collectional shifts and consequent "outside" pitch elements. Might the approach at this point not benefit from, say, certain of Allen Forte's set theoretic formulations? The answer would seem to be possibly—up to a point. Those familiar with Forte's analysis of Stravinsky's early works will doubtless have noted certain correspondences. Forte frequently invokes the octatonic collection, the "superset" 8–28, and in connection with a passage from *Zvezdoliki* (1911–1912), cites it as "one of Stravinsky's hallmarks."[9] In *The Harmonic Organization of The Rite of Spring,* the (0 2 3 5) tetrachord, pitch-class set 4–10, is encountered throughout, while its (0 2 5/0 3 5) incomplete form, 3–7, is identified as "a kind of motto trichord."[10] In fact, most of the prominent sets in Forte's analysis are subsets of the octatonic collection. Of his two hundred twenty pitch-class sets (sets of from three to nine elements, reduced to a "best normal order" by means of transposition or inversion followed by transposition), thirty-four are octatonic: seven from a possible twelve three-element sets, thirteen from the twenty-nine four-element sets, seven from thirty-eight five-element sets, six from fifty hexachords, and one from the thirty-eight seven-element sets, 7–31. These are easily spotted because the pitch numbering of these thirty-four "prime forms" will correspond to that either of the 1–2 half-step–whole-step ordering, (0 1 3 4 6 7 9 10 [0]), or the reverse 2-1 whole-step–half-step ordering, (0 2 3 5 6 8 9 11 [0]).

But beyond this point, the two paths diverge as different concerns and objectives are more intimately brought into play. In particular, the segmentation, or what Forte interprets as cohesive units and groupings in *The Rite,* differs markedly from that proposed here. Reference is occasionally made to the "dominant seventh," 4–27, but the triad, 3–11, is ignored altogether because, as Forte notes, trichords "are easily identifiable components of larger sets."[11] In the current view, however, the triad—not just the three-element trichord, but the *triad*—assumes, even under conditions of superimposition, a registral, instrumental, and notational reality, and to an extent that, on a strictly observational basis, many sections of *The Rite* seem more overtly triadic in construction than many pieces of the later nineteenth-century tonal tradition (pieces on behalf of which the triad is nonetheless routinely invoked as a fundamental unit of musical structure).

Moreover, an emphasis is here placed on disposition, on the fixed, registral identities of recurring tetrachords, 0–5/6,11 vertical spans, triads, and "dominant

---

9. Allen Forte, *The Structure of Atonal Music* (New Haven, 1973), p. 118.

10. Forte, *Harmonic Organization,* p. 36.

11. Ibid.

sevenths." These matters are often obscured when, for purposes of comparison, of gauging the relatedness of sets and complexes of sets, such groupings are regularly reduced to their "prime forms" (by means, as indicated, of transposition or inversion followed by transposition.) Thus, a prime determinancy in part 2's "Introduction" at **79–84** is not the triad *tout court*, 3–11, nor the tight disposition of the triad, but its persistent (0 3 7) "minor" articulation. But because the "major" and "minor" triads are inversionally equivalent and reduce to the single pitch-class set 3–11, the distinction here is likely to be obscured.

Similarly, the two interval orderings of the octatonic collection, along with the three transpositions of distinguishable content, reduce to the single set, 8–28. But the question of an octatonic presence has not merely to do with *the* octatonic collection (that is, 8–28 *tout court*), but equally with *an* octatonic collection. Contexts derive their octatonic character, their symmetrical cohesion, by virtue of their confinement to a single transpositional level for periods of significant duration. All this may point to a hearing and understanding of determinacy in *The Rite* having as much to do with pitch and pitch-class identity as with interval and interval-class identity.

This is not to suggest that Forte ignores these issues. He frequently refers to invariance in pitch-class content between transpositions or transformations of a given set, and then to the Rp relation, which has to do with pitch-class invariance among nonequivalent sets having the same number of elements. But here, too, Forte's conclusions are apt to vary from those reached from a predominantly octatonic or octatonic-diatonic perspective. Thus, Example 8.20 shows twelve single and "composite" sets Forte invokes to identify the verticals and linear successions of block C at **3** in the "Sacrificial Dance" and its subsequent near repeat at **7.** (Although in ascending "normal order," the pitch numbering of these sets has not been reduced to that of the "prime forms." Note that 0 = C.)[12] Only 5–10 and 6-Z23 are octatonic; the others are not subsets of the octatonic collection, 8–28. But the fact that all ten nonoctatonic sets miss the octatonic order by a single step—at pitch number 10 here—or, more important, that all sets, except for a single pitch, the B♭, refer to a single transpositional level, the octatonic collection II, is of the highest priority to an octatonic hearing and understanding.[13] The articulative

12. With 0 = C (and with the sets not reduced to their "prime forms"), a (0 2 3 5 6 8 9 11) numbering will always—as shown in Example 8.20—implicate collection II. However, a (0 1 3 4 6 7 9 10) numbering under these conditions will implicate collection III, while the numbering for collection I (which lacks the C) will conform to neither of the two octatonic pitch numberings.

13. These observations apply equally to Forte's brief analysis of a four-measure passage from *Zvezdoliki* (cited already, from Forte, *Structure of Atonal Music*, p. 114). In the first three of these measures, eighteen sets are identified as cohesive groupings, ten of which are nonoctatonic. Although the significance of 8–28 is recognized, invariance, except insofar as it may be inferred from the pitch numbering, is ignored. As in block C of the "Sacrificial Dance," all the sets refer, but for the single pitch, A♯ (B♭), to a single transpositional level, collection II. A shift to collection III occurs in the fourth measure. Hence, all ten nonoctatonic sets are owing to the single non–collection II A♯ (B♭). Moreover, in articulation, a triadic and "dominant seventh" partitioning of collection II at G♯ (A♭),F,D, and B is in the current view unmistakable.

Example 8.20. Sets in the "Sacrificial Dance" invoked by Allen Forte

makeup of the block is thus conditioned referentially by its confinement to collection II, a confinement that in turn refers back to the initial, punctuating (D C A F♯) "dominant seventh" of block A. Thus, too, more specifically, the two sets 6–Z19 and 6–Z45 that follow one another in block C (see Example 8.17) are "maximally dissimilar" in interval content (the R_0 relation: the interval vectors of the two sets have no common entries) and are said to be "completely detached."[14] Yet from an octatonic standpoint, the sets are close, the distinction having to do with collection II's succession of triads in the lower parts: collection II's (D F♯ A) triad is part of 6-Z19, while (A♭ C E♭) is part of 6–Z45. Furthermore, in comparing versions of equivalent or Z-related sets, the invariants among the three occurrences of the complementary pair, 6–Z23 and 6–Z45, are said to be "of little conse-

14. Forte, *Structure of Atonal Music*, p. 154.

quence," although all three refer, crucially, to collection II.[15] Invariance among the four occurrences of 6–Z43 is likewise deemed "not significant," although this noninvariance crucially concerns the collectional shifts respecting collections II and I, as indicated in Example 8.19. In conclusion, Forte points to "the dearth of strongly represented Rp" in this music and to "the paucity of invariance among equivalent sets," noting that interval content, not pitch-class content, is of "prime importance."[16]

Incompatibility is not really the issue here; it is rather two approaches that differ as to what is ultimately deemed critical to hearing, understanding, and interpreting *The Rite.* A theorist's choices in this respect are obviously determined in large part by his or her preoccupations with other literatures and traditions. But this does not mean—as has been alleged—that the set theoretic approach is without historical foundation. Pieces like *Zvezdoliki* and *The Rite* certainly exhibit a vertical structure that, as Forte has claimed, often comes close to that of the atonal repertory. Moreover, even if the present octatonic-diatonic approach frequently disagrees with both the meaning and significance of Forte's results, the perspective may nonetheless, by taking those results duly into account, be placed in sharper focus.

Neoclassicism

In octatonic contexts of the neoclassical persuasion, the articulation differs from that typical of the "Russian" category. Instead of the (0 2 3 5) tetrachord, a (0 1 3 4) tetrachord may frequently be inferred as a cohesive linear grouping. Indeed, in the *Symphony of Psalms,* it is a kind of "basic cell" in the first and second movements, as Stravinsky himself suggested to Robert Craft.[17] Complementing the (0 1 3 4) tetrachord are the (0 3 4/3 4 7/3 6 7) "minor-major third" units and, perhaps most conspicuously, the (0 3 7/0 4 7) triads and (0 4 7 10) "dominant sevenths," as cited already in connection with Example 8.9 (but in neoclassical works with an overall approach in disposition far more varied than that encountered in *The Rite* or, indeed, in "Russian" pieces generally). The typical neoclassical format is summarized in Example 8.21: a (0,3,6,9) symmetrically defined partitioning of collection I in terms of this collection's (0 1 3 4) tetrachords, (0 3 4/3 4 7/3 6 7) "minor-major thirds," and (0 3 7/0 4 7/0 4 7 10) triads and "dominant sevenths" at E, G, B♭, and D♭. This partitioning implicates the 1–2 half-step–whole-step ordering to which the customary ascending approach in scale formation is applied.

15. Ibid., p. 159.

16. Ibid., p. 166.

17. Igor Stravinsky and Robert Craft, *Dialogues and a Diary* (Garden City, N.Y., 1963), p. 77.

Example 8.21. Typical Use of Octatonicism in the Neoclassical Works

Such changes naturally coincide with changes in the diatonic articulation. Thus, in place of the D-scale ordering so prevalent in "Russian" contexts, the familiar major scale or C scale is typical of neoclassicism, although the E scale and A scale (the descending minor scale in tonal terms) may also at times be inferred. This C-scale reference is implicated not only by the surface gesture and conventions of baroque and classical literature, but occasionally, and in however peripheral a manner, by certain tonally functional relations as well. What is often typical of relations in these contexts, the Stravinskyan stamp, concerns an interacting partitioning of the octatonic collection as shown in Example 8.21—that is, this partitioning's placement in association with the gestures, conventions, and harmonic maneuvers of the baroque and classical C-scale tradition.

These are obviously matters of considerable complexity, and we shall not attempt a detailed scrutiny here. Very briefly, however, consider the tonic-dominant relationship, insofar as this may here and there be felt as assuming a credible presence. The first movement of the *Symphony of Psalms* may be described as a piece wherein octatonic blocks, accountable to collection I with a (0,3,6) "background" partitioning in terms of (E,G,B♭), interact with diatonic blocks implicating the E scale on E. The (E G B) "*Psalms* chord" is punctuated as a spacer, as that which is articulatively shared between these two distinct collections and orderings of reference. Nonetheless, with (G B D F [A♭]) "dominant-seventh" and "minor-ninth" supplementation, the equally shared G steadily gains the advantage and acquires, by virtue of the half-cadence on G that leads to the quasi-C-minor fugal exposition of the second movement, the characteristic "feel" of a dominant. Hence the peculiarity of Stravinsky's dominant. The G or

(G B D) triad in *Psalms* identifies not only with the diatonic E scale on E, or indeed with the quasi-C-minor "resolution" of the second movement, but equally with the octatonic collection I, in which respect it functions as a (E, G, B♭, D♭) symmetrically defined partitioning element, oscillating, or placed in juxtaposition, with this collection's E and B♭ with their (0 1 3 4) tetrachordal and (0 3 7/0 4 7/0 4 7 10) triadic "support." Similar long-term tonic-dominant relationships, entailing collection I and a variety of (C E♭ G/C E G) endings, govern a number of neoclassical ventures, among these the first and third movements of the Symphony in Three Movements (1942–1945).

Hence, the neoclassical perspective is conditioned by considerations of the "Russian" period. And, once again, the attraction of this approach is that a distinctive musical presence is in some measure brought to bear. Although individual pieces naturally yield their own particular rationales, these are always—at least in the current view—most advantageously approached as parts of a greater whole, of a larger listening experience. And since, among most enthusiasts, there can be no mistaking an intuitively grasped distinction (or distinctiveness) on the part of this present composer (however diverse the evidence), speculation along these lines is likely to prove tempting for many years to come.

9 Writing *The Rite* Right

LOUIS CYR

EXAMINATION of all extant, available sources of *The Rite of Spring* from the published sketches to the latest (1967) engraved score reveals a number of variants in the scoring and orchestration of the work. In a way, this is not surprising, especially because Stravinsky himself once admitted having "heard" portions of *The Rite* long before being able to write them. It is also well known that he kept on revising many of his orchestral works during his entire lifetime, not only because of copyright problems. Revisions to *The Rite* have been extensively documented in the last six years by Robert Craft, although not always as systematically and as coherently as one might legitimately expect.[1] But then, a work in progress is inescapably bound to encounter numerous unforeseen hurdles along the way.

Many more things, however, have been tampered with in *The Rite* that cannot be linked with any of the composer's explicit and documented intentions, at least not according to the sources presently available. Some of these variants are all the more intriguing in that Stravinsky himself never abided by them in his own performances and recordings. Moreover, additional variants have crept into other recordings of the work and have acquired a tradition of their own.

The purpose of pinpointing a few of these variants is threefold: (1) to highlight how Stravinsky may have granted spur-of-the-moment concessions to some of his most trusted advisers, mostly conductors, who feared too heavy demands on the orchestra players, only to turn around and stick to the original himself; (2) to raise the question of how attentive or inattentive he was to all the details of the performances of *The Rite* he himself conducted; and (3) to suggest that a certain proportion of surviving discrepancies might actually be attributed to sloppy proofreading of the orchestral parts, which apparently were never systematically recalled and edited since the 1926 initial printing. All three factors have, of course, a direct bearing on the necessity, feasibility, and possibility of a definitive, critical edition of *The Rite*, or of any Stravinsky opus, for that matter.

1. Robert Craft, " 'Le Sacre du Printemps': The Revisions," *Tempo*, no. 122 (September 1977): 2–8. A slightly revised version of this text appears in Vera Stravinsky and Robert Craft, *Stravinsky in Pictures and Documents* (New York, 1978), pp. 526–33. See also his " 'Le Sacre du Printemps': A Chronology of the Revisions," in *Stravinsky: Selected Correspondence*, vol. 1, ed. Robert Craft (New York, 1982), pp. 398–406.

The first audible discrepancy arises at the end of the repetition of the initial bassoon theme, a half-tone lower, at rehearsal number **12** of the "Introduction" to part 1:

Example 9.1. Opening of *The Rite of Spring*, **12**

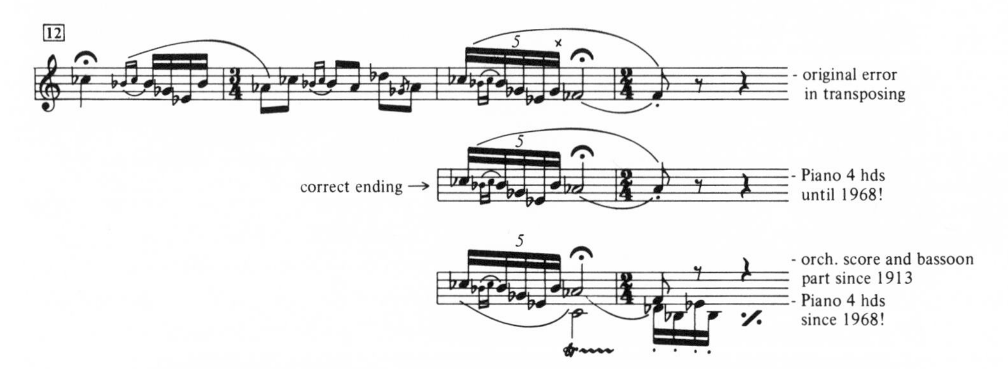

Where 1913 is referred to in Examples 9.1 (first staff), 9.2, 9.4 (first part), 9.5, 9.6, 9.8, 9.9, and 9.10 (parts 2 and 3), the unpublished sources are the following:

1. Autograph full score, now housed at the Stravinsky Archives of the Paul Sacher Foundation, Basel, Switzerland. Used by permission.
2. Manuscript full score, property of Boosey and Hawkes, S.A., Neuilly-sur-Seine, France. Used by permission, and in Example 9.10 (parts 6 and 7).
3. Ansermet's manuscript pages and his handwritten corrections inscribed in his copy of the printed full score (1922), belonging to the Conservatoire de Musique de Genève, Geneva, Switzerland. Used by permission.

The final descent to the note F (on the lowest staff in Example 9.1) simply makes no sense, apart from the fact that hardly any first bassoonist alive ever succeeds in culminating his A♭ pause with an F that is timed exactly with the first pizzicato D♭ of the first violins. For one thing, F would seem obviously foreign to the mode of the theme itself. But above all, as is evident from a close examination of his own autograph manuscript of the score, Stravinsky, in writing down the bassoon lead in the tenor C clef, made a transposition error regarding the last two notes, changing them inadvertently into G♭ and F♭ (see uppermost staff of Example 9.1). The mistake was eventually noticed, and both notes were corrrected back into B♭ and A♭, but an erroneous F♭ was overlooked and left dangling on the other side of the bar line without its accidental. The A♭ half-note was thus simply slurred to the indomitable F♮ that has plagued the orchestral score and bassoon part ever since. Incredibly enough, the piano reduction, which had always carried the correct reading (see middle staff of Example 9.1), was itself purged of its correct tied-over A♭ in 1968 and has been provided with the impossible F♮. At least Stravinsky, Monteux, Ansermet, Boulez, and a few other conductors have noticed the discrepancy and, as is obvious from their phonograph recordings, let the first bassoon's A♭ gradually and inconspicuously die out by itself. But most conductors unknowingly continue to expose the already strained first bassoon to the torture of fitting in an F♮ just when he is about to run out of breath!

A second, albeit, less immediately noticeable variant appears after the restatement *f* *(forte)* of the initial eight-bar setting of the thumping chords of "The Augurs of Spring" at **18.** Following them, *p sub. (subito piano),* come twenty-seven measures of the same chord as a backdrop to a short melodic fragment played by bassoons and trombone and later joined by flute and oboes. The thumping accom-

Example 9.2. "The Augurs of Spring," **18**

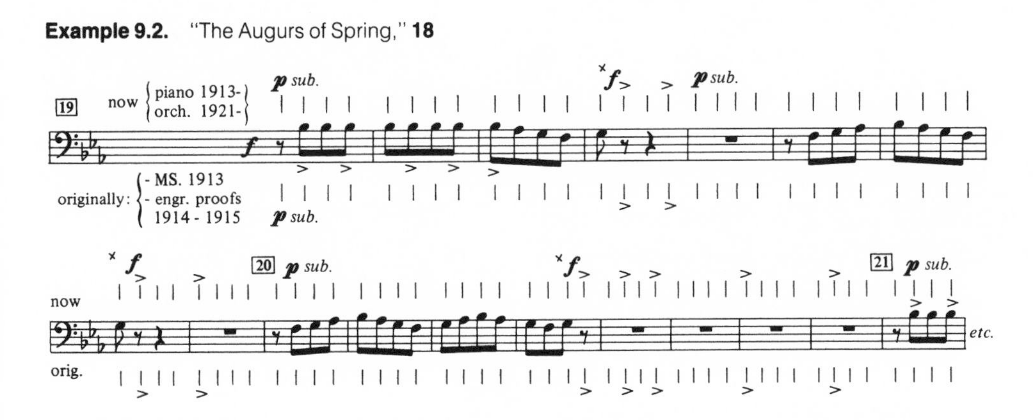

paniment, as it stands in the orchestral score and parts since 1922 and as it apparently stood in the first printing in 1913 of the piano reduction, suddenly detaches itself with *f* outbursts and accents at each bridge section between statements of the melodic fragment and just as suddenly withdraws again *p sub.* into the background with each successive re-entry of the bassoons or trombone (see indications above staff of Example 9.2). The trouble is that these changes from *p* to *f* and vice versa to *p sub.* were originally not to be found in Stravinsky's manuscript scores or in the Leipzig copyist's manuscript from which Pierre Monteux conducted the world premiere of *The Rite.* And if one examines closely the 1922 first printing of the full score, one will see that the subsequent *p sub.* and *f* are also later additions to the engraved proof score of 1914–1915. I might never have stumbled onto this detail were it not for the three Stravinsky recordings and for three of the five Monteux recordings of *The Rite,* which all strictly adhere to the even *p* continuum throughout the entire section (see indications below staff of Example 9.2). The steadier, more stable, and restful texture of this discretely *martellato* accompaniment speaks for itself. However, the question of whether Stravinsky really intended the dynamics of the 1913 piano reduction or those of the 1913 full score, which he subsequently respected to the letter, remains. Who took it upon themselves in 1922 to make the orchestral score and materials conform to the piano reduction, without at least notifying the composer and Monteux?

The next intriguing variant occurs a few measures later in "The Augurs": it is the extensive *col legno (battuto)* of part of the string accompaniment to **24–27** inclusive. Both the celli and violas strike their repeated C's and F's with the wood of the bow from the very onset. The mystery arises from the rather late addition of the *col legno* indication to the second violins and from the utter confusion concerning its duration. Only in 1926 is there any evidence of this *col legno* prescribed for the second violin part, for the alternating eighths G–A beginning in the fourth measure of **24**; but then mention of it is surprisingly repeated at **28**, precisely at the moment the celli and violas stop beating *col legno*, and even for leaping intervals of fifths and sixths in an orchestral environment of increasingly louder texture. To make matters worse, the full score only introduced the *col legno* for the second violins at **24** in 1965 (the study score has it as of 1951, but the mention of it at **28** in the second violin part had been deleted by then). The confusion had in the meantime arisen as to where the second violins should stop beating *col legno*. Only in 1967 is the *col legno (al segno)* direction complete at **24** and its cancellation (the *segno*) located, albeit incredibly, at the end of **29**! Now apart from being practically ineffective in sounding their thematic cells of seconds, fifths, and sixths as such, were the second violins ever really intended to be struck *col legno* or not? If so, why as if as an afterthought, unsystematically, and to what purpose? If not, who is responsible for introducing the *col legno* prescription, for protracting it until **30** only as of 1967 (actually 1971, if one considers the orchestral parts)? Among the dozen or so phonograph recordings in which the second violins play this section either *arco* or possibly *col legno (tratto)* (one would possibly have to include here the earliest Stravinsky, Stokowski, and van Beinum 78 r.p.m. issues), one might single out Monteux, who consistently has the second violins play *arco legato* at the beginning, then *arco staccato* as of **28.** One need only check his next to last

Example 9.3. "The Augurs of Spring," **24–27**

recording of *The Rite* with the Paris Conservatory Orchestra (1956) to perceive this quite clearly. Thus, here again, may we ask, how close is the present score to Stravinsky's real intent in the matter? No reference is made to any such second violin *col legno* in any extant errata list or correspondence. Still, one might reasonably argue that the thematic anacrusis supplied to the imminent thematic statements of both horns and flutes by the rocking seconds of the second violins would warrant the latter being more prominent and audible than any *col legno* beating, however forceful.

The original orchestration of **28** and **29** of "The Augurs" was completely crossed out in Stravinsky's manuscript and replaced by him, in time for the premiere, with the present version. This was apparently done at Monteux's suggestion that some orchestral weaknesses and imbalances needed retouching, following early March 1913 rehearsals of part 1 of *The Rite.*[2] One amazing thing about this revision is that none of the present percussion instruments (timpani, triangle, antique cymbals) had a place in the original orchestral texture. It is interesting to speculate about what prompted the composer to introduce such instrumental novelties at that late stage of rehearsing *The Rite,* and it would be of special

---

2. See the following excerpt of a letter of 30 March 1913 from Monteux to the composer, in *Stravinsky: Selected Correspondence,* vol. 2, ed. Robert Craft (New York, 1984), p. 53:

> The passages to which I refer and which perhaps will need to be slightly altered are the following:
>
> > At **28,** beginning with measure 5, [4-hand piano score, p. 22, first measure], I do not hear the horns loudly enough (unless the rest of the orchestra plays ***pp***), and if I make a little crescendo, I do not hear them at all.
> >
> > At **37,** measures 3 and 4 [4-hand piano score, p. 25, measure 3], it is impossible to hear a single note of the flute accompanied by four horns and four trumpets ***ff***, and first and second violins, also ***ff***. The first flute plays the theme alone in the middle of all this noise.
> >
> > At **41,** measures 1 and 2 [4-hand piano score, p. 27, measures 1], you have first, the *tubas,* which, in spite of ***ff***, produce only a very weak sound; second, the seventh and eighth horns, which one does not hear at all in the low register; third, the trombones, which are extremely loud; fourth, the first six horns, which one hears only moderately in comparison with the trombones. I have added the fourth horn to the seventh and eighth, but without achieving an equilibrium for the four groups. One hears:
> >
> > 1. ***mf***
> > 2. nothing
> > 3. ***ff***
> > 4. ***f***
> >
> > At **65,** measure 3 [4-hand piano score, p. 39, measure 10], the first four horns have ***ff*** but they play with mutes, and I can hear them only with difficulty.
>
> This is all that seems to me not to sound the way you want it, and nothing here is of great importance.

interest to try out the older version and thus test Monteux's acuity of perception as against the possible inadequacies of the orchestral players of that 1913 version.[3]

If we move on to the "Games of the Rival Tribes," at measures 6–10 after **58,** we are in for a few more puzzling inconsistencies:

Example 9.4. "Games of the Rival Tribes," **58** + 6

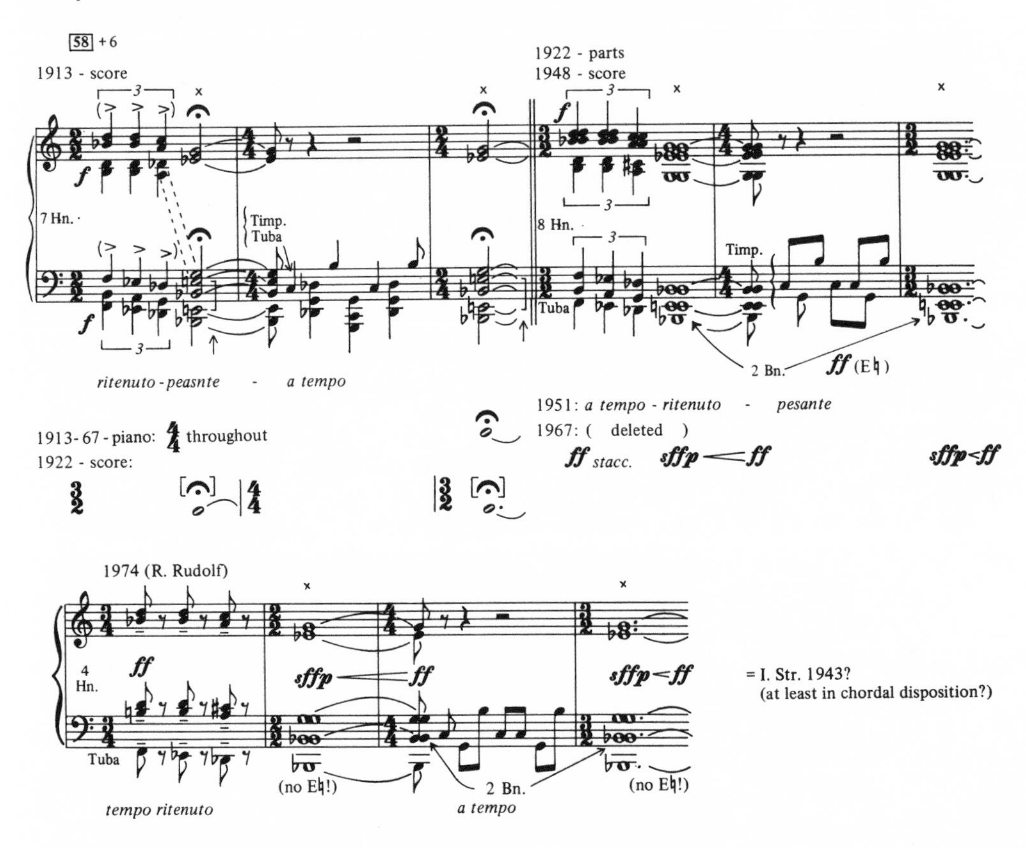

Notice the prolonged chord, marked "x," in the three versions of this passage. Originally played by seven different horns, the seven-note chord involved a grinding E octave stubbornly entrenched within the second inversion of an E♭ major chord. This jarring dissonance is consistent in texture with the chords immediately preceding. Someone obviously advised Stravinsky in 1921 to strengthen the upper thirds by simply doubling them, but in the process, the up-

3. The original version of **28–29** has been transcribed and published by Volker Scherliess in his "Bemerkungen zum Autograph des 'Sacre du Printemps,' " *Musikforschung* (July–September 1982): 238–41.

permost E♮ was eliminated or lowered an octave, both unisono E's then being entrusted to two bassoons, which even in *ff* can hardly compete with the rest of the blaring brass. In any event, the jarring effect of the original E octave was definitely weakened. Surprising as this development is, Robert Rudolf, in his revised version of *The Rite* for reduced instrumentation (1974, but apparently begun as early as 1954 with the composer's approval), makes bold to eliminate any E♮ whatsoever. Thus, American audiences may now be confronted with a pure, unblemished, and beaming 6/4 E♭-major triad.[4] All the more astonishing then is Craft's revelation that this exact chordal disposition is evidenced as early as 1943 in Stravinsky's own sketches for an all-encompassing revision of the entire *Rite*.[5] This indeed raises questions as to the composer's real intentions. At least in his 1929 and 1940 recordings, Stravinsky would seem to have stuck to the earlier version with seven horns; the same seems to hold true for Monteux's San Francisco (1945) and Boston (1951 and 1957) recordings, for Ansermet's first (1951), and for the Karel Ancerl (1963) recording. Markevitch and Goossens both let the upper E♮ sound clearly, at least in the chord's second statement. Whether all these conductors purposely resorted to the older version or just happened by chance on uncorrected orchestral materials must remain an open question. But why then has the piano reduction always clung to the original chordal disposition?

Other aspects of the various strange metamorphoses of this passage need only be mentioned briefly. For example, who is responsible for altering the timpani part into a solo-bravuro of cascading eighths, thereby blurring the rhythmic and motivic connection with the simple alternating C–B quarter-note cell of the "Ritual of Abduction"? Here again we are confronted with a fait accompli, noted in Ansermet's 1921 errata list, but for which both origin and motive have yet to be elucidated. This passage also underwent other rhythmic and metric alterations, including the inconceivable scrambling of the original *ritenuto—pesante—a tempo* into an impossible *a tempo—ritenuto—pesante*(!) that plagued all the study scores from 1951 to 1965 and even the full orchestral score reprinted in 1965. What about the dynamics and staccato articulation of the brass chords, with a 1967 (final?) version of *sffp* crescending to *ff*, which does not even match Stravinsky's own performance practice? In other words, what did Stravinsky really intend here? Did his own perceptions change so drastically over the years, or were such modifications prompted by suggestions from still unidentified sources?

The next example provides us with the seemingly banal case of an undetected mistaken transposition to which we—like the composer from the outset?—have become so accustomed that its recent (1967) correction leaves an uncomfortable void. It is the omnious junction between "Mystic Circles of the Young Girls"

4. *The Rite of Spring*, Full Score, Revised Version and Reduced Instrumentation, Belwin-Mills Publ. Corp., Melville, N.Y., EL 2458, 1974, p. 47. This version may be performed only in the United States.

5. Stravinsky and Craft, *Pictures and Documents*, p. 531.

Example 9.5. Conclusion of the "Mystic Circles of the Young Girls," **103**

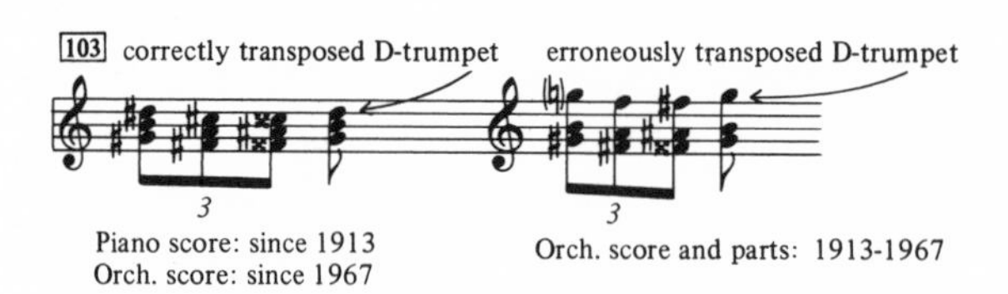

and "Glorification of the Chosen One" in part 2, just at the onset of the rising crescendo, that rolls over into those eleven thunderous string and timpani chords. The piano reduction has always been correct. But just imagine for one moment, as must have happened to Stravinsky, that you forgot that the upper voice was being taken over by a piccolo D trumpet and that you inadvertently wrote the transposition for a B♭ trumpet instead. Your transposition, written of course a whole-tone higher, if read by the D trumpeter, would actually sound an extra whole-tone higher still, with the end result that, instead of crowning the perfect fifth of four successive minor triads, your D trumpet sounds a shrill succession of jarring major sevenths! The simple question here is why did no one, apparently not even the composer, ever notice the mistake until its revision in the newly engraved score of 1967. No less disturbing and indicative of the state of the orchestral parts still being widely circulated is the fact that, of the thirty-five phonograph recordings made of the orchestral version since 1968, only five (all recorded since 1977) make the correction: S. Rattle (Enigma), S. Skrowaczewski (Vox-Candide), A. Lombard (Erato), R. Muti (Angel), and A. Dorati (London).

Example 9.6 raises the question of the motivic, rhythmic, and metronomic link Stravinsky actually had in mind between the prominent horn figure of the 5/8 cell so characteristic of the "Glorification of the Chosen One" and its exact reiterated equivalent in the crashing timpani and lower strings of the "Evocation of the Ancestors" immediately following. If in fact the rhythmic and metronomic connection were so binding, what might have motivated Stravinsky—if the alteration does stem from himself, as his last performance of *The Rite* in Stockholm in

Example 9.6. Rhythmic and Metronomic Connections

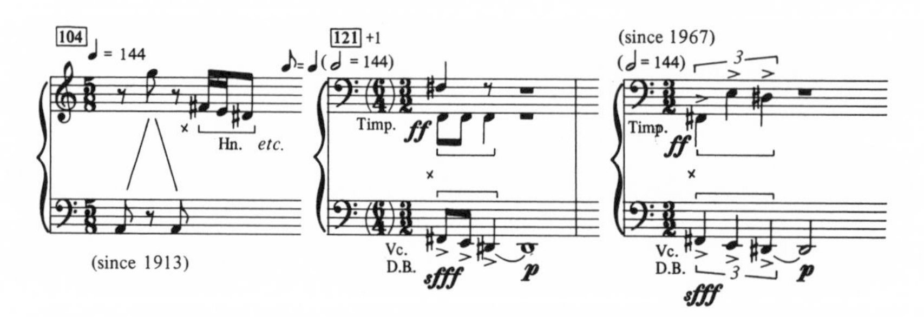

1961 would tend to prove—to attempt to emphasize the melodic contour of this motive by changing it into triplet quarter-notes?[6] At a speed of 144 to a half-note, which he is obviously maintaining, such a change can hardly ever be perceived because it implies taking an extra tenth (7/100, to be precise) of a second to cover the distance between F♯ and D♯. Apart from visually blurring the link between the two motive forms, the shift to the melodic emphasis can thus be made effective only by slowing down the tempo of "Evocation" quite radically, which would be contrary to Stravinsky's own consistent practice. Another solution could have been to ascribe a *ritenuto* or *allargando* only to each statement of this timpani and string motive in "Evocation"; however, no such mention was deemed necessary in the 1967 score revision. Here again we are faced with the question of practice versus analysis versus Stravinsky's real intentions.

Example 9.7, with its added accents, illustrates how in their performances and phonograph recordings Stravinsky and a few other conductors have outlined the melodic contours of this closely knit string duet passage as it occurs in the "Ritual Action." If such emphasis on the initial impulse of each alternating

Example 9.7. "Ritual Action of the Ancestors"

eighth-note was intended from the very beginning, why did Stravinsky not mark all the scores, orchestral and piano reduction, accordingly?

The biggest challenge is yet to come, in the "Sacrificial Dance." The music of Examples 9.8 and 9.9 is one continuous passage at the opening of the "Sacrificial Dance"—**142–147.** At **167–172**, it is repeated literally a half-tone lower (except for two additional timpani strokes, one at the beginning of **167** and the other—strangely enough—on the downbeat one measure before **169**).[7] In these examples, three versions of the bass voice are compared, one above the other: (1) the original 1913 setting, together with its 1922 printing and variants, (2) the

6. A phonograph recording of both rehearsal excerpts and complete live recording of *The Rite* under Stravinsky in Stockholm in September 1961 is in the planning stage by Discocorp. A short, unfortunately edited fragment concerning the passage discussed here is included among the rehearsal excerpts retained.

7. The partial suppression in 1943 of one upbeat chord in one measure before **6** and its complete suppression at **31** remain a mystery, just as does the elimination of the bass upbeat in the following measure.

Example 9.8. Opening of the "Sacrificial Dance," **142–145**

Example 9.9. "Sacrificial Dance," **146–147**

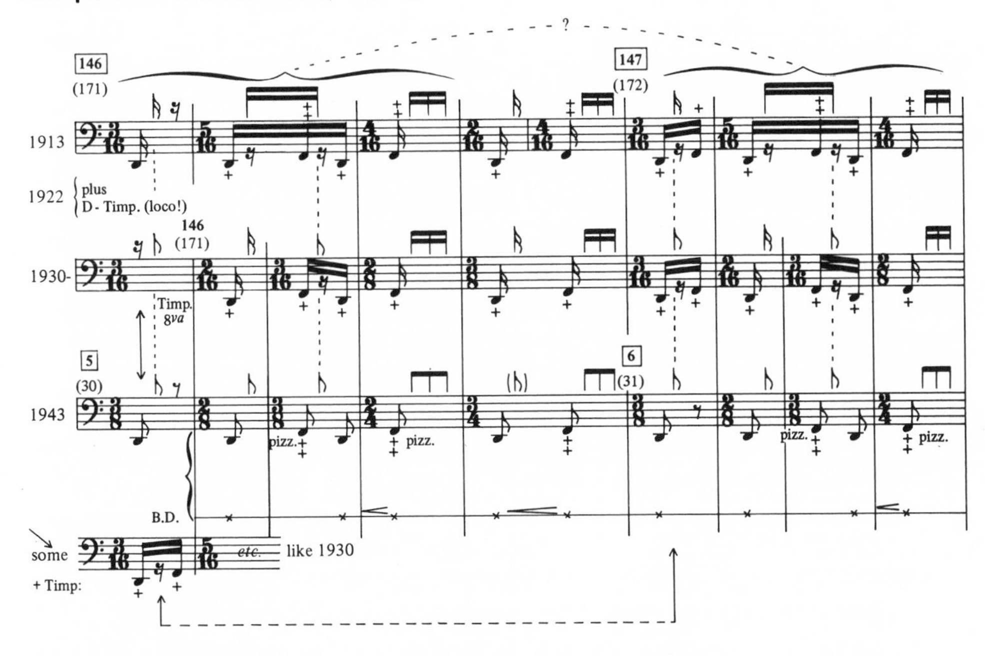

In 1913/1922 at the reprise (**171–172**), the two timpani F-octave gives way to a single stroke that is reinforced each time by the bass drum.

present Boosey & Hawkes edition, which basically reproduces the 1930 revision, and (3) the 1943 revision printed separately by Associated Music Publishers.[8] Stravinsky doubled the rhythmic values in this last version. The alternating string and tutti chords are simply cued in. The + signs indicate timpani strokes that usually sound an octave higher (except in **146–147** of the 1922 version).

Of all the differences that can be pinpointed here, five are most important. First, Stravinsky's 1913 autograph score and the earliest copies of it had some of the string chords plucked pizzicato (see parentheses over the top staff of Example

8. The separately published 1943 revision of "Sacrificial Dance" has not supplanted the Boosey & Hawkes version and was apparently not meant to. It is in any event very rarely heard. Steinberg and Ormandy are the only conductors, besides the composer, ever to have used it for their (monaural) phonograph recordings of *The Rite* (1954–1955). As for Stravinsky, his 1960 recording includes the only extant (stereophonic) recording of "Sacrificial Dance" in its 1943 version. The 1961 Stockholm rehearsal and performance under the composer, scheduled to be issued in the near future (see n. 6) also contain the latter. Explicit rehearsal excerpts even pertain to its central section, where Stravinsky makes bold—in his eightieth year—to experiment with some new percussion scoring! The composer, however, does not go on record as having made the 1943 revision of "Sacrificial Dance" compulsory from 1945 onward in all performances of *The Rite*. This fact does not preclude considering it as yet another step in the composer's unending experimentation with his famous ballet score. Whether he might ultimately have revised the entire *Rite* in a like manner cannot presently be ascertained beyond any doubt.

9.8, **142–145**). This indication disappeared from the printed 1922 score; however, there is no evidence that Stravinsky intended this deletion. Note how Stravinsky resorted to pizzicato strings anew, albeit differently, in 1943 to give added punch to the downbeats of the bass and even to punctuate the climax of the crescendoing orchestral suspensions.

Second, the dotted lines marked in between the staves in both examples underscore the fact that some string chords were perceptibly doubled in length to a full eighth-note in 1930, only to be restored temporarily to their original shorter values in 1943. Some conductors emphasize the difference; others overlook it completely. Again the 1930 score contains this variant as a fait accompli, without any clue as to its origins. It seems strange that Stravinsky would have reinstated the original short chords in 1943 if he had been so convinced of the need for the change in 1930.

Third, the sections linked via brackets along with a dotted line and a question mark in both examples are, chordally speaking, strict repetitions. This has led some conductors to infer that the bass downbeats should also be strictly the same in respective parallel passages—hence their assumption that Stravinsky erred in omitting a timpani stroke in an analogous place at **143** (indicated in parentheses). But did the composer intend a strict repetition here? If so, why did he not correct his own score accordingly, either in 1930 or even in 1943? Note also how the revised 1930 version adds complete down- and upbeats in the bass at the third measure of **144,** as a direct parallel to the third measure of **145.** Such a bass lead was not there in 1913, nor was it taken over in 1943. Similarly, the D-bass note in the fourth measure after **145** was added in 1930, parallel to its previous presence in the corresponding measure of **144.** But this extra note was not there in 1913 and was not kept over in 1943. Are such inconsistencies of Stravinsky's doing or not?

Fourth, another blatant example of obsession with parallel bass leading is to be noted in Example 9.9. Some conductors add a complete timpani motive in the first measure, as being strictly parallel to that of the first measure of **147.** In 1930, Stravinsky (or someone else?) actually deleted the lone bass D, which was nonetheless reinstated in 1943. Charles White, for forty years principal timpanist of the Los Angeles Symphony Orchestra, strongly advocated this additional timpani measure in his published timpani part and apparently always played it accordingly.[9] But he was at least honest enough to include in his text his letter to Stravinsky asking permission to add those two timpani strokes, which the composer promptly returned with a flat "no" written in the margin. When I questioned Igor Markevitch about the basis for his own conviction that this timpani measure was a legitimate addition, he replied:

---

9. *Tympani—Instructions for Playing Igor Stravinsky's 'Sacre du Printemps'—'Rite of Spring'* (Los Angeles, 1965), p. 22a.

> Concerning the timpani in the "Sacrificial Dance": it is on the basis of a conversation with Charles Peschier, timpanist of the Orchestre de la Suisse Romande (who was to record the *Histoire du soldat* with me in 1962), that I adopted this variant. He claimed having taken it over directly from Stravinsky himself. At my first recording of *The Rite*, I really hesitated in introducing it but finally did so, after consulting Walter Legge, who, like myself, considered this timpani addition to be superior, musically speaking. It is therefore quite possible that my recording and performances led other conductors to do the same. I must add that we sent a copy of my recording to Stravinsky, who subsequently told Walter Legge he was perfectly satisfied with it. Nevertheless, during the time I was preparing *The Rake's Progress* for performance in Venice at Stravinsky's request, I spoke to him about this timpani bit, with the score in hand, reminding him of Peschier, etc. He took a long and careful look at the variant, gave me back the score and said: "Well, basically speaking, I am really not opposed to it."[10]

How many other professional musicians have taken it upon themselves to decide what mistakes and omissions Stravinsky was guilty of and what other parallel inferences are thus to be considered "musically superior"? Tony Palmer's film on Stravinsky shows the Russian timpanist playing the controversial added timpani measure with unswerving assurance and authority twice over, including the reprise just before **171.**[11] One wonders what the composer's reaction might have been to such unequivocally immortalized, "musically superior" timpani playing in the "Sacrificial Dance."

Fifth, one final item of note in Example 9.9 is that the oldest version of 1913 implied only timpani octaves for each bass note F; in 1922, all the D's were also entrusted to the timpanist but incorrectly notated an octave lower. In 1930, the timpani part was located "correctly," and all octave doublings disappeared. But in 1943, Stravinsky returned to the old F octaves, adding pizzicati celli F's to them for good measure and introducing thumping bass drum strokes for additional punch to the D's and F's. How does one establish the composer's real intentions for this entire bass lead through all this inextricable maze of variants? Is he basically attached to any so-called "original" version, no matter its "implied" irregularities, shortcomings, or musical "inferiority"?

A rapid examination of the table of variants concerning the last section of the "Sacrificial Dance" (**186–201**) will highlight another confusing situation surrounding the presence or absence of pizzicati strings. If one again considers the separately published 1943 revision, one must question the Stravinskyan origin of

---

10. Letter to Louis Cyr of 13 August 1982, original in French.

11. A phonograph recording has since been issued of *The Rite* with the same performers (Moscow Radio Symphony Orchestra under Vladimir Fedoseev): Vox Cum Laude, D–VCL 9054. The added timpani motive is unmistakably present.

Table 9.1. "Sacrificial Dance" (strings)

Rehearsal numbers	1913 (Ms. + ERM proofs)	1922 (ERM)	1930 (ERM)	Since 1948 (B. + H.)	1943 A.M.P.	Rehearsal numbers
186–188	pizz. for all strings	pizz. deleted	pizz. reinstated (exc. Bassi)	pizz. deleted	pizz. to each "C" of Celli	**45–48**
189	pizz. for all strings	pizz. deleted	pizz. reinstated (exc. Bassi)	pizz. deleted	pizz. for all strings	**49**
190–191	upper strings: alternating pizz.-arco Bassi: pizz. continuous	pizz. deleted	pizz. deleted	pizz. deleted	pizz. remain deleted	**50–53** + 2
192–end	alternating pizz.-arco for all strings	parts: pizz. deleted score: as 1913	alternating pizz.-arco (exc. Bassi)	pizz. deleted	pizz. reinstated for all strings (as in 1913)	**53** + 3–end

the total suppression of any pizzicati whatsoever in the current Boosey & Hawkes edition of *The Rite*. In this connection, a letter from Ernest Ansermet to Stravinsky dated 14 August 1922 provides an important clue:

> . . . I would like to come back to some correction details (involved in drawing up this [1921] errata list). The corrections in the old proof score, which served as the basis for the present (newly) engraved score . . . were made during rehearsals, thus without the care one usually applies to correcting proofs. Thus, for the "Sacrificial Dance," it was decided to delete the pizzicati, and they were in fact eliminated, but not completely, since I notice that some still survive in the score after **192**. . . .
>
> But what bothers me the most are these pizzicati in the entire "Sacrificial Dance." They were deleted as a matter of principle, because we were being rushed, there were few string players available, and even these were below average; we had enough trouble in coping with the rhythmic complexities alone. But now I am seriously pondering if we do right in sticking to that decision. After all, some day we shall be blessed with better performers and performing conditions. In that case, wouldn't writing the strings [alternately] *unisono pizz.* and *divisi arco* be the better solution? And won't the dryness of pizz. strings accompanying the oboes provide a more concise and clear-cut rhythm than any bowing ever could? Perpetual *arco* bowing seems to me (but I am only at the conductor's stand) only to produce a sound

> that is constantly thick and undifferentiated, whereas intervening pizz. would provide clarity and definite contours to the music.[12]

Stravinsky nevertheless stuck to his guns and in his reply to Ansermet decreed anew the perpetual and total deletion of all pizzicati in the "Sacrificial Dance" because "orchestra players will always remain nitwits." Still, the—purely circumstantial?—spite and frustration contained in this last remark are sufficient to make one question the severity and resolve behind such an uncompromising ban.

A final example of behind-the-scenes tampering with *The Rite* concerns the fate of both cymbal and guero on the last page of the "Sacrificial Dance." Once again, I might never have discovered a problem even existed were it not for a certain number of recordings that unmistakably included some rather unexpected cymbal clashes, scraped cymbal swishes, or even, quite plausibly, a scraped guero (as in Ansermet's second recording of *The Rite* [1958]). All these variants may be checked out and verified. But the same old questions are raised anew by the completely haphazard way in which both cymbal and guero evolved in written sources from the sketches onward, only to disappear entirely in 1930 without any evidence pointing to Stravinsky as the origin of both deletions. How many tamperings, inconsistencies, discrepancies, changes, variants in *The Rite* can be attributed to Stravinsky? How many are the responsibility of Monteux, Ansermet, Markevitch, Peschier, Charles White, and of still other unidentified, albeit well-meaning proponents of the "musically superior" or of the technically feasible?

The incredibly confused state of the source materials for Stravinsky's *The Rite* at least partly reflects the composer's own persistent dissatisfaction with any fixed, petrified, so-called "original" state for any of his works.[13] As a conductor, he subsequently, and often reluctantly, had to busy himself with them anew, so he simply made the best of it by enjoying tampering with them and experiencing them in different ways, prompted as he was by aggravating mistakes in the parts, by the performers' unpredictable moods, by tricky acoustics, or even by the sometimes annoying demands of recording engineers. Some of the changes or variants that thus arose led to revisions in the scores. But most of them came and went without any visible effort on the composer's part to collect and edit them systematically, especially if someone else had suggested them to him, no matter

12. "Une lettre inédite d'Ansermet à Stravinsky à propos du 'Sacre du Printemps,' " *Revue musicale de Suisse romande* (December 1980): 210–15. Author's translation.

13. Readers looking for a detailed list of the various manuscripts and printed editions of *The Rite* should refer to the two tableaux in Louis Cyr, "Le Sacre du printemps: petite histoire d'une grande partition," in *Stravinsky: Etudes et témoignages*, ed. François Lesure (Paris, 1982), pp. 89–147.

Example 9.10. Conclusion of the "Sacrificial Dance"

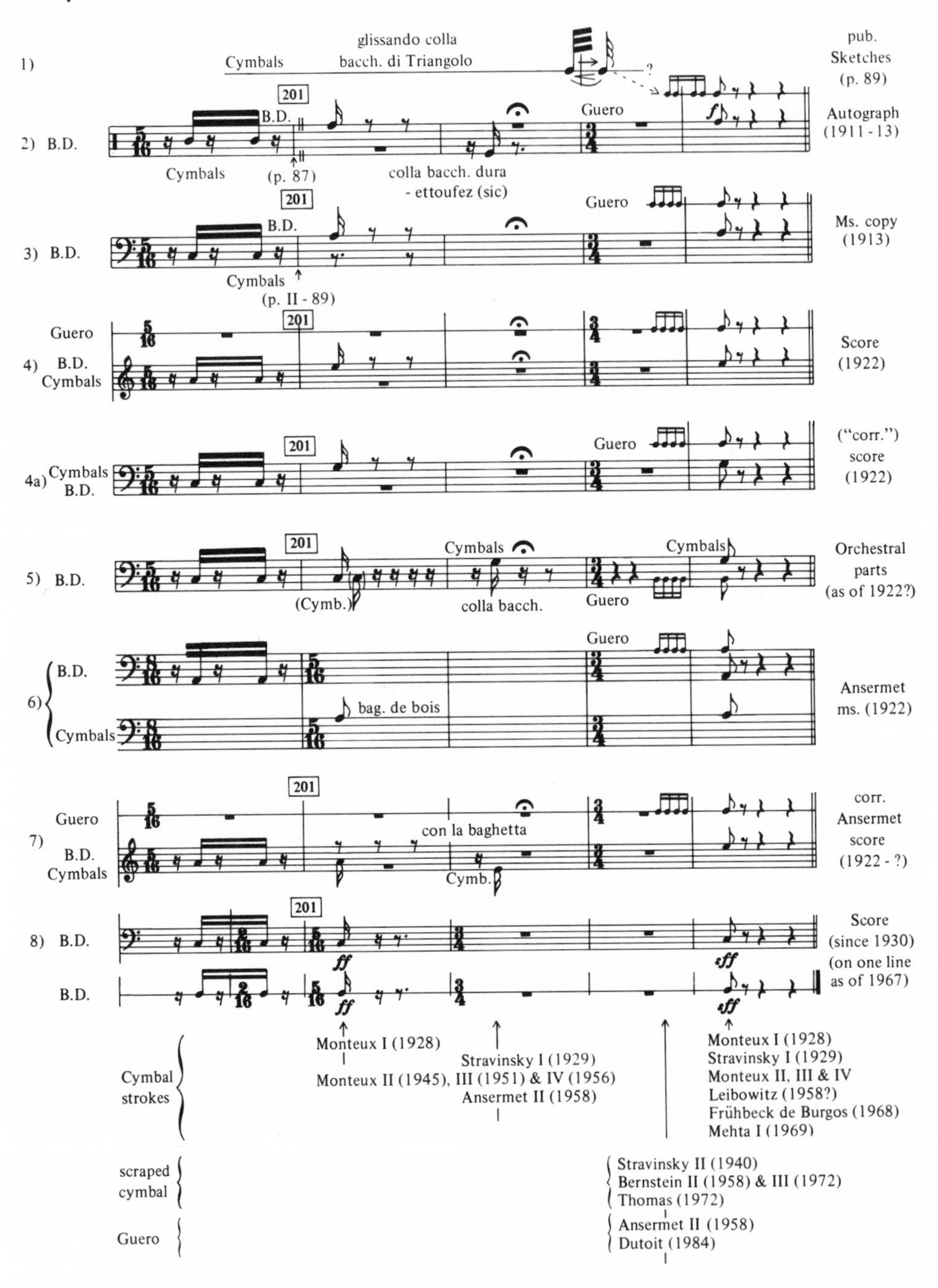

how valid the reasons put forth. Many of *The Rite* variants taken stock of here seem to belong to the latter category. Were the composer alive today, one would be tempted to paraphrase Diaghilev's famous question about the endless repetition of the famous thumping chord of "The Augurs of Spring": "But Igor, will such tampering and fooling around with your *Rite* go on much longer this way?" The composer's huge smile and disarming answer would most likely be exactly the same: "Forever, my dear!"

10 Discontinuity and Proportion in the Music of Stravinsky

JONATHAN D. KRAMER

CRITICS AND ANALYSTS of Igor Stravinsky's music have often noted his predilection for harmonic stasis. Particularly in music written during the 1910s, he created extended passages based on single chords or on the alternation of two chords. One plausible reason for this stylistic trait is that he wanted to focus the listener's attention on rhythm. Whatever the motivation, there are important consequences of his use of frozen harmonies. When a section uses an unchanging harmonic area, the move into the subsequent section necessarily entails discontinuity. There is an inevitable break in the harmonic continuum, and the result is overtly sectionalized music.[1] Although the delineation of sharply juxtaposed sections has its origin in harmonic stasis, the resulting discontinuity is generally supported by other means—contrast of instrumentation, texture, motivic material, tempo, formal design, and even compositional procedure. Not all of Stravinsky's music is discontinuous, of course, just as not all of his harmonies are static, but discontinuity is crucial to his style.

His harmonically static sections unfold more through permutation and variation than through progression and development. The lengths of such sections are thus less internally predictable than are traditional tonal durations. Stravinsky often ends a section at what seems to be the exact right point, despite the impossibility of our forecasting this arrival. The unpredictability comes from the lack of goal-directed development within sections; the sense of rightness comes from the context of the whole piece.

Harmonic stasis implies a relatively small number of structural levels. When the foreground not merely prolongs but actually sustains middleground harmonies, the number of distinct levels between the details and the deep structure cannot be many. Thus, sections of different lengths can function on the same hierarchical level. That a section of a few seconds' duration can be the structural equivalent of one over a minute long makes Stravinsky's music utterly unlike tonal

This article is dedicated to the memory of Norman Dinerstein, with whom I had several fruitful discussions on Stravinsky's music while preparing the original draft.

1. Discontinuity in Stravinsky's music is also discussed in Pasler's article in this collection, in which she analyzes the juxtapositions of sections in the early ballets.

compositions, in which shorter passages are usually subsidiary to longer sections.

Stravinsky's originality has influenced subsequent generations. The Darmstadt composers, for example (Stockhausen, Nono, Zimmermann and others), made his concept into both an aesthetic manifesto and a compositional technique, as shown by Stockhausen's formulation of "moment form." Moments are self-contained sections created by internal stasis or by processes that complete themselves within the moments.[2] A moment-form composition does not have an underlying progressive logic propelling it from beginning to end; rather, it is a mosaic of *seemingly* independent sections assembled in *apparently* arbitrary order. Because one moment does not progress to another, the form does not unfold linearly. Instead, an immobile whole is unveiled gradually. As we hear more of a performance, we acquire more information that allows us to apprehend the formal balance. It almost (and in some cases literally) does not matter in what order moments are heard, as long as we come to understand their proportional interrelationships. Stravinsky never composed a true moment form; there is always some degree of linearity, however disguised, and stasis is never absolute. Hearing his discontinuous compositions as mosaics is nonetheless appropriate. Just as a moment form's purposeful impoverishment of structural levels forces us to hear all moments as having equal importance regardless of their lengths, so in Stravinsky's sectionalized music, formal coherence comes from balance between relatively static sections that are heard as equivalent, no matter what their durations.

Stravinsky's music is, as I have indicated, unlike tonal music. When we speak of balance between sections in tonal music, we have trouble offering convincing evidence to support our intuitions. The experience of musical time, after all, is not much like the experience of clock time. Changes in harmonic rhythm, in the rate of information flow, in densities, and in degrees of predictability create a malleable temporality that is the essence of tonality's linearity. The pacing by which tonal music reaches its (predictable) goals is what that music is all about. Thus, the relative durations of two sections *as experienced* may not have much to do with their "actual" lengths as measured by the clock. The kineticism of tonality distorts (though not unpleasantly) our perception of time. We therefore cannot learn much about the experience of tonal form by counting beats, bar lines, or seconds.[3]

In Stravinsky's music, however, the problem is much simpler. Sections that are self-contained and static within their contexts do not appreciably distort our sense of time. We can compare the measurable lengths of sections. The stasis and consistency of the moments, along with the high degree of discontinuity that sep-

2. Jonathan D. Kramer, "Moment Form in Twentieth Century Music," *Musical Quarterly* 64 (April 1978): 177–94.

3. Some quantitative analyses have shown interesting equivalences in tonal music, but I question how *perceptually* relevant such observations really are.

arates them, makes experiential time correspond much more closely to clock time than in tonal music. Thus, we can investigate proportional lengths of sections objectively with some confidence that what we are talking about is perceived.

The first step in studying proportions is to decide which sections to compare. The concept of a moment is a useful starting point. Assuming that a moment is a clearly defined, self-contained section, we can readily decide where the moment divisions are. Although the designation of moment boundaries is initially an intuitive decision, we can always discover a given composition's rationale for moment definition. In *Symphonies of Wind Instruments* (1920; revised 1947), for example, moments are delineated by discontinuity in three "parameters": harmony, motivic material, and tempo.

With the moments defined, we can look for meaningful subdivisions and groupings of moments. We can demarcate submoments, again using *Symphonies* as the example, by noticing change in two of the three parameters. In other compositions, different factors may create moments, submoments, and moment groups. But in every case, we are dealing with about three distinct yet adjacent structural levels.

Once the section boundaries on each level have been located, the third step is to calculate the durations of the sections using Stravinsky's metronome markings (fermatas must be estimated). Then we can compare the lengths of sections in order to uncover possibly consistent relationships between durations of adjacent sections and of sections with similar material and between durations of section subdivisions.

By subjecting a number of Stravinsky's works to such analyses, I have made some interesting discoveries. He seems initially to have been attracted to discontinuities primarily for their expressive impact (and because they correspond to individual dances of the ballet). *The Rite of Spring*, for example, appears to display no overall pattern of temporal proportions. The aesthetic of discontinuity emerges in the early ballets, but the creation of formal balance by overall proportional consistencies is a later development, perhaps a consequence of Stravinsky's increasingly classical aesthetic.

After experimenting with overt discontinuities in the second and third of the Three Pieces for String Quartet (1914), the composer began to organize his forms temporally. Because that work is a miniature, the lengths of moments vary in accordance with typical additive rhythmic procedures—each time certain figures return, they are a beat or two longer or shorter. But we do feel in this piece an embryonic sense of balance between unequals. More sophisticated is the first tableau of *Les Noces* (1914–1917, but revised through 1923), where sections vary in length from 6 to 35 seconds. Stravinsky convinces us to hear these moments as of equivalent weight by giving several independent, nonadjacent sections the same duration (see Table 10.2). Not all the moments, however, participate in equality relationships.

The real breakthrough piece is *Symphonies*. Here the composer moves beyond additive durations and identity relationships to discover a principle that he was to develop and refine during the remainder of his life: the use of a single multiplicative ratio to determine most of the moment durations of an entire (or at least a major portion of a) piece. The ratio in this case is 3:2, probably the most readily perceived relationship beyond identity (1:1) and doubling (2:1). However, the actual ratio is less important than the consistency with which it is used. Every moment in the first half of the piece (and most of the submoments as well) is in a 3:2 relationship of duration with another moment, and all these relationships are perceptible because they are between adjacent or similar moments. The economy and consistency of a system that determines proportional lengths from the smallest (7 seconds) up to the largest (80 seconds) moments have a lot to do with why the work seems carefully balanced despite frequent discontinuities and extremely disparate section durations.

The neoclassical music is often less overtly discontinuous than the earlier works, and it is not always blatantly static within sections. Nonetheless, the pieces are often sectionalized, and the sectional lengths are usually determined by consistent proportions. For example, the Sonata for Two Pianos (1943–1944), especially in its first movement, is concerned with ratios slightly greater than 1:1 (see Table 10.4). To generate proportions from a ratio such as 1.1:1.0 is to create a compromise between additive and multiplicative procedures.

The most pervasive and elegant proportioning I have found in Stravinsky's music is in *Agon* (1953–1957). This highly discontinuous work has puzzled commentators by its disparity of materials yet unmistakable unity. Part of the reason is the incredible sense of balance Stravinsky creates by utilizing one ratio to determine virtually all the important durations, from the level of the submoment (as brief as 14 seconds) to the entire 18-minute composition. The sections in *Agon* are delineated by a great variety of means, including but not limited to harmonic stasis, and even the compositional methods (serial versus neotonal) vary. Yet *Agon* magically coheres. The pervasiveness of one proportional ratio offers the single-mindedness absent from the work's surface.

Stravinsky's proportional consistencies are never exact, which implies that he did not consciously calculate sectional durations (the first movement of Three Pieces is probably an exception—see Table 10.1). We should not be surprised that a composer as sensitive to surface rhythms as Stravinsky should also have a finely developed intuitive sense of temporal middleground. His intuition operated within the limits of perception. Thus, a section lasting 20 seconds can be heard as equivalent to one 20-1/2 seconds long, in the appropriate context. We do not know what degree of deviation is so slight that it cannot be perceived, but it is surely significant that Stravinsky's choice of tempos as a performer often only approximated his metronome indications.[4]

4. I am indebted for this observation to Jeremy Noble.

Stravinsky's sense of timing became more acute as he matured, so deviations from exactness are smaller in later than in earlier works. This refinement allowed him to work with more complex ratios. In *Symphonies,* for example, most deviations from 3:2 are within a range of 7 percent; in other words, proportions in the range from 1.40 to 1.61 function as approximations of 1.50 (=3:2). Thus, a 30-second section (in 3:2 relationship to a 20-second section) can be approximated by durations lying between 28.0 and 32.2 seconds. This range of approximation is acceptable *in context* because other simple ratios do not fall within the range 1.40 to 1.61—4:3 = 1.33, 5:3 = 1.67, 5:4 = 1.25, the golden mean = 1.62, and so on.

In *Agon,* Stravinsky uses a more sophisticated ratio—1.19:1. No longer is a 7 percent deviation acceptable because it would allow ratios ranging from 1.11 to 1.27. In such a context, durations ranging, for example, from 18.7 seconds to 21.4 seconds cannot approximate 20.0 seconds because durations in the proportion 1.19:1 to 20 seconds are 16.8 and 23.8 seconds; 21.4 (7 percent approximation of 20.0) is not so far from 23.8 after all. Almost all the approximations in *Agon* are within 2.7 percent of accuracy; thus, 20.0 seconds is approximated by durations between 19.5 and 20.5 seconds, which are considerably closer to 20.0 than to, respectively, 16.8 and 23.8. Such close approximations are surely well within the limits of perception. That *Agon* utilizes its proportional ratio as consistently and on as many structural levels and that it does so to such a high degree of accuracy is remarkable. Stravinsky's sensitivity to formal proportions is truly impressive.

Three Pieces for String Quartet is a frankly experimental work.[5] The first movement, which is thoroughly static harmonically and repetitious melodically, is a deliberate exploration of proportional control, although it differs from Stravinsky's subsequent procedures. The third and especially the second movements are experiments in extreme discontinuity. The composer's later methods seem to develop from the implications of both the quantitative durations in the first and the discontinuities in the other movements. The lengths of sections in the later movements result from additive rhythms, and the durations in the first movement are *simultaneous* time spans of unequal duration.

Table 10.1 explains the unique approach to duration in the opening movement. There are three continually repeating cycles (actually four, but the viola-cello 7-beat cycle coincides with and thus supports the second violin 21-beat cycle). The 23-beat melodic pattern in the first violin and the second violin's 21-beat duration are completely regular while the other second violin span varies irregularly within narrow limits. The number of beats between the relaunching of different spans varies because the spans are of unequal length. The relationship is

---

5. Forte, in his article in this collection, singles out this work for its important advances in Stravinsky's pitch language.

Table 10.1. Three Pieces for String Quartet, First Movement—An Experiment in Harmonic Stasis and Additive Durations

A	15	22	19	21	22	13						
AB	7	8	15	7	16	3	20	1	22	13		
B	7	23	23	23	23	13						
BC	4	3	18	5	16	7	14	9	12	11	10	3
C	4	21	21	21	21	21	3					
AC	4	11	10	12	9	10	11	10	11	11	10	3
A	15	22	19	21	22	13						

There are three main ideas of differing lengths that cycle continually throughout the movement. "A" is the duration initiated by 4 (but *not* 8) eighth-notes in the second violin; the average length of this slightly varying cycle is 21 beats. "B" is the first violin's melodic line, which repeats literally after 23 beats. "C" is the duration initiated by 8 (not 4) eighth-notes in the second violin; the length of each of these cycles is 21 beats, supported throughout by the 7-beat cycles in the viola and cello. The chart shows the cycles and their mutual interaction throughout the 112-beat movement.

"AB" shows where within the B cycle each A cycle starts (and conversely, where within the A cycle each B cycle begins); in other words, "AB" shows how many beats, after each melodic relaunching in the first violin, the second violin plays 4 eighth-notes: 8, 7, 3, 1, and 0 beats, respectively. "BC" shows where within the B cycle each C cycle commences; in other words, "BC" indicates that, respectively, 18, 16, 14, 12, and (theoretically) 10 beats after the first violin begins its melodic statement, the second violin plays 8 eighth-notes. Conversely, after the second violin starts its 8-eighth-note figure, the first violin begins its next melodic cycle, respectively 3 (theoretically), 5, 7, 9, and 11 beats. "AC" shows where within each A cycle a new C cycle begins (and conversely). In other words, the duration from the start of one 8-eighth-note figure in the second violin to the start of the next is approximately evenly subdivided by the start of a 4-eighth-note figure, also in the second violin. The slight exception occurs in the second C cycle, which is subdivided 12 + 9 rather than the more nearly even 11 + 10 or 10 + 11. It is difficult to explain this anomaly in an otherwise quite regular scheme other than by suggesting a slight (and typical) degree of unpredictability. Or was this exception an oversight during the compositional process?

The basic additive duration is 2 beats, which derives from the difference in length between the two regular cycles—B (23 beats) and C (21 beats). This duration accounts for the gradual lengthening in the time between the start of an 8-eighth-note cycle and the start of the subsequent melodic cycle.

The cycles are potentially infinitely repeatable. The movement starts so that it avoids the overlapping of the end of an 8-eighth-note figure and the start of a melodic cycle (shown theoretically in the chart). The movement ends after the 4-eighth-note and the melodic cycles ("A" and "B") have begun together.

Table 10.2. ***Les Noces.* First Tableau**—Moment and Submoment Durations and Proportions

Section	Rehearsal Numbers	Duration in Seconds
whole tableau	**0** to **27**	293.3
	moments	
A0 + B1 + C2	**0** to **4**	69.5
A4 + B5 + C7	**4** to **8** +3	68.2
A8	**8** + 3 to **9**	10.5
D9 + E10 + F11 + G12 + D14 + H16 + D18	**9** to **21**	82.9
A21 + C24	**21** to **27**	62.2
	submoments	
A0	**0** to **1**	20.2
B1	**1** to **2**	28.1
C2	**2** to **4**	21.2
A4	**4** to **5**	27.8
B5	**5** to **7**	27.4
C7	**7** to **8** + 3	13.0
D9	**9** to **10**	6.0
E10	**10** to **11** +	7.0
F11	**11** + to **12**	10.0
G12	**12** to **14**	14.2
D14	**14** to **16**	13.0
H16	**16** to **18**	12.2
D18	**18** to **21**	20.5
A21	**21** to **24**	35.2
C24	**24** to **27**	27.0

Submoment durations have a tendency to cluster around certain values (6.5, 10.2, 12.8, 20.6, 27.4), but consistent proportional ratios are not in evidence. This clustering indicates a concern with approximate equality of durations for different sections:

D9 = 6.0	F11 = 10.0	H16 = 12.2	A0 = 20.2	C24 = 27.0
E10 = 7.0	A8 = 10.5	C7 = 13.0	D18 = 20.5	B5 = 27.4
		D14 = 13.0	C2 = 21.2	A4 = 27.8
		D9 + E10 = 13.0		

A0 + B1 + C2 = 69.5
A4 + B5 + C7 = 68.2

A0 + B1 + C2 + A4 + B5 + C7 + A8 = 148.2

D9 + E10 + F11 + G12 + D14 + H16 + D18 + A21 + C24 = 145.1

additive because this number of beats increases or decreases by 2 each cycle. Details are shown in Table 10.1.

Perhaps this experiment taught Stravinsky that carefully controlled durations can have a perceivable effect and that they can generate a form. The use of simultaneous cycles of different lengths must have proved too constricting, however, and he never again used such a procedure. Rather, he began to control durations of separate sections, such as those created by the discontinuities in the last two movements.

In *Les Noces,* one of the first works to control section durations, Stravinsky does not yet relate different lengths by means of consistent ratios, but his concern with overall formal balance is evidenced by a tendency to make disparate moments (that is, those that are neither adjacent nor motivically similar) equal in length. As Table 10.2 shows, the first tableau has eight motivically distinguishable submoments: A, B, C, D, E, F, G, and H. These submoments are grouped into five movements: ABC, ABC, A, DEFGDHD, and AC. As Table 10.2 indicates, several distinct submoments share lengths. These equalities unify a movement that contains 16 sections ranging from 6.0 to 35.2 seconds. Discontinuity is maximized by keeping transitions small; thus, the equal lengths of passages placed in different parts of the tableau definitely contribute to the form. Moments as well as submoments are balanced by durational equality: the first two ABC moments (respectively from the beginning to rehearsal number **4** and from **4** to three measures after **8**) are of equal duration. The largest internal discontinuity (at **9**, where a new tempo and new motivic materials are introduced) divides the tableau into two virtually equal durations.

These equalities lend a subliminal sense of balance to this collection of harmonically static sections. There is, of course, an underlying progression, and return of materials from earlier submoments does round out the form. Nonetheless, the equality of (sub)moment durations is more important to the form than their order of succession, and thus the structure is more nonlinear than linear.

Equalities of durations proved to be a viable but restricted solution to the problem of static form. In *Symphonies of Wind Instruments,* Stravinsky relates section lengths not by identity but by the ratio 3:2, which allows him to project a sense of relatedness between different durations. To make such balances perceivable, he applies the proportional ratio to sections whose relatedness is already suggested by adjacency or similarity.

As in *Les Noces,* transitions are short so that discontinuity is maintained. The sectionalization created by harmony, motivic material, and tempo is supported by changes in instrumentation and texture. Table 10.3 shows several manifestations of 3:2 proportions in the first half of the piece. Included are the submoments of the first long moment, a chain of moment durations from large to small involving all the D moments and all but the final A moment, relationships between the D moments and their submoments, the last three moments, and the remaining two moments. Table 10.3 also shows several larger scale meaningful

Table 10.3. ***Symphonies of Wind Instruments.* Portion up to 42—** Durations and Proportions

Section	Rehearsal Numbers	Duration in Seconds	Tempo	Defining Characteristics
				moments
A0	**0** to **6**	49.6	Tempo I	F and B♭ in bass
B6	**6** to **8**	12.2	Tempo II	modal flute tune with static harmony
C8	**8** to **9**	7.8	Tempo II	3-note bassoon melody with static harmony
A9	**9** to **11**	14.2	Tempo I	clarinet and trumpet fanfare
D11	**11** to **26**	80.0	Tempo II	consistent high register B
A26	**26** to **29**	22.5	Tempo I	clarinet and trumpet fanfare
D29	**29** to **37**	35.3	Tempo II	flute and clarinet duet with punctuations
A37	**37** to **38**	9.6	Tempo I	clarinet and trumpet fanfare
C38	**38** to **39**	7.5	Tempo II	3-note bassoon melody with static harmony
A39	**39** to **40**	10.8	Tempo I	clarinet and trumpet fanfare
B40	**40** to **42**	16.1	Tempo II	modal tune with new continuation
				submoments
a0	**0** to **1**	7.9	Tempo I	clarinet and trumpet fanfare
a1	**1** to **2**	12.9	Tempo I	block chords
a2	**2** to **3**	5.2	Tempo I	clarinet and trumpet fanfare
a3	**3** to **4**	3.6	Tempo I	foreshadowing of **44, 46,** and **58** in oboes
a4	**4** to **6**	20.0	Tempo I	block chords
d11	**11** to **15**	26.1	Tempo II	ascending motive
d15	**15** to **26**	53.9	Tempo II	flute and clarinet duet with punctuations
b40	**40** to **41**	8.6	Tempo II	modal flute tune with static harmony
b41	**41** to **42**	7.5	Tempo II	cadential harmonic stasis

The melodic material, basic harmonies, moment types, and proportional system change after **42.** The new system is less economical than the one used before **42.** The fermata duration is averaged from several recordings considered authentic and/or accurate (Craft, Stravinsky, Boulez). Section durations are calculated according to Stravinsky's metronome markings (in the 1947 version), from the first attack point of a section to the first attack point of the following section.

The analytic decision of what constitutes a moment in the context of *Symphonies* is perceptual and (initially) intuitive. Justifications for such decisions can, in every case, be given: when there is a change in harmony, melodic material, and tempo, a new moment has arrived; when only two of these three "parameters" change, a new submoment has arrived. The one exception is the move from B6 to C8, which share tempo II. Because of the highly restricted nature of the melodic material and harmonies in both these moments, their contrast is sufficiently great for them to be heard as separate moments. The "defining characteristics" listed in the chart indicate some, but never all, of the factors that suggest hearing the indicated sections as moments or submoments. The transitions that appear at the ends of some moments are too brief to upset either the essential discontinuity of the form or the stasis of the harmony within each moment.

Table 10.3. *continued*

"Meaningful" proportions are those between adjacent or similar (sub)moments. The pervasive ratio of proportions is 3:2 = 1.50. Each moment and every submoment except those of B40 is in an approximate 3:2 relationship with an adjacent or similar (sub)moment. These approximations are usually, but not quite always, close. The relevant 3:2 approximations are:

submoments of A0

a4 : a1 = 1.55 (similar submoments)
a1 : a0 = 1.63 (adjacent submoments)
a0 : a2 = 1.52 (similar submoments)
a2 : a3 = 1.44 (adjacent submoments)

chain from large to small involving all A and D moments except A39

D11 : A0 = 1.61 (longest moments)
A0 : D29 = 1.41
D29 : A26 = 1.57 (adjacent moments)
A26 : A9 = 1.58 (similar moments)
A9 : A37 = 1.48 (similar moments)

submoments of D

D11 : d15 = 1.48 (subdivision of D11)
d15 : D29 = 1.53 (D29 is a condensation by omissions of d15)

last three moments

B40 : A39 = 1.49 (adjacent moments)
A39 : C38 = 1.44 (adjacent moments)

only adjacent moments with same tempo

B6 : C8 = 1.56 (adjacent moments)

3:2 approximations involving groups of adjacent moments

(B6 + C8) : A9 = 1.41
(three adjacent moments)

(A9 + D11) : (A26 + D29) = 1.63
(both D moments and their respective preceding A moments)

(A39 + B40) : (A37 + C38) = 1.57
(last four moments)

(A0 + B6 + C8) : (A37 + C38 + A39 + B40) = 1.58
(first three moments compared to last four moments)

(A0 + B6 + C8 + A9 + D11) : (A26 + D29 + A37 + C38 + A39 + B40) = 1.61
(all moments, partitioned after longest moment)

3:2 proportions involving groups of adjacent moments, including the subdivision of the whole first half of the piece according to 3:2.

Moments range in length from 7.5 to 80.0 seconds, submoments from 3.6 to 53.9 seconds. Yet, because of carefully controlled degrees of discontinuity, the moments all function on the same structural level and the submoments on the next level "down." The pervasiveness of the 3:2 proportional ratio has a lot to do with the equivalence of sections of vastly unequal durations. Not every meaningful ratio in *Symphonies* approximates 3:2, but there is sufficient consistency of proportions to unite disparate lengths. Because discontinuities are frequent and transitions are minimal, some means other than foreground continuity are needed for formal coherence. Stravinsky chose two means: stepwise background connections (to show these would require a detailed reductive analysis, which is beyond the scope of this chapter) and consistent proportions. He was thus able to compose a work of stark, almost violent, contrast, a work that nonetheless seems somehow economical, self-motivated, self-actualizing. This is an achievement of stunning imagination and originality. Stravinsky created a music in which proportions not only matter to the form but actually generate it. Tonal music traditionally concerns itself with rates of motion, but in *Symphonies,* we feel proportions of blocks—durations of stasis.

Stravinsky's neoclassical music is in some ways more subtle than his earlier music. When it is discontinuous, juxtapositions are less stark. When harmonies seem static, they are not necessarily totally unchanging. Often the harmonies are not static at all. After a decade of deep involvement with frozen chords, the composer embraced the music most deeply involved with motion. He was able to strip tonal sounds of their kinetic implications and to freeze them in motionless nonprogressions. There is usually background motion, although it is created by other than tonal-triadic means. The materials he uses imply a motion that only rarely occurs *on its own level.* There is irony in this music: the tonal materials suggest movement, but they do not move; in the background, the pieces do move, but by nontonal means.

The Sonata for Two Pianos is a typical neoclassical work. The first movement adheres to the outlines of classical sonata-allegro form, but each section is motivically self-contained and harmonically static. The "bridge" section is in no real sense a transition, but rather a short yet independent static block. Even the "development" section, though less overtly static, does not have the sense of drive common in tonal music. Thus, the sections are really moments. Not surprisingly, the proportions contribute to the form. As Table 10.4 demonstrates, many contextually significant proportions derive from a single ratio. Because the ratio is slightly more than 1:1, the proportions are close to equality. The subtlety is greater than in *Les Noces,* however, where Stravinsky uses approximations of equality. In the Sonata, the ratios range up to 1.11 (with an exception at 1.20); the general feeling, then, is of moments of slightly greater length than other sections.

Table 10.4. Sonata for Two Pianos—Sectional Durations and Proportions

Section	Duration in Seconds	Pitch Centricity (static sections only)
	movements	
I	242.4	
II	262.5	
III	100.4	
	main sections	
I. exposition	124.8	
development	38.1	
recapitulation	64.3	
coda	15.2	F
II. theme	96.0	G
variations	166.5	
III. theme 1	41.6	
theme 2	28.7	
transition	4.2	G
recap. theme 1	25.9	
	subsections	
I. exp. theme 1	27.6	F
exp. bridge	4.3	G
exp. theme 2	30.5	C
recap. theme 1	33.3	C
recap. bridge	4.3	C
recap. theme 2	26.7	F
II. variation 1	41.1	G "root"; "key" of D
variation 2	40.0	
variation 3	49.4	
variation 4	36.0	D

Proportional ratios slightly greater than 1:1 (first two movements only):

(exp. repeated) : (devel. + recap. + coda) = 1.06
(exp. theme 1 + bridge) : (exp. theme 2) = 1.11
(exp. theme 2) : (exp. theme 1) = 1.11
(recap. theme 1) : (recap. theme 2 + bridge) = 1.07
(recap. theme 2 + coda) : (recap. theme 1 + bridge) = 1.11
(exp. theme 1) : (recap. theme 2) = 1.03 (both themes "in" F)

continued

Table 10.4. *continued*

(recap. theme 1) : (exp. theme 2) = 1.09 (both themes "in" C)
(recap. without coda) : (exp. not repeated) = 1.03
(static "in" C) : (static "in" F) = 1.02
(theme + var. 4) : (var. 1 + var. 2 + var. 3) = 1.01
(var. 3) : (var. 1) = 1.20
(var. 1) : (var. 2) = 1.03
(var. 2) : (var. 4) = 1.11
(mvt. II) : (mvt. I) = 1.08

The third movement, which is not harmonically static, uses different proportions—3:2 (1.50), 5:4 (1.25), and golden mean (1.62) :

3:2 (mvt. III) : (theme 1 + recap. theme 1) = 1.49
(theme 1) : (theme 2) = 1.45

5:4 (theme 1) : (theme 2 + trans.) = 1.26
(theme 2 + trans.) : (recap. theme 1) = 1.27
(theme 1 + theme 2 + trans.) : (theme 2 + trans. + recap. theme 1) = 1.27

golden mean (theme 1 + recap. theme 1) : (theme 1) = 1.62
(theme 1) : (recap. theme 1) = 1.61

Also, interestingly:
(mvt. II + mvt. III) : (mvt. I) = 1.50

The following durations indicate the total time spent in each centricity throughout the Sonata. Durations take into account both harmonically static *and* active passages. The decision of what pitch class (if any) governs a passage in a chromatic and/or transitional context is sometimes difficult to determine; thus, the following durations should be considered approximate:

Movement I	"in" F	97.1
	"in" C	120.0
	"in" G	4.3
	"in" A♭	21.0
Movement II	"in" G	131.8
	"in" D	89.8
	"in" C	40.9
Movement III	"in" F	67.5
	"in" G	32.9

Proportional ratios of time spent in main centricities (both slightly greater than 1:1):
("in" G) : ("in" F) = 1.03
("in" F) : ("in" C) = 1.02

This proportional idea is carried over into the second movement, a set of variations. The theme and the first and fourth variations are static; the second and third variations are not. This introduction of motion is significant because the finale is rarely static. Thus, internal proportions in the last movement are not as important to formal coherence as in the earlier movements—progression takes over as the form becomes linear. We should not be surprised that the proportions between the clearly delineated large sections of the finale do not continue the subtle ratio of the first two movements: hearing sophisticated balances when motion influences our perception of time is difficult.

There is one further consequence of the "slightly greater than 1" ratio. As Table 10.4 shows, this ratio is reflected in the total amounts of time spent in each of the three main pitch centricities of the Sonata—the "keys" of F, G, and C. Applying the basic ratio to total amounts of time spent in tonal areas is apparently a new development for Stravinsky; it does not depend directly on either stasis or sectionalization. The Sonata thus extends the principle of proportional balance into a new realm, and the result is an elegantly proportioned work.

Agon is possibly Stravinsky's most discontinuous conception. Moments (which do not always coincide with the movements as labeled in the score) are differentiated by instrumentation, tempo, compositional procedures (some of the music is twelve-tone), harmony, recapitulation, and melodic material. Many moments contain submoments, and moments are grouped into five types. Some of these groups are contiguous but others include sections from different parts of the piece (see Table 10.5).

Table 10.6 shows the proportional system. The basic ratio is 1.19:1. This ratio is not as strange as it might seem because it is really $\sqrt[4]{2}$:1. The musical significance of $\sqrt[4]{2}$ is that the series doubles every fourth term (for example, the subseries 40.2, 80.4, 160.8, 321.6, 643.2 is in the ratio 2:1). Thus, sections twice as long as other sections are often encountered in *Agon*. The composer is therefore able to utilize a sophisticated series that also provides readily perceivable doubling of durations.

The series in the first column of Table 14.6, a sequence of numbers increasing according to the basic ratio, is simply a reference. The second column gives actual durations of all moments (except the longest one, E411) plus selected moment groups. Comparison of these two columns shows how very close to the $\sqrt[4]{2}$:1 series the sectional durations are (the fourth column gives the percentage of deviation)—only one approximation is poor. Equally amazing is the range of the series: durations ranging from 40.7 to 1109.5 seconds approximate terms of the reference series.

The series in Table 10.6 does not explain durations of submoments. Another series, using the same ratio $\sqrt[4]{2}$:1 but starting from a different number, determines the durations of submoments from A61 and E411 (see Table 10.7). The approximations are as close as in Table 10.6, and the series is carried onto large structural levels by the durations of groups of adjacent submoments. The series of

Table 10.5. ***Agon*—Delineation of Sections**

Section	Measures	Duration in Seconds	Name in Score	Defining Characteristics
		moments groups		
A	1–121; 561–620	296.0		framing fanfares
B	122-145; 254-277; 387-410	122.1		refrain
C	146–253	194.4		neoclassical dances
D	278–386	161.6		"ABA" forms
E	411–560	335.4		serial
		moments		
A1	1–60	81.5	Pas-de-Quatre	fanfarelike
A61	61–121	133.7	Double and Triple	attacca between Double and Triple
B122	122–145	40.7	Prelude	
C146	146–163	65.8	Saraband-Step	solo vln, xyl., 2 trb.
C164	164–184	60.6	Gailliarde	fls., solo strings, harp, mand., piano
C185	185–253	68.0	Coda	chamber orchestration
B254	254–277	40.7	Interlude	return of B122
D278	278–309	47.6	Bransle Simple	"ABA" form
D310	310–335	47.0	Bransle Gay	castanets ostinato; "ABA" form
D336	336–386	67.0	Bransle Double	"ABA" form
B387	387–410	40.7	Interlude	return of B122
E411	411–560	335.4	(several)	serial
A561	561–620	80.8	Coda	recapitulation
		submoments		
a61	61–80	41.9	Double Pas-de-Quatre	4/8 time
a81	81–95	38.3	Double Pas-de-Quatre	5/8 time, more pointillistic
a96	96–121	53.5	Triple Pas-de-Quatre	4/8 time, coda
b122	122–135	20.7	Prelude	overlapping figures
b136	136–145	20.0	Meno mosso	high cb., low fls., etc.
c146	146–153	29.8	Saraband-Step	ends with strong cadence
c154	154–163	36.0	Saraband-Step	answering section
c164	164–170	17.6	Gailliarde	
c171	171–178	28.3	Gailliarde	add piano and timp., repeat
c179	179–184	14.7	Gailliarde	recapitulation of c164
b254	254–267	20.7	Interlude	overlapping figures
b268	268–277	20.0	Meno mosso	high cb., low fls., etc.
d278	278–287	13.9	Bransle Simple	trumpets fanfare

Table 10.5. *continued*

Section	Measures	Duration in Seconds	Name in Score	Defining Characteristics
		submoments continued		
d288	288–298	15.7	Bransle Simple	pointillistic orchestration
d299	299–309	18.1	Bransle Simple	recapitulation of d278
d310	310–320	21.5	Bransle Gay	flutes and bassoons
d321	321–331	17.9	Bransle Gay	flute solo
d332	332–335	7.5	Bransle Gay	recapitulation of d310
d336	336–351	25.7	Bransle Double	tpt., trb., strings
d352	352–364	13.9	Bransle Double	add flute and piano
d365	365–372	12.9	Bransle Double	recapitulation of d336
d373	373–386	14.5	Bransle Double	coda
b387	387–400	20.7	Interlude	overlapping figures
b401	401–410	20.0	Meno mosso	high cb., low fls., etc.
e411	411–451	121.7	Pas-de-Deux	violin solo with strings
e452	452–462	16.5	Pas-de-Deux	strings; irregular meters
e463	463–494	44.8	Pas-de-Deux	"ABA" form
e495	495–503	16.5	Coda	energetic
e504	504–511	45.0	Doppio lento	mand., harp, solo strings
e512	512–519	13.9	Quasi stretto	first real transition
e520	520–538	33.0	Four Duos	lower strings pizz., trbs.
e539	539–552	27.5	Four Trios	string fugato
e553	553–560	16.5	Four Trios	transition to recap. of A1

"Moment groups," "moments," and "submoments" represent three distinct but hierarchically adjacent levels of structure. Moments are self-contained sections defined by some of the following characteristics: static harmony, texture, compositional procedure, orchestration, tempo, melodic material, form. The analytic decision of what constitutes a moment in the context of *Agon* is perceptual and (initially) intuitive. Justifications for such decisions can be given—"defining characteristics" indicate some, but never all, of the pertinent factors that suggest hearing the sections on the indicated structural levels. Moments that share common materials, textures, and/or procedures are grouped together into moment groups, whether or not the constituent moments are temporally adjacent. Distinct sections that are not as strongly delineated as moments are labeled submoments. Most, but not all, moments contain submoments.

"Duration" is calculated according to Stravinsky's metronome indications, from the first attack point of a section to the end of the final sound of that section (if it is followed by a between-movement pause of indeterminate length) or to the first attack point of the subsequent section (if it follows *attacca*).

Fermatas are estimated to add one second.

Table 10.6. ***Agon*—Proportional Relationships Between Moments and Moment Groups**

1:1.19 Series	Duration in Seconds	Moments	% Deviation from Series	Remarks
40.2	40.7	B122	1.2%	
	40.7	B254	1.2%	
	40.7	B387	1.2%	
47.8	47.0	D310	1.7%	
	47.6	D278	0.4%	
56.8	60.6	C164	6.7%	poor approximation
67.6	65.8	C146	2.7%	
	67.0	D336	0.9%	
	68.0	C185	0.6%	
80.4	80.8	A561	0.5%	
	81.5	A1	1.4%	
95.6	94.6	D278 + D310	1.0%	two adjacent moments
113.6	114.0	D310 + D336	0.4%	two adjacent moments
135.2	133.7	A61	1.1%	
160.8	161.6	D	0.5%	moment group D
191.2	194.4	C	1.7%	moment group C
227.2	235.1	(B122 + C) or (C + B254)	3.5%	group C + one framing B moment; weak approximation
270.4	275.8	B122 + C + B254	2.0%	group C + both framing B moments
321.6	321.7	A1 + A61 + B122 + C146	0.0%	first four moments
382.4	376.1	B387 + E411	1.6%	two adjacent moments
454.2	456.9	B387 + E411 + A561	0.6%	last three moments
540.8	537.7	D + B387 + E411	0.6%	five adjacent moments
643.2	631.4	A + E	1.8%	two moment groups
764.8	753.5	A + B + E	1.5%	three moment groups
908.4	915.1	A + B + D + E	0.7%	four moment groups
1081.6	1109.5	A + B + C + D + E	2.6%	five moment groups (entire composition)

All moments other than the exceptionally long E411 have durations approximating a 1:1.19 series (all approximations are remarkably close, except for C164). This series is shown for comparison with the actual durations—it has no direct relevance to *Agon* except by such comparison. This series is interesting, however, because its ratio is 1 to the fourth root of 2; in other words, the $(n+4)$th term of the series is twice the nth term. Thus, many moments are twice as long as other moments (for example, A561 and A1 are twice B122, B254, and B387; A61 is twice C146, D336, and C185; and so forth). Such nearly exact doublings of duration have a decided impact on the sense of formal balance in *Agon*. Also important are certain virtually identical durations—A1 and A561, the framing moments of the entire composition; B122, B254, and B387, the virtually identical Prelude and Interludes; adjacent moments D278 and D310, whose combined duration is also significant in the proportional scheme.

The chart goes well beyond the three structural levels of submoments, moments, and moment groups. It goes to the ultimate background—the duration of the entire piece. It is remarkable that this one proportional scheme governs durations from the individual moments through perceptually relevant "meaningful" (that is, adjacent or similar) groupings of moments to the total span of the work.

Notice the tendency of certain durations to cluster around certain terms of the main series (40.2, 47.8, 67.6, 80.4). This indicates further the pervasiveness of the ratio. The duration of every moment except E411 is determined by the series; every term of the series approximates at least one significant duration; many chains of adjacent moments figure in the higher durations of the series; sums of durations of moment groups are also determined by the series. These facts go a long way toward explaining the mysterious sense of unity in *Agon*, despite the disparity in materials and compositional procedures and despite the extreme discontinuity between moments.

Table 10.7. ***Agon*—Proportional Relationships Between Submoments of A and E**

1:1.19 Series	Duration in Seconds	Submoments	% Deviation from Series	Remarks
13.7	13.9	e512	1.5%	
16.3	16.5	e452	1.2%	
	16.5	e495	1.2%	
	16.5	e553	1.2%	
19.3	19.6	e495+	1.6%	includes preceding silence
23.0	22.5	e504	2.2%	not counting repeat
27.4	27.5	e539	0.4%	
32.6	33.0	e520	1.2%	
38.7	38.3	a81	1.0%	
46.0	44.8	e463	2.6%	
	45.0	e504	2.2%	
54.8	53.5	a96	2.4%	
65.2				no meaningful approximation
77.4	77.0	e520 + e539 + e553	0.5%	
	75.4	e495 + e504 + e512	2.6%	preceding three submoments; "Coda"
92.0	91.9	e504 + e512 + e520	0.1%	three adjacent submoments
	90.9	e512 + e520 + e539 + e553	1.2%	last four submoments
	91.8	a81 + a96	0.2%	two adjacent submoments
109.6				no meaningful approximation
130.4				no meaningful approximation
154.8	152.4	e495 + e504 + e512 + e520 + e539 + e553	1.6%	last six submoments
184.0	182.9	e411 + e452 + e463	0.6%	other submoments of E411
219.0	215.2	A1 + A61	1.8%	first three submoments
260.8	256.0	A1 + A61 + B122	1.8%	first three moments

All submoments of A61 and E411 are involved in this series of approximations of a 1:1.19 series (a series different from but having the same ratio as the approximation series for moments shown in Table 10.6). All approximations are remarkably close, although three terms of the series do not correspond to perceptually meaningful durations in *Agon*. Most submoments (except a61 and e411) appear as entities. For approximations of larger durations, adjacent submoments (usually from the beginning or ending [except for the recapitulatory coda] of the piece) are summed. This procedure reflects the framing nature of the opening and closing of the work—not only the material but also the proportions produce an archlike structure. As in the previous analysis of moment lengths, we find doublings of length (for example, e539 is twice e512; e520 is twice e452, e495, and e553, and so forth). Also important are such identities of duration as e452, e495, and e553; e463 and e504; the successive groups of submoments e495 + e504 + e512 and e520 + e539 + e553; the interlocking groups of submoments e504 + e512 + e520 and e512 + e520 + e539 + e553; also significant is the fact that e539 + e553 = e504.

Table 10.8. ***Agon*****—Other Significant Proportions in Submoments**

Moments A1 and A61

a61 = a81, to within 1.6 seconds
a61 + a81 = A1, to within 1.3 seconds
(a81 + a96) : A1 = 1.13

Moments B122, B254, and B387

b122 = b136 = b254 = b268 = b387 = b401, to within 0.7 seconds

Moments C146, C164, and C185

C185 = C146, to within 2.2 seconds
c164 + c179 = c154, to within 1.7 seconds
c154 : c146 = 1.21 (adjacent submoments of C146)
c164 : c179 = 1.20 (similar submoments of C146)
(c164 + c179) : c171 = 1.14 (all submoments of C146)

Moments D278, D310, and D336

adjacent submoments increasing in duration according to ratio:
d288 : d278 = 1.13
d299 : d288 = 1.15
d310 : d299 = 1.19
d321 = d299, to within 0.2 seconds
d352 + d365 = d365 + d373 = d336, to within 1.7 seconds (all submoments of D336)
d336 : d310 = 1.20 (first submoments of two successive moments)
(d321 + d332) : d310 = 1.18 (adjacent submoments)
d310 : d321 = 1.20 (adjacent submoments)

Moment E411

e463 = e504 = e539 + e553, to within 1.0 seconds
e539 is twice the length of e512, to within 0.3 seconds
e520 is exactly twice the length of e452, e495, and e553
(e411 + e452 + e463) : (e495 + e504 + e512 + e520 + e539 + e553) = 1.20 (subdivision of E411 at largest silence)
e520 : e539 = 1.20 (adjacent submoments)
(e411 + e452) : e411 = 1.14
e452 : e512 = e495 : e512 = e553 : e512 = 1.19

Table 10.7, like that of Table 10.6, contains several doubling relationships. There are also a number of significant equalities of durations shown in Tables 10.6 and 10.7. Table 10.8 demonstrates additional manifestations of the basic ratio, several equalities of durations and further doublings of durations.

Careful study of Tables 10.6, 10.7, and 10.8 should indicate the impressive pervasiveness of the basic ratio. The choice of this particular ratio was fruitful because it allows for two long chains of proportionally related durations and includes several 2:1 ratios. The closeness of approximation is strong evidence that these series do indeed operate structurally. The participation of every moment and submoment (except the single longest moment, the twelve-tone E411, which is carefully set apart) in one of the two series testifies to the thoroughness of Stravinsky's system. The fact that both series are projected onto high levels, thus determining durations up to that of the entire composition, is further proof of the significance of this construction. The higher order terms of both series are approximated by groups of moments chosen not randomly but in accordance with temporal adjacency and/or motivic similarity. *Agon*, Stravinsky's most mosaiclike, most discontinuous, seemingly least consistent work, is in fact unified by a tight system of durational proportions. What results from his great sensitivity to sectional lengths is a beautifully balanced composition in which diverse sections balance one another in numerous sophisticated ways. The composer's achievement is extraordinary; it bespeaks both an incredibly well developed intuition and a deep understanding of the implications of discontinuity.

Discontinuity implies nonlinearity of musical time. The idea that time does not progress from moment to moment, does not even really flow, is common to much twentieth-century music; this notion is not only Stravinsky's. There is, in addition, ample evidence that such a conception of time is endemic to much contemporary art and culture. Despite the irrationality of time, despite the fragmented nature of human existence (surely made painfully acute to Stravinsky and his contemporaries by World War I), we do grow up, and grow old, and die. Our bodies progress inexorably through time, even if our daily lives do not. This contradiction between a middleground life of discrete moments and a background life of process aimed toward the grave parallels (all too neatly?) the formal procedures of Stravinsky's discontinuous works. If he were an isolated composer, this comparison between musical logic and twentieth-century concepts of time might be too pat. But Stravinsky's discontinuities derive in part from those of Debussy, parallel those of Ives, Webern, and Varèse, and anticipate those of Messiaen and the Darmstadt school. Stravinsky's aesthetic belongs to an important mainstream of modern musical thought.

His formulation of discontinuous time is particularly elegant because his music's unexpected juxtapositions are the starting point, not the whole essence, of his aesthetic. Stravinsky deals with the formal implications of discontinuity—the creation of static forms that are revealed moment by moment. There is a subtle tension in his music, as this middleground stasis of form is contradicted by foreground details and background pitch connections that do progress through time.

Stravinsky went beyond the creation of discontinuities and static forms and found a way to convince the ear of the functional equivalence of sections of different lengths. Therein lies his great originality. He invented a compositional technique, apparently intuitively, that provided the means to create structures that cohere despite vastly different durations and extreme discontinuities. This technique allowed him to compose pieces that are beautiful statements of the contemporary aesthetic of nonlinear time.

11 Aspects of the Religious Music of Igor Stravinsky

GILBERT AMY

THE STRAVINSKY family, in true Russian fashion, chose to live surrounded by icons and pious images. But finding any evidence of a sentimental attitude toward the sacred in Igor Fyodorovitch's religious music would be difficult. On the contrary, this music is characterized by the starkness of its content and the sharp clarity of its lines, the absence of pathos or bombast but not of eloquence. Economy, clarity, objectivity, and exclusion of "personal" emotion are the hallmarks of Igor Stravinsky's style. The nature and function of his religious and liturgical music in no way invalidates them. It enhances and *exalts* them. The religious aspects of Stravinsky's art are essentially nonrepresentational, but not by any means abstract—far from it. In his religious music, Stravinsky re-establishes links with a distant past and at the same time breaks new ground. The religious music displays specific characteristics and has its own color, reminiscent not so much of the glowing reds and gold of icons as of the cool, severe grisaille of stained glass windows. A description and comparison of certain aspects of this complex art will reveal what creates unity despite the music's apparent diversity.

Stravinsky's religious music falls into two distinct categories: (1) liturgical (for example, the Mass, *Pater Noster, Introitus* [T. S. Eliot in Memoriam], *Requiem Canticles*) and (2) works of biblical inspiration (for example, *Symphony of Psalms, Threni, Canticum Sacrum*). This is not an arbitrary division. The liturgical works draw upon Latin texts from Roman Catholic ritual and are "functional."[1] The works of biblical origin, most of them also in Latin (with the exception of *A Sermon, a Narrative, and a Prayer* and *Abraham and Isaac*) are "free." Stravinsky had a natural predilection for texts of supplication, invocation, and praise. Like the psalmist, he had a very personal relationship with the divine. He felt any setback or loss in the family, so I have been told, as an ordeal directly inflicted upon him by God. But "personal" relationship does not imply a psychological transposition into his music. There is eloquence, but it is not overdone, and tragedy, but without pathos.

For Pierre Souvtchinsky

Translated by Nancy François and Jann Pasler

1. With the exception of the a capella pieces *(Pater, Ave Maria, Credo)*, which use the Slavonic ritual.

That Stravinsky did not turn to religious music before his fiftieth year should not surprise us. Two reasons are possible, one musical and spiritual, the other psychological. First, he had gained an intimate knowledge of Latin, the sacred language of Roman ritual, already exploited with such felicity in *Oedipus Rex,* and had come to revel in the language, wrapping himself in it like some spiritual garment of sound.[2] Second, he had arrived at middle age, for him a period of difficulty and sadness, after his brilliant younger years and the successes of the Ballets Russes.[3]

The experience of creating the great ballets and the more significant among the works that followed (*Symphonies of Wind Instruments, Pulcinella, Oedipus Rex,* works for piano) was a necessary preliminary that *permitted* the musician to approach the domain of religious music with an extraordinary serenity of mind. Can one then induce that Stravinsky's religious music is a synthesis of his works from 1910 to 1925? I would say no. Rather than representing a synthesis, his religious music reflects another side of his musical and spiritual sensibility, one hidden but powerfully present in his earlier works. The orchestral sonorities of the *Symphony of Psalms* or the Mass, for example, are foreshadowed in the *Symphonies of Wind Instruments.* To my mind, the "Lacrimosa" from the *Requiem Canticles* is overwhelmingly evocative of the deep voice of Jocasta in the second act of *Oedipus Rex.* In both cases, the sonorities have lost something of their abrasive, almost cynical contour; they have been *interiorized, sublimated.*

Whenever one speaks of religious music, one normally thinks of the presence of a chorus. In Stravinsky's music, it may play a central role, representing a people on the march or in procession (as in *Symphony of Psalms*), or, as in Greek tragedy, it may assume the role of commentator on the monologues of the main characters *(Threni).* Taking its cue from the Catholic mass, it can also alternate with or be superimposed on soli voices whose role is only episodic (as in the "Gloria" and "Sanctus" in the Mass, the "Libera me" in the *Requiem Canticles*). In the choral domain, Stravinsky is not the innovator we find in his orchestral works. The risks he took in *Zvezdoliki* (1911–1912)—writing for male voices only, the use of many subdivisions, and the inherent intonation difficulties—were not to be repeated. The brisk and colorful syllabification of *Les Noces* is replaced in the Latin music by more subdued prosodic writing for four voices; extreme registers are

---

2. About this time, Schoenberg was also moving spiritually and musically closer to the religion of his forefathers. He began the opera *Moses and Aaron* on 17 July 1930, the year of Stravinsky's *Symphony of Psalms.*

3. "Having lived close to Stravinsky for nearly a quarter of a century, and much of that time in the same house with him, I knew him to be, as the expression goes, 'profoundly religious.' . . . That Stravinsky had reached a spiritual crisis in 1944 [the year he began work on his Mass] is evident in his reading, which consisted of parts of the *Summa,* Bossuet's *Lettres sur l'Evangile,* Bloy, Bernanos, and T. S. Eliot." Robert Craft, "Stravinsky—Relevance and Problems of Biography," in his *Prejudices in Disguise* (New York, 1974), pp. 290–91. [Editor's note]

avoided and subdivisions are few indeed. There is a distinct preference for the middle register. In the *Symphony of Psalms*, the long coda never exceeds a total range of two and a half octaves (Example 11.1), and the whole third movement never more than three; whereas *Les Noces* (Example 11.2) ranges over three octaves and a fourth.

Example 11.1. Range of the Coda of *Symphony of Psalms* (1930)

Example 11.2. Range of *Les Noces* (1914–1917, 1921–1923)

The adoption of the serial system in the later years of his creative life did not significantly change Stravinsky's choral writing. In *Threni*, the choruses remain confined to the middle range, and the extremely tense voice leadings are given to the soloists (almost two octaves to the basso profundo). In the *Requiem Canticles*, the framework is even tighter (Example 11.3)—the sopranos have only one high C and the bass, only one low A. Stravinsky's approach is the opposite of his Viennese contemporaries, whose use of the serial system led to considerable extension of the vocal register compared with their works of the post-tonal or nonserial period (Example 11.4). (In his Second Cantata, Webern's total range extends to three and a half octaves for the chorus, almost two of which are for the first sopranos.)

Example 11.3. Range of *Requiem Canticles* (1965–1966)

Example 11.4. Range of Webern's Second Cantata (1943)

Syllabification of a Latin text is common practice in Stravinsky's choral writing. Sometimes this is nothing more than the simplest psalm tone writing slightly modulated and inflected, as in the "Credo" of the Mass, or even rhythmic speech ("Elegia Prima" in *Threni,* occasionally also in the *Introitus*).[4] It can even be non-rhythmic speech that almost certainly has definite links to the practices of Slavonic ritual Stravinsky used in the a capella pieces ('Libera me" in the *Requiem Canticles*). The prosody is disconcerting at times, especially in the melodic litanies, a device Stravinsky really used successfully only in the famous coda of the *Symphony of Psalms.*[5] The following example shows that the accents of the Latin phrase do not necessarily correspond to the phrase divisions and create several "hiatuses" incompatible with good elocution:

Example 11.5. Prosody in *Symphony of Psalms* (1930)

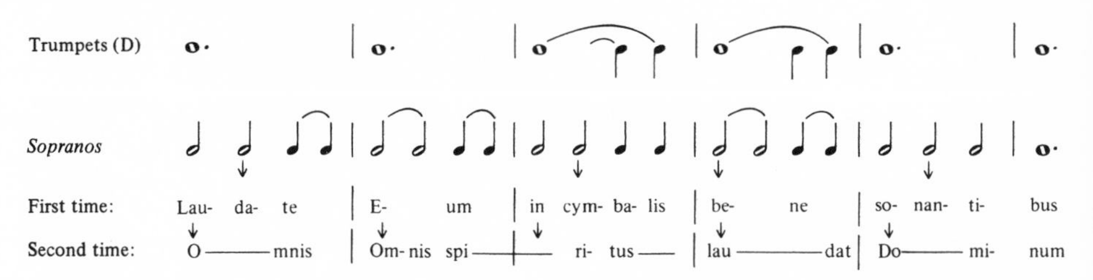

Remember that Stravinsky had announced "the true" rhythmic profile in the introduction of this third movement:

Example 11.6. *Symphony of Psalms* (1930)

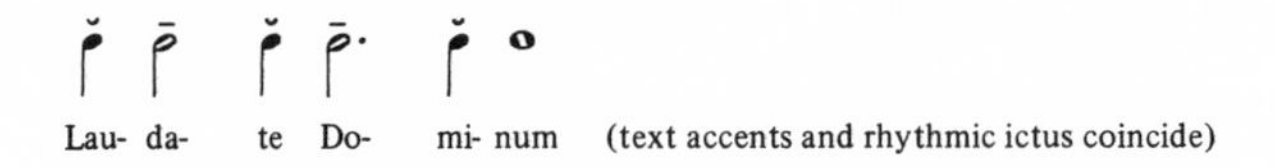

4. On this point, see Pierre Souvtchinsky's enlightening text in "Sur la genèse de la musique russe" [The genesis of Russian music], *Contrepoints* 6 (1949): 79–101. "In Russian plainsong, syllabic articulation and the flow of musical time become one, a synthesis generating so high a degree of spirituality that this music, in which there is no development, is heard in a 'permanent present,' surely the essential nature of a state of religious concentration." See also, in the same article, the definition of "homony" (somewhat like homophony) with reference to the syllabification of the liturgical text (pp. 96–101).

5. By "melodic litany," I mean any formula repeated several times without development.

Stravinsky frequently trusts his own instinct rather than inductive reasoning and so "proposes" several prosodic solutions when logically one would have been sufficient. In the "Credo" in the Mass, he enunciates:

Vi - si - bi - lium, but then: in - vi - si - bi - li - um

To quote Stravinsky on the subject in *An Autobiography:* "The text thus becomes purely phonetic material for the composer. He can dissect it at will and concentrate all his attention on its primary constituent element—that is to say, on the syllable."[6] Thus, the musical rhythm is not subordinate to the prosody: just the opposite. In this sense, he is re-establishing links with the musicians of isorhythmic motets. As we see in the Mass, the "rhythmic theme" must impose its order on the Latin phrase even if this involves some mispronunciation. Of course, the reverse occurs in plainsong, where the freedom of the musical phrase depends on its following the contour of the text. Once he has "found" a "litanic motive," Stravinsky's prosodic process is the same for Latin, Russian, or French:[7]

Example 11.7. A "litanic motive" in the Coda of *Les Noces* (1914–1917, 1921–1923)

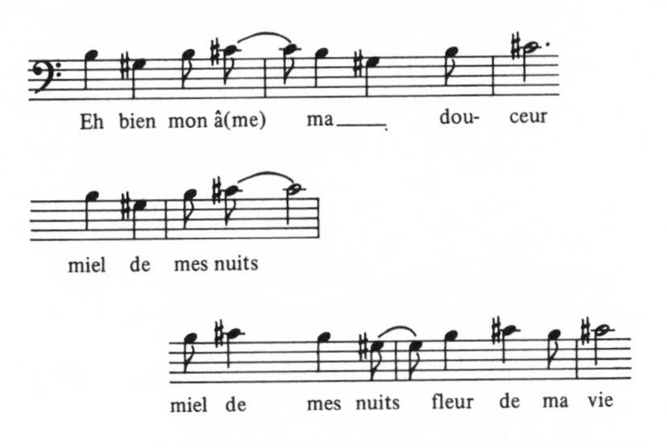

Stravinsky is always extremely careful to give clarity and prominence to the chorus. In his accompaniments, he does not double individual polyphonic parts. Or he does so only briefly to support the initial statement of a fugato (rehearsal number **5** in the second movement of the *Symphony of Psalms*), or occasionally in a homophony, to strengthen a particular accent (third movement, **11–12**) or to serve as guide to an eminently "litanic" voice (role of the D trumpet in the coda from **22** onward). Moreover, we never find straight doublings, but rather an

6. Igor Stravinsky, *An Autobiography* (New York, 1936), p. 128.

7. Messiaen uses the expression "litanic motive" to denote a motive that repeats with little variation, as in the litanies of the Catholic liturgy.

added structure with its own shape, rhythmic values, and articulations. When unaccompanied, the chorus does not sound "vulnerable," likely to sing out of tune; rather, it appears to emerge in the continuity of its own universe, its own ethereal region (second movement, **10**).

The chorus should in fact be heard as a second orchestra, having its own sound *within* the instrumental orchestra, but never doubling it. The *Threni* coda provides a good example: the orchestra is reduced to four French horns whose parts are rhythmically and melodically independent of the homophonic chorus. However, from time to time, several notes are allowed to stray in and discreetly establish points of contact between the two groups (measures 405 to the end). The same impression of interiority, of reflective tranquillity, occurs in the coda of the *Symphony of Psalms,* which is, however, more cathedral-like and beautifully proportioned than the coda of *Threni.*

These remarks bring us to the subject of the orchestra in Stravinsky's religious music. Can we in fact speak of an orchestra specific to the religious music? If so, can we define its specificities? More important, what new elements distinguish them from what we already know about the Stravinskyan orchestra, from his familiar repertory of sounds? To put it very simply, in the religious works, one finds a "ritual" approach to instrumentation, that is, one can find an archetypical use of certain sonorities. Until the 1930s, Stravinsky's instrumentation was colorful, powerful, structural, architectonic, always wonderfully appropriate, not really "ritual," except in certain pages of *The Rite* and probably in *Les Noces.* It then became both "ritual" and pragmatic in the sense of using certain instruments, chords with harmonics, and particular ways of blending timbres.

This "ritual" instrumentation will become clear when we compare works a decade apart in time—the *Symphony of Psalms,* the Mass, *Threni,* and the *Requiem Canticles:*

Symphony of Psalms: winds "by five" (but no clarinets), timpani, harp, two pianos, bass drum, strings *without* violins and violas

Mass: double wind quintet (no clarinet, no French horn)

Threni: winds "by two or three," brass *without* trumpets, timpani, percussion, celesta, harp, strings; addition of special instruments: alto bugle, sarrusophone; absence of bassoons

Requiem Canticles: four flutes, two bassoons, brass, timpani, harp, percussion, piano, celesta, strings

At times, whole families of instruments are missing. Wind instruments predominate in the orchestration. Stravinsky could have intended to form groups harmonized like an organ with superimposed doublings of four- or five-note chords (four, eight, sixteen, and even thirty-two feet), eliminating families likely to produce unwanted doublings in particular ranges. (Examples can be seen in the *Symphony of Psalms:* 4/16 in the beginning of the first movement and at **7,** 8/4 in the third movement, **11** and **26,** and 32/16/8/4 in three measures before **3** and the final C-major chord.) Or Stravinsky could have sought a medieval sonority by eliminating the "modern" instruments—clarinets and French horns—in favor of the older ones: flutes, oboes, trumpets, trombones. Or he could deliberately have selected timbres rarely used in the orchestra, such as alto clarinet, bugle, sarrusophone in *Threni,* to create a very specific color.

Stravinsky usually avoids percussion instruments of indeterminate pitch, but he gives keyboards, xylophone and metallophones included, a prominent place, especially in the later works. (Is this evidence of influence by the new generation of serial musicians?) Their use in some ways recalls the scoring of *Les Noces.* The group of two pianos-timpani-harp in the *Symphony of Psalms* becomes piano-chimes and celesta-vibraphone in the *Requiem Canticles,* but their musical role is unchanged.

The strings, with the exception of the celli and basses in the *Symphony of Psalms,* play a minor role; they are almost relegated to that of a bare outline or to being used for mixture sounds ("Lacrimosa" in the *Requiem Canticles*). These factors, through a series of meticulous and sometimes unexpected choices, a rigorous process of selection and elimination, and a supreme economy of means, together create this "ritual sound." This highly original creation is due solely to the ear of Igor Fyodorovitch, who succeeded in turning earlier skills to good account, stripping away their stylistic references and erasing any theatrical imagery.[8]

Let us turn now to the musical language itself, the shape of its homophonies, the organization of its polyphonies, of its ostinati or its melodic and rhythmic litanies, and its ornamentation. A series of comparisons will highlight the extraordinary continuity of the Stravinskyan style throughout all the transformations of his musical language. Consider the first part of the *Symphony of Psalms* and the "Exaudi" from *Requiem Canticles.* Both use the verse of a psalm beginning with the words: "Exaudi orationem meam." In the *Symphony of Psalms,* it is treated as a melodic litany on E and F:

Example 11.8. *Symphony of Psalms* (1930)

8. "It would seem that something more than theoretical and speculative thought sustained and guided I. S. It must surely be the phenomenon of his musical ear, incomparably imaginative, evocative, provocative, controlled, demanding and true at the highest level of sound perception, linked in a mysterious way to a fount of intelligence and spirituality." Pierre Souvtchinsky, "Stravinsky auprès et au loin," in *Stravinsky: Etudes et témoignages,* ed. François Lesure (Paris, 1982), pp. 11–52.

We find the embryo of a litany in the corresponding passage of the *Requiem Canticles:*

Example 11.9. *Requiem Canticles* (1965–1966)

Note the parallelism of the two structures in the progression of the incipit and in the "litanic" movement in equal rhythmic values, the similarity of the inflections, ascending and descending in the "Exaudi" regardless of the intervallic differences, and the ascending litany, two notes by two notes, on "orationem meam."

Example 11.10.

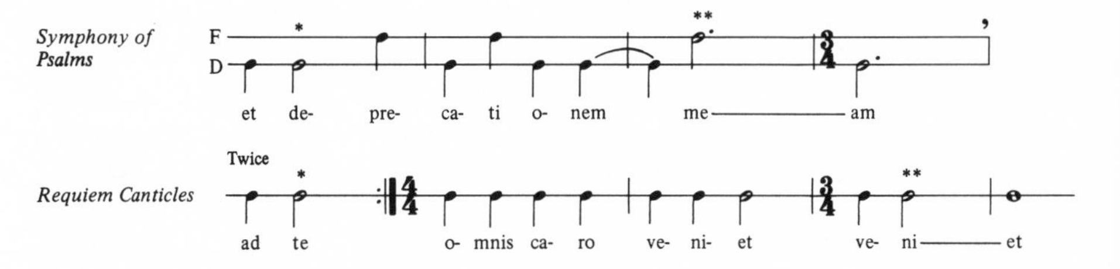

Examining the rhythm of the fragments in Example 11.10, we find, despite the difference between the literary text and the voice leading, the same elongation of the second beat (the weak beat) and the same eloquent prolongation of the penultimate value on the weak part of the measure, although it is more expressive, because longer, in the *Symphony of Psalms.* Despite differences of harmonic language, an all-pervading sense of peace and a manifest spirituality resounds through both passages.

Another, perhaps even more striking, connection can be observed between the "Sanctus" of the Mass and the "Lacrimosa" in the *Requiem Canticles.* Both examples use the same type of design. One instrument gives the "pitch"; the voice embellishes a pivot note; and the chorus, then orchestra, answer, tutti, with the same iambic rhythm (♫). In the "Lacrimosa," there is no chorus, but the rhythmic sequence between voice and orchestra unfolds in exactly the same way.

The "technical" difference between these two musical examples lies in the

Example 11.11.

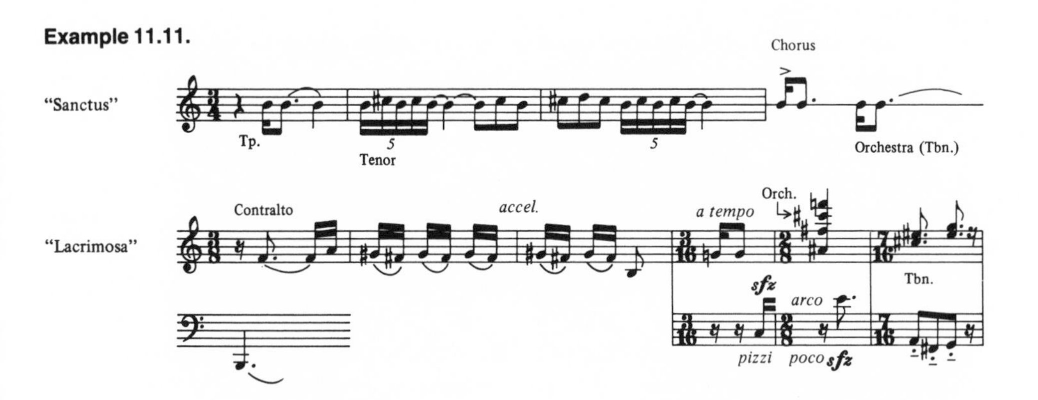

nature of the intervals. They are stepwise and diatonic in the "Sanctus" (around the playing and continued holding of the B) and more disjunct and chromatic in the "Lacrimosa" (with the playing and then removal of the B pedal). But because the dissimilar nature of the intervals is here allied to other opposing factors (accentuation, dynamics, instrumentation), it generates a fundamental difference in expression in the two passages. Open and straightforward in the "Sanctus," it becomes somber and spasmodic in the "Lacrimosa," where the impression is intensified by the rhythmic precipitation of the accelerando and the 3/16. The adoption of a neomodal language ("defective" modes) inclined Stravinsky—especially in the *Symphony of Psalms*—to use melodic litanies that, through their endless repetitions, induce an overwhelming sense of peace. But his adoption of a language whose essential nature is one of permanent variation led him in *Threni*, on the contrary, to vary the initial statement when repeating it.

Example 11.12. Melodic Litanies in *Symphony of Psalms* (1930) and *Threni* (1957–1958)

Despite apparent differences, the overall structures of the two passages in Example 11.12 are similar. Both have the same contrapuntal contour in their two principal voices, each filling the open spaces of the other. Both build the same tension toward a culminating point (arsis/thesis) and end with final repose, even though the sonorities and what one might call the emotional charge of the two passages are of a very different nature. Stravinsky clearly transfers a sense of the value of variation—variation that can be applied to any parameter, melodic, rhythmic, accented, or dynamic—from one work to the next. In the *Symphony of Psalms,* a feeling of absolute stability, eternity, is realized, but within a general cadential movement toward C major. In *Threni,* we find an almost incantatory repetition of the incipit, but within an atmosphere of pervasive anxiety created by the syncopation of the pizzicati in counterpoint with each entry of the chorus. A release of the tension comes on an a capella chord that serves as harmonic resolution:

Example 11.13. *Threni*

This same incipit treated thirty years earlier by Stravinsky probably would not have had the same exacerbated character of tension/release, for his musical language would not have been so oriented.

In referring to the Mass, we have already noted a return to medieval sonorities and practices: diaphonies (in the "Gloria"), predominance of the "open" intervals (fourths and fifths on open strings), specific instrumentation, and so forth. This practice too seems to have followed an evolution parallel to that of Stravinskyan syntax. One of its most interesting aspects is to be found in the rhythmic movement of the lines. Besides setting formulas syllabically like the verses of the "Credo," Stravinsky frequently uses the iambic or anapestic rhythms with which he was familiar, accenting the first value, and less frequently uses isochronous rhythmic patterns. Stravinsky would probably have dismissed them as too caricatural, and they are certainly outside his rhythmic style! There is no direct reproduction of musical sources five or six hundred years old, but rather a re-creation of them, filtered through the ear of an architect of twentieth-century music.

Example 11.14. Iambic and Anapestic Rhythms

Example 11.14. *continued*

Notice that even when adopting the constraining system of serially organized pitches, Stravinsky, as if to mitigate its severity, but in fact following his own behavioral patterns, continues to use repeated pitches:

Example 11.15. Use of Repeated Pitches

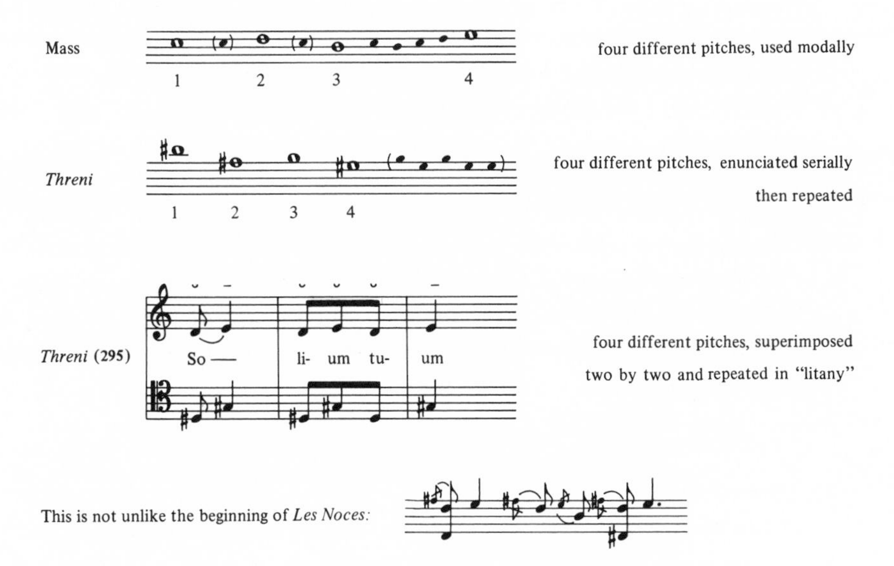

Another "archaistic" practice is the use of canon and fugato. Stravinsky turns to them not for the system they offer, but as architectural processes, inherited from the past but capable of being regenerated. In the second movement of the *Symphony of Psalms,* we find an example of fugue exposition, followed by a brief episode and the beginning of a stretto (**10**). Afterward the composer abandons fugal polyphony, retaining only certain compositional devices such as compression and rhythmic diminution. In the Mass, only one real canon, a fairly short one, appears in the "Sanctus" (Example 11.16) on the words "Pleni sunt coeli et terra"; even this is really a "false canon," insofar as the rhythms of the antecedent and its consequents are stuck back to back, not forming a true polyphony.

Example 11.16. Canon in the "Sanctus" of the Mass (1944–1948)

Stravinsky becomes more excited about canonic writing as he becomes more involved with serial technique.[9] In the third elegy of *Threni,* we find a two-voice canon ("Vetustam . . ."), a three-voice canon ("Et fregit . . ."), and a double, four-voice canon ("Recordare paupertatis . . ."). In the *Canticum Sacrum,* there is a three-voice inverted canon ("Diliges Dominum . . .") and a four-voice canon ("Ego autem . . ."). These are extremely strict forms, intended to convey noble texts, wherein Stravinsky draws upon past masters as well as upon the most rigorous of his peers.[10] It never becomes a mannerism or a technical trick. When he needs something more compact and concise, a tragic or fiery expression, as in the *Requiem Canticles,* he does not hesitate to abandon canonic models and revert to almost ritual statements, rather like certain choral sequences in *Oedipus Rex,* or to fairly free though still tight polyphonies, as in "Rex tremendae."

Whatever the transformations of Stravinsky's musical language, neotonal or modal in the *Symphony of Psalms* or in the Mass, neoserial in *Threni* or in the *Requiem Canticles,* its global sound in the ontological sense of the word maintains an impregnable unity. As we have seen, the intervals may change, the rhythmic contours may change or be tightened as they integrate the irregularities and variation principle of a serial technique. Expression and meaning will thus be modified, but not the style or the manner. Such eloquent unity of basic structure and such rich diversity of expression is one with the mystery of Stravinsky's style itself.

---

9. See Watkins's essay in this anthology.

10. I am thinking of Webern's Second Cantata, written a little more than a decade earlier.

12 The Utopian Unison

ELMER SCHÖNBERGER AND LOUIS ANDRIESSEN

POLYPHONY, harmony, unison, writing in one part, two-part writing, doublings—for centuries, these notions were sufficient to describe musical compositions. They unambiguously classified unambiguous musical structures. Twentieth-century music has forced theoreticians to redefine some of them. When redefinition resulted in vagueness because of excessive generality, entirely new notions had to be introduced. Polyphony now no longer means only a fabric of independent voices, but can also mean a fabric of independent chord sequences. Harmony has lost its general meaning and has become a special case of "density" or "field."

Stravinsky's music, too, has left Theory 101 in disarray—not only because his music inflates these notions out of proportion (Stravinsky, after all, is a composer of twentieth-century music), but also, and especially, because his music questions them. Is one-part writing by definition one-part writing? Is two-part writing by definition two-part writing? Are doublings by definition doublings?

Example 12.1. *Orpheus*, **101** + 6

In *Orpheus*, Orpheus has his Euridice back again. He dances a quiet *pas-de-deux* with her while still blindfolded. The music accompanying their steps can be seen as a portrayal of the situation on stage. This situation is dubious. Everything

Adapted from Part 2, Chapter 4 of *The Apollonian Clockwork: About Stravinsky*, orig. in Dutch, trans. Jeff Hamburg (Amsterdam, 1983).

seems to be working out fine, but the audience knows it will not work out at all. There is a one-part melody, doubled one, sometimes two, octaves lower. Then and again the doubling derails. *And* there is a one-part melody doubled one, sometimes two, octaves higher. This paradoxical musical situation asks for a paradoxical definition—parallel counterpoint. The notion of counterpoint is justifiable because if the one voice is doubling the other and the other is doubling the one, then both are independent voices and neither is a doubling (as there is no third voice that each is doubling).

The paradox of parallel counterpoint gives listeners a choice that they cannot really make. In the simplest form, the choice sounds like this:

Example 12.2. *Ebony Concerto,* **9** + 6 (only Clarinet and Trombone)

This example from the *Ebony Concerto* can be described as a melody in octaves with wrong notes. But who is playing the wrong notes, the trombonist or the clarinetist, the left hand or the right hand?

Example 12.3. Symphony in C, beginning of second movement

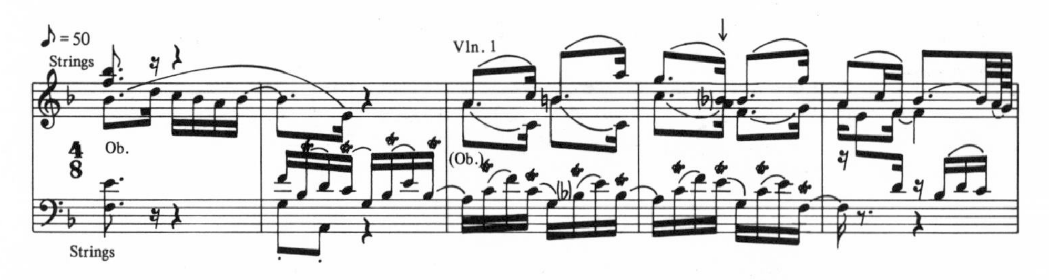

Another dilemma involves the dividing up of the parts. The second movement of the Symphony in C begins with a melody in the oboe. Two measures later the oboe is joined by the first violins. Along the way, as a result of "mistakes" in the placement of the octaves, one-part writing tends to sound like two-part writing. The character of this two-part writing is a special kind of one-part writing. In the fourth measure, the listener who chooses two-part writing gets into trouble. If there is going to be discussion about two voices, it will be difficult to make out which voice is the one and which voice is the other. In this example, made comparatively simple by the absence of voice crossings and by the recognizability of the distinct timbres, the answer seems obvious: the first violins are the one voice (always the upper voice), and the oboe is the other (always the lower voice). But as soon as we arrive at the arrow (➡), we are not so sure of ourselves anymore. Is that an "out-of-tune" prime? Then who is playing the "out-of-tune" note? Is the violin "early" with the B♭? In that case, the A in the oboe is the "right" note, making the upper voice G A B♭ G, not G B♭ B♭ G. In other words, without the voices crossing at the arrow, they nevertheless exchange functions—or do they? That is up to the listeners who might just change their minds with repeated hearings.

Stravinsky reconnoiters the border between unison and not-unison in countless ways. What often occurs is that the unison gets out of hand:

Example 12.4. *Octet,* **6**

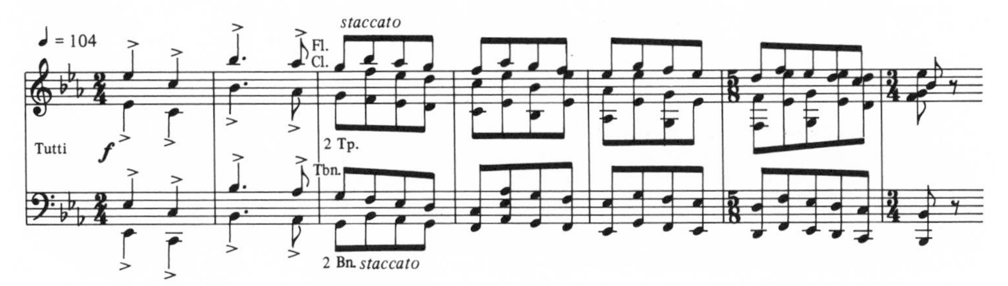

The performers really all want the same thing, but the brass players—always considered the proletarians of the orchestra—have abandoned their comrades and have formed an opposition party that yields a unison or octave every once in a while, but mostly results in seconds. The 5/8 bar (the 2/4 bar that lasts too long) is the straw that breaks the camel's back. Or was there a revolution in which the woodwinds were bested? That seems perhaps more reasonable. Not only is the sequence in the woodwinds rather insipid; they would never have arrived safely if the 5/8 bar had been a 4/8 bar. (In the *Octet,* at least two measures come out alright. There are cases where things go wrong from the start, such as rehearsal number **9** in the *Symphony of Psalms* or **19** in *Babel.* Here other voices also have the principal voice, only twice as fast. The effect is not merely of a traditional diminution; it is as if the copyist made a mistake in the tempo markings in some of the parts. But even in *Babel,* the voices that run themselves ragged just hit the dead-end sooner.) The voice leading in the example from the *Octet* is divergent; the voice leading also can be convergent:

Example 12.5. Conclusion of "Española," from Five Easy Pieces

or:

Example 12.6. Symphony in Three Movements, **63** + 3

The last example calls to mind Bach, that other great illusionist of voice leading. These measures resemble the bass in the Brandenburg Concerto, No. 6, with their quasi-two-part writing (heterophony):

Example 12.7. Brandenburg Concerto, No. 6, "Adagio," m. 27–28

and the "Allemande" from the English Suite, No. 3, with their motion:

Example 12.8. English Suite, No. 3, "Allemande," m. 10–11

But there is much more at Stravinsky's switching yard of voice leading that recalls Bach, from the opening of the Dumbarton Oaks Concerto, a two-part string theme that sounds like one-part:

Example 12.9. Beginning of the Concerto in E♭ ("Dumbarton Oaks")

to the two bassoons that trample over each other in the last movement of Symphony in Three Movements.

Example 12.10. Symphony in Three Movements, **148**

Play the example under tempo and two octaves higher, and the bassoons begin to resemble the sighing recorders of *Actus Tragicus:*

Example 12.11. *Actus tragicus,* "Sonatina," m. 7–8

Stravinsky, as well as Bach, used canonlike techniques. The slightly archaic word for canon is *catch*. The voices almost catch each other in these canons—almost, but not quite.

The unisons and octaves in Stravinsky's music start to sound like a musical utopia—much coveted, rarely reached. In his old age, after a lifetime filled with shattered octaves, unisons slipping and sliding, and doublings unraveling, Stravinsky permitted himself the luxury every so often of a "grandiose unison." But even then he seldom gave in to a perfectly concordant passage of the voices:

Example 12.12. *Agon,* m. 512–514

When the perfect consonant actually is reached, it sounds more unison than unison—it sounds not-not-unison. This not-not-unison can be considered the culmination, in the opposite direction, of the emancipation of the "wrong" note, as there it all began—with women who sing together and not together (heterophony):

Example 12.13. *Les Noces*, **115** (without orchestra)

and with musicians who let their fancy have free reign:

Example 12.14. "Marche," m. 26 from Three Easy Pieces

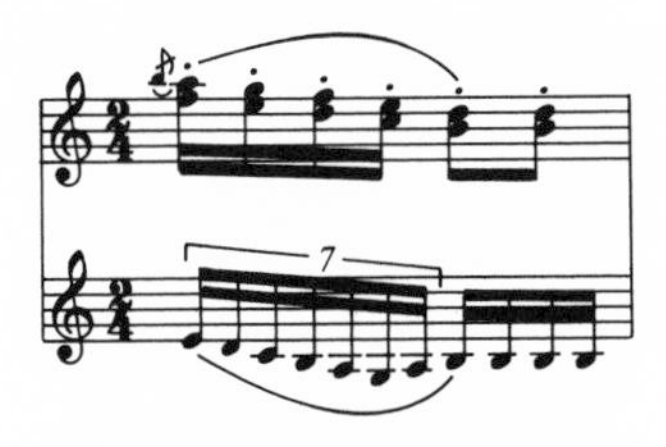

But it is more than just the emancipation of the "wrong" note. It is also the emancipation of hard-core playing around, when wrong notes become so prevalent that they become the norm.

Example 12.15. *Concertino* for String Quartet, m. 1–2

It went so far that Stravinsky could make the octave sound like a dissonance.

Compositional Practices in the Late Music

13 The Canon and Stravinsky's Late Style

GLENN WATKINS

"... anyone who has spent two minutes in the same room with I. S. has a theory about him, and a self-including story to put at the disposal of a potential biographer."

Robert Craft, *Chronicle of a Friendship*

ALTHOUGH audible canonic structures appear as early as *Fireworks* (1908), Stravinsky gave special attention to the canon in the period extending from the Cantata (1951–1952) to his last creations. Its application in original compositions, in commentary on other composers' music, and in revised versions of his earlier music invites consideration of the appeal of canonic structures to Stravinsky and their importance to his stylistic profile.

By the term "canon" I mean to define a strict and rigorously imitative form, all of whose parts "could be reduced to, and be performed from, a single written line,"[1] and to eschew expressions such as "freely canonic," which could more properly read "freely imitative." Canon so defined has a solid foundation in the history of polyphony from the thirteenth century to the present, and its position has varied from one of preeminence to that of a suspicious academic exercise. Yet no period from the Middle Ages to the present is without its examples, and among those composers whom Stravinsky admired, Machaut, Isaac, Josquin, Gesualdo, Purcell, Bach, Mozart, and Beethoven all indulged in it. Although canon may be considered more characteristic of Renaissance and Baroque than Classical and Romantic music, no picture of Schumann or Brahms, for example, would be complete without a consideration of the technique.

Although an increasing emphasis upon linear qualities in the twentieth century may have naturally favored a resubscription of canonic principles, its appearance in the works of composers of widely divergent aesthetic bases does not

1. Hans T. David, *J. S. Bach's Musical Offering* (1945; rpt. New York, 1972), p. 22. For the evolution of the term "canon," see *The New Grove Dictionary of Music and Musicians* (1980), s. v. "Canon," v. 3, p. 689, and especially Edward Lowinsky, "Music in Titian's *Bacchanal of the Adrians:* Origin and History of the *Canon per tonos,*" in *Titian, His World and His Legacy*, ed. David Rosand (New York, 1982), p. 209–14.

really explain the consistent and prominent appearance of canon in Stravinsky's late style. I do not intend to describe in detail the various canonic structures of Stravinsky's compositions following *The Rake's Progress,* but a list of the most prominent appearances of the technique will be useful.

ORIGINAL WORKS

Cantata (1951–1952)

Septet (1953)

In Memoriam Dylan Thomas (1954)

Canticum Sacrum (1955)

Agon (1953–1957)

Threni (1957–1958)

Double Canon for String Quartet: "Raoul Dufy in Memoriam" (1959)

A Sermon, a Narrative, and a Prayer (1960–1961)

REWORKING OF PRE-EXISTENT MATERIAL

Greeting Prelude (1955)

(Bach) Choral-Variations on "Vom Himmel hoch" (1955–1956)

(Gesualdo) *Tres sacre cantiones:* "Assumpta est Maria," "Da pacem Domine" (1959)

REVISED VERSIONS OF HIS EARLY WORKS

Eight Instrumental Miniatures (1962) after *Five Fingers* (Eight Very Easy Pieces) (1921)

Canon on a Russian Popular Tune (1965) on a theme from *The Firebird* (1910)

Original Works

Three categories appear in this list, preeminent among which are the original works beginning with the Cantata of 1952. The first two movements of this work, generously titled "Ricercar," "Cantus cancrizans," and "Canon," were described by Stravinsky thus:

> *The Maidens Came* is a Ricercar for soprano and instrumental quintet. I use the term *"Ricercar"* not in the sense that Bach used it to distinguish certain strict *alla breve* fugues, as for example the six-part Ricercar in the *Musical Offering,* but in its earlier designation of a composition in canonic style. In *The Maidens Came* the

canonic structure is obvious. . . . *Tomorrow will be my dancing day*. . . . is also a Ricercar in the sense that it is a canonic composition.[2]

In addition to a preoccupation with counterpoint and especially canonic manipulation, this statement betrays a "not this . . . but that" attitude that emphasizes historical models. But such distinctions create a certain confusion, for Bach never used the term "ricercar" outside the *Musical Offering*, and the only *alla breve* fugue so designated by him is the six-voice one later arranged by Webern to which Stravinsky obviously refers. In addition, while the ricercar exists as an imitative type from Willaert through Frescobaldi and Froberger to Bach, none of them is canonic.[3] But then neither are all of Stravinsky's, in spite of his claims and labels. Indeed the canons Stravinsky claims for Ricercar I are strict only with respect to pitch in the A sections, the rhythms being altered in the first one and registral changes taking place in the last. Although the B sections of Ricercar I (Example 13.1a) are genuine canons between the soprano and oboe, except for

Example 13.1. Cantata (1951–1952)

(a) "Ricercar I": Three-voice canon, direct and by inversion; registral changes at cadence.

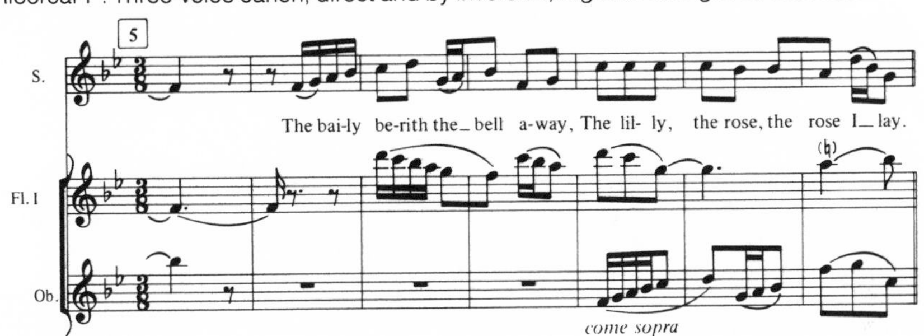

continued

2. Stravinsky's complete analysis of the work appeared in a program note for the first performance quoted in Eric Walter White, *Stravinsky: The Composer and His Works* (Berkeley and Los Angeles, 1966), pp. 428–29.

3. I am grateful to Prof. H. Colin Slim for corroborating this point.

Example 13.1. *continued*

(b) "Ricercar II": "Cantus cancrizans" presents P, R, I, RI of eleven-note series used as a basis for nine labeled "canons" that employ changes of rhythm, register, and color. Canons 1, 3, 5, 7, and 9 serve as ritornello.

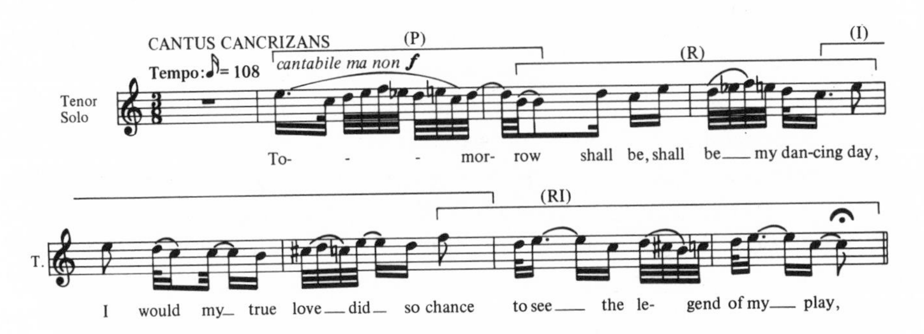

the registral changes at the cadence, in Ricercar II, pitch succession functioning as a series, as opposed to canon, becomes paramount (Example 13.1b).[4] Here nine sections are labeled "Canon," but the word should be placed in quotes for the imitations are of the pitches only, both rhythm and register being subjected to constant change. However, the idea of the pitch series as a "rule" or "precept" analogous to canon is employed in the Cantata in anything but a trivial fashion, and its role in defining the overall structure is fundamental. Stravinsky's special definition of the term "ricercar" is also in harmony with his predilection for designations with historical implications and calls to mind his use of terms like "capriccio" and "symphonies" with special connotations. Although his claim for a specifically canonic type of ricercar is historically in error, his view of the term as one both imitative and emblematic of a rigorously learned style is accurate. His feelings about the adoption of such forms is clarified as early as the *Poetics of Music*, where he announced:

> We can make use of academic forms without running the risk of becoming academic ourselves. The person who is loath to borrow these forms when he has need of them clearly betrays his weakness.[5] . . . I myself have . . . often borrowed academic attitudes with no thought of concealing the pleasure I found in them. . . . I always use academic formulas knowingly and voluntarily. I use them quite as knowingly as I would use folklore.[6]

The fact that the ricercar is essentially an instrumental form also raises questions with respect to its use by Stravinsky to describe a texted, vocal piece. Yet he had also addressed this point in the *Poetics* with the observation:

> It is customary to distinguish instrumental forms from vocal forms. . . . Basically, such distinctions constitute only artificial categories . . . each medium so readily borrows forms that were developed by other media that the mingling of styles is constant and makes discrimination impossible.[7]

Stravinsky's association of canon with ritornello designs in the Cantata (canons 1, 3, 5, 7, 9 of Ricercar II, for example, are essentially the same and used in conjunction with a noncanonic ritornello), the clear sectionalization, and a distinct color component (in Ricercar II the canons are restricted to voice, two oboes, and cello) also speak of the past as much as the future. In fact, the use of the ri-

4. The serial implications of the Cantata were first discussed by George Perle, *Serial Composition and Atonality* (Berkeley and Los Angeles, 1963), p. 37, and Donald C. Johns, "An Early Serial Idea of Stravinsky," *Music Review* 23, no. 4 (1962): 305–13.

5. Cf. Schoenberg's remarks, quoted in this essay, pp. 239–40.

6. Igor Stravinsky, *Poetics of Music*, trans. Arthur Knodel and Ingolf Dahl (Cambridge, 1947), pp. 83–84.

7. Stravinsky, *Poetics of Music*, p. 42. Yet see note 12.

tornello as a formal principle and even the employment of canon between voice and instruments can be found in the secular cantatas of the most renowned practitioner of the genre, Alessandro Scarlatti.

We have it from Klemperer, who saw Stravinsky frequently during the time of the Cantata's composition, that Bach's *Well-Tempered Clavier* was his daily fare and from Craft that Stravinsky was introduced to Webern's Quartet, Opus 22, just before writing Ricercar II. Although the association of these two composers with canon as a fundamental precept is perhaps unmatched, strictly speaking, neither of the previously-mentioned works is devoted to the art of canon. Yet both Bach's and Webern's infatuation with a rigorous species of canon, not only as a personal modus but as a historical concept, is patently demonstrable. Webern's edition of Isaac's *Choralis Constantinus*, Book II, for example, carries the following remarks in the preface to the published version of 1909:

> In the second part of his *Choralis Constantinus*, Isaac uses artful canonic devices in the greatest profusion: two-voiced canons at the unison, the fourth above and below, the fifth and the octave, or the twelfth. Then it may happen that one voice is so derived from another that, entering at the same time as the latter, it imitates it in notes of double the value or, likewise starting at the same time, transposes the other to the third above. . . . Isaac further constructs three-voiced canons, one of four voices, three double canons, and finally two crab canons . . .[8]

We may suppose that Stravinsky took his cue from Webern in expressing his fascination for Isaac about this time—an infatuation that apparently lasted a number of years.[9]

Having established the Cantata as a beachhead for contrapuntal practice in Stravinsky's late works, let us briefly consider the role of canon in the principal works of the following decade.

With *In Memoriam Dylan Thomas* of 1954, the composer once more introduces the term "canon" in the score, this time in the title "Dirge-Canons" that frames the central song. But the designation invites scrutiny in light of our discussion of the Cantata, and indeed analysis reveals that the principal technique at work is that of a five-note pitch series. With the exception of trombones I, II, and IV in the first statement of the "Prelude" (Example 13.2a), the variable rhythms of these "canons" identify them as pitch canons only (see Example 13.2b, "Postlude"). As

---

8. Hans Moldenhauer, *Webern* (New York, 1979), p. 85.

9. Stravinsky wrote to Nadia Boulanger in a letter of 12 May 1957: "I never received the microfilm (Isaac-Webern) that you promised to send through Georges Sachs, who was supposed to come to the U.S. at Easter. I have heard nothing from her." What could this have been other than a microfilm of Webern's edition of the second book of the *Choralis Constantinus* published in *DTOe* in 1909, and if so, why would he have been after Boulanger to provide a microfilm when a copy undoubtedly resided in the music library at nearby UCLA? See *Stravinsky: Selected Correspondence*, vol. 1, ed. Robert Craft (New York, 1982), p. 259.

Example 13.2. *In Memoriam Dylan Thomas* (1954)

(a) "Dirge-Canons (Prelude)": Pitch-canons based on five-note series; opening theme of Trombones I, II, IV yields genuine canons, remainder are pitch-canons.

(b) "Dirge-Canons (Postlude)": Pitch-canons only on a five-note series. B section ritornello of Prelude becomes A section; strings and trombones exchange roles.

in the Cantata, three features confirm early habits that were to remain important for the years ahead: (1) the use of ritornello as a formal device, (2) the use of immiscible colors (strings and trombones) as a structural component, (3) serial imitation (shall we say "canon"?) as an architectural principle.

The canonic markings in the score of the "Prelude" were, according to Stravinsky, an oversight: "In correcting the proofs I forgot to erase in the Prelude these brackets left over from my final sketches where they were put *throughout* the work. . . ."[10] When one recalls, however, the canonic designation and the "Cantus cancrizans" bracketing in the Cantata as well as the presentation of the various pitch rows above the staff in the "Gigue" of the Septet, where the printing

Example 13.3. *Canticum Sacrum* (1955)

(a) "Caritas": Three-voice vocal canons direct and by inversion; registral changes; trumpet-bassoon double note values, introduce "Klangfarben" element. Entrance levels: C, C♯, D, D♯.

10. Quoted by White, *Stravinsky*, p. 440, who in a footnote says it appeared first in Hans Keller, "In Memoriam Dylan Thomas: Stravinsky's Schoenbergian Technique," *Tempo* (Spring 1955).

Example 13.3. *continued*

(b) "Fides": Twelve-note canon based on preceding choral unison series analogous to "Cantus cancrizans" in Cantata; instrumental canon in augmented values (equal dotted half-notes).

format looks back to the *Five Fingers* as much as forward to any serial adventure—all of this without later disavowal—one is inclined to believe that all such markings are rightly interpreted as overt methodological advertisements.

Examples from the first twelve-tone works, *Agon, Canticum Sacrum, Threni,* and *A Sermon, a Narrative, and a Prayer,* presented in Examples 13.3 through 13.6, provide evidence of a continuing interest in the idea of canon. To summarize, in both labeled and nonlabeled canons of the decade, there is a range of structures from classically defined canon to those that may be classified only as pitch-canons, rhythm-canons, or pitch-rhythm canons with registral freedom. The progressive buildup in the number of voices in *Threni* (Example 13.5) suggests a compendium analogous to numerous canon sequences in Bach's late works; the simultaneous statement in different rhythms (Example 13.6a) or proportionally augmented rhythms (Example 13.3a) recalls Webern's description of Isaac's canons and Stravinsky's own reference to a type of High Renaissance mensuration

Example 13.4. *Agon* (1953–1957)

(a) "Gailliarde" (two female dancers): Two-voice canon, registral changes, free cadence.

Example 13.4. *continued*

(b) "Bransle Simple" (two male dancers): Classic two-voice canon between trumpets with freely composed cadence for woodwinds.

canon in Josquin (Example 13.6b). The use of a solo voice, labeled "Cantus cancrizans," prior to the presentation of the canons in Ricercar II of the Cantata; the use of unison chorus as an introduction to the canons on this material in *Canticum Sacrum;* and the appearance of a "Monodia" as a preface to the sequence of two-, three-, and four-voice canons in *Threni* are not only analogous to each other but suggestive of canon as an idea that is reducible to and performable from a single written line. Thus, in a variety of ways, Stravinsky acknowledges not only the classic canons of Josquin and Bach, but also the procedures of the serialists. His rhythmic canons (Example 13.6c) may remind us of contemporaneous developments in the music of Messiaen and Boulez. Or we may see in them a reflection of medieval isorhythms, or, as he claimed for the barless canons of *Threni* (Example 13.5), a reference to the motet style of Josquin. At the same time, Stravinsky's own voice can be heard in his formalistic deployment of canon as ritornello, rondo, and reprise, or, using different material but maintaining canonic structure, as frame promoting audible symmetricalities (as in the flanking virtues of the central movement of *Canticum Sacrum*).

Example 13.5. *Threni* (1957–1958). "Monodia" presentation of twelve-note series before canons analogous to Cantata (Example 13.1b) and *Canticum Sacrum* (Example 13.3b). Canons are labeled, strict, and progressive. Stravinsky claimed that the lack of bar lines mirrored Josquin motet style.

Example 13.5. *continued*

Example 13.6.

(a) *Threni*: "Quomodo sedet"; simultaneous presentation of same pitches in different rhythms. Serves as refrain.

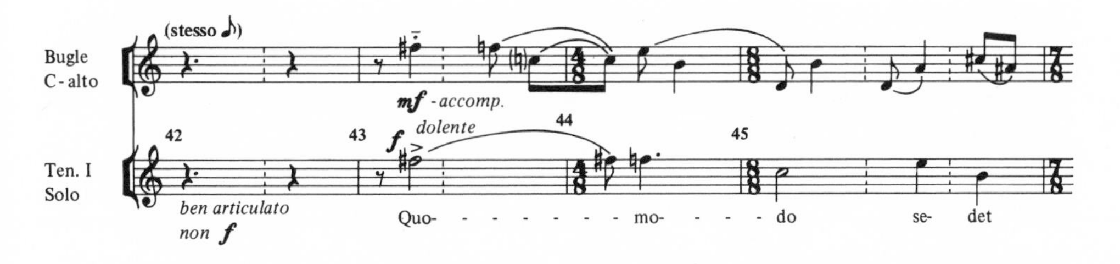

(b) *Missa l'homme armé super voces musicales:* "Agnus Dei II"; mensuration canon mentioned by Stravinsky with respect to rhythmic polyphony of *Movements.*

continued

Example 13.6. *continued*

(c) *A Sermon, a Narrative, and a Prayer:* "Prayer" opening, direct rhythm canon

Reworking of Pre-Existent Material and Revised Versions of His Early Works

In the reworking of pre-existent material during the 1950s, Stravinsky confirms his addiction to canon. In the setting of the (Bach) Choral-Variations on "Vom Himmel hoch," composed to accompany the premiere performance of *Canticum Sacrum,* we can spot most clearly his multiple affections for the device. By choosing one of the archetypal canonic sets by the greatest contrapuntal practitioner of all time, Stravinsky not only bows to his model but introduces personal habits of old as well as those of his contemporaries: the former in his introduction of a canon at the seventh in the third variation, which is already a canon "alla settima" (Example 13.7b), the latter through a Webernian color component visible throughout the work (Example 13.7a). Stravinsky's endorsement of *Klangfarben* technique in lieu of his former preference for immiscible colors in the presentation of canon is redolent of Webern's treatment of Bach's six-voice ricercar from *The Musical Offering*.[11]

Beyond this color component, something of Stravinsky's harmonic manner, particularly his preference for seconds and sevenths observable from his earliest

Example 13.7. (Bach) Choral-Variations on "Vom Himmel hoch" (1955–1956)

(a) "Klangfarben" elements

continued

11. This coloristic attitude was to reappear later in a noncanonic context in *Monumentum pro Gesualdo* (1960) and suggests its appeal as a modus of commentary on pre-existent material.

Example 13.7. *continued*

(b) Added canon at seventh in Bach's canon "alla settima"; color and registral changes

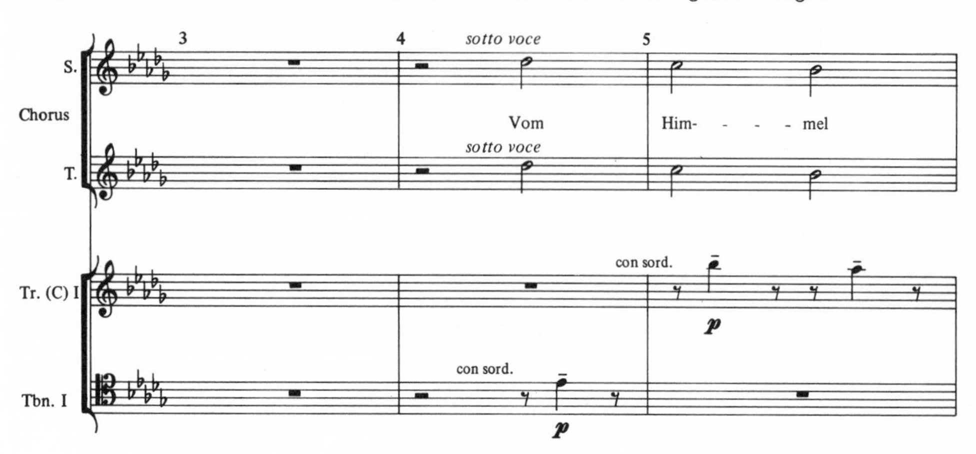

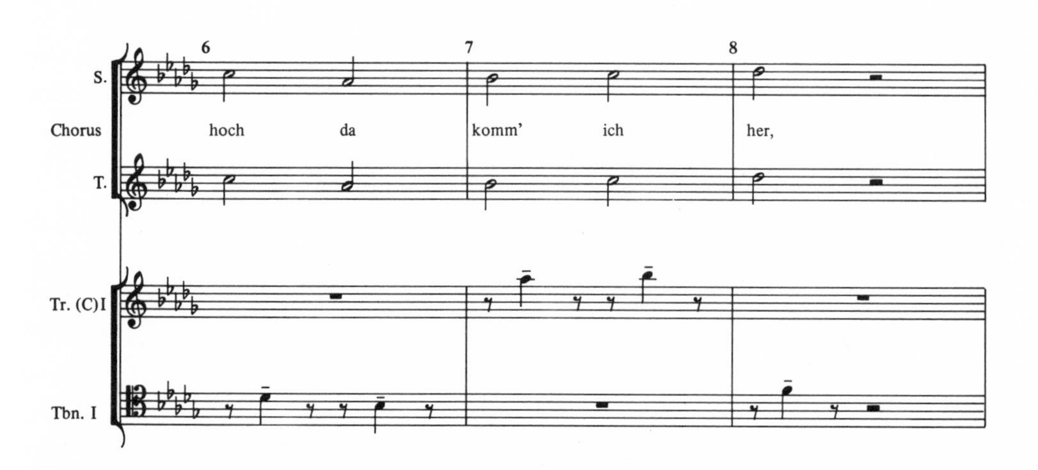

ballets to the harmonization of the "Vom Himmel hoch" chorale (Example 13.8a), can also be seen in his 1959 commentary on Gesualdo's two canonic motets, where his only task was to supply a missing bass line.

Stravinsky had already added the missing bass part to Gesualdo's "Illumina nos" in 1956 for possible inclusion with the *Canticum Sacrum* premiere. In preparing the entire collection of 1603 from whence it came for publication as part of the composer's *Opera omnia,* I encountered canonic indications in the motets "Da pacem Domine" and "Assumpta est Maria"—unique examples of canon in

Example 13.8.

(a) (Bach) Choral-Variations on "Vom Himmel hoch" (1955–1956) Stravinsky's harmonization adds non-Bachian sevenths and seconds (*).

(b) (Gesualdo) "Da pacem Domine" (1959): Stravinsky's bass creates non-Gesualdine sevenths and seconds (*).

continued

Example 13.8. *continued*

(c) (Gesualdo) "Assumpta est Maria" (1959): Same as (b) above.

Gesualdo's music. I conveyed my enthusiasm at once. The following excerpts of letters from Craft to me suggest the genesis of Stravinsky's final contribution:

> Hollywood, California
> June 19, 1959
>
> What exciting news about the strict canon motets. Since there is only one part missing in two of these pieces would you care to try to complete them—or shall I try—or shall I ask Stravinsky? I would so much like to have these pieces for the recording.

I had completely forgotten until I recently reread this correspondence that I did, indeed, complete the canonic motets. In retrospect, I cannot imagine having had the nerve—nor did I save copies of my solutions. However, I am sure they were "academic," with appropriate attention paid to matters of dissonance control. Nevertheless, the following appears in a note from Craft of 1 August 1959:

> Stravinsky wouldn't look at the motets at first because he was finishing his *Movements for Piano and Orchestra* or, rather, adding a fifth movement, but now he has seen them, and pronounced your solutions good, and won't tamper with them.

Hollywood, California
August 16, 1959

> I'm delighted you will complete the 6-part motet book. . . . It is still possible that Stravinsky will add a voice to the two canon pieces—send him directly (not through me) a copy of each one, but on transparencies, so he can make his own copy there without copying the whole out—to Hotel Bauer Grunwald, Venice—hold for arrival Sept. 15. He will be in a wonderful mood—he always is when he arrives in Venice—and I can guarantee he will add the missing line.

Venice
September 27, 1959

> Stravinsky got your letter—has completed both motets now. . . . The 2nd motet, too, becomes rather dissonant—more S. than Ges.[12]

Examples 13.8b and c, of which only the bass line is by Stravinsky, verify Craft's observations regarding Stravinsky's contribution (the asterisks indicate crucial dissonance points). As with the (Bach) "Vom Himmel hoch" Variations, however, it takes a careful listener to identify the thrust of his musical commentary. The original motets are not chromatic and thus do not sound like familiar Gesualdo, and Stravinsky fails to introduce any notable degree of rhythmic spice. But the diatonicism (Stravinsky introduces nary a sharp or flat outside the orbit of Gesualdo's upper parts) and the dissonance factors (a plethora of accented seconds and sevenths in both motets totally outside Gesualdo's vocabulary) are traceable throughout Stravinsky's career. Listening to these works, one easily hears Stravinsky's new bass while Gesualdo's canons disappear, like those in Josquin's "Faulte d'argent," in the inner voices.

I was to have a second brush with Stravinsky's involvement with canon within a year. Having written early in 1961 that, lacking any original organ works by Stravinsky, I proposed to arrange a group of pieces from the *Five Fingers* for that instrument, I received a note on 17 January 1961 in which Craft indicated that

> Mr. S. says he trusts you to make a good arrangement of the little pieces . . . but he won't add anything.

As it happened, the scenario for the Gesualdo motets was to be repeated—Stravinsky eventually did "add something," including canons, but not in a ver-

12. Although not directed to the question of canon, the following communication from Craft of 1 March 1960 caught me standing up: "The big news I have, however, is that I. S. has just completed a *Gesualdo Monumentum*—all unbeknownst to me—are you sitting down . . . instrumentations of certain madrigals with additions. I haven't seen or heard it yet, but he says it's the most difficult thing he ever did, and no less than a 'definition of what is vocal and what instrumental.' " See Stravinsky's remarks regarding distinctions between vocal and instrumental forms, p. 221.

sion for organ. A further entreaty in a letter of 14 February 1961 to write a totally new work for organ fell on deaf ears, so I returned to the idea of refurbishing the *Five Fingers*. Before I could send him my version for organ, however, I was informed that Stravinsky had transformed them into the *Eight Instrumental Miniatures*. Not only had he exchanged the monochrome palette of his early piano pieces for an instrumental ensemble, but he had reworked the material in various ways among which the employment of canon played a prominent part. Number 1 of the set (Example 13.9) is illustrative: the opening now simultaneously presents the inversion of the principal melody; the middle section has a canon between oboe and horn; and the reprise is a third-voice canon between two oboes and bassoon over a free voice in the horn. None of these canonic features was anywhere implied in the originals. A similar elaboration occurs in the canon between the two oboes in number 7 from the same set. Hearing these pieces in their new guise at the premiere in Toronto, 29 April 1962, I felt they had found a new home and altogether abandoned my organ transcriptions based on the originals.

Example 13.9. *Eight Instrumental Miniatures*, No. 1 (1962)

(a) Oboes and bassoons move simultaneously by inversion
(b) Oboes and horn imitate by inversion
(c) Three-voice "strict" canon between oboes and bassoon (n.b. *)
(d) J. S. Bach, Two-Part Invention in D minor, m. 28

Example 13.9. *continued*

Stravinsky and Canon Prior to the Cantata

Given his early inclination toward counterpoint and a capacity for writing canons as early as *Fireworks* (1908), Stravinsky's neoclassicism would lead one to expect far more use of this technique. However, a perusal of the works written between 1920 and 1950 reveals that, while imitation and fugue are common features, works that employ canon in any significant way are relatively rare. Despite all of Stravinsky's pronouncements during this time to the effect that "My freedom thus consists in moving about within the narrow frame that I have assigned myself for each one of my undertakings," or "Let us take the best example: the fugue. . . . Doesn't the fugue imply the composer's submission to rules?", the canon fails to appear as an embodiment of such sentiments in any recurrent fashion.[13]

The decade of the 1920s, was, as all students of the period know, a time that saw the apparent division of the musical world into two camps centering around Stravinsky and Schoenberg. Although at the opening of the decade it was not clear that such a schism was destined to develop, by 1924–1925, the dualism was already firmly established, as can be seen from the following chronology.[14]

20 July 1924: Schoenberg's *Serenade* premiered (Donaueschingen)

25 July 1925: Stravinsky's Sonata premiered (Donaueschingen)

7 September 1925: Schoenberg's *Serenade* (Venice-ISCM Festival)

8 September 1925: Stravinsky's Sonata (Venice-ISCM Festival)

9 September 1925: Stravinsky completes *Serenade en la* (Venice)

31 December 1925: Schoenberg completes *Drei Satiren* (Vienna)

The chronology is dramatic and the events of early September 1925, pivotal—Stravinsky and Schoenberg placed back to back with their newest wares in Venice and writing works whose titles suggest something of a collision course. Schoenberg's *Satires,* written shortly thereafter, sealed the relationship for the remainder of his life, and in the preface that accompanied its publication, he left no doubt as to his sentiments. The text of the second satire, of course, includes the reference to "kleine Modernsky" all dressed up in his wig and looking just like Papa Bach.

Even more important for the present discussion is the fact that his satire on Stravinsky was written in the form of a mirror canon in the old clefs. As if to affirm his point, Schoenberg titled his third satire "Die Neue Klassizismus," and he rounded off the entire set with a set of mirror canons also in the old clefs and all in C major. The thrust of the Opus 28 set is therefore two pronged: (1) The adoption of the older contrapuntal techniques is a game that any respectable composer can play. (2) Lest anyone think that atonal canons are easier to write than tonal ones, Schoenberg hastens to illustrate his canonic prowess in tonal surroundings as well.[15]

The last piece of the appendix to Opus 28 is a canon dedicated to George Bernard Shaw on his seventieth birthday and, with the title "Legitimation als

13. Stravinsky, *Poetics of Music,* pp. 65, 76.

14. I am grateful to Scott Messing for bringing this chronology into focus. See Stein's essay in this anthology for further information.

15. In the preface to the Appendix itself, which includes the tonal canons, Schoenberg confesses that his purpose was to answer would-be critics and to show "That someone who wrote the present (twelve-tone) compositions does not absolutely have to have things made easy for him in that way, and that even with seven tones he can manage to produce a good deal that is, if not highly valued, at least counted difficult." See Willi Reich, *Schoenberg,* trans. Leo Black (London, 1971), p. 155.

Canon," it rounds off the set as a compendium of canonic writing with diverse messages. That Stravinsky smarted from Schoenberg's attack is attested to by a comment many years later in *Conversations*: ". . . in 1925 he [Schoenberg] wrote a nasty verse about me (though I almost forgive him, for setting it to such a remarkable mirror canon)." The verb "forgive" is in the present tense (1959). What may be a more nearly contemporaneous reaction can be found in an article titled "Avertissement" ["A Warning"] that appeared in *The Dominant* of December 1927.[16]

In *Von Heute auf Morgen* and *Moses and Aaron,* which immediately followed the *Satires,* canon served for Schoenberg two principal functions—to satirize and to moralize or pay homage, but not as a routine accessory to his use of the series. To these, one might add a third purpose, implied by the other two: to demonstrate his craft, perhaps as a recompense for his almost total lack of formal music training (a matter over which he was acutely sensitive). This judgment is borne out in the numerous tonal canons of the period, many written in the old clefs and frequently carrying texts in the manner of a puzzle canon that provides the clue to the resolution of a single notated voice.[17] That Schoenberg frequently felt a private anxiety over the results of his tonal canons is attested to by scattered remarks written in the margins of his scores. Number 7 (1934) in Rufer's listing contains the note, "Sick two days, can write nothing better today"; number II (1933), "I hope that all these canons are not as ghastly as these two, but I fear so. It is unbelievably difficult to achieve even this much"; and finally, in number 16 from 1936, the simple judgment: "Poor."

Schoenberg addressed the issue of canon in the works of the neoclassicists as early as 1931 in an article entitled "Linear Counterpoint" wherein he decried their writing of toccatas *à la Handel* with their motor rhythms, their assumed "cantata tone," and their favoring of

> canons in fifteenth-century style, or inexact ones . . . and a new imitative style . . . which I had to call "imitation-imitation." . . . One hardly need waste words on the canons—they bear witness

16. White, *Stravinsky,* appendix A, no. 3. In a letter of 30 September 1927 to Lifar detailing a visit he had just paid to Stravinsky in Nice, Diaghilev wrote: "The Adagio *(pas d'action)* has a broad theme very germane to us today; it runs concurrently in four different tempos and yet, generally speaking, the harmony is most satisfactory (see White, *Stravinsky,* p. 303). The passage presents the main theme in canon in the interior voices while it appears simultaneously in augmentation in the top and in diminution in the bass. Shades of Renaissance mensuration canons? A potent though brief hint of canonic prowess? Although this short passage is probably not a direct response to Schoenberg, Diaghilev's citation of it while the work was still in progress indicates that the composer must have pointed it out to him and with some pride.

17. As early as 1922, Schoenberg had written a "4-voice mirror- and clef-canon in Netherlands style," which suggests evidence of his association with Webern—a point confirmed in the dedication of a canon for the jubilee of the Concertgebouw in 1928: "For truly Netherlandish arts the undersigned can thank you only with imitated ones." See Josef Rufer, *The Works of Arnold Schoenberg* (London, 1962), p. 102.

> to the most utter ignorance, so far as understanding the essence of contrapuntal composition is concerned. . . . What could the other parts, the accompanying parts do? Imitate—inexactly, like the stuff found in junk shops.[18]

Later in his article titled "Composition with Twelve Tones (I)" of 1941, Schoenberg left no doubt as to his feelings about canons in twelve-tone music. Speaking of the canonic structure of the Trio to his own Minuet in the Suite, Opus 25, he stated:

> The possibility of such canons and imitations, and even fugues and fugatos, has been overestimated by analysts of this style. Of course, for a beginner it might be as difficult to avoid octave doubling here as it is difficult for the poor composers to avoid parallel octaves in the "tonal" style. But while a "tonal" composer still has to lead his parts into consonances or catalogued dissonances, a composer with twelve independent tones apparently possesses the kind of freedom which many would characterize by saying: "everything is allowed." "Everything" has always been allowed to two kinds of artists: to masters on the one hand, and to ignoramuses on the other. However, the meaning of composing in imitative style here is not the same as it is in counterpoint. It is only one of the ways of adding a coherent accompaniment, or subordinate voices, to the main theme, whose character it thus helps to express more intensively.[19]

In the second part of the same article from circa 1948, he presses the point in what proves to be the conclusion of the essay:

> It is quite easy to repeat a basic set in one or more voices over and over again. There is no merit in writing canons of two or more voices. . . . I believe canonic or other imitation should serve only in order to base accompanying voices . . . on a more intimate relation to the main voice. Even the writing of whole fugues is a little too easy under these circumstances. Composing of these forms in which the highest achievement has already been reached by composers whose form of expression was that of contrapuntal combinations—composing of these forms should only be undertaken for some special reason. For instance, if a composer feels he must calm down a sort of nostalgic longing for old-time beauty; or because in the course of a huge work—an opera, an oratorio, a cantata, etc., one of the parts must be in old style. There are certainly few reasons which might oblige a composer to compete with those *hors-concours* achievements of such great masters, whose native language was counterpoint.[20]

---

18. Arnold Schoenberg, *Style and Idea,* ed. Leonard Stein (London, 1975), pp. 292–93. Schoenberg's use of the word "junk" may have been a conscious reference to the *Merz* ("junk") style of Kurt Schwitters (1887–1948), which was flourishing at precisely this time.

19. Ibid., p. 235.

20. Ibid., pp. 248–49.

In the period 1928–1931, following Schoenberg's *Satires* and contemporaneous with his essay "Linear Counterpoint," canon per se is only occasionally evident in the works of Stravinsky, but fugal sections achieve a notable prominence in such works as the *Capriccio* (1928–1929), the *Symphony of Psalms* (1930), and the Concerto for Two Solo Pianos (1931–1935), which in its last movement employs a fugue by inversion modeled directly after the concluding movement of Beethoven's Opus 110. In the "Eglogue I" of his *Duo concertant* (1931–1932), however, Stravinsky composed an extended and genuinely canonic prelude between violin and piano that could easily have filled Franck with envy and that in its lack of bar lines looks forward to Stravinsky's remarks concerning the nonaccentual quality of the canons in *Threni* and their relation to the metric world of Josquin. The fashion in which the two instruments exchange roles as Dux and Comes is illustrated in Example 13.10.

The only *canon d'occasion* from the period 1930–1950, and the first one since his Canon for Two Horns of 1917, is for Nadia Boulanger on her sixtieth birthday

Example 13.10. *Duo concertant* (1931–1932). "Eglogue I": Canonic prelude with reversal of Dux and Comes

in 1947. Attempts to emphasize the canonic aspect of Stravinsky's technical arsenal elsewhere during this time have led periodically to exaggerated claims about works where its presence might be suspected (the Mass and the Sonata for Two Pianos in particular). Contrarily, there have been oversights where its appearance was unanticipated: the prime example may be found in *The Rake's Progress,* written just prior to the Cantata. Tom's opening aria provides evidence not only of the composer's canonic prowess but of his concern for projecting such structures within a clearly defined formal plan. Here the formal division (A B C A B′) is articulated by the presence of a strict canon between tenor and answering bassoon in the opening A and, reversing the role of Dux and Comes, between instruments and answering tenor in its reprise (Example 13.11).

Although a conspicuous use of canon appears in Stravinsky's neoclassical valedictory, the absence of extended canon in the remainder of the work suggests it functions at a localized level without the larger formal consequences of the im-

Example 13.11. *The Rake's Progress* (1948–1951). Tom's Aria, Act I, scene 1. Form ABCAB'; at reprise of "A" Dux and Comes reverse.

Stravinsky: "Since it is not by merit, We rise or we fall . . ."

Schoenberg: "There is no merit in writing canons of two or more voices." (c. 1948)

mediately ensuing Cantata and *In Memoriam Dylan Thomas*.[21] Yet between the completion of *The Rake* in April 1951 and its premiere in September, Schoenberg died on July 12. Although the canonic structures of the Cantata and *In Memoriam Dylan Thomas* would seem to spell the coda to the neoclassical period and at the same time reflect his new interest in Webern-Isaac, Stravinsky may also have been addressing, on the eve of Schoenberg's passing, the most potent and direct challenge that Schoenberg ever laid at his door, namely, the triple-pronged indictment of the *Satires* whose focus was canon, tonality, and the series.[22]

Conclusion

Why did both Schoenberg and Stravinsky pay such circumspect attention to the question of imitative forms, and canon in particular, at some point in their careers? There appears to be a complex of reasons. For Schoenberg, the loss of a tonal base without a compensating set of guidelines for harmony virtually invalidated the idea of canon as the supreme emblem of craft that it had historically enjoyed. Arguments that the harmonic realm was guided by Schoenberg's attention to factors of combinatoriality relate primarily to matters of pitch redundancy and not to classic relations of consonance-dissonance formation and resolution that are fundamental to the construction of tonal canons. At the same time, the attention paid to the construction of twelve-tone sets with special hexachordal properties in conjunction with various inverted and retrograde formations (all possessing classic associations with modes of canonic manipulation) may be seen in part as an attempt to confect an analogy to the idea of canon viewed as a supreme demonstration of contrapuntal-harmonic control. Schoenberg's choice of canon to satirize the neoclassicists in his Opus 28 and his pointed discussion of canonic technique in the preface to that collection (as well as in essays from 1928, 1931, 1941, and 1948) help us understand the decidedly limited role for canon in his early twelve-tone works and his disclaimer regarding its appropriateness. Yet his continuing preoccupation with tonal canons throughout these years clearly points to a sense of loss for the serial composer.

Stravinsky's earliest poststudent forays into canon and imitative counter-

21. In spite of the brevity of such occurrences elsewhere in *The Rake*, Stravinsky's awareness of and satisfaction in such constructions is dramatized by the following: "It was a pleasure to share Stravinsky's own delight in his handiwork (*The Rake's Progress*). At the beginning of the C-minor aria in the second act, where there is a short imitative passage in the orchestra, Stravinsky nudged me and whispered proudly, 'canon.' " Ralph Kirkpatrick, "Recollections of Two Composers," *Yale Review* 71 (Summer 1982): 637.

22. In support of this theory, see Vera Stravinsky and Robert Craft, *Stravinsky in Pictures and Documents* (New York, 1978), pp. 411, 421, 423.

point not unexpectedly confirm the solidity of his training. The adoption of canon and fugue after 1920 carried a neoclassical overtone, but their limited and localized application suggests the composer's caution in relying too heavily upon pro forma "fugues with subjects at least thirty-two bars long," as he deprecatingly spoke of Hindemith's music and later of his own *Symphony of Psalms*.[23] Perhaps Stravinsky realized that, in spite of a demonstrable preference for certain vertical collections and an abiding tonal inclination, his harmonic-contrapuntal vocabulary lacked a rigorous definition for the control of dissonance. By this I do not mean to suggest the absence of a describable harmonic language or attention to the question of voice leading, only the absence of a metrically defined consonance-dissonance relationship that historically has lain at the heart of the canonic challenge. The acerbic use of a freely dissonating yet diatonic language, which Slonimsky dubbed "pandiatonicism" as early as 1937, made canon virtually no more difficult to employ than in Schoenberg's serial terrain.[24] At the same time, passages such as bar 28 of Bach's two-part invention in D minor (Example 13.9d), which Dahlhaus suggests "would be absurd if it were not heard as an embellishment of the chord of A minor,"[25] can stand as a precedent for Stravinsky's own dissonating but tonally directed canons such as we find in Examples 13.9, 13.10, and 13.11.

Stravinsky's later guardedness with respect to the idea of canon in the works of those for whom he had a newly won admiration is pointed:

> Even Webern, having allowed the canon in the first movement of the Quartet, Opus 22, to become too overt, cannot save us from the impression that we are following a too protracted game of tag.[26]

Why then was Stravinsky drawn to the technique in the 1950s in a way he never was during the neoclassical years? The dramatically increased attention to canon in his last works comes at a time of both consolidation and expansion—the consolidation of the contrapuntal techniques of the period 1920–1950 and the expansion of his horizons to accommodate many of the propositions of the serialists. That Stravinsky saw in the series a technical challenge comparable to earlier contrapuntal ones he made clear when he stated:

> The rules and restrictions of serial writing differ little from the rigidity of the great contrapuntal schools of old. . . . The serial technique I use impels me to greater discipline than ever before.[27]

---

23. Igor Stravinsky and Robert Craft, *Memories and Commentaries* (New York, 1960), pp. 117–18.
24. Nicolas Slonimsky, *Music Since 1900*, 4th ed. (New York, 1971), p. xxii.
25. *The New Grove Dictionary*, s.v. "Counterpoint, #15, Bach," v. 4, p. 847.
26. Igor Stravinsky and Robert Craft, *Expositions and Developments* (New York, 1962), p. 124.
27. Igor Stravinsky and Robert Craft, *Conversations with Stravinsky* (New York, 1959), p. 22.

Stravinsky's invocation of canon to perform a central role in effecting a synthesis was a masterstroke. The familiar dictum from the *Poetics* that "my freedom will be so much the greater . . . the more narrowly I limit my field of action and the more I surround myself with obstacles" is once again put into play.[28] Such a synthetic and retrospective compendium of uses meshes naturally with the seemingly effortless but virtuosic resolution of compositional problems by the artist in old age.

The retrospective and technical aspect apparent in Stravinsky's use of canon in his last years is manifest in the late style of numerous artists throughout history. We are reminded in this regard of Bach's interest in canon, which was at its highest in his final years, as well as the "conscious return to Renaissance ideals" in the fourteen canons on the bass part of the *Goldberg Variations*, *The Musical Offering*, the canonic variations on "Vom Himmel hoch," and *The Art of Fugue*.[29] Bach's retrospective endorsement of the *stile antico* in his late masterworks is patently self-conscious. The same claim may fairly be made of Beethoven's application of inversion as a prominent structural device signaled in the title of the fugue of his sonata, Opus 110, and in the revival of crab motion in the final fugue of the *Hammerklavier Sonata*, Opus 106. Both are from the composer's late style and signal the beginning of a preoccupation with canon, of which some three dozen examples come from the last decade of his life.[30]

Similarly, Stravinsky's invocation of canon as an emblem of craft blends with the idea of canon as both neoclassical and serial device. If it was also the natural agent for the recognition of a new influence, that of Anton Webern, this is perhaps most demonstrable in Stravinsky's occasional instrumental colorings and in their common veneration of the masters of the High Renaissance and Bach. Contrarily, for Webern, canonic principles served for the rigorous construction of the series, "which has itself assumed the function of 'rule' or 'precept' by which the composition unfolds."[31] This was not true of Stravinsky's approach to the series.

But Webern's use of canon also carried its own models from the remote past, and Stravinsky's acknowledgment of Webern simultaneously acknowledges those models, many of whom had been his own. The prominence Stravinsky accorded Webern gave the impression of a rapprochement between two principal styles of the first half of the twentieth century. The point was not obliquely made and in itself seemed to sound a note of reconciliation. From Stravinsky's point of view, however, the acknowledgment of Webern did not represent a capitulation so much as it confirmed a lifelong commitment to synthesis. Stravinsky, whose historical sense was acute, no doubt understood that the compatibility of the canon with the series made it a natural agent both for the dissolution of old

28. Stravinsky, *Poetics of Music*, p. 68.

29. *The New Grove Dictionary*, s.v. "J. S. Bach," v. 1, p. 817.

30. *The New Grove Dictionary*, s.v. "Beethoven," v. 2, p. 386.

31. *The New Grove Dictionary*, s.v. "Canon," v. 3, p. 693.

boundaries and for a technical reconciliation with powerful historical implications. A composer always in search of rules whereby he might play the game, Stravinsky in the 1950s found in canon a wedge to the future as well as a bridge to the past. As with all stylizations, a source is acknowledged and a license is taken. In the interpretation, the fingerprints of a master are revealed.

14 Order, Symmetry, and Centricity in Late Stravinsky

MILTON BABBITT

WERE I, inhibitedly aware of the inceptually festive character of symposia and the particularly celebrative function of this symposium, thereby to feel defensively paranoid in my choice of a subject that might appear to some simply—or complexly—"technical," so narrowly theoretical as to capture and embrace little of those deep human concerns that have made music what it is today, I might seek vindication by responding, by observing, by asserting that "the slow climb through the 1950s eventually brought Stravinsky to the *Movements* for Piano and Orchestra, the cornerstone of his later work,"[1] in which he discovered "new serial combinations, and which was the most advanced music from the point of view of construction of anything he had composed. Every aspect of the composition was guided by serial forms, the sixes, quadrilaterals, triangles, *et cetera*. The fifth movement, for instance, uses a construction of twelve verticals."[2] I could continue to heap such hyperbole upon the probably elliptic, but the words—of course—are not, could not be, mine. They are Stravinsky's, except for the trivial alteration of a rigid designator or two in order to "conceal" the identity of the source. For this occasion the fact that these were Stravinsky's views of this music is itself a matter of justificatory public interest, but—in the larger view—such an invocation is susceptible to the criticism of one's indulging in or—at least—indulging a fatal form of the intentional error. But whether Stravinsky may have been dissembling, or mistaken, or merely not have provided the most satisfactory construal of his own creation does not concern me, for I—as an "hypothetical other" engaged in rational analytical reconstruction, and thereby neither presuming nor concerned to suggest the mode of begetting but rather attempting to provide a mode of "understanding"—am prepared to stake the same claims and raise them, in generality, scope, and significance. For the shared compositional modes of the major works beginning with *Movements* and ending with the *Requiem Canticles* not only affected and engaged all the dimensions of these compositions in a manner unprecedented for Stravinsky personally, but remarkably define a different position for Stravinsky vis-à-vis the music which preceded

1. Igor Stravinsky and Robert Craft, *Themes and Episodes* (New York, 1966), p. 23.
2. Igor Stravinsky and Robert Craft, *Memories and Commentaries* (New York, 1960), p. 100.

these works, both his own and that of others. They seem to occupy a different kind of historical site, and these surely are not Stravinsky's words or—very likely—his slightest concern; his sense of historical position never burdened him, never obliged him to manufacture a history of music (both past and present) to which he could define his own relation in the most favorable way. He never felt impelled verbally, or even analytically, to characterize composers of the past as his predecessors, and even his alleged "back to Bach" was far more a forward to the *Movements*. But before I proceed from the surely overly general to the probably unduly specific, permit me to enter the celebrative and personal spirit of this occasion by recalling two personal moments from the time of the *Movements*. They are intended to prove nothing, but I hope they will say something.

In late December 1958 Stravinsky came to New York from London. He was to conduct the first performance of *Threni*, but was working on a new composition: *Movements*. Mrs. Stravinsky, Robert Craft, and I were sitting in the living room (as it turned out, anteroom) of the Stravinskys' suite at the Gladstone Hotel waiting for Stravinsky to join us for dinner; he was in the bedroom, doing we knew not what until he suddenly bolted out of the room in his robe, waving a page of manuscript paper, smiling broadly that pixylike smile, and shouting: "I found a mistake, and the right note sounds so much better." In addition to all its other lovely implications (and they should be inferrable from the later parts of this paper), the remark serves to explicate what Stravinsky meant when, in speaking of the *Requiem Canticles*, he observed that he continued "to follow the logic of my ear."[3] And although some might seize upon that remark to argue that the music is less "out of ear" than "out of mind," among all the rich ramifications of his only seemingly innocent metaphor is the realization of the profoundly experienced composer that "the ear" is at least as theory laden as the eye or mind, and only the mind's ear and the ear's mind can provide the vehicles for the necessary filtering, sorting, and discriminating.

On the morning of 9 January 1960 Stravinsky conducted the final rehearsal for the first, so to speak, performance of the *Movements*, after which he lunched with the pianist for whom the work was commissioned, her husband, and others of us. Although or perhaps because the luncheon wine had been ordinary neither in quality nor quantity, Stravinsky—at the conclusion of lunch—insisted that Claudio Spies and I escort him from the Ambassador Hotel—the luncheon scene—down the street to, again, the Gladstone, and then up to his suite, where he further insisted that we sit, surrounding him, while he produced and displayed all of his copious notes, alphanumerical and musical, for the *Movements*, and then proceeded, as if to restore for himself and convey to us his original, unsullied image of the work, to lead us on a charted voyage of rediscovery. I do not know how long his exegesis lasted, but I do recall that dusk arrived and we

3. Stravinsky and Craft, *Themes and Episodes*, p. 23.

scarcely could follow visually the paths and patterns that his finger fashioned from his arrays of pitch-class letters, but we dared not switch on the light for fear it would disrupt the flow of his discourse and the train of his rethinking. But I doubt that it would have, for he did not drop a syllable in whatever language he was speaking at that moment when I, in a spontaneous burst of détente, observed that the hexachord of the *Movements* was, in content, that of Schoenberg's *De Profundis*.

If I do not recall when that extraordinary exposition ended, I surely cannot recall how, but I do recall how Claudio Spies and I attempted immediately, collaboratively, and subsequently to reconstruct that grand tour.

The next evening the *Movements* received its first "performance," accompanied by program notes in which Stravinsky wrote of the hexachords, the verticals, and others of the preceding day's "secrets," which were out, or in, then and even now. And still after seventeen years, those program notes could induce a cry of outrage from a violated British dilettante, who branded them "claptrap" and with the modesty characteristic of his clan, suggested the assistance of an "astrological chart" for the "average music lover."[4] But those program notes, the *Movements*, the subsequent works and words are the astonishing evidence of what those ideas and conceptions meant to Stravinsky; I propose to attempt to remind you of, to suggest what they mean in and to his music.

Here I dare step slightly out of my purely reconstructive role to suggest that—however Stravinsky discovered or had uncovered for him (by Craft or by Ernst Krenek) the procedure that spawned such a congeries of relations and references as appear so suddenly and intricately in the *Movements*—it was as a profound compounding of two necessary conditions of musical "serialism" (in any discriminating sense): pitch-class ordering and pitch-class interval, rather than as the isolated acquisition of the not unprecedented but peripheral and compositionally and systematically largely unassimilated "primitive" of "rotation," that Stravinsky viewed and employed as his primary "new discovery" which induced his verticals. Surely, from the standpoint of reconstruction, such a view binds that discovery to the past of music and of Stravinsky and to the deepest dynamics of serialism in all its musical manifestations. The notion of "rotation"—at least initially—not only obscures and confuses such sources and attributes, but tends to trivialize the transformation and—thus—its consequences, by seeming to introduce but yet another possible from a profusion of apparently equally reasonable or unreasonable possibles. If, however, the procedure is characterized as the generation of a succession of transpositions, determined by the order of the pitch classes of the constructed referential set (as if the familiar 12 × 12 array) and—particularly—of the constituent, disjoint hexachords, then the historical associations and the systematic orientation are immediately apparent and vivid.

4. Neil Tierney, *The Unknown Country* (London, 1977), pp. 175–76.

I do not know whether Stravinsky knew or cared that the canonic relations among the "voices" (lines of the series) necessarily induced by the ordered transpositions can be regarded as "structural" imitations, and were—chronologically—significantly adumbrated by Wagner and explicitly celebrated by Schoenberg, particularly in his Opus 16, no. 3, where—for all that the underlying canon is both in pitch and rhythmic form a literal, traditional canon—the primary effect seems to have been to project the resultant "chords," "simultaneities," "verticals," so much so that even one of the titles imposed on that movement was "The Changing Chord." And the chord that is so changed, canonically, is yet another point of strong consilience between that work and Stravinsky's "new combinations." Further, this canonic procedure is itself but a special case of that contextually determined "motivic" voice leading, that polyphony in which the component lines derive their individual coherence from and by their direct transformational relations to one another rather than as instances of formations and progressions derived from the same context-independent common types. Stravinsky's verticals, as such, in their compositional employment, had no predecessor in serial composition, but—if only anecdotally—do have attitudinal predecessors in—above all—his Russian antecedents: in Rimsky's harmony book and his music, which both regard the chord far more as a sonic thing in itself, a collection of pitches and—therefore—intervals, than in its extensive functional role; in Scriabin's minute compositional dissections and revelations of his composition's singular "chord"; in the notion of the "sonorous object" or "complex," which came to be termed, not too fortunately, a "tonic sonority." And the associations necessarily induced among the verticals by the generating operations are generalizations of the notion of associative harmony, which is just "contextually coherent" harmony.

Regarding verticals as deriving from the relation of order and the operation of transposition is ultimately less important in identifying the traditional affinities of this procedure than in disclosing, in a relatively unfamiliar guise, the singular role of transposition in the deep structure of twelve-tone serialism.[5] It is the system's "Sheffer stroke," the only operation which need be postulated to induce inversion within an array of sets, and inversion—therefore—can be viewed as a "supervenient," an abbreviational definition rather than as a primary, independent transformation generalized from the however suggestive genesis of contour inversion. And the application of the transposition operation to order number (rather than pitch-class number) creates "rotation" in the Stravinskyan sense.

But whatever the historical and heuristic advantages of the idea of transposition, it—itself—can be dependently generated from the fundamental relation of directed distance, "interval" (in the customary sense) taken together with, again, the relation of linear ordering, by taking each successive pitch class of the set as

5. For a fuller discussion, see Milton Babbitt, "Since Schoenberg," *Perspectives of New Music* 12, nos. 1 and 2 (Fall 1973, Spring–Summer 1974): 25–27.

the origin of the series. When these pitch-class origins are interpreted as order number origins, Stravinsky's verticals appear.[6] It is, then, as a consolidated extension of his own compositional ontogeny that Stravinsky's technique of verticals can, biographically, be best understood. Indeed, when he began composing works that suggested being construed as "serial," he asserted no one should be shocked or even surprised for, after all, he had always "composed with intervals," and those who knew—say—the *Octet,* the *Capriccio,* the *Symphony of Psalms,* the Symphony in C, knew of what he spoke, while being delightedly impressed by Stravinsky's perception of that relation which is the central, irreducible determinant of the relations, constancies, invariants of the twelve-tone syntax. And Stravinsky's vertical arrays are supersaturated with the influence of the intervals of the set and its hexachords, since each vertical, in turn, is determined by the successive pitch-class intervals created by the successive order number intervals; that is, every interval in the set collection (including complements), not just successive intervals formed by adjacent elements, determines the exact content of the verticals. Then, the intervals within the verticals are the intervals of the intervals of the original series, the differences between interval sizes in the initial collection. For all that the dual reference of every entry in the 12 × 12 array, as pitch-class and interval number, long has been understood, the interpreting of such an entry, which—in the pitch-class domain—represents pitch classes in four different set forms, as a pitch class in yet another formation, appeared a highly "theoretical" notion, and—therefore—had no phanic—or even latent—function in previous serial composition. From the *Movements* on, the "new" interval becomes a foreground feature of significant discriminative value.

In Table 14.1, the first line of the array is "the" set or series of the *Movements,* analytically decided by virtue of primary, strategic occurrence and referential centrality. The upper left 6 × 6 array, and the upper right 6 × 6 array, are derived respectively from the first and second discrete hexachords by the described process (which also may be viewed as complementing—mod. 12 and mod. 6 respectively—the pitch-class and order numbers, by analogy with the comparable complementations, mod. 12 and 11, respectively, which yield the traditional inversion and retrogression). There is no interval of 3 (or, of course, 9) present in the hexachordal collection, but that interval arises immediately as an adjacency defined interval in the third vertical and—necessarily—(and necessarily adjacently) in the fifth vertical. When such verticals, so dissimilar from any set form, are presented compositionally, vertically or horizontally, with no explicit compositional exposition of their derivation, the work may appear, that is "sound," "hermetic," as it has been described by a Stravinsky biographer.[7] As the listener

6. This relation and the general subject of order transposition are discussed in Charles Wuorinen, *Simple Composition* (New York and London, 1979), pp. 101–109.

7. Eric Walter White, *Stravinsky: The Composer and His Works* (Berkeley and Los Angeles, 1966), pp. 464–66.

Table 14.1. *Movements* for Piano and Orchestra

	E♭ = 0	H_1						H_2						
	t = 0	0	1	7	5	6	11	9	8	10	3	4	2	0
	11	0	6	4	5	10	11	9	11	4	5	3	10	1
S	5	0	10	11	4	5	6	9	2	3	1	8	7	11
	7	0	1	6	7	8	2	9	10	8	3	2	4	6
	6	0	5	6	7	1	11	9	7	2	1	3	8	5
	1	0	1	2	8	6	7	9	4	3	5	10	11	7
	0	0	11	5	7	6	1	3	4	2	9	8	10	0
	1	0	6	8	7	2	1	3	1	8	7	9	2	11
I	7	0	2	1	8	7	6	3	10	9	11	4	5	1
	5	0	11	6	5	4	10	3	2	4	9	10	8	6
	6	0	7	6	5	11	1	3	5	10	11	9	4	7
	11	0	11	10	4	6	5	3	8	9	7	2	1	5
	0	11	6	5	7	1	0	2	4	3	10	8	9	0
	5	11	10	0	6	5	4	2	1	8	6	7	0	10
R	6	11	1	7	6	5	0	2	9	7	8	1	3	11
	4	11	5	4	3	10	9	2	0	1	6	8	7	4
	10	11	10	9	4	3	5	2	3	8	10	9	4	6
	11	11	10	5	4	6	0	2	7	9	8	3	1	5
	0	1	6	7	5	11	0	10	8	9	2	4	3	0
	7	1	2	0	6	7	8	10	11	4	6	5	0	2
RI	6	1	11	5	6	7	0	10	3	5	4	11	9	1
	8	1	7	8	9	2	3	10	0	11	6	4	5	8
	2	1	2	3	8	9	7	10	9	4	2	3	8	6
	1	1	2	7	8	6	0	10	5	3	4	9	11	7

	3	3	4	10	8	9	2	0	11	1	6	7	5	3
	2	3	9	7	8	1	2	0	2	7	8	6	1	4
S	8	3	1	2	7	8	9	0	5	6	4	11	10	2
	10	3	4	9	10	11	5	0	11	1	6	5	7	9
	9	3	8	9	10	4	2	0	10	5	4	6	11	8
	4	3	4	5	11	9	10	0	7	6	8	1	2	10
	9	9	8	2	4	3	10	0	1	11	6	5	7	9
	10	9	3	5	4	11	10	0	10	5	4	6	11	8
I	4	9	11	10	5	4	3	0	7	6	8	1	2	10
	2	9	8	3	2	1	7	0	1	11	6	7	5	3
	3	9	4	3	2	8	10	0	2	7	8	6	1	4
	8	9	8	7	1	3	2	0	5	6	4	11	10	2

engages in the epistemological act of acquiring familiarity with, knowledge of the composition as it proceeds, the bases of association, of cumulative continuity, may seem elusive, opaque, and tenuous, with no reassuring, putative "form" worn on the composition's sleeve. Yet, even in the *Movements*, the network of dependencies is so multiply reinforced, powerfully transitive, subtly redundant, that the very pace of the cohesive transformational process is a decisive temporal, rhythmic, cognitive property of the work. Particularly since Stravinsky's method is so exceptionally sensitive to order, in time and space.

The minimal alteration of the order of pitch-class components—say, the interchange of just one pair of adjacent elements—will, in general, transform violently the structure of the vertical, not merely the verticals of which they are immediate constituents, but all of the verticals, because of the dependency of every vertical upon all of the intervals of the hexachordal collection. Such alterations are not employed by Stravinsky, but the observation is meant to emphasize the care and consideration he had to expend on the ordering of his series in order to achieve a family of verticals with the properties he desired. In the *Movements*, the absence of an interval class of 3 (or 9) in the set is a pervasive determinant of further choices and of local and global consequences. Because of this absence, there can be no pitch class (3 or 9) in the array of verticals generated by the first hexachord (see the 6 × 6 array in the upper left, Table 14.1), for if there were, it would contradictorily—and impossibly—create an interval of 3 (or 9) with the initial pitch class 0. (Observe that every numerical entry in the array represents a pitch class in a transposition, a pitch class in a vertical, and an *interval* in the original *ordered* hexachord.) The succession of transposition numbers determined by the successive "rotations" yields, necessarily and independently of the structure of the hexachord, an inversion of the hexachord corresponding, again necessarily, to the inversion occupying the first line of the 6 × 6 array directly under the one we have been examining; this line can be derived by the customary inversion operation of complementation.

Because of the absence of 3 and 9 as pitch classes in the array induced by the first hexachord, Stravinsky begins the second hexachord of his set with a 9, thereby securing a complete balance of pitch-class multiplicities: each pitch-class occurs exactly six times in the two arrays generated by the two hexachords. Had he chosen, for example, an 8 as the initial element of the second hexachord (following the traditional principle of producing, at the nexus of the second hexachord (following the traditional principle of producing, at the nexus of the hexachords, an—or the—interval absent from the hexachords) 8's—and 2's—would dominate the two arrays. Also, remarkably and independently, Stravinsky selected the final pitch class of each of the hexachords (11 and 2, respectively) which also are related by the excluded intervals, so that the "rotational" derivations of R and RI arrays display the same balance of pitch classes. Table 14.2 offers the more humanistically inclined reader the equivalent of the upper arrays of Table 14.1 in pitch-class letters, as Stravinsky represented them to himself. Such a representa-

Table 14.2.

H_1						H_2					
E♭	E	B♭	A♭	A	D	C	B	C♯	F♯	G	F
E♭	A	G	A♭	D♭	D	C	D	G	A♭	F♯	C♯
E♭	C♯	D	G	A♭	A	C	F	F♯	E	B	B♭
E♭	E	A	B♭	B	F	C	C♯	B	F♯	F	G
E♭	A♭	A	B♭	F	D	C	B♭	F	E	F♯	B
E♭	E	F	B	A	G	C	G	F♯	A♭	C♯	D
E♭	D	A♭	B♭	A	E	F♯	G	F	C	B	C♯
E♭	A	B	B♭	F	E	F♯	E	B	B♭	A	F
E♭	F	E	B	B♭	A	F♯	C♯	C	D	G	A♭
E♭	D	A	A♭	G	C♯	F♯	F	G	C	D♭	B
E♭	B♭	A	A♭	D	E	F♯	A♭	C♯	D	C	G
E♭	D	D♭	G	A	A♭	F♯	B	C	B♭	F	E

tion has no other advantages, but the serious disadvantages of obscuring, beyond possible discovery, the duality of pitch-class and interval numbers.

One of the motives that seemingly impelled Stravinsky in his search for this "new procedure" was his often expressed unease with the notion (or, perhaps more accurately, the slogan) "the identification of the vertical with the horizontal." However this discomfort may have reflected a perpetuated misunderstanding of an expression which, if Schoenberg ever used it, was the characterization of a subtle process of deriving contextual polyphony from the properties of a single line, which itself was the source of the constituents of the polyphony, it led Stravinsky to seek a basis of differentiation of the two dimensions comparable with the tonal distinction of the triad as the vertical norm, and the scale as the horizontal norm. Such differentiation he secured strikingly, as has been noted, between his (inceptually) horizontal series and his (precompositionally) vertical "verticals," but—characteristically enough—he resorted to various local techniques to obtain whatever immediate identity was available between the verticals and their horizontal origin, as Jerome Kohl has so clearly demonstrated in his valuable article on the *Variations* (Aldous Huxley in Memoriam),[8] and—ultimately of greater consequence—the "identification" is built subtly but essentially into his basic process, since the successive elements of each vertical are successive elements of the original set, each transposed by the appropriate interval of

8. Jerome Kohl, "Exposition in Stravinsky's Orchestral Variations," *Perspectives of New Music* 18, nos. 1 and 2 (Fall 1979, Spring 1980): 391–405.

the set. So, order is preserved within the verticals, while pitch-class succession and, even, content are altered.

Further, the successive lines of the hexachordal array do not and cannot (except in the case of the whole-tone hexachord) preserve the content of the initial hexachord, and the hierarchization of differences of order demanded by the permutations induced by set transposition in twelve-tone serialism (which Schoenberg secured by the combinational identity of segments within and between differently ordered sets) is not pertinent here, and even the lines created by the concatenation of the two disjunct hexachords do not constitute, in general, an aggregate. But a truly new criterion of linear association is created. Such a path of affinity is stated explicitly as early as measure 13 of the *Movements* (Example 14.1), where the linear progression from the piano through the clarinets moves through the second hexachord of the second line of Table 14.1 (where t = 1), followed by the first hexachord of the same line of the array (t = 11) (a "horizontal" created by the technique of deriving "verticals"), and then the second hexachord of t = 11. The middle hexachord, then, is the link between the newly created linear association and the "traditional" transpositional association, the latter creating an aggregate (but, of course, not a transposition of the original set, in the usual sense).

The statement of a line of such structure (followed by its partial retrograde) in combination with its notorious polyphonic fellow (including the B♭–G of m. 14, which is "unorganized"[9] only to those who fail to recognize the strategic first two pitch classes of the third vertical of Table 14.1) so early in the work may be a source of the work's "difficulty"; although Stravinsky shared with Schoenberg the taste for an explicit, foreground presentation of his set at the outset, very quickly—by m. 3 in the *Movements*—it recedes to exert its pervasive, persistent influence and control, acting at ever-varying distances from the musical surface data, re-emerging at the end of the movement, and the end of the work. But, there are compensating associative immediacies; for instance, in m. 13–14 (Example 14.1), the isolated G♭–D♭ in the clarinet (singularly "doubling" the preceding and following piano pitches) is "prepared" by the same pitch interval in m. 2, 4, 6 (in two different appearances), and 12.

The *Movements* is unique among Stravinsky's late works in employing a set whose two hexachords are so related (as transpositions of one another) that the transposition numbers identified with the six transformations of the two hexachords are the same, securing closure among the pairs of 6 × 6 arrays associated with S, I, R, and RI. In the *Requiem Canticles*,[10] two structurally apparently dissimilar sets are used, deployed symmetrically about the middle movement, where the two appear simultaneously at the mid-moment of that movement. From Table

---

9. White, *Stravinsky*, p. 466.

10. For a thorough discussion of all aspects of this composition, see Claudio Spies, "Some Notes on Stravinsky's Requiem Settings," in *Perspectives on Schoenberg and Stravinsky*, rev. ed., ed. Benjamin Boretz and Edward T. Cone, (New York, 1972), pp. 233–49.

Example 14.1. *Movements* for Piano and Orchestra (1958–1959)

Example 14.1. *continued*

14.3 one can infer a deep relation between the two sets, both of which yield the same number of t numbers in common between the two hexachords. The first set produces 0, 5, 6, 7; the second, 11, 0, 1, 2. Both are the pitch-class numbers of all-combinatorial tetrachords. An examination of Table 14.1, including all the transpositions, should reveal something of the chain of effects of such properties.

Since the discrete hexachords are usually employed independently, acting individually, the condition that they are the hexachords of a set assures that they

Table 14.3. ***Requiem Canticles***

	F = 0	H$_1$						H$_2$						
	t = 0	0	7	6	4	5	9	8	10	3	1	11	2	0
	5	0	11	9	10	2	5	8	1	11	9	0	6	10
S	6	0	10	11	3	6	1	8	6	4	7	1	3	5
	8	0	1	5	8	3	2	8	6	9	3	5	10	7
	7	0	4	7	2	1	11	8	11	5	7	0	10	9
	3	0	3	10	9	7	8	8	2	4	9	7	5	6
	0	0	5	6	8	7	3	4	2	9	11	1	10	0
	7	0	1	3	2	10	7	4	11	1	3	0	6	2
I	6	0	2	1	9	6	11	4	6	8	5	11	9	7
	4	0	11	7	4	9	10	4	6	3	9	7	2	5
	5	0	8	5	10	11	1	4	1	7	5	0	2	3
	9	0	9	2	3	5	4	4	10	8	3	5	7	6

		H$_1$						H$_2$						
	t = 0	0	2	10	11	1	8	6	7	9	4	3	5	0
	10	0	8	9	11	6	10	6	8	3	2	4	5	11
	2	0	1	3	10	2	4	6	1	0	2	3	4	9
S	1	0	2	9	1	3	11	6	5	7	8	9	11	2
	11	0	7	11	1	9	10	6	8	9	10	0	7	3
	4	0	4	6	2	3	5	6	7	8	10	5	4	1
	0	0	10	2	1	11	4	6	5	3	8	9	7	0
	2	0	4	3	1	6	2	6	4	9	10	8	7	1
I	10	0	11	9	2	10	8	6	11	0	10	9	8	3
	11	0	10	3	11	9	1	6	7	5	4	3	1	10
	1	0	5	1	11	3	2	6	4	3	2	0	5	9
	8	0	8	6	10	9	7	6	5	4	2	7	8	11

are structurally analogous in the usual, hierarchical sense, so that each stands intersectionally in the same similarity relation to corresponding transpositions and—most relevantly—to transpositional segments.

An apparently unanticipated, by Stravinsky, bonus induced by his production of verticals was the systematic relations that obtained among the verticals, created by the double transposition, of pitch-class and order numbers. Disregarding the first vertical (whose internal symmetry is evident enough) and counting it as the zeroth vertical, as it should be in terms of its derivation from order no. 0, that those verticals symmetrically disposed around the middle vertical are cyclically permuted inversions of one another, and that—therefore—the middle vertical is self-inversional, is but another instance of the identical consequences of retrogression and inversion.[11] Just as, in the small, they produce intervallic complementation, in the large, in which successive retrogression produces "rotation," total inversion results. And the notion of a symmetrically constructed vertical, such as the mid-vertical, is not merely metaphorical or "geometrical"; it describes intervallic redundancy, patterned redundancy. So that in the five-part chord of Schoenberg's Opus 16, no. 3 (consisting of the opening three-note motive of the work compounded with its own inversion), the center of symmetry is E (the note in common between the two forms of the motive), which is compositionally noted and exploited as such, while the canonic theme (by which the "chord" is "changed") is itself symmetrical around its initial note.

The inversion of the hexachordal arrays, by direct complementation or by "rotating" from the inverted set, yields verticals that are identical in pitch-class content (and only cyclically reordered) with those of the S array, but they are reversed in order; that is, the verticals are symmetrically interchanged, the mid-vertical—therefore—remains unchanged. Again, pitch-class inversion produces retrogression of the order of the verticals: the inversion, retrogression duality again. The combinatorial structure of the hexachords of the *Movements* permits yet further identities within the general symmetries. The second order structure of the hexachord allows Stravinsky to shape his second hexachord as two successive inversionally related trichords. As a consequence, the symmetrically placed verticals of the second hexachord are not only inversionally related, but identical in pitch content (while, in the middle vertical, each pitch class occurs the same number of times). This would not have been the case had the two discrete trichords been disposed as transpositions (say: 8, 9, 10, 2, 3, 4); thus, an inversional

11. See Milton Babbitt, "Contemporary Music Composition and Music Theory as Contemporary Intellectual History," in *Perspectives in Musicology*, ed. Barry S. Brook, Edward Downes, and Sherman van Salkema (New York, 1972), pp. 166–67. But a thorough investigation of the properties of the array of verticals and its extensions can be found in a series of articles by John Rogers, "Toward a System of Rotational Arrays," *American Society of University Composers, Proceedings of the Second Annual Conference*, April 1967, pp. 61–74; "Some Properties of Non-Duplicating Rotational Arrays," *Perspectives of New Music* (Fall–Winter 1968): 80–102; and, with Barry Mitchell, "A Problem in Mathematics and Music," *American Mathematical Monthly* (October 1968).

relation yields a "simpler" relation (an identity) than does the "simpler" transposition, reflecting again the nature of the foundations of Stravinsky's procedure.

Symmetry requires and defines a center of symmetry. The pitch-class center for all the pairs of verticals and the middle vertical is the initial of each of the hexachordal lines, which—thereby—is distinguished not just by primacy and multiplicity, but by being the referent of symmetry. (The tritone-related pitch class is, necessarily, also so symmetrically oriented.) The E♭ of the *Movements,* the F—with which the *Requiem Canticles* begins and ends—are compositionally explicit projections of such centers of symmetry. In this respect, too, the past has been recaptured and enhanced by Stravinsky. He had long been fond of explaining that his Concerto for Piano and Wind Instruments was not "in A," but "on A," that the pitch class A was a contextually weighted and emphasized center of reference rather than a functionally defined and influential "tonic" class. In his new cosmos, pitch-class centricity is the point of convergence for all the symmetries, the patterns of redundancy, and—even—the local harmony and polyphony. For example, in m. 40 of the *Movements,* the two part retrograde pitch-class canon between the flute and the bass clarinet, bassoon contains just one contrapuntal doubling of a pitch class, the E♭.

The realization of the new relations affected not only all the dimensions of his last music, but his thinking about these dimensions.[12] He spoke, again elliptically, of the "hint of serialism" in the "rhythmic language" and the "instrumental structure" of the *Movements.* I suspect that this, and other comparable remarks are intended to designate less of serious seriation than of a far greater degree of self-reference, within and between dimensions, than appears in his earlier works, even earlier serial works. At the very onset, in m. 1, the three instrumentally differentiated (by trumpet, violin, and piano) E♭'s are expressed as three successive, thus temporally differentiated E♭'s in a single instrument, the piano, in m. 3. The two hexachords are disposed each within the first two measures of the work, thus placing D and F in the final positions of the measures (as the E♭ and C are in the initial positions) setting off, by metrical placement and analogy, the excluded intervals of 9 and 3, "preparing" the juxtaposed D and F of m. 3, signaling the independent use of the discrete hexachords.

There is further evidence of Stravinsky's extending his earlier method of slicing and intercalating continuities to serial succession and contingency.[13] The E♭ of the piano in m. 18 connects two instrumentally disjoint (except for the solo piano) passages by continuing, from the preceding A of the bass clarinet, the pitch retrograde begun by the clarinet in m. 16–17. The F, pizzicato and in the lowest register of the viola in m. 21, obviously is picked up by the G of the viola,

12. Milton Babbitt, "Remarks on the Recent Stravinsky," in Boretz and Cone, *Perspectives on Schoenberg and Stravinsky,* p. 182.

13. Edward T. Cone, "Stravinsky: The Progress of a Method," in Boretz and Cone, *Perspectives on Schoenberg and Stravinsky,* pp. 155–64.

pizzicato and in the lowest register, at m. 40, continuing the presentation of the second hexachord at t = 0, in retrograde, of which F was the initial note. And the clearly omitted A of the clarinet at m. 137 in its presentation of the RI form of the second hexachord is provided by the first note of its next entry in m. 143 et cetera, et cetera.

In 1962, when Stravinsky's eightieth birth year was being celebrated in Santa Fe and he was just beginning the composition of *Abraham and Isaac,* he spent an afternoon hearing and seeing the works of a group of young composers who had been imported for the occasion. He was unusually pensive and meditative during the journey back from that ceremony, and finally—with not, for him, exceptional insight and foresight—he quietly remarked that music already had and probably would continue to retreat from the kind of luxuriant complexity that now engaged him. It would retreat, he conjectured, not just back to his *Firebird,* but to his *Fireworks.*

15 On the Significance of Stravinsky's Last Works

CHARLES WUORINEN AND JEFFREY KRESKY

MOST JOURNALISTS and critics—among so many others—prefer to see in Stravinsky's stylistic periods a youthful exuberance, followed by an elegant and controlled middle age, all culminating in a disappointing experimental dotage. But some of us, as composers, have been so profoundly affected by the late works, in which are first exhibited techniques and devices we have extracted to employ and extend, as to want to predict that the final chapter of his output will be the most significant in the long run. In our view, these "serial" works do not simply treat the received twelve-tone system to the celebrated Stravinskyan "ear"—or, worse, bend it unwillingly and ungracefully to the attractive Stravinsky aesthetic. Rather, they suggest an important extension and generalization of Schoenberg's contribution to include some of the fundamental bases of tonality, pointing even to a possible synthesis of the tonal and twelve-tone approaches.

Some general observations about Stravinsky's diatonic music can shed light on the achievement of the late works. The neoclassical period is often thought of as a collection of pieces that work like various distorting mirrors held up to the functional relationships of genuine tonal music. Without trying to suggest Stravinsky's attitudes toward his music of this period, or even to judge something about his actual creative procedures of that time, one can still react critically to general effects contained in typical passages to arrive at a different description. For example, the result of so simple a device as fusing a dominant chord and a tonic chord into a single chordal entity can be seen as destroying the time dependency that is essential to the ordered hierarchical relationships that inform the local and large-scale continuities of tonal pieces; these relationships then give way, such that (for example, in this case) the role usually assumed by the tonic note or tonic triad is transferred onto the entire scale collection of the key being uttered at the moment. An immediate surface consequence of this particular phenomenon might well be the relative freedom in the choice of pausing notes, semicadential and cadential tones, and so forth, found in a wide variety of passages in these pieces. Although the musical situations resulting from such a transfer of role from a particular to a generality (or, really, to an *expanded* particular) might seem to represent an internally weakened and thereby restricted functional tonality, there is perhaps a compensating sense in which the entire functional arena is at the same time enlarged, for entire key collections—whole scales—become the "notes" to manipulate. Therefore, without necessarily sacrificing coherence, keys can be juxtaposed and interrelated in ways that would seem prohibitively complex, or at least abrupt, in normal tonality. In the *Duo concertant,* for example, the "Gigue" spends a lot of time articulating the A♭ scale collection, which seems to be unprepared by what precedes it and unresolved by what follows. But the A♭ scale may "mean" the A♭ pitch class, echoing the F major/minor tonality so important elsewhere in the work, and introduced and left by way of its dominant E♭, which stands in the same relation to the equally important C major/minor.

Now this denial of the functional distinctions among the notes of the present scale would, among other things, affect the local successions of pitches in such a way as to elevate the importance of the *absolute* order of notes (as opposed to the more usual contextual time dependency that reflects and establishes their standard functional relationships). Here we may see a first suggestion in Stravinsky's work of a breakdown in terms of Babbitt's well-known distinction between content-significant ("tonal") and order-significant ("twelve-tone") systems. An example of this might be seen in the first of the Three Pieces for String Quartet, in which a neatly stratified texture consisting of melody (first violin), vamp (second violin), accompaniment (cello), and minor-ninth drone (viola) depends to a large extent upon the permutation and reconfiguration of the several discrete elements to achieve forward motion.[1]

If we are seeing in Stravinsky's "tonal" works a presence of an important ingredient of serial music, we can discern in the twelve-tone works the exact opposite and corresponding preoccupation with *content*—that is, some denial of what is supposed to be the very essence of the serial twelve-tone way, in favor of what is usually thought of as a systematic feature of tonality. Here we refer to the general world of the "rotation" and its chordal derivative, the "vertical." The technical aspects of these related devices are by now well known, but the point of emphasis here is that the practice of transposing the successive forms in the cyclic permutation of the (for Stravinsky, six) elements in the rotated chain *by* the successive intervals of that chain brings each product "down" to the "zero" level, with all forms starting in the same pitch class. Thus, a centricity is automatically achieved, even if only in terms of frequency and regularity of occurrence: if, at the simplest, a hexachord is fully rotated in this standard way, and the rotations are presented in straightforward linear form—as a tune in a single instrument—then the "zero" pitch would occur every six attacks, and each time initiate a chain of intervals representing the looped or closed intervallic definition of the original hexachord. In fact, even in this direct way, examples in late Stravinsky abound. (The steady unfolding contralto line in the "Lacrimosa" of *Requiem Canticles* is a particularly uncluttered case.) At the same time, this "centric" feature, so unmis-

1. For further discussion of this work, see Kramer's essay in this collection.

takably reminiscent of the tonal world, is coupled in such passages with the restricted content and content changes that likewise recall the scale-and-key tradition, because Stravinsky always rotates hexachords by themselves, split off from their full-set contexts. (The technique itself, however, is applicable to any size ordered unit, with or without duplications.) Thus, not only is the unit that repeatedly starts with the center note only six pitches in size, but which six they are changes with each rotation, with intersections between groups of six *not* resulting from operations familiar from usual (say, combinatorial) set-manipulation practices.

If this appearance of tonal echo from quite strict twelve-tone situations in the late works seems like an end-of-life looking back, matching the foretaste of the serial we have noted in the diatonic works, then this can be seen as just another example of the celebrated "continuity" across the vast stylistic changes in Stravinsky's output. This example is as abstract as others may be strikingly specific, such as the reuse of particular instrumental utterances from work to work, even the reappearance of the same isolated pitches in the same instruments (witness, for example, the use of G and B♭ in the timpani in works as diverse but chronologically close as *Oedipus Rex* and the *Capriccio* for Piano and Orchestra—in terms of which one may also think of the repeated G/B♭—containing timpani chords in the Interlude of *Requiem Canticles;* or see the sixteenth-note repetitions of F C B that form the first moments of both the *Requiem* and *Agon*).

On the surface of these late works, Stravinsky often seems to hint at this rapprochement of tonal and serial ways through various kinds of puns on tonal functionality, expressed nevertheless in direct serial means (often as plain as the mere straightforward statement of a set-form). The following passage in *Threni* (Example 15.1) just unfolds a set-form (RI^6), but the phraseologic, registral, and instrumental deployments yield strong associative outlines to G♯ minor (together with its dominant), then A minor (a "6–5–1" statement), and then G major. Only the last two notes, C♯ and C, do not join in these suggestions: and it is this part of the set that is now extracted for use underneath the choral chant that follows. Similarly, the opening of *Movements* for Piano and Orchestra (Example 15.2) promotes an E♭ that introduces a quick unfolding of twelve different notes, the last of which, F, is likewise promoted (doubled, sustained, spatially moved) in preparation for a reintroduced E♭, which is again stressed. Thus, a kind of "2–1" tonal arrival back to E♭ is superimposed on the set (complete even with a D "leading tone"); and the set can then have been heard as *an expression of E♭ from a particular point of view.* And when the passage is heard again, after the repeat sign at measure 26, it is prepared in just that way, for E♭ is again emphasized (with the registral change adding particular weight).

These suggestions perhaps reach their strongest voice in the *Requiem Canticles,* in which not one but two distinct sets that begin on F form the sources of all pitch situations in the work, with the F serving not just as the arbitrary first of twelve notes that describe a fixed interval pattern, but as some kind of "special"

Example 15.1. *Threni* (1957–1958)

or "favorite" note. So not just the sets, but the individual movements, become "F expressions." This idea is clearest in the "Postlude," where the long-sustained F in the horn, under the bell-like chords that make up the motion of the movement, turns out to be the start of a slow-motion pun—a full, broad F-minor triad (which, for reasons best known to the composer alone, is spelled F G♯ B♯) that spans the

Example 15.2. *Movements* for Piano and Orchestra (1958–1959)

movement, underlies its phrase plan, and rounds out back to F an octave lower under the final chord (in exactly the register where F began the *Canticles* in the first place).[2]

But it is in the use of the so-called "verticals" that these works depart from standard serial practice in the direction of the tonal world in a way capable of significant generalization and compositional expansion—that is, independent of the particular compositional idiosyncracies observed above. For the centric rotation-beginning pitch (which, after all, can be treated compositionally on any level, to any extent) presents itself in a most striking way when chords are made by reading vertically in the chart array of rotationally produced set-forms. It is these chords—verticalizations of corresponding order positions of all the rotations—that are designated "verticals" (*not*, for example, mere vertical statements of rotations themselves, which, by eliminating considerations of order, would actually, in Stravinsky, reduce simply to original hexachord transpositions): and, by definition, one of them consists *only* of the generating pitch. A simplest compositional interpretation of this strange property can easily be seen in the closing measures of *Variations* (Aldous Huxley in Memoriam):

2. The influence of this F-minor triad on the movement as a whole is discussed in Jeffrey Kresky, "A Study in Analysis," (Ann Arbor: University Microfilms, 1974), where a full account of the pitch world of the other movements of the *Canticles* will also be found.

Example 15.3. *Variations* (Aldous Huxley in Memoriam) (1963–1964)

Here we have five string chords, each containing six notes, all omitting G♯, and then, in a different timbre (the bass clarinet) and under a cadential fermata, the lone G♯. In fact, these six attacks are the six verticals of the second hexachord of the set of the piece: G♯ D♭ E♭ G G♭ F. If this hexachord is rotated and transposed cyclically to produce the typical six-by-six rotational array, these chords are the columns (played from last to first), with the grand G♯ a kind of metaphor for the sixfold G♯ vertical, representing the starting pitch of the hexachord.

This isolation and promotion of the rotational zero pitch class occurs even more explicitly in this fragment that appears in sketches for an unfinished orchestral piece Stravinsky worked on at the end of his life.[3] The passage describes two sets of hexachordal verticals. The two octaves are the respective hexachordal local zeros. As in the Huxley *Variations* example, the chords proceed backward along the rotational array, so the zeros come last in each group of six. Thus, again by definition (because these are twelve-tone hexachords), these zero pitches appear only as the first notes of each rotation, and thus are excluded from the chords *until* the chord consisting of the first (same) note of all the rotations. And when they arrive, they are composed so as to declare their uniqueness, their very arrival. This situation can be heard in a way quite analogous to that of the arriving tonic at a cadence in a tonal piece. Furthermore, the descending stepwise relation of the two special pitches, B and A, invokes the familiar tonal upper-voice arrival, 2–1.

Now the first two of these chordal statements are arpeggiated, and this fact introduces the next phase in the direction in which these examples can point. For

3. This fragment is quoted exactly in Charles Wuorinen's *Reliquary for Igor Stravinsky*, which uses these sketches and from which the printed example is taken.

Example 15.4. Charles Wuorinen, *A Reliquary for Igor Stravinsky*, pp. 8, 9

it is a short step from arpeggiation to treating these constructs not as chords at all, but as linear successions in themselves. This development may indeed have been in Stravinsky's mind in his last years, for it seems rather clear from these final sketches and fragments, in which verticals written out horizontally can be found, that he did intend to convert these materials into lines, to arrive at essentially new kinds of continuity.

Not to be found in Stravinsky's work is a first obvious extension of this notion. One can take a vertical, itself derived as above, and then having linearized it, use *it* as the linear basis for generating a new rotational array. (Again, the size of the new generating element need not be limited to the hexachordal six first compositionally present in these developments.) Of course this plan can be followed globally, with a six-by-six array immediately producing thirty-six new constructs, of which each could then yield six of its own, and so on. The calculations for this

Example 15.4. *continued*

potentially overwhelming amount of generated material can best be handled by computer, with, moreover, programs that can be adjusted to weed out or otherwise deal with undesirable redundancies (degeneracies incapable of yielding new material further on down the line, and so on). But other, more selective ways are possible, such as at each transformation choosing only *one* vertical (always, perhaps, at the same order position) to produce the next stage—a process that can continue on until (again, for example) a loop is formed by the reappearance of an early form (a strange and as yet unanalyzed feature of these operations). And in this kind of scheme, chains of considerably different length would result from the same transformations being made on the same size originals, with, thus, minuscule differences among starting materials reflecting in quite obvious macrostructural ramifications.

Because they admit so much local duplication of notes and are inevitably centric by virtue of their very mode of generation, these practices, together with other possible related techniques, may then show the possibility of convergence and direct continuity between the diatonic past and what can in a very general way be called the chromatic present—with these remarkable, spare last works of the master as the precious link. To be sure, such a convergence would be so much more definitively important than, say, the low-grade neotonality that is often expressed these days in semipop or trancelike terms involving diatonic figures, and that is perhaps a relatively transient phenomenon. It is an intriguing matter to realize that it was only after Schoenberg's death that Stravinsky came to express his own concerns through his colleague's procedures: for we can never know what Schoenberg's response, musical and otherwise, might have been.

Currents and Contemporaries

16 *Three Japanese Lyrics* and Japonisme

TAKASHI FUNAYAMA

IGOR STRAVINSKY began work on the *Three Japanese Lyrics* for high voice and chamber orchestra at Ustilug during the autumn of 1912 and completed the composition at Clarens at the beginning of 1913. Where *The Rite of Spring*, composed in the same place at almost the same time, is regarded as one of the twentieth century's great musical masterpieces, these three short pieces based on Japanese poems tend to be overlooked, lurking as they do in the shadow of *The Rite.*

Even disregarding the works' artistic value, comparing the *Three Japanese Lyrics,* a chamber work for ten performers lasting scarcely three minutes, with *The Rite,* a major work for large orchestra lasting more than thirty-five minutes, would be stretching a point. The *Three Japanese Lyrics* are miniatures, dealing with sound on a small scale and arguably composed as a result of the overflow of creative energy that Stravinsky expended on *The Rite.*[1] Still, minor works composed in the intervals between major ones often illuminate a composer's overall image from an unexpected angle. In examining the *Three Japanese Lyrics,* I do not intend to reassess their artistic merit, but to use them as the basis for considering Stravinsky's relationship with "Japonisme," a phenomenon that appeared in France in the latter half of the nineteenth century, and more directly, his relationship with the "Apaches," a group of Parisian artists, composers, and poets (including Maurice Ravel and Maurice Delage) who provided a base of support for Stravinsky's creative activity beginning in 1910.

Stravinsky often spoke of his fascination with Japanese art. For example, in *An Autobiography,* he writes:

> While putting the finishing touches to the orchestration of the *Sacre,* I was busy with another composition which was very close to my heart. In the summer I had read a little anthology of Japanese lyrics—short poems of a few lines each, selected from the old poets. The impression which they made on me was exactly like that made by Japanese paintings and engravings. The graphic solution of problems of perspective and space shown by their art incited me to find something analogous in music. Nothing could have lent itself better to this than the Russian version of

1. In fact, the sketches for both works appear in the same notebook. [Editor's note]

> the Japanese poems, owing to the well-known fact that Russian verse allows the tonic accent only. I gave myself up to this task, and succeeded by a metrical and rhythmic process too complex to be explained here.[2]

When he first visited Japan in May 1959, Stravinsky told an interviewer:

> I came into contact with Japan in the course of my work many years ago. In 1913, I composed a small work which used three short Japanese poems for its texts. I was interested at the time in Japanese woodblock prints. What attracted me was that this was a two-dimensional art without any sense of solidity. I discovered this sense of the two-dimensional in some Russian translations of poetry, and attempted to express this sense in my music. However, the Russian critics of the time attacked me severely for creating two-dimensional music. Well, you know how critics are. . . .[3]

The music critic Hans Pringsheim, who lives in Tokyo and acted as Stravinsky's interpreter during his stay in Japan, elaborated further in another article published at the time:

> Stravinsky spent more than one hour at an exhibition of Ukiyo-e masterpieces which was being held in Osaka in coordination with the International Festival of the Arts, after which he had the following to say: "I have long been fond of Japanese art, and I used to own some prints by Hokusai and Hiroshige about fifty years ago. I have the feeling that some of the prints which I used to own are included amongst the views of Mount Fuji by Hokusai and the Fifty-three Stages of the Tokaido by Hiroshige which I have seen here today. Unfortunately, many of my most treasured possessions disappeared at the time the First World War broke out."[4]

Yet, in none of these statements does Stravinsky mention the circumstances in which he became acquainted with the poems he set in his *Three Japanese Lyrics,* and Stravinsky's biographers and researchers have not investigated this point. A short look at the history of Japonisme from the latter half of the nineteenth century into the twentieth may suggest how Stravinsky developed his keen interest in the arts of Japan by the time he was composing *The Rite.*

In the mid-nineteenth century, the Meiji restoration ended the exclusionist policies that had prevailed from the middle of the seventeenth century, and Japan joined the three great international exhibitions that took place in Paris in 1867, 1878, and 1900. After more than two centuries of national isolation, during which only an infinitesimally small number of art objects had been exported in Dutch

2. Igor Stravinsky, *An Autobiography* (New York, 1936), p. 45.

3. Report of a press conference, *Mainichi Shimbun,* 8 April 1959.

4. H. Pringsheim, "Conversation with Stravinsky," *Asahi Shimbun,* 5 May 1959.

trading vessels, Ukiyo-e prints and other "Japonaiserie" were taken overseas in large quantities. The art dealer Tadamasa Hayashi (1853–1907), who first traveled to France in 1878, collected and sold literally hundreds of thousands of Ukiyo-e prints. He later became director of the 1900 exhibition.

Europe and France, in particular, responded enthusiastically to this influx of Japanese art and culture. An 1886 number of the magazine *Paris illustré* was devoted entirely to Japan. The issue was compiled by Tadamasa Hayashi. It included articles on Japanese history and culture written by Hayashi among others and sold perhaps twenty-five thousand copies.

Research into Japan was undertaken in earnest by French scholars. Edmond Goncourt, with cooperation from Hayashi, wrote his famous studies of Utamaro (1891) and Hokusai (1896). The Hamburg-born art dealer Samuel Bing (1838–1905) published thirty-six issues of the art magazine *Le Japon Artistique* in Paris over a period of three years between May 1888 and April 1891. Invariably included in this magazine was one long essay by a European scholar on the Japanese visual arts or culture in general. Overall, it attempted to provide a panoramic view of Japanese art, using a large number of color plates. According to Bing's preface in the first edition of the magazine, Japanese artists "learn geometry from spider's webs, observe decorative motifs in the footprints of birds in the snow, and obtain inspiration for their use of curves and shapes in the ripples formed on the surface of water by the breeze. . . . This is the most important and the most valuable lesson which we can draw from the examples of this art with which we have been provided."

For the twentieth issue of *Le Japon Artistique,* Justis Brickmann submitted an article entitled "La tradition poétique dans l'art du Japon" in which the second of the texts in the *Three Japanese Lyrics,* the poem by Miyamoto Masazumi, was presented. Brickmann here argues that the image of ice melted by the spring breeze blowing through a valley was an example of the peculiarly Japanese sense of decoration. Knowledge of the particular poetic form used in this poem, the Waka, was increased further in late nineteenth-century France as a result of the publication of a collection of translations, entitled *Poèmes de la libellule* (Paris, 1884), made by Judith Gautier and the Japanese politician Kinmochi Saionji (1849–1940), who had spent some of his student days in France.

Arguably, Japonisme reached its peak in France with the great international exhibition held in Paris in 1900. Ukiyo-e's influence upon Edouard Manet, Claude Monet, and other members of the impressionist school, as well as upon other leading artists such as Van Gogh, Gauguin, and Toulouse-Lautrec, has been studied in detail by Japanese art historians.[5] In contrast, the question of Japonisme in music has been almost completely overlooked. Whereas Japonaiserie

5. The following are the two major works in Japanese dealing with Japonisme and the visual arts: Kiyoji Ōshima, *Japonisumu—Inshōha to Ukiyo-e no Shūhen* [Japonisme—the impressionists and Ukiyo-e] (Tokyo, 1980), and Taketoshi Sadazuka, *Umi o Wataru Ukiyo-e—Hayashi Tadamasa no Shōgai* [Ukiyo-e over the seas—the life of Tadamasa Hayashi] (Tokyo, 1981).

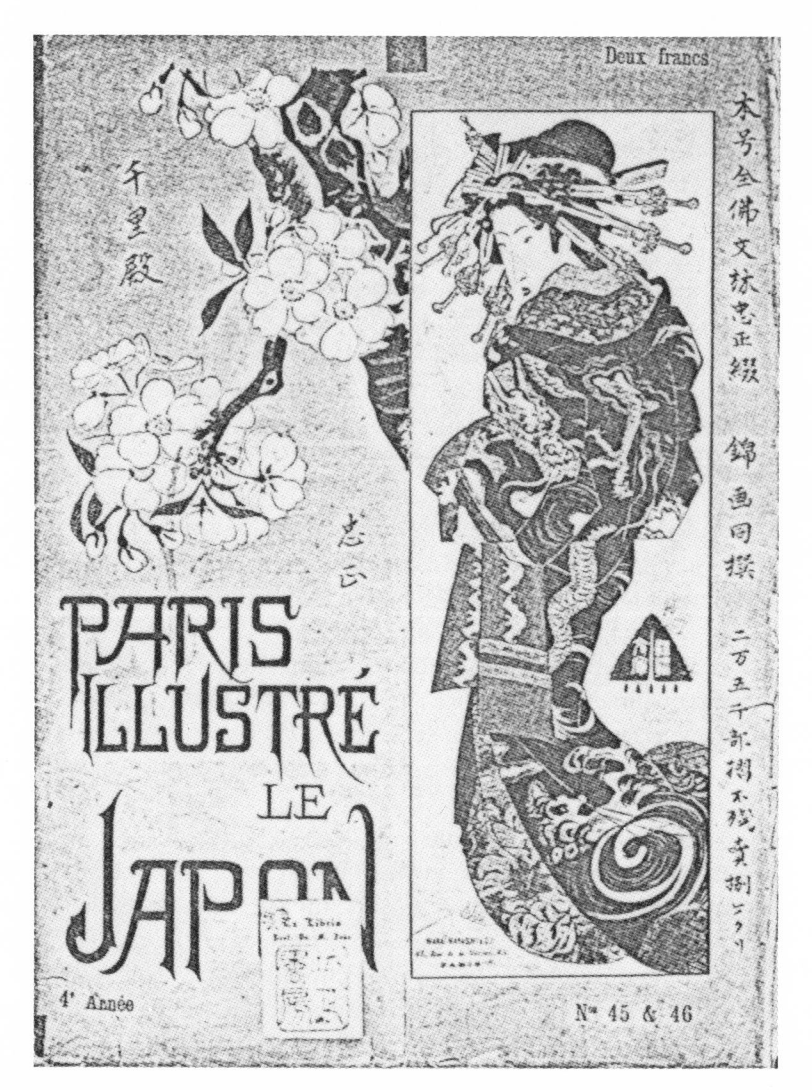

Figure 16.1 Cover of May 1886 issue of *Paris illustré*, "Le Japon," on which Van Gogh based his painting *Japonaiserie*.

in its manifold forms was introduced into Europe on occasions like the three great international exhibitions, Japanese traditional music was almost never performed in Europe. French musicians who attended the 1900 exhibition, such as Debussy, Satie, Ravel, and Chabrier, were deeply moved upon hearing Indonesian gamelan music, but they had no knowledge whatsoever of Japanese music. However, these musicians could scarcely have remained unaffected by the phenomenon of Japonisme that was exerting such a strong influence upon European culture as a whole at the time. It is commonly known that Debussy, who was an enthusiastic collector of woodblock prints and other manifestations of Japonaiserie, employed

Figure 16.2 Vincent Van Gogh's *Japonaiserie: The Courtesan (after Kesai Eisen).*

a print of waves taken from Hokusai's series of prints entitled "Thirty-six Views of Mount Fuji" to decorate the cover of the score of his symphonic poem *La Mer*. Many other composers besides Debussy obtained inspiration and even the titles of their works from Japanese prints, poems, and stories. For example, in 1883, the composer and conductor André Messager wrote an opera in four acts entitled *Madame Chrysanthème* based upon the novel of the same name by Pierre Loti. In 1908, Désire-Emile Inghelbrecht composed a piece for orchestra entitled *Pour le jour de la première neige au vieux Japon* on the basis of an article in the special Japan issue of *Paris illustré* edited by Tadamasa Hayashi. In 1943, the Japanese music critic Tarō Matsumoto published a detailed survey of pieces that use Japanese materials and were composed in France during the early years of the twentieth century. This study provides evidence that approximately seventy such pieces were composed over a thirty-year period.[6] Such a figure indicates the extent of the influence of Japonisme upon the Parisian musical world at the beginning of this century.

The Apaches, formed at the beginning of the twentieth century, included some of the most devoted Japanese enthusiasts. Jann Pasler's "Stravinsky and the Apaches" has brought to light this group's role in Stravinsky's creative development at the time of *The Rite of Spring*.[7] Stravinsky was on intimate terms with the most fervent devotee of Japonisme in the group, Maurice Delage. After accompanying his father on a business trip to India and Japan in spring 1912, Delage wrote a number of compositions reflecting his fascination with the East. These include the *Quatres poèmes Hindous* (1913), which received their first performance together with the *Three Japanese Lyrics*, the *Sept Haikai* (1925), and *In Morte di un samurai* (1952).

The two Maurices who were members of the Apaches shared a common Japanese acquaintance: Jirohachi Satsuma (1901–1976). This Japanese gentleman of not inconsiderable means was an habitué of Parisian high society in the 1920s. He went under the sobriquet of "Baron" Satsuma and was a classic example of a rich profligate devoted to ensuring that not a penny of his immense fortune remained after his death. Satsuma provided the Apaches with information about Japan, and when the Japanese shamisen virtuoso Sakichi Kineya the Fourth visited Paris in 1925, Satsuma arranged a shamisen recital for the Apaches. The following episode is contained in his autobiography, to which he gave the French title *C'est si bon*.

> I immediately consulted Ravel and Delage, and decided to hold a welcoming party for Sakichi and his wife at the home of the pianist, Gil-Marchex. Sakichi performed on a red blanket surrounded by a golden folding screen. Ravel and Delage were enthralled by the performance. That was all well and good, but Sakichi had brought along with him from Japan a Shinto fox image, his object of religious devotion, which he placed on the mantelpiece in his hotel room and would worship reverently without fail in the morning and the evening by clapping his hands in front of it.

---

6. Tarō Matsumoto, "Furansu no Ongakukai ni Arawareta Nihon" [Japan in the French musical world], *Ongaku Kenkyu* [Music research] no. 2 (1943).

7. Jann Pasler, "Stravinsky and the Apaches," *Musical Times* (June 1982): 403–407.

> However, upon their return to the hotel later in the evening, Sakichi and his wife were dismayed to find that the underwear which Mrs. Kineya was in the custom of wearing beneath her travelling kimono had been placed by a hotel employee on top of this sacred altar which Sakichi had created, as a result no doubt of ignorance of its actual function.

Recently I investigated the estate left by Jirohachi Satsuma and discovered there a score of *Sept Haikai* (Editions Jobert) presented to Satsuma by Delage, as well as a manuscript in the composer's own hand of an eight-bar piece composed for Satsuma by Delage, using the original Japanese text of Basho's Haiku about the sound of a frog jumping into a pond. Figure 16.3 shows the hitherto unpublished score of this piece by Delage, entitled *Bashō*. It is a typical example of the Japonisme of this age. Another find was a letter, dated 18 May 1925 (?), sent to Satsuma in Japan by Delage and addressed from 3 rue de Civry, the headquarters of the Apaches. The noteworthy feature of this letter is the envelope, which is written in an elegant Japanese script, indicating that Delage was able both to read and write Japanese to some extent.

Surely if Stravinsky was not familiar with Japanese prints and poetry before his acquaintance with the Apaches, his frequent stays in Delage's "little hotel" at 3 rue de Civry would have brought him into contact with Japonisme. The *Three Japanese Lyrics* are in fact dedicated to the Apaches, the first to Delage, the second to Florent Schmitt, the third to Ravel.

Turning to the poems that Stravinsky selected, we encounter a number of difficulties. The texts are taken from classical Japanese poetry. Attached to the vocal score are translations of the poems into Russian by A. Brandt, into French by Delage, into English by Robert Burness, and into German by Ernst Roth. From Stravinsky's comment in his autobiography, it is clear that he composed the songs using Brandt's Russian translations.

These poems are known as "Waka" (literally, "Japanese songs") or "Tanka" (literally, "short songs"). Waka or Tanka are short poems of thirty-one syllables arranged in five lines with a syllabic structure of 5–7–5–7–7. They appear in Japanese literature around the eighth century and considerably predate the Haiku form that arose in the fourteenth century and developed through the Edo period. Thus, the poetic form of the Waka or Tanka has been a vehicle of Japanese poetic expression for at least twelve centuries. (Even today the major Japanese newspapers carry weekly sections featuring Waka submitted by readers, a fact indicating the great regard in which this poetic form is held in Japan.) Between 1901 and 1925, Daizaburo Matsushita, a scholar of Japanese literature, compiled and indexed two volumes of representative Waka. This work, known as the *Kokka Taikan* [Great collection of Japanese poetry] contains 43,613 poems in its first volume and 41,069 poems in its second. All the poems are arranged and numbered for easy reference.

The poems' brevity and the Waka's frequently appearing stereotyped expressions made it difficult to find the original texts from the translations on

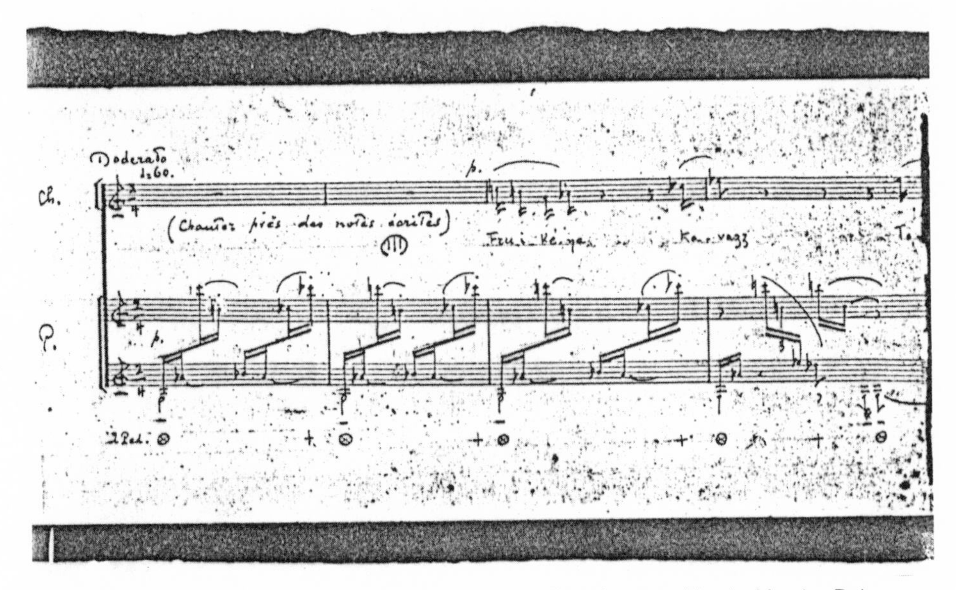

Figure 16.3 Manuscript facsimile of "Bashō," an unpublished composition by Maurice Delage inscribed to Jirohachi Satsuma.

Stravinsky's score. I searched through the *Kokka Taikan* and found the following Waka.

1. "Akahito"
   Written by Akahito Yamanobe, *Kokka Taikan* No. 1426 (Manyo-shu)
      Waga seko ni
      Misenu to omoishi
      Sakurabana
      Sore to mo miezu
      Yuki no furureba
2. "Mazatsumi"
   Written by Masazumi Miyamoto, *Kokka Taikan* No. 12 (Kokin-shu)
      Tani kaze ni
      Tokuru kori no
      Hima goto ni
      Uchi-izuru nami ya
      Haru no hatsuhana
3. "Tsaraiuki"
   Written by Tsurayuki Ki no, *Kokka Taikan* No. 59 (Kokin-shu)
      Sakurabana
      Sakinikerashina
      Ashibiki no
      Yama no kai yori
      Miyuru shirayuki

Figure 16.3 *continued.*

Each of these poems is named for a Japanese poet. "Akahito," the poet of the first piece, refers to Akahito Yamanobe, a famous court poet who lived in the Nara period during the eighth century. His fifty most notable poems are contained in Japan's oldest collection of poetry, the *Manyo-shu.* The second piece, however, presents a problem, for no poet named "Mazatsumi" appears to have existed. Yet a virtually unknown poet named Masazumi Miyamoto, who lived in the latter half of the ninth century, composed a poem likening the ice that melts in the wind blowing through the valleys in spring to the first blossoms of spring. Clearly, this is the poet in question. Strictly speaking, then, Stravinsky's orthography is incorrect. The title of the piece should be "Masazumi."

Another case of faulty orthography occurs in the third piece. The poet in question is clearly Tsurayuki Ki no, one of Japan's most renowned poets and the compiler of the *Kokin-shu,* Japan's earliest and most famous collection of Waka. Tsurayuki lived during the latter half of the ninth century and the first half of the tenth. The image of cherry blossoms that bloom in the spring and are likened to white clouds appears in at least five of Tsurayuki's poems. Considering certain aspects of the translations, I have concluded that the poem Stravinsky chose was "Kokin-shu," number 59 in the *Kokka Taikan.* In short, I was able to extract the original versions of the three poems used in the *Three Japanese Lyrics* from the many thousand poems contained in the *Kokka Taikan.* My conclusion is that Stravinsky composed *Three Japanese Lyrics* on the basis of texts written by Japanese poets between the eighth and ninth centuries.

The one central idea unifying the Waka upon which the *Three Japanese Lyrics* are based is that of spring. In each song, Stravinsky portrays the aspect of nature represented in the poems in a faithful manner. In "Akahito," an ostinato in eighth-notes using the four pitches B♭, C♭, C♮, and D♭ and two grace notes on the pitches A♭ and E♭ at both extremes of the constituent pitches of the ostinato, portrays an image of snow gently falling during spring. In "Mazatsumi," rapid passages making effective use of continuous time values (from single quarter-notes to thirty-second-notes and division of the quarter-notes in from one to ten beats) depict the water created by the thawing of the winter snow flowing rapidly through a valley. In "Tsaraiuki," fast passages played by the wind instruments reflect the color of the cherry blossoms seen on a distant mountain. With a few exceptions, the vocal part moves entirely in eighth-notes, this being one of the principal characteristics of the piece as a whole. Stravinsky's compositional technique is evident throughout, such as the B♭, C♭, C♮, D♭ ostinato in the first piece, the B, C ostinato in the third piece, the polydivision of time values and the bitonality in the second piece, and the clear texture with the emphasis placed upon the sound of the individual instruments within the chamber orchestra.

The main feature of this work lies, to borrow Stravinsky's words, in its striving toward "a two-dimensional art without any sense of solidity." Although the piece is dominated by a sense of linear counterpoint, the linear technique involved is what Pierre Boulez has referred to as "*faux contrepoint*" or false counterpoint.[8] There is no arrival at a single center with the maintenance of close interconnection between the parts. In contrast to the way in which a self-enclosed and complete world is created in Western painting by means of the "vanishing point" in traditional perspective technique and of the techniques of symmetry, the *Lyrics* as it were erect a number of "vanishing points" outside the picture itself. They employ asymmetrical techniques, as the result of which a unique, open world, hitherto unknown to Western music, is created.

Many scholars have expressed the opinion that the *Three Japanese Lyrics* were influenced, especially in respect to instrumentation, by Schoenberg's *Pierrot Lunaire*. However, documentary evidence shows that the *Lyrics* were begun before Stravinsky had heard *Pierrot* in December 1912.[9] Stravinsky's work belongs in a world totally different from *Pierrot*, which has its roots thoroughly within the Austro-Germanic tradition. The musical world created by the *Three Japanese Lyrics*, simple pieces composed in accordance with a unique technical method, was explored further in *Pribaoutki* (1914) and attained perfection in *Histoire du soldat* (1918).

Finally, I shall briefly trace the introduction and reception of Stravinsky's work in Japan. Stravinsky's name was introduced into Japan by the country's first music critic, Motoo Otaguro (1893–1979). Otaguro studied in London during the

8. Pierre Boulez, *Relèves d'Apprenti* (Paris, 1966), p. 247.

9. Vera Stravinsky and Robert Craft, *Stravinsky in Pictures and Documents* (New York, 1978), pp. 107–109.

early 1910s and wrote a book, *From Bach to Schoenberg*, published in May 1915. In it, he devotes ten pages to Stravinsky, including the following passage:

> Only a short time has passed since the name of Stravinsky has become known to the world. Before that time not only was he unknown to the world but almost unknown even in his homeland, Russia. . . . However, in whichever direction he advances, his development and his works will never fail to attract people's attention. Irrespective of success or failure, he will undoubtedly continue to the end as a musician of the greatest originality and with an abhorrence of the imitation of others.

In this, the first of his more than one hundred publications devoted to the introduction of Western music in Japan, Otaguro thus expressed his high opinion of Stravinsky's abilities. Only much later, during the 1930s and 1940s, were Stravinsky's works actually performed for the first time in Japan. The NHK Symphony Orchestra gave the premiere performances of many of Stravinsky's works in Japan, including *Fireworks* on 8 March 1931 under Hidemaro Konoe, *The Firebird* on 29 April 1931 under Nicolai Schifferblatt, *Pulcinella* on 30 September 1934 under Hidemaro Konoe, and *Petrushka* on 21 April 1937 under Josef Rosenstock. *The Rite* had to wait until after World War II. Its first performance in Japan took place on 21 September 1950 under the baton of Kazuo Yamada.

Despite the generally belated introduction of Stravinsky's work in Japan, the *Three Japanese Lyrics* received their Japanese premiere at an exceptionally early juncture. Attracted by the title of the work, the Japanese tenor Yoshie Fujiwara included it in his recital at the Wigmore Hall in London on 30 October 1922. On 9 June 1925, he gave the work its premiere in Japan. His performance of the *Three Japanese Lyrics* was thus not only the first time Stravinsky's music was heard in Japan, but also the first interpretation made of this work by a Japanese artist.

17 Stravinsky and the Pianola

REX LAWSON

AMONG SUCH a polyphony of musicologists, I confess to feeling somewhat abashed; I am no expert on Stravinsky's life, or his character, or even his harmony. My task is simply to persuade you that he had, so to speak, a great foot for music. But if you are to place his player piano compositions in perspective, it is important that I first provide you with a brief historical survey of the player piano's technical evolution and musical traditions.

In 1882, the year of Stravinsky's birth, the Pianola had not yet been invented. Already, however, there were many roll-operated musical instruments in the drawing rooms of American and European high society. Usually reed organs, these instruments were given voice by wind; they were descended, on the one hand, from the pinned barrel organ and musical box and, on the other, from the Jacquard loom, which used punched cards to mechanize complex weaving patterns in the textile industry. During the late 1890s, much research into pneumatic piano-playing devices was carried out in the United States. The results of this activity became apparent in 1897, when the first Pianolas went on sale.

The Pianola was the Aeolian Company's brand of piano player, a device that fitted in front of the keyboard of an ordinary piano and played it by means of a number of felt-covered wooden fingers controlled by a pianolist with the aid of a music roll. From around 1902, pianos were also manufactured with the roll-playing action inside them. These were known as "player pianos" (the reverse of "piano players") or, in the case of the Aeolian Company, as Pianola Pianos.

A similar development took place in Europe, notably in Germany, where in January 1905 Edwin Welte began recording the actual playing of contemporary pianists for his newly invented reproducing piano.[1] This instrument was generally known as the Welte-Mignon, though this title really applies to only one model—a keyboardless instrument designed to resemble an elegant sideboard.[2] But it was Great Britain, France, and the United States that influenced Stra-

1. The earliest Welte-Mignon rolls carry recording dates on their labels.

2. "Player piano" is usually taken to refer to all types of pianos operated by a music roll, whether foot pedaled or not. As the paper roll moves around on the instrument, it passes over a brass or wooden tracker bar that is drilled with a number of tiny holes, one for each note. Suction is applied through these holes, holding the paper flush against the tracker bar as it rolls down. When a perforation in the roll uncovers one of the holes in the tracker bar, free air is allowed to pass

vinsky's player piano activities; in fact, his interest in the Pianola lasted for over fifteen years.[3]

The Pianola and Its Competitors

For the first few years of the century, both Britain and France were largely importers of American pneumatic instruments, not only from the Aeolian Company, but also from its many competitors. The Pianola thus vied with the Angelus, the Cecilian, the Simplex, the Triumph, and the Rex, not to mention the Tonkunst and many others, in attempting to capture the lion's share of the European export market.[4] Most of these early piano players used sixty-five-note rolls or something similar. Not until a 1908 conference in Buffalo did all manufacturers agree to a common standard for the new eighty-eight-note or full-scale rolls.

By 1914, when Stravinsky visited Aeolian Hall in London, the Orchestrelle Company was well established as the major player piano manufacturer in the country, with the Pianola and Pianola Piano acknowledged as the leading instruments on the market.[5] Easthope Martin, the Worcestershire song composer, had

down this hole to a small pneumatic valve, deep inside the mechanism. The operation of this valve allows suction to pass to a pneumatic motor for the appropriate piano note. The motor is like a small bellows but in reverse: instead of the sides being squeezed in order to force air out, the air is actively sucked out, causing the motor sides to collapse together. The motion thus generated operates the piano, and the chain from perforated roll to audible motor is complete.

Reproducing pianos are a particular type of player piano that use specially recorded and coded rolls to reproduce the exact playing of well-known pianists. They too are usually powered pneumatically, with an electric pump supplying suction. Operating a mains switch sets them happily on their way.

Alas, we lack a neat term to define a foot-pedaled player piano. I favor the word "Pianola," but I am aware this is still a registered trademark of the Aeolian Company, although no longer used by it to refer to the type of instrument to which it originally applied. However, the European use of the word "gramophone" to refer to all types of record player in no way diminishes the memory of the Gramophone Company as pioneers in that industry, and I suggest that the Aeolian Company would do great service to the world and to itself by allowing "Pianola" to develop into the generic term it has so long sought to become. In this chapter, I use the word with a capital letter to refer to the Aeolian Company's specific product.

3. I here wish to express my gratitude to Louis Cyr, who generously made available to me all his extensive research concerning Stravinsky and the player piano.

4. Regular perusers of the *Denkmäler Deutscher Tonkunst* will be surprised to learn that the Tonkunst was indeed an American instrument, manufactured by the evidently erudite Mr. William Tonk of New York City and his brother.

5. The legal name of what is generally known as the Aeolian Company has varied from time to time. Its full title in America in the early part of this century was the Aeolian, Weber Piano, and Pianola Company because it manufactured Aeolians (roll-operated organs), Weber Pianos, and Pianolas. In Britain, it was known as the Orchestrelle Company until around 1920, when it gradually took on the name of Aeolian and began making rolls through its wholly owned subsidiary, the Universal Music Company. This latter firm made rolls not only for its parent company, but also for nearly all its competitors, which accounts for the fact that many rolls were issued both as Aeolian Themodist and as Universal.

been the company's chief pianolist for several years, having pedaled the Grieg Piano Concerto in 1912 with the London Symphony Orchestra under Nikisch. Now, owing to ill health, he was giving up his position in favor of Reginald Reynolds, lately employed as the expert Cecilian player by the Farrand Company.[6]

It may appear an unwarranted luxury to invent a special title like "pianolist" for a humble player piano operator. You may think the roll does all the work, leaving the operator only to pedal with great force and little understanding—like someone conducting a phonograph record in front of a mirror. This is not the case. Although the pianolist is relieved of the necessity of pushing down the notes of the piano with his own fingers, he must nevertheless control the dynamic force of them all with the pressure of his feet; he must acquire a subtle and fluent use of the tempo lever; and his left hand must carry out the functions of sustaining and una corda, which his feet are too preoccupied to manage. Despite the publicity that reproducing piano systems such as the Duo-Art and Ampico receive nowadays, most piano roll master copies were not recorded at all but simply perforated by hand with a hammer and punch, after being marked up in pencil with reference to the original sheet music. Unthoughtful pedaling will produce unthoughtful music, devoid of light and shade and without the slightest signs of life.

Nearly all foot-operated player pianos made before World War II were designed, in theory at least, to allow for good musical performances. Despite these worthy intentions, most performers lacked the musical understanding to use such an easily acquired digital technique. As a result, the mistaken impression was created that the player piano had its own unique sound, characterized by inexorable tempi and terrace dynamics with only one terrace.

Besides providing hand controls for tempo, sustaining, and half-blow pedals, the Pianola used two patented systems, the Metrostyle and the Themodist. The first worked by means of a wavy red line printed on each roll, which was to be followed by a pointer attached to the tempo lever mechanism. In this way, a red line supervised by a composer or pianist could provide an authoritative guide to the phrasing of a particular piece of music. This, at any rate, was the theory. In practice, most Metrostyle lines on rolls made in Britain from around 1911 were copied by operatives paid piecework rates; as a result, their accuracy is somewhat suspect. Yet when these limitations are understood, Metrostyle lines can be a useful guide to a composer's intentions.

The Themodist allowed the performer to bring individual notes or chords into relief. The pneumatic operation of the Pianola was split into treble and bass between E and F above middle C. Two graduated accompaniment levers progressively reduced the suction provided by the feet to either or both halves of the pi-

6. Reginald Reynold's memoirs were serialized in the *Player-Piano Group Bulletin*, no. 60 (January 1976): 23–29, 61: 16–23, 62: 24–29, 64: 10–14, 65: 14–18, 66: 17–19, 67 (October 1977): 16–17. Copies of this privately printed journal, subsequently referred to as *PPG Bulletin*, are on deposit with the British Library.

ano, which in no way absolved the pianolist from providing as subtle and varied an overall level as possible. In combination with this process of throttling back, tiny marginal performations on the roll, rather like ditto marks, allowed full pedal suction to reach whichever half they controlled for a split second, thereby causing individual notes to become prominent, according to the editing of the roll. Thus, the pianolist could control both solo and accompaniment levels.

The London office of the Orchestrelle Company directed Aeolian operations throughout Europe, the British Empire, and South America, so, short of a trip to New York, Stravinsky's visit to Aeolian Hall was the closest he could come to the center of worldwide pianolistic activity. In some ways, it *was* indeed the center. In the United States, the Aeolian Company's reproducing piano, the Duo-Art, had already been launched in competition with the Welte-Mignon; their recorded rolls were soon to capture the market on the other side of the Atlantic as well. Because of World War I and the subsequent introduction of import duties, the Duo-Art was not "pushed" in Britain until the early 1920s. Local staff thus had to be trained to manufacture both instruments and rolls.

The British tradition of expert pedaling remained strong; in addition, the choice of repertoire on rolls was noticeably adventurous because the financial directives of H. B. Tremaine, who ran the Aeolian Company, were less harshly felt three thousand miles away.

In France, the Aeolian Company ran a thriving business from the Salle Pleyel on the Avenue de l'Opéra, but the team of Pleyel quickly became a strong competitor. Indeed, Pleyel may be said to have dominated the piano and player piano business in Paris, owing to the great energy of Gustave Lyon, who controlled the firm. Many technical experiments were carried out, notably those resulting in Wanda Landowska's famous harpsichords and in the double grand pianos used in the premiere of the final version of *Les Noces*.[7] In the field of player pianos, the firm manufactured the Pleyela and, from the mid-1920s, the Autopleyela, a somewhat simplified form of reproducing piano.[8]

Like the Pianola, the Pleyela split its pneumatic mechanism into treble and bass between E and F above middle C, and its overall dynamic level was controlled by the feet. In addition, it incorporated a device known as the "Chanteur," somewhat like the Themodist on the Pianola but not quite as subtle. Because no evidence suggests that Stravinsky's works found their way onto Autopleyela rolls, no great purpose would be served by a detailed description of the system.

Unfortunately, there does not seem to have been many adequate pianolists in Paris at the time. Stravinsky abandoned the intermediate version of *Les Noces* due to difficulties of synchronization with the pianolists. Exactly the same problem prevented George Antheil's *Ballet Mécanique* from being performed with sev-

---

7. Information kindly provided by Théodore Strawinsky, who was present.

8. Lyon even caused at least one double Pleyela grand to be made, which played genuine two-piano music from gigantic rolls.

enteen Pleyelas, as intended. The first private performance of this ballet is described in some detail by Bravig Imbs, a friend of the composer, who relates how a young girl employed by Pleyel strenuously exerted her way through the three rolls involved and "glowed" very freely as a result of the experience.[9] That a young person should have been employed in Paris in a position for which a trained musician in his forties was required in London seems to reflect a difference in attitude toward the player piano. In any case, undue perspiration is a sure sign of inexpert pedaling.

According to Jacques Brillouin, a leading French player piano expert, the aim of a good piano roll should be to provide all the nuances of tempo from a recorded performance, leaving dynamic control to the operator.[10] No suggestion is made that the pianolist should do other in matters of tempo than set the roll at a constant speed. Although this use of the player piano precludes its synchronization with any live performers, it is easy to perceive how it accorded with Stravinsky's desire to fix his own ideas of tempi in a permanent record.

By the time Stravinsky paid his first visit to the United States in 1925, the reproducing piano had reached its maturity. The Aeolian Company's Duo-Art was in competition with the Ampico, the Welte-Mignon and Welte Licensee, the Angelus Artrio, the ArtEcho, and various less successful makes. Although widespread, the foot-operated player piano was definitely regarded as a poor alternative to these highly publicized, more glamorous recording systems. Of course, perhaps in the early years of the century, considerable expertise was to be found in the operation of foot-pedaled instruments, but after World War I, the Aeolian Company's advertising centered mainly around the Duo-Art Pianola Piano and the Aeolian Duo-Art Pipe Organ, to give the company's chief products their correct names.

Like other reproducing pianos, the Duo-Art needs no human intervention beyond the operation of a mains switch. Rolls run at a fixed speed, and all the original pianist's variations of tempo are thus reproduced. At the Aeolian London studio, rolls were recorded at a special Weber grand piano that had series of contacts below each key, not all of which were used. The operational contacts were connected to a very fast perforating machine in another room, which created an instant record of the tempo by punching at a frequency of four thousand holes per minute. A recording producer, Reginald Reynolds, sat beside the piano at a specially made console, his hands controlling two large knobs, rather like oversized amplifier volume controls. He thus caused dynamic coding perforations to be punched onto the recorded roll at the same time as the pianist was playing. Clearly, this was a far from accurate way of recording dynamics, but af-

9. Bravig Imbs, *Confessions of Another Young Man* (New York, 1936), p. 56.

10. Jacques Brillouin, "Premiers Contacts avec le Piano Automatique," *La Revue Musicale* (February 1928): 53–58 and "La Musique Perforée," *La Revue Musicale* (April 1928): 280–83.

ter repeated editing, and approval from the artist in question, many rolls achieved a remarkable fidelity.[11]

The Duo-Art system of dynamic coding uses two sets of four perforations, located toward each side of the roll in the positions where perforations for the bottom four and top four notes of the piano are usually to be found, thus rendering these notes inoperative when the Duo-Art is in use. Each set of four holes combines its information according to the binary system, allowing sixteen different combinations in each case. These work upon two pneumatic regulators in order to provide graduated degrees of touch upon the piano. The coding of the left-hand side of the roll controls what is known as the "Accompaniment" regulator, which in normal circumstances provides suction for the whole piano. But whenever a Themodist-type ditto mark perforation appears on either the left or right margin of the roll, the appropriate half of the piano is transferred for a split second to the "Theme" regulator, always kept at least one degree louder than the "Accompaniment," and controlled by the four coding perforations toward the right-hand edge of the roll. In this way, instantaneous accents and changes of level can be obtained.

In practice, Duo-Art rolls were edited until they sounded satisfactory, and not simply according to the theory of the system. Consequently, it is pointless to place too much importance on the thirty-two degrees of touch the instrument is supposed to possess. Because of the way in which rolls were edited, performances on the Duo-Art can be a great deal more subtle than such a rigid theoretical description may suggest.[12]

Stravinsky's Music for Pianola

These different avenues of development in the three countries in which Stravinsky worked with the player piano are reflected not only in contemporary writings about his work, but also in his published recollections of the instruments. Having noted these differences in attitude, albeit briefly, we are now in a position to examine Stravinsky's uses of the player piano more closely.

Stravinsky's music first appeared on piano roll toward the end of 1914, when the Orchestrelle Company of London issued four rolls of the Four Studies, Opus

11. Reginald Reynolds, "A Note on the Technique of Recording," *Gramophone Player-Piano Supplement* (February 1924): 4, 7; rpt. in *PPG Bulletin*, no. 66 (July 1977): 22–24. See also Roger Buckley, "An Interview with Gordon Iles," *PPG Bulletin*, no. 61 (April 1976): 13–16.

12. Of course, given an editor on a bad day and a pianist fed up with listening to playbacks of his or her rolls, performances can also be terrible. This dependence on editing standards applies to all reproducing piano systems and is the main reason why Ampico rolls, whose editing processes were minutely painstaking, have consistently high standards.

7.[13] Evidence on certain rolls indicate that these were commissioned by Claude Johnson, a wealthy amateur musician who was later managing director of Rolls-Royce Motors, and then released to the general public.[14] They are not recorded rolls; yet Stravinsky must have heard them when he visited Aeolian Hall in mid-1914 for a demonstration of the company's instruments.

About a year later, Esther Willis, a member of the famous British organ-building family, cut a private set of rolls. The commission came from Philip Heseltine ("Peter Warlock"), the English composer. The titles include such early works as the *Scherzo fantastique* and *Fireworks.* As far as I can tell, these rolls carried no "imprimatur"—perhaps I should say "perforetur"—from Stravinsky. But in any event, two of them, *Fireworks* and the "Chinese March" from *The Nightingale,* were performed by the photographer Alvin Langdon Coburn at Aeolian Hall in 1916.[15]

Stravinsky's 1914 visit to Aeolian Hall led him to consider the Pianola, with its facilities for speed, spacing, and spectacularly sized chords, as a solo instrument. He mentioned this in conversation to Edwin Evans, the British music critic, and in 1917, Evans enlarged on the idea and wrote to a number of European composers asking for Pianola compositions. Thus, the Etude for Pianola, although conceived as a unique entity, was in fact issued as part of a series, along with works by Malipiero, Casella, Eugene Goossens, Herbert Howells, and several others.[16] It was not, however, the first work to be written for the Pianola. The Orchestrelle Company's 1914 catalogue lists several such compositions, although all by minor composers, in addition to many special arrangements of existing works, notably by Busoni, Scharwenka, and Percy Grainger.

The music of the Etude is deliberately mechanical in sound, full of fragmented Spanish dance tunes, overlapping and competing with each other as Stravinsky sought to capture the atmosphere of the Madrid streets, which he had experienced firsthand during a visit in 1916. What Charles Ives's *Fourth of July* is to the brass band, the Etude for Pianola is to the cafe piano and barrel organ. The piece makes a virtue of the chunky musical texture the player piano can sometimes produce. Stravinsky may have supervised the Metrostyle line on the roll;

---

13. I base what is admittedly a supposition on the fact that the Orchestrelle Company's June 1914 catalogue lists rolls to within one hundred of the serial numbers of the Four Studies, Opus 7. In 1914, rolls were being issued in this series at a rate of about thirty-five per month, with reasonable regularity.

14. There is a set of rolls in England, formerly the file copies of the Universal Music Company, bearing on it the heading, "Specially Manufactured for Claude Johnson, Es." I can conceive of no reason why Mr. Johnson should have needed to have these rolls specially made if they were already freely available. For this reason, I conclude that it was he who investigated the manufacture of the Four Studies, Opus 7, as well as of a good deal of music by Debussy, Ravel, and others.

15. Information kindly provided by Miss Willis and also gleaned from concert programs in the writer's possession.

16. Edwin Evans, "Pianola Music," *Musical Times* (November 1921): 761–64.

many other rolls in the same series were marked in this way by their composers.[17] Reginald Reynolds gave the first public performance of the Etude on 13 October 1921 at Aeolian Hall, London.[18]

At the same concert, there was also a performance of one of the four rolls of *The Rite of Spring,* which Aeolian had just manufactured. This set was based on the four-hand arrangement.[19] It has the advantage, underlined by Percy Scholes in a book entitled *Crotchets,* of saving the performers from coming to blows over wrong notes.[20] But by 1921, Stravinsky's imagination left the realm of mere four-hand versions. That year he moved into a studio in the Pleyel building in Paris, setting the scene for a musical collaboration that was to result in fifty rolls being made of his works, at least forty of them special arrangements.[21]

In *An Autobiography,* Stravinsky describes his labors with a mixture of affection and regret:

> It was at this time that my connection with the Pleyel Company began. They had suggested that I should make a transcription of my works for their Pleyela mechanical piano.
>
> My interest in the work was twofold. In order to prevent the distortion of my compositions by future interpreters, I had always been anxious to find a means of imposing some restriction on the notorious liberty, especially widespread today, which prevents the public from obtaining a correct idea of the author's intentions. This possibility was now afforded by the rolls of the mechanical piano, and, a little later, by gramophone records.
>
> The means enabled me to determine for the future the relationships of the movements *(tempi)* and the nuances in accordance with my wishes. It is true that this guaranteed nothing, and in the ten years which have since elapsed I have, alas! had ample opportunity of seeing how ineffective it has proved in practice. But these transcriptions nevertheless enabled me to create a lasting document which should be of service to those executants who would rather know and follow my intentions than stray into irresponsible interpretations of my musical text.
>
> There was a second direction in which this work gave me satisfaction. This was not simply the reduction of an orchestral work to the limitations of a piano of seven octaves. It was the process of adaptation to an instrument which had, on the one hand, unlim-

17. Information taken from an Aeolian selected roll list, for use with a book by Percy Scholes, *The Appreciation of Music by Means of the Pianola and Duo-Art* (London, 1925). The list is found attached to the rear cover of only a few copies of this book.

18. The performance occurred during a talk given by Edwin Evans and transcribed by him for publication as the article referred to in n. 16.

19. I say this having played the rolls many times but without yet having specifically set out to analyze them.

20. Percy Scholes, *Crochets* (London, 1924), pp. 157–58.

21. Fifty-one rolls were originally advertised, but no evidence has been found that any copies of *Rag-time* ever existed.

> ited possibilities of precision, velocity, and polyphony, but which, on the other hand, constantly presented serious difficulties in establishing dynamic relationships. These tasks developed and exercised my imagination by constantly presenting new problems of an instrumental nature closely connected with the questions of acoustics, harmony, and part writing.[22]

More detailed research is needed to discover exactly how Stravinsky worked at Pleyel. Mayakovsky describes how he could "hand his work directly in to the factory, trying the musical proof on the Pianola."[23] The implication of this is that Stravinsky's product was in the form of manuscript, which was then transcribed onto master rolls by a Pleyel musician. We know, however, from Jacques Brillouin that Pleyel master rolls were of the same length as their usual issued copies and that these masters could be directly played on a piano without the need for producing multiple rolls.[24] Thus, Stravinsky may have drawn his transcriptions on a master, leaving the laborious process of punching for a technician. Whichever is the case, and the former seems more likely to me, it would be unwise to assume that Mayakovsky's brief description, made in 1922, refers to the only process Stravinsky carried out during his years at the Pleyel factory. For example, Pleyel certainly possessed a recording piano that allowed concert pianists to make rolls of their own playing, and in such simple pieces as the *Five Fingers*, it would have been much more sensible for Stravinsky actually to record at such an instrument.

The master's own description of one of his techniques appears in *Expositions and Developments:*

> I discovered the chief problem [of the Pleyela] to be in the restrictive application of the pedals caused by the division of the keyboard into two parts; it was like Cinerama, or a film shown half and half from two projectors. I solved this problem by employing two secretaries to sit one on either side of me as I stood facing the keyboard; I then dictated as I transcribed from right to left and to each in turn.[25]

This statement's full meaning is not immediately clear, but I can think of only one set of circumstances that accords with all the details of Stravinsky's description. In the first place, the pedals he mentions are certainly not the sustaining and una corda, nor even the Pleyela pedals in a literal sense; rather the word is used as a nontechnical substitute for "pneumatic mechanism." In other words, Stravinsky had to work within the framework of an instrument in which the rela-

22. Igor Stravinsky, *An Autobiography* (1936; rpt. New York, 1962), p. 101.

23. Vera Stravinsky and Robert Craft, *Stravinsky in Pictures and Documents* (New York, 1978), p. 213.

24. Brillouin, "*La Musique Perforée,*" p. 282.

25. Igor Stravinsky and Robert Craft, *Expositions and Developments* (London, 1962), pp. 69, 70.

tive levels of bass and treble could be varied, but in which chords overlapping both halves of the piano could be emphasized only by means of the Chanteur device. In both cases, the lower of the two levels on the Pleyela, if not actually fixed, was nevertheless automatically regulated to remain in a loose dynamic relationship with the higher level. This automatic control must be what caused Stravinsky the problems of dynamic balance.

The two secretaries cannot have been working for the benefit of the roll technician, who would certainly have found it a hindrance to have to use two manuscripts to cut one roll. Similarly, there would have been no point to the secretaries making up two half–master rolls when only one complete one would play on the test Pleyela. The only possible explanation I can find is that Stravinsky not only worked quickly but also wanted to check and revise his dictation before it was transcribed onto the roll. A dual manuscript would have saved him having to remember in every bar the division between treble and bass at E and F and would thus have eased his task of balancing the two halves of the Pleyela.

So although Stravinsky's Pleyela rolls state they are "adapté et joué par l'auteur" or some variant of this, in fact, a variety of transcriptional processes was probably used. To a confirmed pneumatic addict like myself, it seems easy to understand Stravinsky's fascination with this kind of technical and intellectual challenge. In a socialite Paris brimming with rich princesses, worthy musicians, and adoring acolytes, donning a metaphorical boiler suit and joining the musical mechanics must on occasion have been a great relief.

The results of this factory work deserve to be better known. The titles can be found in the Appendix. They include *The Firebird, Petrushka, The Rite of Spring,* the *Song of the Nightingale,* and *Pulcinella.* Even *Piano-Rag-Music* was specially arranged for the Pleyela, thus out-Rubinsteining its dedicatee. It would take a separate chapter to discuss the problems involved in interpreting these rolls. Suffice it to say, they do need interpretation, with regard to the dynamics indicated by the instructions on the roll and, more reliably, by the appropriate printed score. In the case of the tempo level, it is only necessary to compensate for those factors in the player piano that cause a performance to sound mechanical, as opposed to merely regular. Clearly, much of Stravinsky's arranging was done with a view to creating a precise, clear, and consistent sound. What can make a performance sound mechanical is not excessive regularity, but regularity without dynamic interest, or illogical hiccups in that regularity. These faults must be avoided.

In 1924, Stravinsky enlarged his player piano activities to include the Duo-Art reproducing piano, signing a contract with the Aeolian Company in October of that year. His first recording sessions came in early 1925 in New York, when at least the first movement of the Concerto for Piano and Wind Instruments was automatically transcribed onto roll from his own playing.[26] But the total number of these recorded Duo-Art rolls was small, only one movement of the Concerto

26. Stravinsky and Craft, *Pictures and Documents*, pp. 622–23.

and three rolls of the 1924 Sonata for Piano, although further movements of the Concerto were listed in various catalogues as being in preparation. There was also a roll of the "Berceuse" and "Finale" from *The Firebird* for the Aeolian Duo-Art Pipe Organ, a large and sophisticated breed of residence organ with automatic changes of registration and swell pedaling, much prized nowadays by those collectors who value rarity above all else. The organ repertoire was not great, and its tone colors were those of a home orchestra. So a roll of *The Firebird* no doubt represents one of the pinnacles of its achievement. At any rate, it would be most interesting to hear.

Besides these recorded rolls, a set of *The Firebird* was produced for the Duo-Art piano in the AudioGraphic series masterminded by Percy Scholes, the British music critic.[27] From the style of the dynamic coding and from the fact that the tempo lever has to be reset during the course of certain rolls, it appears the Pleyela *Firebird* was used as a basis for the Duo-Art set, but this is still a rich field for further research. One obvious difference, however, can be seen in the fact that the Duo-Art *Firebird* begins with the "Introduction." The Pleyela version omits it. Stravinsky clearly must have been involved in at least a modicum of extra transcription. In any case, the Duo-Art coding must have required the composer's own suggestions and approval.

Two AudioGraphic series, one issued in London and the other in New York, ran roughly concurrently. The Aeolian Company in Britain was the originator of the scheme, owing not only to Percy Scholes, but also to an American, George Whitefield Fay Reed, the deputy managing director in London, who was less of an accountant than most of his colleagues and was prepared to risk the enormous investment involved.[28] As a result, the British AudioGraphic series is the more important of the two. In the absence of evidence to the contrary, I would suggest that Stravinsky carried out the necessary work for London. For the non-Duo-Art owner, the chief attraction of these series lies in the lengthy illustrated program notes printed on paper left unperforated at the start of each roll. A running commentary is also printed as the music unrolls, as are slurlike lines of several colors that visually emphasize the various themes. Because the program notes are in part autobiographical, it would be useful to have them reprinted—an easy task in these days of cheap photolithography but one that underlines the enormous expense Aeolian undertook in making printing plattens of extreme length.

27. Scholes edited the *Oxford Companion to Music,* which up to its eighth edition prints an excellent illustrated article on the "Mechanical Reproduction of Music," including details of the Audiographic series. In subsequent editions, the article is somewhat curtailed.

28. Was Mr. Reed related to Amy Fay, the pupil of Liszt, who wrote *Music Study in Germany?* The name is sufficiently unusual to suggest some connection, and clearly the family was strongly musical. Amy's sister Rose married Theodore Thomas, who founded the Chicago Symphony Orchestra with the aid of her brother, C. Norman Fay.

Projects were also in hand to include *Petrushka, The Rite of Spring*, and the *Song of the Nightingale* in this series.[29] However, in 1930, the American Aeolian Company, in a bid to survive, bought out its main rival, the American Piano Corporation, makers of the Ampico. Needing cash for this purpose, it sent a hatchet man in the shape of Myers Wayman, its former metropolitan sales manager for New York, to take charge of the British Aeolian Company and to sell off everything he could.[30] Thus, the AudioGraphic project came to an untimely end through no great fault of its own. It certainly provided a unique and intimate way of linking printed commentaries to the actual music and could easily have become a major force in musical education.

At this point, Stravinsky's direct involvement with the player piano ceased so far as I am aware.[31] The intermediate version of *Les Noces,* which includes a part for Pianola, was not given its first performance until 1981. The instrumentation of this 1919 version was Pianola, harmonium, two cymbaloms, and percussion. According to *An Autobiography,* it was never performed at the time, owing to the difficulty of synchronizing the many electrical instruments with the live performers.[32] What Stravinsky means by "electric instruments" is not clear: the harmonium cannot have been intended to be powered by electricity because the manuscript specifies the occasional use of the expression stop. This device was designed so that the feet could control the instrument's dynamics, accents, and hairpins. Stravinsky probably did not intend an electric player piano because accents and forte-pianos abound in the music, and these are not easy to achieve well with a nonreproducing, electric instrument. It seems to me that the part is

---

29. Information on many unissued AudioGraphic rolls is to be found in the *Duo-Art Numerical Catalog,* compiled by Alkert M. Petrak and published privately by him in Cleveland, Ohio in 1963.

30. Information kindly provided by the late Bob Good, formerly roll librarian and Pianola salesman at Aeolian Hall, London.

31. Two Ampico rolls of his works were recorded during the 1920s, the fourth of the Four Studies, Opus 7 (1908) by Alexander Brailowsky and, in the normal piano arrangement, the "Russian Dance" from *Petrushka* made by Paul Doguereau. Anxious as I am that no corner of Stravinskyan research remain unexplored, I should report that the 1925 Ampico catalogue (New York, 1925), p. 25, prints the following inspired program note for the Brailowsky study:

> Delightfully picturesque in its suggestion, the mock anguish of hordes of little sprites smarting under the lash of a burly and loud-mouthed master, one who would govern by force and brawling rather than by kindness and friendly interest. The little fellows rush headlong, the noise of their pattering feet mingling with their cries and complaints. Now and again a gentler note is heard, and there is a suspicion of humor and burlesque underlying it all, which leads one to believe things are not so bad as they seem.

See also Elaine Obenchain, *The Complete Catalog of Ampico Reproducing Piano Rolls* (Darien, Conn., 1977), p. 25.

32. Stravinsky, *An Autobiography,* pp. 104–105.

meant for a foot-operated Pianola, which Stravinsky would have heard in London, and that his later association with Pleyel, and the electric Pleyela he had in his studio in Paris, became uppermost in his mind when he thought and wrote of player pianos thereafter.[33]

Synchronization of a Pianola with other instruments is quite demanding but not impossible, although the difficulty is all the greater when the tempo is strict. Sheltering the odd late note under the wing of a slight rubato is only too easy, but not in *Les Noces!* For the world premiere in Paris in June 1981, I was asked to prepare the music roll, which I did with the aid of many razor blades and a special ruler. There are some fourteen thousand individual holes, and the roll runs for something over ten minutes. I began the cutting process at the Macon municipal camping site in Burgundy, continued it in a tent in Paris by the banks of the Seine, and finished on returning from holiday at my home in south London. This is not the place for a detailed analysis of the music, but the Pianola is called on to provide musical resources beyond the number, span, and speed of the human fingers. Individual notes repeat at six hundred forty per minute in many instances; yet I found only one bar containing a musical impossibility in the shape of three pairs of notes repeated at nine hundred sixty per minute, which is attainable by the Pianola mechanism, but alas not by the piano keyboard. As luck would have it, the octave above is sounded with the first note of each pair, so the omission of the lower pitch is barely noticeable, especially at such a high speed.

Igor Stravinsky spent some fifteen years, about one-sixth of his life, in close and sustained contact with many types of player pianos. This activity was far from being some unfortunate form of aberration, but the sad state into which the player piano has fallen over the years has colored critical opinion of this part of Stravinsky's oeuvre as well as the composer's own memories. If this distortion is to be made good, it must be realized that the player piano, like any other instrument, takes years of practice to master. I hope this essay will mark the beginning of a renewed interest not only in Stravinsky's own player piano activities, but also in the instrument and its repertoire as a whole.[34]

---

33. The electric Pleyela in Stravinsky's Paris studio is mentioned by George Antheil, *Bad Boy of Music* (London, 1947).

34. When an earlier version of this paper was delivered at the International Stravinsky Symposium, the following rolls were played:

a. Stravinsky—Piano-Rag-Music (Pleyela 8438)
b. Rachmaninov—Polka de W. R. (Themodist T24316B)
c. Stravinsky—Etude for Pianola (Themodist T967B)
d. Stravinsky—*Petrushka* [excerpt] (Pleyela)
e. Stravinsky—*The Rite of Spring* [excerpt] (Pleyela)
f. Stravinsky—*Song of the Nightingale* [excerpt] (Pleyela)
g. Stravinsky—*Les Noces* [Pianola part] (U.S. premiere)

Appendix: Igor Stravinsky—His Music on Piano Roll

Table 17.1 contains all the rolls I have been able to trace. Others may exist, but they cannot be numerous. The four columns supply the title of the work, the roll number, the label under which the roll was published, and the original date of issue. All the rolls referred to, with the exception of two, are intended for use on eighty-eight-note player pianos, or reproducing pianos. The two exceptions are the rolls mentioned in section E for the Duo-Art Pipe Organ. This instrument used large, complex rolls to reproduce two manuals and pedals, with automatic changes of registration and swell pedaling.

Only those dates without parentheses are certain. In such cases, I have read a contemporary roll bulletin or press announcement or have seen such a specific source quoted. Dates in parentheses are probably as accurate as they claim to be. Sources for these include the factory date codes on individual rolls, projection from annual roll catalogues, and deduction from composite roll advertisements, when new numbers appear between two particular months, without any specific issue announcement being made. To achieve complete accuracy of these dates will take several more years of research.

Table 17.1. Igor Stravinsky: His Music on Piano Roll

UNIVERSAL MUSIC COMPANY, Hayes, Middlesex, England			
1) Four Studies, Opus 7, No. 1 Mechanically Perforated	TL 22596 T 22596 A	Aeolian Co. Themodist	(Late 1914)
	S 7546 S 7546 A	Universal Accentuated	(Late 1914)
2) Four Studies, Opus 7, No. 2 Mechanically Perforated	TL 22597 T 22597 B	Aeolian Co. Themodist	(Late 1914)
	S 7548 S 7548 B	Universal Accentuated	(Late 1914)
3) Four Studies, Opus 7, No. 3 Mechanically Perforated	TL 22598 T 22598 A	Aeolian Co. Themodist	(Late 1914)
	S 7550 S 7550 A	Universal Accentuated	(Late 1914)
4) Four Studies, Opus 7, No. 4 Mechanically Perforated	TL 22599 T 22599 A	Aeolian Co. Themodist	(Late 1914)
	S 7552 S 7552 A	Universal Accentuated	(Late 1914)
5) Etude for Pianola Mechanically Perforated	T 967 B	Aeolian Co. Themodist	(Sept. 1921)
	S 13842 B	Universal Accentuated	(Nov. 1929)

continued

Table 17.1. *continued*

6) *The Rite of Spring* (1) Mechanically Perforated	T 24150 C	Aeolian Co. Themodist	(June 1921)
	S 11900 C	Universal Accentuated	(June 1921)
	84545 C	Triumph	
7) *The Rite of Spring* (2) Mechanically Perforated	T 24151 C	Aeolian Co. Themodist	(June 1921)
	S 11902 C	Universal Accentuated	(June 1921)
	84546 C	Triumph	
8) *The Rite of Spring* (3) Mechanically Perforated	T 24152 C	Aeolian Co. Themodist	(June 1921)
	S 11904 C	Universal Accentuated	(June 1921)
	84547 C	Triumph	
9) *The Rite of Spring* (4) Mechanically Perforated	T 24153 C	Aeolian Co. Themodist	(June 1921)
	S 11906 C	Universal Accentuated	(June 1921)
	84548 C	Triumph	
10) Sonata for Piano (1) Recorded by Stravinsky	D 231	Duo-Art AudioGraphic	(Early 1927)
	(D 232)	Pianola AudioGraphic	(Early 1927)
11) *The Firebird* (1) Interpreted by Stravinsky	D 759	Duo-Art AudioGraphic	(Oct. 1928)
	D 760	Pianola AudioGraphic	(Oct. 1928)
12) *The Firebird* (2) Interpreted by Stravinsky	D 761	Duo-Art AudioGraphic	(Jan. 1929)
	D 762	Pianola AudioGraphic	(Jan. 1929)
13) *The Firebird* (3) Interpreted by Stravinsky	D 763	Duo-Art Audiographic	(Jan. 1929)
	D 764	Pianola AudioGraphic	(Jan. 1929)
14) *The Firebird* (4) Interpreted by Stravinsky	D 765	Duo-Art AudioGraphic	(Mar. 1929)
	D 766	Pianola AudioGraphic	(Mar. 1929)
15) *The Firebird* (5) Interpreted by Stravinsky	D 767	Duo-Art AudioGraphic	(Mar. 1929)
	D 768	Pianola AudioGraphic	(Mar. 1929)
16) *The Firebird* (6) Interpreted by Stravinsky	D 769	Duo-Art AudioGraphic	(Mar. 1929)
	D 770	Pianola AudioGraphic	(Mar. 1929)

The Universal Music Company manufactured rolls not only for the Aeolian Company, its parent, but also for most of its competitors on a wholesale basis. Consequently, most Aeolian themodist rolls

Table 17.1. *continued*

are duplicated by the Universal accentuated series, which was often overprinted with the names of smaller music roll dealers. The two series are identical, except for the red metrostyle line, which appears only on Aeolian rolls.

Rolls 1–4 were probably originally commissioned by Claude Johnson and released to the general public later, at the date indicated. Roll 10 was originally issued in the United States (see below) but had its AudioGraphic program notes added in Britain. Rolls 11–16 were not directly recorded by Stravinsky, but over his signature on each he attests to the fact that they are his interpretations.

Rolls 1–9 have price code suffixes. These were introduced in about 1920, at the same time the "L" prefix (signifying Aeolian rolls whose masters originated in London) was dropped. Both styles are given for rolls 1–4.

ESTHER WILLIS, Brentford, Middlesex, England

1) *Faun and Shepherdess* Mechanically Perforated	Unnumbered	Private	(1915)
2) Two Melodies, Opus 6 Mechanically Perforated	Unnumbered	Private	(1915)
3) *Scherzo fantastique* Mechanically Perforated	Unnumbered	Private	(1915)
4) *Fireworks* Mechanically Perforated	Unnumbered	Private	(1915)
5) *Zvezdoliki* Mechanically Perforated	Unnumbered	Private	(1915)
6) *The Nightingale* (Chinese March) Mechanically Perforated	Unnumbered	Private	(1915)
7) *The Nightingale* (excerpt) Mechanically Perforated	Unnumbered	Private	(1915)

These rolls were cut by hand by Miss Willis for Philip Heseltine, Alvin Langdon Coburn, and possibly Edwin Evans. There is no suggestion that Stravinsky was involved.

PLEYEL, LYON & CIE, Paris, France

1) *Pulcinella* (1)	8421	Pleyela/Odéola	(1921)
2) *Pulcinella* (2)	8422	Pleyela/Odéola	(1921)
3) *Pulcinella* (3)	8423	Pleyela/Odéola	(1921)
4) *Pulcinella* (4)	8424	Pleyela/Odéola	(1921)
5) *Pulcinella* (5)	8425	Pleyela/Odéola	(1921)
6) *Pulcinella* (6)	8426	Pleyela/Odéola	(1921)
7) *Pulcinella* (7)	8427	Pleyela/Odéola	(1921)
8) *Pulcinella* (8)	8428	Pleyela/Odéola	(1921)
9) *The Rite of Spring* (1)	8429	Pleyela/Odéola	(1921)
10) *The Rite of Spring* (2)	8430	Pleyela/Odéola	(1921)
11) *The Rite of Spring* (3)	8431	Pleyela/Odéola	(1921)
12) *The Rite of Spring* (4)	8432	Pleyela/Odéola	(1921)
13) *The Rite of Spring* (5)	8433	Pleyela/Odéola	(1921)
14) *The Rite of Spring* (6)	8434	Pleyela/Odéola	(1921)
15) *The Rite of Spring* (7)	8435	Pleyela/Odéola	(1921)
16) *The Rite of Spring* (8)	8436	Pleyela/Odéola	(1921)
17) *The Rite of Spring* (9)	8437	Pleyela/Odéola	(1921)

continued

Table 17.1. *continued*

18) *Piano-Rag-Music*	8438	Pleyela/Odéola	(1921)
19) Three Easy Pieces	8439	Pleyela/Odéola	(1922–1923)
20) Five Easy Pieces	8440	Pleyela/Odéola	(Jan. 1923)
21) *Petrushka* (1)	8441	Pleyela/Odéola	(Late 1922)
22) *Petrushka* (2)	8442	Pleyela/Odéola	(Late 1922)
23) *Petrushka* (3)	8443	Pleyela/Odéola	(Late 1922)
24) *Petrushka* (4)	8444	Pleyela/Odéola	(Late 1922)
25) *Petrushka* (5)	8445	Pleyela/Odéola	(Late 1922)
26) *Petrushka* (6)	8446	Pleyela/Odéola	(Late 1922)
27) *Petrushka* (7)	8447	Pleyela/Odéola	(Late 1922)
28) *Five Fingers* (1)	8448	Pleyela/Odéola	(Nov. 1922)
29) *Five Fingers* (2)	8449	Pleyela/Odéola	(Nov. 1922)
30) *Rag-time*	8450	Pleyela/Odéola	(1921)
31) *Song of the Nightingale* (1)	8451	Pleyela/Odéola	(1922–1923)
32) *Song of the Nightingale* (2)	8452	Pleyela/Odéola	(1922–1923)
33) *Song of the Nightingale* (3)	8453	Pleyela/Odéola	(1922–1923)
34) Three Tales for Children	8454	Pleyela/Odéola	(1922–1923)
35) Four Russian Peasant Songs	8455	Pleyela/Odéola	(1922–1923)
36) *Concertino* (1920)	8456	Pleyela/Odéola	(Late 1923)
37) *Les Noces* (1)	8831	Pleyela/Odéola	(Late 1923)
38) *Les Noces* (2)	8832	Pleyela/Odéola	(Late 1923)
39) *Les Noces* (3)	8833	Pleyela/Odéola	(Late 1923)
40) *Les Noces* (4)	8834	Pleyela/Odéola	(Late 1923)
41) *Les Noces* (5)	8861	Pleyela/Odéola	(1924–1925)
42) *The Firebird* (1)	10039	Pleyela/Odéola	Aug. 1926
43) *The Firebird* (2)	10040	Pleyela/Odéola	Aug. 1926
44) *The Firebird* (3)	10041	Pleyela/Odéola	Aug. 1926
45) *The Firebird* (4)	10042	Pleyela/Odéola	Aug. 1926
46) *The Firebird* (5)	10043	Pleyela/Odéola	Aug. 1926
47) *The Firebird* (6)	10044	Pleyela/Odéola	Aug. 1926
48) *The Firebird* (7)	10045	Pleyela/Odéola	Aug. 1926
49) Sonata for Piano (1)	8457	Pleyela/Odéola	Apr. 1927
50) Sonata for Piano (2)	8458	Pleyela/Odéola	Apr. 1927
51) Sonata for Piano (3)	8459	Pleyela/Odéola	Apr. 1927

Many types of roll preparation were used for this series. For this reason, it is impossible at present to state which processes were used for each roll. *Pulcinella, The Rite of Spring, Piano-Rag-Music, Petrushka, Song of the Nightingale,* Four Russian Peasant Songs ("Saucers."), *Concertino, Les Noces,* and *The Firebird* are all specially arranged for the player piano, and some of the other rolls may also have been. Pleyel also manufactured rolls for its competitors, including Odéola, which used the same numbers.

The existence of roll 30 is in some doubt, as it disappears from advertised lists in 1924. Rolls 40 and 41 are each half of the final tableau of *Les Noces. The Firebird* series (rolls 42–48) omits the "Introduction" and begins instead with the "Firebird's Dance." Whether there was any duplication of arrangements or recordings with Aeolian is a subject for further research.

Table 17.1. *continued*

AMERICAN PIANO COMPANY, New York, NY, USA			
1) Study for Piano, Opus 7/4 Recorded by Alexander Brailowsky	64011 H	Ampico	Feb. 1925
2) *Petrushka* ("Russian Dance") Recorded by Paul Doguereau	66861 H	Ampico	Dec. 1926
AEOLIAN, WEBER PIANO AND PIANOLA COMPANY, New York, NY, USA			
1) Concerto for Piano and Wind Instruments (first movement) Recorded by Stravinsky	528	Duo-Art	
2) Sonata for Piano (1) Recorded by Stravinsky	6867	Duo-Art	Apr. 1925
3) Sonata for Piano (2) Recorded by Stravinsky	6956	Duo-Art	
4) Sonata for Piano (3) Recorded by Stravinsky	7003	Duo-Art	
5) *The Firebird* (1) Interpreted by Stravinsky	A 95	Duo-Art AudioGraphic	(May 1929)
6) *The Firebird* (2) Interpreted by Stravinsky	A 96	Duo-Art AudioGraphic	(May 1929)
7) *The Firebird* (3) Interpreted by Stravinsky	A 97	Duo-Art AudioGraphic	(May 1929)
8) *The Firebird* (4) Interpreted by Stravinsky	A 98	Duo-Art AudioGraphic	(May 1929)
9) *The Firebird* (5) Interpreted by Stravinsky	A 99	Duo-Art AudioGraphic	(May 1929)
10) *The Firebird* (6) Interpreted by Stravinsky	A 100	Duo-Art AudioGraphic	(May 1929)
11) *The Firebird* ("Berceuse" and "Finale")		Duo-Art Pipe Organ	
12) *Symphonies of Wind Instruments* ("Chorale")		Duo-Art Pipe Organ	

It is possible that rolls 1–4 were also issued in Great Britain, with the same serial numbers. Roll 2 was issued there, in the AudioGraphic series, under a different number (see above). Rolls 5–10 are a reissue of the AudioGraphic *Firebird* series prepared in London (see above).

The April 1925 issue of *Duo-Art Monthly*, published in New York, announces the imminent issue of the two organ rolls without specifying numbers.

REX LAWSON, Honor Oak Park, London, England.			
1) *Les Noces* (solo part)		Private	June 1981

This roll was hand cut from a photocopy of the manuscript and first used for a performance of the work at Radio France in June 1981, conducted by Pierre Boulez. The final perforation, being the top note of the last chord, was carried out under strict supervision by Lesley Lawson some two years after our own wedding!

18 Stravinsky, Dushkin, and the Violin

BORIS SCHWARZ

ALL GREAT COMPOSERS of the past had a personal concept of violin sound that served their expressive needs. Bach's ideal was sturdy; Mozart's was limpid and graceful; Beethoven's was lyrical with a few dramatic accents. Mendelssohn sought a warm and romantic sound; Brahms was massive; Tchaikovsky was elegant; César Franck was sensuous and seductive. The twentieth century brought changes, including a new "functionalism": the violin sound became lean, objective, unsentimental; the bow attack became precise and springy; vibrato and glissando were minimized while such special sonoric effects as harmonics and pizzicato were used ingeniously. The violin became functional rather than emotional; even expressive phrases acquired a certain angularity. After World War I, the so-called *Neue Sachlichkeit* became widespread. Among the leaders and pioneers of this "new functionalism" were—each in his own way—Stravinsky, Prokofiev, Hindemith, Milhaud, and to a lesser degree Bartok.

Stravinsky, in pursuing his own concept of violin style, displayed a high degree of originality and sophistication, with no regard for ease of execution. (Composers who do not play the violin are usually more ruthless in making technical demands. They challenge the virtuosos, who in turn rise to the challenge. The term "playable" has disappeared from the vocabulary. Did not Arnold Schoenberg recommend a six-fingered violinist for his Violin Concerto?)

Stravinsky's preference for a "lean" violin sound is clearly demonstrated in *Histoire du soldat* (1918), followed by the *Concertino* for String Quartet (1920) with its prominent first violin part. The leader of the Pro Arte Quartet, Alphonse Onnou, once said in mock despair, "You have no idea how completely one has to forget Spohr in order to be able to play this sort of music."[1] Violinist Fernand Closset played the first performance of *Histoire* and Alfred Pochon, the *Concertino*. Remembering the premiere of the *Concertino*, the composer Casella remarked, "Its performance by the Flonzaley Quartet showed an almost complete lack of

Boris Schwarz, who was a musicologist, conductor, and violinist, died in December 1983. This essay was one of the last of his many valuable contributions to musical scholarship. [Editor's note]

1. Eric Walter White, *Stravinsky: The Composer and His Works*, 2d. ed. (Berkeley and Los Angeles, 1979), p. 291.

artistic understanding and resulted in a clamorous failure."[2] The inability of four such excellent artists, steeped in the classical tradition, to grasp Stravinsky's style merely showed the need for a new breed of executants (I am using Stravinsky's favorite substitute word for "interpreter").

The year 1918 was the heyday of the eloquently emotional, throbbing violin style. Ysäye, Kreisler, Elman, Thibaud, and Zimbalist were the reigning violinists—Heifetz was yet to make his impact. Stravinsky wanted the antithesis of a Kreisler. The music of Stravinsky, like that of Prokofiev and Hindemith, required a new approach to the violin, stressing motion rather than emotion, a style intense but unsentimental, rhythmic and crisp, at times brittle. As the new music appeared, so did a string of new violinists—all excellent instrumentalists who were willing to deglamorize the violin. Among them were Kochanski, Szigeti, Josef Wolfsthal (Klemperer's concertmaster at the Berlin Kroll Opera), Alma Moodie, Jeanne Gautier, Licco Amar, Stefan Frenkel, Georg Kulenkampff, and Samuel Dushkin. The next step was to educate the public in the new sound.

In 1925, Stravinsky arranged five movements from the *Pulcinella* ballet into a suite for violin and piano and dedicated it to his close friend Paul Kochanski, a Russian-Polish violinist then living in New York. However, for reasons that are still not clear, Stravinsky withheld the privilege of a premiere from Kochanski and played the first performance in Frankfurt with the young violinist Alma Moodie, famous for her interpretations of contemporary music. To pacify Kochanski, Stravinsky gave him the dedication of two arrangements from *The Firebird* (Lullaby" and "Prelude and the Princesses' Round Dance"). Though Kochanski was now the recipient of three dedications, he had no active part in shaping the violin parts of any of these works. But the incident with the *Pulcinella* Suite had no ill effect on their friendship, which remained close until Kochanski's death in 1934 and continued with his widow Zosia.

In 1930, Samuel Dushkin, an American violinist of Russian birth, entered the Stravinsky circle. For the next decade, he was to become the master's trusted collaborator and concert partner both in Europe and America. At the time, Dushkin was in his mid-thirties, with a modest reputation as a soloist, still struggling for a major career. He had a wealthy patron, the American composer Blair Fairchild, who had sponsored Dushkin's musical education in New York and Paris since he had left Russia as a child. His principal teacher was G. Rémy, a professor at the Paris Conservatoire, though he also had some lessons with Leopold Auer. Dushkin had made his Paris debut in 1918, his New York debut in 1924, but he was actually better known in Europe. In 1930, Dushkin and Stravinsky were brought together by Willy Strecker, head of the Schott Publishing House in Mainz. They worked out an arrangement whereby Stravinsky accepted a commission to compose a violin concerto for Dushkin, provided he could count on the violinist's presence during the genesis of the work. Dushkin was overawed

2. Ibid.

by the older master and agreed to all conditions; in fact, during the summer of 1931, he followed the Stravinsky household from Nice to Grenoble in order to be available at all times. Stravinsky enjoyed his work with Dushkin and wrote in *An Autobiography* (1936):

> . . . I was very glad to find in him, besides his remarkable gifts as a born violinist, a musical culture, a delicate understanding, and—in the exercise of his profession—an abnegation that is very rare.[3]

By "abnegation," Stravinsky meant the absence of a "virtuoso" mentality that he abhorred:

> In order to succeed, they [virtuosi] are obliged to seek immediate triumphs and to lend themselves to the wishes of the public, the great majority of whom demand sensational effects from the player. This preoccupation naturally influences their taste, their choice of music, and their manner of treating the piece.[4]

Having decided to write a violin concerto, Stravinsky had to come to terms with virtuosity. Here he made several contradictory statements. "I want to write a true virtuoso concerto," Stravinsky said to his publisher Strecker, "and the whole spirit of the violin must be in every measure of the composition."[5] But later he declared, "Virtuosity for its own sake plays little part in my Concerto."[6] And he explained further, "I did not write a cadenza for the reason that I was not interested in violin virtuosity."[7] But he is wrong in assuming that "the technical difficulties of the piece are relatively tame."[8] In fact, it is a very difficult work, though Dushkin's collaboration gave the solo part an idiomatic shape.

When questioned by Robert Craft about his Concerto in D for Violin and Orchestra (1931), Stravinsky made a curious statement that was printed on the record liner of the concerto as recorded in 1962 by Stravinsky with Isaac Stern as soloist:

> The Violin Concerto was not inspired by or modeled on any example. I do not like the standard violin concertos—not Mo-

---

3. Igor Stravinsky, *An Autobiography* (1936; rpt. New York, 1962), p. 166.

4. Ibid.

5. Vera Stravinsky and Robert Craft, *Stravinsky in Pictures and Documents* (New York, 1978), pp. 306–7.

6. Quoted on the record cover of Columbia Stereo MS 6331; the source given is Igor Stravinsky and Robert Craft, *Dialogues and a Diary*, which was copyright 1962. However, there are discrepancies with the printed book (New York, 1963). For example, the parallel passage in *Dialogues* reads, "I did not compose a cadenza, not because I did not care about exploiting violin virtuosity, but because the violin in combination was my real interest" (p. 80).

7. Ibid.

8. Ibid.

> zart's, Beethoven's, Mendelssohn's or Brahms's. To my mind, the only masterpiece in the field is Schoenberg's, and that was written several years after mine. . . .[9]

Indeed, Schoenberg's concerto was completed in 1936. The previous comment was made in 1962, after Schoenberg's death and after Stravinsky's "conversion" to serialism—which may explain the lavish praise. Nevertheless, the comment is somewhat eccentric and was toned down by a solicitous editor for inclusion in *Dialogues and a Diary*, where it reads:

> I did not find that the standard violin concertos—Mozart's Beethoven's, Mendelssohn's, or even Brahms's—were among their composers' best works. (The Schoenberg Concerto is an exception, but that is hardly standard yet.)[10]

After denying he had any "models," Stravinsky then admits to at least one:

> The subtitles of my Concerto—Toccata, Aria, Capriccio—may suggest Bach, though, and so, in a superficial way, might the musical substance. I am very fond of the Bach Concerto for Two Violins, as the duet of the soloist with a violin from the orchestra in the last movement of my own Concerto possibly may show.[11]

The friendship between Stravinsky and Dushkin lasted far beyond the concerto. During the 1930s, Stravinsky developed an interest in performing as a pianist and conductor, and the partnership with Dushkin fitted into his plans. Within a few years, Stravinsky created a repertory of works for violin and piano done in close collaboration with Dushkin, whose advice was obviously so valuable to the master that he permitted Dushkin's name to be listed as co-author on most of these pieces. The concerto stood apart because it could not be performed with piano, but Stravinsky conducted the premiere in Berlin on 23 October 1931, with Dushkin as soloist, and performances followed in Paris, Florence, Madrid, as well as in Germany, Switzerland, Belgium, Holland, and Scandinavia. On 28–29 October 1935, they recorded the concerto for Polydor in Paris.

At the same time, the duo Stravinsky-Dushkin appeared in Europe during 1932–1934 in a varied program consisting of the following Stravinsky works for violin and piano: the *Duo concertant* (1931–1932), the *Divertimento* (1932) (after *The Fairy's Kiss*), the *Suite Italienne* (a new transcription of the *Pulcinella* Suite), and a few shorter arrangements from *The Firebird, Mavra, Petrushka*, and *The Nightingale*. They brought a similar program to the United States in 1935 and again in 1937.

9. Liner notes, Columbia Record MS 6331.

10. Stravinsky and Craft, *Dialogues*, p. 80.

11. Ibid.

After a concert at New York's Town Hall on 27 January 1937, Olin Downes wrote in the *New York Times:*

> Mr. Stravinsky . . . had never played the piano so smoothly and clearly . . . with polish, almost with zest. . . . Mr. Dushkin was efficient and authoritative. The ensemble was excellently adjusted.[12]

In 1940, George Balanchine choreographed a ballet based on the music of the Violin Concerto that he named *Balustrade.* Stravinsky agreed to conduct the premiere in New York City, and Dushkin played the solo part. I remember the occasion vividly because I served as concertmaster of the ballet orchestra under Stravinsky. During the first rehearsal, the maestro lost a beat during a tricky change of meter in the first movement and found himself waving his hands in the wrong direction, muttering angrily under his breath, "Mais qu'est ce qu'il y a? Mais qu'est ce qu'ils font?" But the evening performance went faultlessly, Dushkin played with authority, though the public's attention was focused on the stage.

The Violin Concerto bears no formal dedication to Dushkin, but the printed edition is prefaced by a note in French in the composer's facsimile handwriting:

> Cette oeuvre a été créée sous ma direction le 23 octobre 1931 au concert du Rundfunk de Berlin par Samuel Dushkin auquel je garde une reconnaissance profonde et une grande admiration pour la valeur hautement artistique de son jeu.[13]
>
> Igor Strawinsky
>
> [This work was premiered under my direction on 23 October 1931 at a concert of the Berlin Rundfunk by Samuel Dushkin to whom I profess a profound gratitude and a great admiration for the highly artistic excellence of his playing.]

The piano score bears a footnote in English, "Violin part in collaboration with Samuel Dushkin." The visible part of Dushkin's hand consists of excellent fingerings and bowings, but there was certainly more to his collaboration. In his affectionate memoir "Working with Stravinsky," published in 1949, Dushkin described his role in modest words:

> My function was to advise Stravinsky how his ideas could best be adapted to the exigencies of the violin as a concert display instrument. At various intervals he would show me what he had written. . . . Then we discussed whatever suggestions I was able to make.[14]

12. *New York Times,* 28 January 1937.

13. *Concerto en Re* (Mainz: Edition Schott No. 2190, 1931).

14. Merle Armitage and Edwin Corle, eds., *Stravinsky* (New York, 1949), p. 186.

In the matter of transcriptions—that is, adaptations of existing music to the violin—Dushkin seems to have been given much latitude, as he writes:

> My role was to extract from the original scores of former works we were transcribing a violin part which I thought appropriate for the violin as a virtuoso instrument and characteristic of his musical intentions. After I had written out the violin part, we would meet, and Stravinsky then wrote the piano part which very often resulted in something different from the original composition. Stravinsky sometimes also altered details of the violin part which I had extracted.[15]

In fact, the master did not hesitate to reject the entire first version of the "Berceuse" from *The Firebird* (as prepared by Dushkin) because it sounded to him too much like a Kreisler arrangement of Rimsky-Korsakov. Ultimately, they agreed on a version: Dushkin wanted to make it simple to play, but Stravinsky became involved and made it more complicated. When Dushkin objected, the master retorted angrily, "What can it matter to me if all the fools do not play my music."[16] On other occasions, Stravinsky would reject a particularly brilliant passage of Dushkin's invention as too virtuosic, somewhat out of style. To what extent Stravinsky accepted Dushkin's suggestions is difficult to tell. Errors could be made by either side. Asked how he liked working with Dushkin, he replied good-humoredly, "When I show Sam a new passage, he is deeply moved, very excited—then a few days later he asks me to make changes."[17] There is the famous case when Stravinsky showed Dushkin a certain chord and asked whether it was playable. Dushkin glanced at it and said, "No." "Too bad," replied Stravinsky. Once at home, Dushkin took out the violin and found that the chord—though unusual—was indeed playable, and he phoned Stravinsky at once to give him the good news.[18] This chord served as "motto" for all the movements of the violin concerto—a characteristically strange and exciting sound. But Stravinsky could be changeable and even unpredictable. He permitted two arrangements of his *Tango* to be made for violin and piano, one by Babitz, the other by Dushkin, but neither was released for publication. He approved Dushkin's arrangement of the "Ballade" from the *Divertimento* and proofread it twice, but ultimately he did not include it in the printed version. A decade later he authorized Jeanne Gautier's transcription of the same piece to be published separately.

A surprising change of direction is evident in Stravinsky's publication of *two* versions for violin of his *Pulcinella* Suite—the first dedicated to Kochanski dated 1925, the other made in 1933 with Dushkin's assistance. The second version

15. Ibid., p. 190.

16. Ibid., p. 188.

17. Ibid., p. 187.

18. Ibid., p. 182.

(known as *Suite Italienne*) shows a radical change of approach in favor of a certain idiomatic slickness; in my opinion, it represents an impoverishment, stripped of the austere flashes of Stravinsky's ingeniousness and transformed into a far more ordinary "tuneful" piece. Gone are the biting angular chords; gone is the even-handed relationship between piano and violin in favor of violin tunes accompanied by the piano. Dushkin must have convinced the master that the first version was not very idiomatic—or perhaps Piatigorsky did the convincing, for he worked on a cello version at about the same time that shows a comparable simplification. (Stravinsky may have listened to Piatigorsky more willingly because he was less sure about the cello than the violin, as we learn from Robert Craft.)

Looking through the half-dozen or so violin transcriptions published under the joint authorship of Stravinsky and Dushkin, one finds that Stravinsky became more tolerant of virtuoso display: such pieces as the "Russian Dance" from *Petrushka* or the "Scherzo" from *The Firebird* are violinistically brilliant, yet in excellent taste.[19] Being constantly exposed to audiences while concertizing as a pianist, Stravinsky may have become more attuned to the public's immediate reactions. Virtuosity lost its sinfulness; he began to enjoy it.

The ultimate question is what Stravinsky considered a satisfactory rendering of his violin pieces. The recordings he made with Dushkin during the 1930s should be a guideline, but unfortunately, only one of these records has been reissued recently: the *Duo concertant* (made in April 1933) on Seraphim (Angel) Mono 60183. The sound is perhaps not as rich as later stereophonic tapings, but it gives us a good understanding of the honest, straightforward, unadorned execution, guided by the composer's spirit and ably partnered by the violinist. The *Duo concertant* is not a transcription of existing material but Stravinsky's concept of music for two equal partners, both masters of their respective instruments, motivated by a unity of approach. It was composed immediately after the Violin Concerto—a direct outgrowth of the collaboration between Stravinsky and Dushkin—and it has a freshness and originality unequaled by the other violin pieces.

In 1940, Stravinsky moved to California. Dushkin remained in New York, pursuing his independent concert career. They remained friends throughout their lives (Stravinsky died in 1971, Dushkin in 1976), but their collaboration ceased. (Their joint performance of the violin concerto for Balanchine's ballet *Balustrade* in 1940 was an exceptional event.)

Throughout the 1950s and 1960s, Stravinsky's Violin Concerto continued to be slow in attracting converts. Violinists were reluctant to accept the work as a repertoire item, a fact of which Stravinsky was all too aware when he complained in 1967, "Why is my Violin Concerto not mentioned in Szigeti's book? It is not a

---

19. Dushkin's exceptional skill as a transcriber is demonstrated in the more than twenty transcriptions published by Schott as a series under his own name.

bad work."[20] An important milestone was achieved in 1961, when it was recorded with Isaac Stern as soloist and Stravinsky as conductor. More recently, the Violin Concerto has begun to receive performances and recordings by many great violinists, from Menuhin to Perlman. No one discusses "functional" violin playing anymore: Stravinsky has entered the mainstream of great music and has shaped its course.

20. Stravinsky and Craft, *Pictures and Documents*, p. 307.

19 Schoenberg and "Kleine Modernsky"

LEONARD STEIN

WHILE COMPILING the second edition of *Style and Idea: Selected Writings of Arnold Schoenberg*, I came across an item in Josef Rufer's *The Works of Arnold Schoenberg* whose title had been translated into English as "The Restaurant Owner." (See appendix 1.) On examining the original manuscript, which was eventually incorporated into *Style and Idea*, I discovered it was a one-page commentary on a newspaper interview that a certain N. Roerig conducted with Stravinsky in 1925.[1] Although the interview took place in New York, presumably in English, the news report in Schoenberg's possession had been clipped from a German newspaper. (See Figure 19.1 in appendix 2.)[2] Schoenberg's heading to his commentary, most likely added later and in blue pencil, was "Der Restaurateur," a term that the German dictionary informs us is, indeed, "the restaurant owner." However, because the article has nothing to do with Stravinsky's culinary interests, we are led to consider the French alternatives, "restaurant owner" and "restorer."[3] Knowing the lexicographic interests of both composers, one might take this title to be some kind of a pun; but, for reasons that reflect the serious tone of the commentary, one would rather opt for "restoration" as the true intended meaning.

Stravinsky mentions this interview in *Conversations*, stating that he did not have Schoenberg in mind but was criticizing those who presumed to be discovering the "music of the future" instead of trying to compose the "music of the

1. The manuscript is to be found in the archives of the Arnold Schoenberg Institute, Los Angeles. Stravinsky's first visit to the United States took place in 1925. The date is further corroborated by the newspaper clipping, which refers to Stravinsky's Concerto for Piano and Wind Instruments, composed eight months earlier (in 1923–1924) and performed on tour by the composer. See Leonard Stein, ed. *Style and Idea: Selected Writings of Arnold Schoenberg* (London, 1975), pp. 481–82, and Josef Rufer, *The Works of Arnold Schoenberg*, trans. Dika Newlin (London, 1962), p. 166.

2. The clipping is in the archives of the Arnold Schoenberg Institute. As was his habit, Schoenberg clipped out the interview without identifying either the newspaper or the date. Schoenberg dated his "Restorer" article 24 July 1926, apparently a good year after the newspaper interview. His marginal comments, however, bear the date of 1932. So he must have kept the clipping for some six years before writing these comments and evidently was still upset by the interview (note the reference to "the little Modernsky," a line taken out of the text of Schoenberg's *Satires* of 1925).

3. Actually, the German word for "restorer" is *der Restaurator*. In any case, the German and French terms are easily confused.

present," as he did himself.[4] However, Schoenberg assumed that the reference was aimed at him personally and had reason to believe it was a continuation of the feud that began at the ISCM Festival in Venice in September 1925, when Schoenberg's *Serenade,* Opus 24, and Stravinsky's Sonata for Piano were performed on successive days.[5] In some respects, the juxtaposing of these two works is rather ironic: the *Serenade* is probably the one work of Schoenberg closest in style to neoclassicism, of which the Sonata is one of the most representative examples.

We have no reports as to what happened at the festival, although we might assume that the followers of both composers took up the cudgels on behalf of their masters, such being the musical climate of the time. Schoenberg's twelve-tone method was barely into its third year; it was displayed here for nearly the first time, and in its most elementary form, in the "Sonnet" movement of the *Serenade.* The opposite directions taken in these two works—the one codifying atonal chromaticism, the other relying on tonal references to the past, must have been apparent to all observers. Stravinsky asserts that neither heard the other's composition, so reports about their reactions in either camp must have been purely a matter of hearsay.

Whatever reports Schoenberg heard from his pupils or friends caused him to take immediate offense and led directly to the expression of his resentment in a musical work entitled *Three Satires* (Opus 28). About these pieces he wrote later: "I wrote them when I was very much angered by some of my younger contemporaries at this time and I wanted to give them a warning that it is not good to attack me."[6] Note that Stravinsky is not mentioned here directly; actually, most of Schoenberg's polemics during this period were directed toward the younger German-Austrian composers, like Krenek and Hindemith, who were identified with the prevalent *Neue Sachlichkeit* movement. Nevertheless, there is no doubt as to whom Schoenberg is referring when we read his text to the second *Satire,* "Vielseitigkeit ("Manysidedness"):

> Ja, wer trommer lt denn da?
> Das ist ja der kleine Modernsky!
> Hat sich ein Bubizopf schneiden lassen;
> sieht ganz gut aus!
> Wie echt falsches Haar!
> Wie eine Perücke!
> Ganz (wie sich ihn der kleine Modernsky vorstellt),
> ganz der Papa Bach!

---

4. Igor Stravinsky and Robert Craft, *Conversations with Igor Stravinsky* (1959; rpt. Berkeley and Los Angeles, 1980), p. 69.

5. The *Serenade* was performed on 7 September, the Sonata on 8 September.

6. Erwin Stein, ed., *Arnold Schoenberg: Letters* (London, 1964), pp. 271–72.

Why who could be drumming away there?
If it isn't little Modernsky!
He's had his pigtails cut.
Looks pretty good!
What authentic false hair!
Like a peruke!
Quite (as little Modernsky conceives of him),
Quite the Papa Bach!

Further, the foreword to the *Satires* expresses forthrightly Schoenberg's objection to what he supposed the tendencies of the neoclassicists to be:

> [Those] who nibble at dissonances, and therefore want to rank as modern, but are too cautious to draw the consequences from it . . . those who figure they are in a position that permits them any shattering of tonality, if only an occasional triad—whether it occurs properly or not—would prove their loyalty to tonality . . . those who pretend to "go back to" . . . finally, all the ". . . ists," who I can only find to be mannerists.

The purpose of the *Three Satires* was to show who the real classical master was by lampooning the "neo"-claimant to this role. It is evident (1) by the reference to false tonal inferences, as in the C-major triad opening to the twelve-tone set of the first canon ("tonal oder atonal") and in the conclusion of the Cantata, "Der neue Klassizismus," where the "obligatory" tonal ending on C, sung in unison by all the voices, fends off the other eleven pitches in the instruments, and (2) by the exhibition of contrapuntal skill in the writing of intricate canons, a reminder that the classical masters were great contrapuntists. (Interestingly enough Stravinsky did not prove himself equally adept in this practice for many years. Did the Schoenberg example serve as a goad or as a model? At the same time, can we not contend that the Cantata of Schoenberg with its fugue and embellished continuo part is "neoclassical" in about every respect other than tonality?)

If Schoenberg is to be criticized for a display of bad manners (or at least heavy-handedness) in these *Satires,* one must take into account the years of controversy in which he had been embroiled and the tradition of the polemic he had inherited in Vienna, as well as his impulsive nature of responding strongly to real or imagined slurs. Some of his later articles also display an aggressive tone close to that of the *Satires*: "Folkloristic Symphonies," "My Blind Alley," "The Blessing of the Dressing," and "New Music, Outmoded Music, Style and Idea" among them.[7]

In regard to the concept of neoclassicism, Stravinsky asserts in *Conversations* that the term embraced not only his own music but "all of the between-the-war

7. The first performance of the *Three Satires* was supposed to have been given by the Choral Society of the Vienna State Opera, conducted by Felix Greissle, but it had to be canceled because the chorus objected to the texts. (Information provided by Berthold Türcke, editor of the unpublished memoirs of Felix Greissle.)

composers" as well.[8] The whole issue is a matter of what musical elements are considered in this category. If it pertains to musical forms, then one most certainly must consider the suites, variations, quartets, and quintets of Schoenberg and Webern as well as the *Octet*, Sonata for Piano, *Serenade*, and concertos (both classical and baroque) of Stravinsky. The formalized movements of the Schoenberg suites and *Serenade* are as much a throwback to classical models as are the Stravinsky Sinfonia, Toccata, *Capriccio*, Cantilena, Arioso, and Rondo, which lead back to an even earlier period. In addition, parodistic references to classical mannerisms that arose in the prewar period, first of all in *Pierrot Lunaire* and then, most notably, in *Histoire du soldat*, persisted into the 1920s in Stravinsky's *Octet* and Schoenberg's *Serenade* and Septet Suite.

We know from various accounts that Stravinsky was impressed by *Pierrot Lunaire*, which he heard in one of its first performances in 1912. He apparently did not care much for the recitation or the poetry, but he was strongly taken by the instrumental settings. This work has long been supposed an influence on Stravinsky's *Three Japanese Lyrics*, composed only a year later, but apart from the use of a chamber ensemble with voice, there is little connection between the two works. In any case, the two composers seem to have been on good terms around that time, so when Schoenberg founded his Society for Private Performances in 1919, he made sure that Stravinsky's music was represented. From April 1919 to October 1921, the following works of Stravinsky were performed at the society's concerts: Three Easy Pieces and Five Easy Pieces for piano duet (parodistic pieces par excellence), *Cat's Cradle Songs* and *Pribaoutki* for voice and instruments, Three Pieces for String Quartet, a four-hand arrangement of *Petrushka* (played by Edward Steuermann and Rudolf Serkin), and the *Piano-Rag-Music*. The response of the Schoenberg circle to this music seems to have been most enthusiastic. Stravinsky in *Themes and Episodes* quotes a letter from Webern to Berg, dated 9 June 1919, in which the former raves about *Cat's Cradle Songs:* "Stravinsky war herrlich! Wunderbar sind diese Lieder . . . wie diese drei Klarinetten klingen!"[9] Of course Webern, of all the Schoenberg pupils, would have shown the greatest appreciation for these short songs.

How much more either composer knew about the other's music is hard to ascertain, but most likely they were so absorbed in their own discoveries that they paid little attention to each other. Schoenberg's remarks about *Oedipus Rex* bear quoting, if only to show how unsympathetic he was to its music:

> I do not know what I am supposed to like in *Oedipus.* At least, it is all negative: unusual theater, unusual setting, unusual resolution of the action, unusual vocal writing, unusual acting, unusual melody, unusual harmony, unusual counterpoint, unusual

8. Stravinsky and Craft, *Conversations*, p. 126.

9. "Stravinsky was masterful! These songs are wonderful. How these three clarinets sounded!"

instrumentation—all this is "un" without *being* anything in particular.[10]

There is no doubt about the wide divergence of their styles after 1920. Schoenberg felt that with his twelve-tone method he was in a position once again to write in the expansive classical instrumental forms he had more or less given up during the preceding—atonal—phase of his career. In any case, the exploitation of fully chromaticized harmony (it was twelve-tone in content if not in order) had gone as far as he could foresee without "the desire for a conscious control of the new means and forms" interceding. So he "laid the foundations for a new procedure in musical construction which seemed fitted to replace those structural differentiations provided formerly by tonal harmonies."[11]

Stravinsky, alienated from his Russian roots, also went through a crisis during this period. But his composition turned in an opposite direction in a sense, transforming a tonality he had never abandoned. Despite the shift in musical language, Schoenberg, continuing the Viennese classical-romantic tradition, picked up the forms of his immediate forebears, particularly the sonata form with its strong elements of contrast, variation, and development—all those matters we consider the provenance of *theme* and all that it implies. He carried these formal attitudes and practices over into his twelve-tone works, including the Wind Quintet, the Third and Fourth String Quartets, and the Violin Concerto. Stravinsky, in contrast, though adhering to tonality in whatever manner of transformation and superimposition, had access to various models of the past that he absorbed into his own inimitable style as the occasion arose. His approach was antidevelopmental, antitraditional, relying instead in many instances on the newfound rhythmic structures he had uncovered in the previous "Russian" period and producing a music full of repetitions and ostinatos, one that relied more on movement and color than on expression. These characteristic differences persisted in each composer's works until the end.

In 1934, Schoenberg came to Los Angeles. Two years later, on being appointed to the UCLA faculty, he settled down in Brentwood Park, West Los Angeles, just north of Sunset Boulevard. Stravinsky arrived in Los Angeles around 1940 and found residence the following year in a house one block north of Sunset Boulevard—but ten miles east of Schoenberg's. However, they might as well have lived a thousand miles apart as far as social contacts were concerned. I believe they glimpsed each other on only a few occasions: once at a rehearsal of the *Genesis Suite* in 1945, at the funeral of Franz Werfel, and, so Stravinsky relates, at a concert of the Los Angeles Chamber Orchestra in 1949, when Schoenberg made a speech on the occasion of his seventy-fifth birthday, accepting the honorary citizenship of Vienna. I believe Stravinsky showed more interest in Schoen-

10. Schoenberg, *Style and Idea*, pp. 482–83.

11. Schoenberg, "Composition with Twelve Tones," in *Style and Idea*, p. 218.

berg than the latter showed in Stravinsky. Stravinsky mentioned to me (when I had been asked to copy some music for him) that he heard Schoenberg was still hostile to him.[12] But this did not prevent him in 1945, I believe, from attending a performance of Schoenberg's Third Quartet, performed by the Pro Arte Quartet (Rudolf Kolisch, first violinist) and expressing considerable interest in the work. This event may have occurred around the time of the *Genesis Suite* project, to which Schoenberg and Stravinsky contributed movements.[13] My job was to collect the various scores of this work and play them for the chorus. So besides copying out Schoenberg's "Prelude" from particell to full score, I also got to talk to Stravinsky about his *Babel*, which used narrator and male chorus. It must have been his first excursion into the English language, because I noticed he attempted to elide "people is" into two syllables, as one would in French. Referring to its measured or monumental manner, he also described the choral setting (treated about as plainly as in any of his works) as being in a "Greek style." The two composers attended the dress rehearsal of their respective works but chose to remain on opposite sides of the hall. Not a word was exchanged. I left the hall with Schoenberg just at the completion of Stravinsky's piece. Only one sentence was forthcoming from Schoenberg when I asked him what he thought of the piece. "It didn't end; it just stopped."

For some reason, many people thought it a shame the two great masters never got together. I would have been intrigued by such a prospect. What would they have talked about? Who would have dominated the conversation? Most likely they would have engaged in small talk about the matters that preoccupied most of the émigrés in Hollywood—affairs of everyday life in a foreign country. What kept them apart was more a matter of cultural background, one that divided the community along national lines—the German-speaking Central Europeans on one side, the French and Russians on the other.

Of equal interest for one growing up in the climate of Los Angeles was the division among American-born musicians who took sides in support of the one master or the other. With the appearance of Mlle Boulanger, whose influence among American composers had been so strong for many years, Stravinsky's followers were in the ascendancy. A composer and teacher such as Ernst Krenek, who also resided in the community, was veritably a voice in the wilderness in his advocacy of twelve-tone composition. The American composers who practiced twelve-tone methods were hardly known outside of academic circles. But perhaps neither Stravinsky nor Schoenberg was as influential at this time as Paul Hindemith, with his base on the East Coast.

---

12. I copied the parts for the revised version of the "Sacrificial Dance" of *The Rite of Spring* in 1943 and saw Stravinsky on quite a few occasions until 1960.

13. Schoenberg contributed the "Prelude," Stravinsky, *Babel*, both written for mixed chorus and orchestra, plus narrator for Stravinsky's piece. *Babel* is dated 1944, the "Prelude," 1945, the latter practically an afterthought by the commissioner, Nathaniel Shilkret.

Stravinsky's "conversion" to twelve-tone or serial methods was thus all the more surprising to most musicians in America. The postwar period (more definitely around 1950) here, as in Europe, was dominated by Webern rather than by either the neoclassically oriented Stravinsky or by Schoenberg, whose major works were scarcely known. Certain events, in retrospect, seem to be of significance in this shift of interest: (1) the demonstration against Stravinsky's neoclassical works, led by Boulez in Paris; (2) the discovery of Webern and the performance and recording of his music (the first performances in Los Angeles date from about 1948); and (3) the Darmstadt summer courses, which began at about the same time. This crisis in music in general affected nearly every composer. Schoenberg's death in 1951, in a certain sense, marks the close of the preceding period. But Stravinsky's "conversion" was doubtless the most important breakthrough of all in fashioning attitudes toward new methods and techniques.

Stravinsky's influence throughout this century has been profound. As Aaron Copland noted, Stravinsky influenced three (perhaps four) generations of American composers—and probably an equal number abroad. Always a public figure, Stravinsky had a good press and a constituency of the widest sort, from the ballet audience who recognized him as the greatest creator in their field and knew his nonballetic works as well (which are also used for the dance), to the serious composers, even the most antagonistic, who were always intrigued and influenced by his mastery and innovations, particularly with regard to his rhythmic structures and instrumental sounds. He was always the embodiment of "modernism" in both its most fashionable and most characteristic aspects. One can well appreciate Ernst Krenek's comments in 1971 about Stravinsky's pervading influence:

> From hindsight one might say that historically Stravinsky's function was to prevent for about thirty years so-called atonality, which was recognized as the revolutionary nucleus and essence of "New Music," from becoming the mainstream of contemporary musical utterance. The victory of Stravinskyan neoclassicism kept dodecaphony in a kind of intellectual ghetto from which it burst forth only after it had acquired a new dimension in total serialism.[14]

Stravinsky did, indeed, make serialism fashionable. With every new work he wrote from 1952 until his death nearly twenty years later, he was in the limelight, becoming as well known to the general public as to the musical one through the published conversations with Robert Craft (which began to appear as early as 1957), recordings, and television. As always, premieres of his works were international events. Musicians and scholars enjoyed meetings on campuses with Stravinsky, in many cases becoming privy to sketches of his latest works, even before they were performed. Access to his works greatly aided the development

---

14. Ernst Krenek, *Perspectives of New Music* 9, no. 2; 10, no. 1 (1971), Stravinsky Memorial Issue, pp. 7–9.

of theory and analysis—and not only of serial works—in music departments throughout the land. The dodecaphonists who had been cloistered in the "intellectual ghetto" now became the kingpins of musical studies and leaders of the new direction in American music.

Relations with the European avant-garde were also salubrious. Boulez, who had led the demonstration against his neoclassical music, became reconciled with Stravinsky. In 1957, *Le Marteau sans maître* was performed in Los Angeles with Boulez conducting. He had come west primarily to meet Stravinsky, who, in turn, attended the rehearsals and performance of the work and let it be known that he thought highly of it. This served as the stamp of approval for Boulez's music and affected, in turn, the attitude of even the most conservative followers of Stravinsky, particularly in France. Although there was some suspicion in avant-garde circles that Stravinsky was jumping on the bandwagon of the young, his patronage was readily accepted. Of course, Boulez has shown his homage to Stravinsky in *Marteau*, whose second movement reminds us of the "Bransle Gay" in *Agon*, though using tom-toms instead of castanets.

It has been pointed out that Stravinsky only absorbed the style of the masters after their deaths; indeed, he did not start writing serial music until the year after Schoenberg's death. There may have been portents in his earlier music tending in this direction, as some commentators have attempted to show, but Stravinsky did not make his move until he became acquainted with some of Schoenberg's music and with Webern's as well. His earliest works of this sort, the Cantata (1951–1952) and the Septet (1953), still cling to tonality (or modality), but his progress in shucking off or disguising tonality takes place gradually, reminding us of Schoenberg's experiments with tones and intervals in Opus 23 and Opus 24, which finally led to his first twelve-tone pieces.

Stravinsky certainly modeled his Septet, or at least part of it, on Schoenberg's Septet Suite, Opus 29. He attended the rehearsals and recording of this work, conducted by Robert Craft, and seems to have studied the piece thoroughly. The two works are most alike in the final "Gigue" movements, although the variations movements in both works bear some resemblance. One must remember that Schoenberg's Septet is a work of the greatest maturity and complexity; Stravinsky's Septet comes at the beginning of a new period with holdovers from the past, trying out devices new to the composer and being purposely limited in design—perhaps even overcautiously so. Both "Gigues" are in bipartite form, both are fuguelike, both invert the subject at the halfway point—all nice archaistic tributes to Papa Bach. But the Schoenberg "Gigue" is expansive, in the thoroughgoing manner of Viennese "developing variation." Stravinsky's "Gigue" is much more modest, limiting each voice to its own series (though all of them are intervallically equivalent). Stravinsky, even in the period of the Sonata for Piano, knew very well how to write counterpoint (though Schoenberg may have felt that it was like Handel's counterpoint), but serial constructions doubtless demanded from him greater contrapuntal concentration and texture, which had decided effect on all Stravinsky's subsequent works.

As to Webern's influence on Stravinsky, compared to Schoenberg, the former's generally simpler, clearer, more transparent and abstract style must have had a great attraction for Stravinsky. Yet, despite their common interest in certain devices, such as the canon, remarkably few of Webern's stylistic traits show through in Stravinsky's serial works. One mentions the mensuration canon in the last movement of Webern's Second Cantata as pertinent to the canons of *Threni*, but actually there is nothing like it in the latter work. Other composers, much less gifted and imaginative than Stravinsky, were to imitate the Webern style more explicitly. Perhaps there was not enough interest on the surface of Webern's music—sonorities, instrumental timbres, rhythms—for it to impress Stravinsky as a good model to follow.[15]

Because academic life in America has tended to lead in the direction of theoretical abstraction and systematic analysis, students today naturally examine in depth more abstruse and complex devices in music and try to relate all composition to a common system in order to discover a unified language, so to speak. The motivation may very well come from the attempt to reconcile the differences in the contributions of the two great masters of our century. Even though their aims and practices may show opposing tendencies, the two composers complement each other in many ways. Stravinsky, in adopting some of Schoenberg's techniques, may have attempted to close the breach. And both of them, in their later works, may have been reaching for a common goal: some of Schoenberg's last works suggest tonality with serial methods; Stravinsky, likewise, in his last works, used his own brand of serialism—verticalization—to achieve another "reformulation" of tonality, of a "tonality beyond tonality."

Appendix 1: *Der Restaurateur*

Stravinsky pokes fun at musicians who are anxious (unlike himself—he wants simply to write the *music of today*) to write the *music of the future.* I could not say such a thing without at least giving an inkling of the reasons why any music that is fully and truly of the present must also belong to the future. But I am not sure that is what Stravinsky means. He seems rather to find it old-fashioned to regard any work of art as significant for any period beyond the present. And he apparently believes this even though elsewhere he actually admits such significance, constantly finding new points to "take up": Bach, Scarlatti, Clementi, etc. It seems to me, furthermore, that this attitude is no more deeply based than a good many other phenomena of mass psychology.

One example (naturally I cannot pursue every piece of rubbish): nowadays it

15. Compare this discussion of Webern's influence with Watkins's and Allen's in this anthology.

is the fashion to find criminals sympathetic. Certain deficiencies of the law, certain lapses by guardians of the law, particularly the police, have fostered this sympathy.

Now surely it is impossible to have a serious discussion with someone unless he admits that the following proposition is true: however imperfect laws and their administration may be, it still remains the duty of the enlightened man, even while he actively opposes a law, not to infringe it. A thief from principle is no less in the wrong than an unprincipled thief. It may be humane to judge the former more leniently, but this has the bad result that the latter then also comes off better. Many present-day people, with their petty journalistic way of thinking, contrast the dull policeman with the interesting, sympathetic offender. But no serious mind will see in this more than a cheap piece of fashionable foolishness.

It is rather the same here. In all fields of thought there is an undeniable need to produce things to last longer than grease-proof paper and neckties. It may be appropriate to build exhibition buildings to be pulled down after three months; to invent machines for weaving fashionable material; even pyramids need not be planned for all eternity. But, on the other hand, the aim in seeking a cancer cure can only be a permanently effective one; we want to know something unchangingly valid about the course of the stars and the fate of the soul after death.

Maybe for Stravinsky art falls not into this last category but among the fashionable materials and neckties. In that case, he is right in trying merely to satisfy the customers.

I, however, never reckoned to fall among window-dressers. Nor, I think, did any of those who are my models. And I believe not even Muzio Clementi may be so assessed, since he is still good enough to serve as a model for Stravinsky.

24 July 1926

Appendix 2: Igor Stravinsky on His Music—A Conversation with the Russian Master

N. ROERIG (NEW YORK) *[Here translated from the German. See Figure 19.1]*

The first impression I got from Stravinsky was when I met him at a rehearsal in Carnegie Hall, New York. The hall was dark; on the stage there was a small square-built man in an orange sweater of light silk, a man who continuously stamped his feet and wildly gestured and shouted with temperament to a group of musicians who were sitting in front of him: "One, two, three—one, two, three." Already with the first sounding notes I recognized his jazz composition *Rag-time.* Between his frequent foot stampings and his one, two, three, I could hear him singing: "Tum-tum-ta-ta." His musicians grinned with their whole faces and could not get enough of him during this rehearsal.

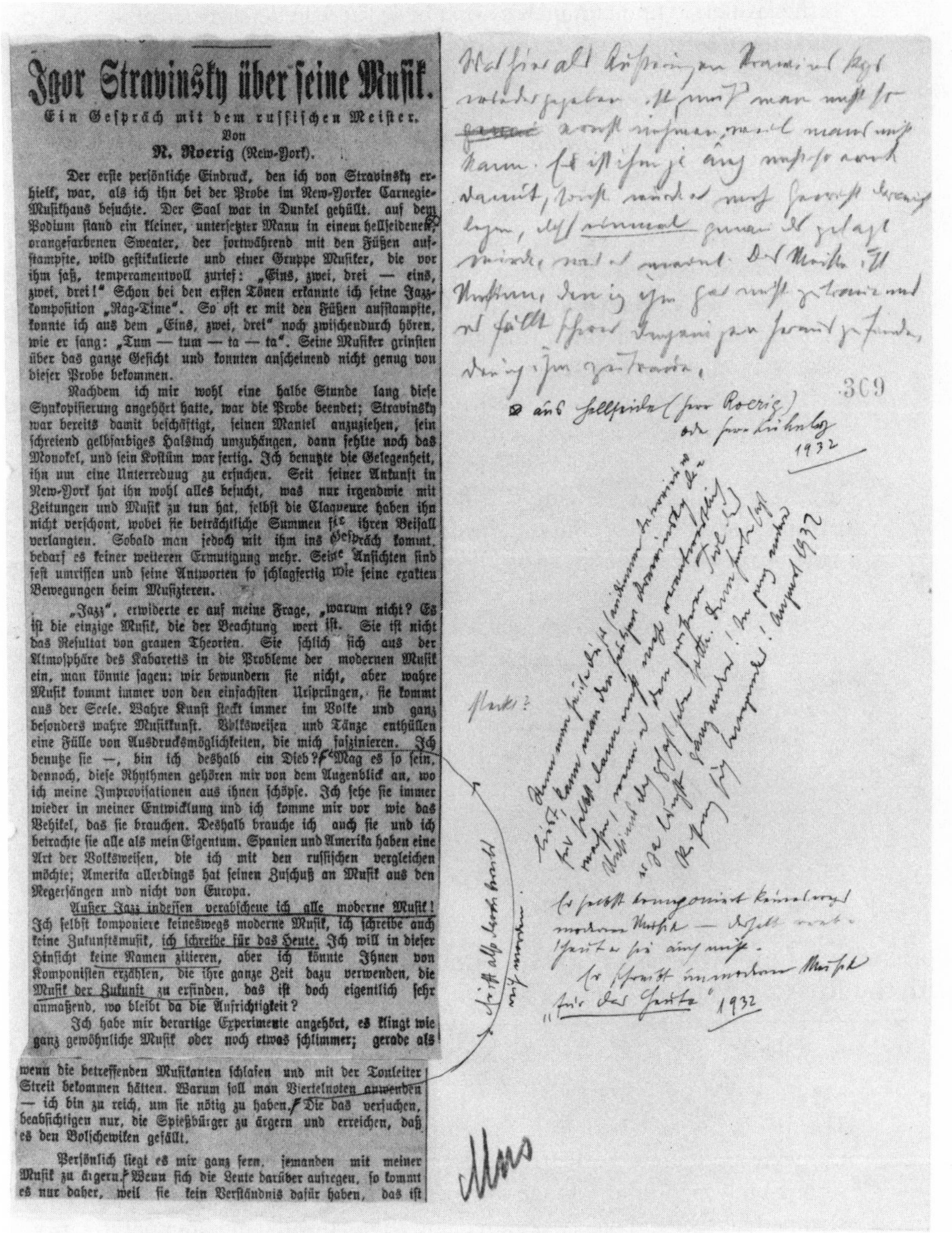

Igor Stravinsky über seine Musik.

Ein Gespräch mit dem russischen Meister.

Von

N. Roerig (New-York).

Der erste persönliche Eindruck, den ich von Stravinsky erhielt, war, als ich ihn bei der Probe im New-Yorker Carnegie-Musikhaus besuchte. Der Saal war in Dunkel gehüllt. auf dem Podium stand ein kleiner, untersetzter Mann in einem hellseidenen, orangefarbenen Sweater, der fortwährend mit den Füßen aufstampfte, wild gestikulierte und einer Gruppe Musiker, die vor ihm saß, temperamentvoll zurief: „Eins, zwei, drei — eins, zwei, drei!" Schon bei den ersten Tönen erkannte ich seine Jazzkomposition „Rag-Time". So oft er mit den Füßen aufstampfte, konnte ich aus dem „Eins, zwei, drei" noch zwischendurch hören, wie er sang: „Tum — tum — ta — ta". Seine Musiker grinsten über das ganze Gesicht und konnten anscheinend nicht genug von dieser Probe bekommen.

Nachdem ich mir wohl eine halbe Stunde lang diese Synkopisierung angehört hatte, war die Probe beendet; Stravinsky war bereits damit beschäftigt, seinen Mantel anzuziehen, sein schreiend gelbfarbiges Halstuch umzuhängen, dann fehlte noch das Monokel, und sein Kostüm war fertig. Ich benutzte die Gelegenheit, ihn um eine Unterredung zu ersuchen. Seit seiner Ankunft in New-York hat ihn wohl alles besucht, was nur irgendwie mit Zeitungen und Musik zu tun hat, selbst die Claqueure haben ihn nicht verschont, wobei sie beträchtliche Summen für ihren Beifall verlangten. Sobald man jedoch mit ihm ins Gespräch kommt, bedarf es keiner weiteren Ermutigung mehr. Seine Ansichten sind fest umrissen und seine Antworten so schlagfertig wie seine exakten Bewegungen beim Musizieren.

„Jazz", erwiderte er auf meine Frage, „warum nicht? Es ist die einzige Musik, die der Beachtung wert ist. Sie ist nicht das Resultat von grauen Theorien. Sie schlich sich aus der Atmosphäre des Kabaretts in die Probleme der modernen Musik ein, man könnte sagen: wir bewundern sie nicht, aber wahre Musik kommt immer von den einfachsten Ursprüngen, sie kommt aus der Seele. Wahre Kunst steckt immer im Volke und ganz besonders wahre Musikkunst. Volksweisen und Tänze enthüllen eine Fülle von Ausdrucksmöglichkeiten, die mich faszinieren. Ich benutze sie —, bin ich deshalb ein Dieb? Mag es so sein, dennoch, diese Rhythmen gehören mir von dem Augenblick an, wo ich meine Improvisationen aus ihnen schöpfe. Ich sehe sie immer wieder in meiner Entwicklung und ich komme mir vor wie das Vehikel, das sie brauchen. Deshalb brauche ich auch sie und ich betrachte sie alle als mein Eigentum. Spanien und Amerika haben eine Art der Volksweisen, die ich mit den russischen vergleichen möchte; Amerika allerdings hat seinen Zuschuß an Musik aus den Negersängen und nicht von Europa.

Außer Jazz indessen verabscheue ich alle moderne Musik! Ich selbst komponiere keineswegs moderne Musik, ich schreibe auch keine Zukunftsmusik, ich schreibe für das Heute. Ich will in dieser Hinsicht keine Namen zitieren, aber ich könnte Ihnen von Komponisten erzählen, die ihre ganze Zeit dazu verwenden, die Musik der Zukunft zu erfinden, das ist doch eigentlich sehr anmaßend, wo bleibt da die Aufrichtigkeit?

Ich habe mir derartige Experimente angehört, es klingt wie ganz gewöhnliche Musik oder noch etwas schlimmer; gerade als wenn die betreffenden Musikanten schlafen und mit der Tonleiter Streit bekommen hätten. Warum soll man Viertelnoten anwenden — ich bin zu reich, um sie nötig zu haben. Die das versuchen, beabsichtigen nur, die Spießbürger zu ärgern und erreichen, daß es den Bolschewiken gefällt.

Persönlich liegt es mir ganz fern, jemanden mit meiner Musik zu ärgern. Wenn sich die Leute darüber aufregen, so kommt es nur daher, weil sie kein Verständnis dafür haben, das ist

Figure 19.1 "Igor Stravinsky on his music" by N. Roerig, with marginal comments by Arnold Schoenberg. Courtesy of the Schoenberg Institute, Los Angeles, California. Originally in English, it is translated from the German in appendix 2 of this chapter.

wohl die einfachste Erklärung. Außerdem, wenn das Publikum meine Musik nicht versteht, kommt es meistens auch daher, weil sie nicht richtig gespielt wird. Musik muß unbedingt so wiedergegeben werden, wie sie aufgezeichnet ist, was leider selten geschieht. Sie wird deshalb falsch ausgesprochen, gerade wie mein Englisch, sobald ich in die Versuchung komme, es zu sprechen. Ich selbst hörte vor einiger Zeit meine Symphonie für Blasinstrumente, die so eigenartig gespielt wurde, daß ich selbst nicht wußte, was das eigentlich sein sollte. Ein Dirigent muß unbedingt die Psychologie seiner Zuhörer studieren, so daß er seine persönlichen Impressionen letzten Endes in ein reales Verhältnis zur Musik bringt. In der Symphonie sah ich, wie der Dirigent manchmal auf dem Podium herumtanzte, wobei er ganz fürchterlich seine Arme verrenkte, und dieses ausgerechnet bei einer Passage, in der zwei Instrumente das zarteste Pianissimo zu spielen hatten. Die Zuhörer glauben natürlich, daß hier irgend etwas nicht stimmen dürfte, denn sonst würde doch der Kapellmeister nicht solch ein Aufhebens machen, um solche „geräuschlose" Töne hervorzubringen.

„zarteste" ai, ai! oeuf, oeuf! 1932

Glauben Sie mir, wenn ein modernes Auditorium ein Konzert von Bach vorgesetzt erhielte, wie es eigentlich geschrieben ist, es würde wohl niemand noch etwas von Bach hören, denn man will doch um jeden Preis moderne Auffassung haben. Aber gerade hier bin ich bei dem Ausgangspunkte meiner Auffassung von Musik, diese Art und die russische Kirchenmusik sind meine Quellen. Zum Beispiel in „Les noces" verwende ich einen Kontrapunktchor — Dinge, von denen hier niemand eine Ahnung hat; aber in Rußland singt jeder Chor diese Musik, und es ist ganz selbstverständlich so, denn man singt diese Chöre seit jeher in den Kirchen. Diese Art meiner Musik ist eine Mischung zwischen Blas- und Streichinstrumenten, wobei die menschlichen Stimmen als Blasinstrumente figurieren, denn letzten Endes sind sie es ja auch."

Einen Kontrapunktchor: was sich der kleine Modernsky unter Kontrapunkt vorstellt 1932

Stravinsky machte nach diesen Ausführungen eine Pause, bei der wir uns über andere Dinge unterhielten, schließlich fragte ich ihn über Motive seines „Piano-Rag".

„Ach das? Es ist jetzt acht Monate alt und verkörpert die Idee einer großen Passacaglia oder auch Toccata. Es ist ganz im Stile des 17. Jahrhunderts gehalten, denn dieses Jahrhundert lebte ja in den gleichen Gesichtspunkten, wie sie heute zum Ausdruck gebracht werden. Wie Sie wissen, hat noch niemand dieses Konzert gespielt, und nur ich allein kann es spielen. Ich möchte auch nicht, daß irgendein anderer dieses Konzert spielt, bis ich es selbst nicht mehr für mich brauche.

Passacaglia **oder** auch Toccata; oder ist gut.
der „Stil" des 17. Jhd.
" immer den Stil eines andern 1932

Wie Sie wissen, bin ich richtiggehend verliebt in diejenigen Kompositionen, an denen ich gerade arbeite. Sonst existiert für mich überhaupt nichts —, ich glaube, es muß so sein, weil ich ja auch alles, was ich fühle, hineinlege. Wenn ich meine Arbeit besser machen könnte, würde ich es gewiß tun. Nachher allerdings bin ich nicht immer davon überzeugt, daß es ein geniales Werk wurde."

er fühlt — ah, hört euch an!
Ja darf man denn das? 1932

Nachdem Stravinsky das gesagt hatte, sprang er von seinem Podium herunter mit der Geschmeidigkeit eines Panthers, rückte sein gelbes Halstuch, das er sehr zu lieben scheint, mit einer nervösen Bewegung zurecht, ein kurzer Gruß und schon war er hinter der Türe verschwunden.

Der Sekretär, der die ganze Zeit hinter ihm stand, bemerkte noch: „Bei seiner Lebhaftigkeit ist es schwer, zu glauben, daß er bereits einen Sohn von 17 Jahren hat; insgesamt hat er vier Kinder, und alle sind leidenschaftliche Musiker. Jetzt muß ich sehen, ihn so schnell wie möglich einzuholen, denn er ist sehr zerstreut und wird wieder alles vergessen. Frau Stravinsky hat mich ganz besonders gebeten, auf ihn acht zu geben, denn er ist imstande, alles liegen zu lassen, seinen Hut, Mantel und selbst zu vergessen, wo er hingeht."

⊗ Autorisierte Uebersetzung von Ernst Kühnly.

⊗ Ich erinnere mich an dies Blatt [illegible]
(trotz dieser Unterhaltung) [illegible]
[illegible] Strawinsky. 1932

Figure 19.1 *continued*

After I had been listening to his syncopation for about a half-hour, the rehearsal was over. Stravinsky was already busy putting on his coat and his bright yellow scarf. Then he added his monocle and his costume was complete. I used the opportunity to ask him for an appointment. Ever since he had arrived in New York he was apparently visited by anybody who was connected with newspapers or music in any way. Even the claqueurs did not spare him, asking him for a considerable amount of money for their applause. As soon as one starts a conversation with him, however, one does not need courage any longer. His ideas are sharply laid out, and his answers are delivered with as much punch as his movements while he conducts.

"Jazz," he replied to my question, "why not? It is the only kind of music that is worth being paid attention to. It is not a result of dull theories. This music sneaked into the problems of modern music out of the atmosphere of the cabaret and one could say we don't admire it, but true music always has the most simple origin. It comes from the soul. True art is always inherent in the people and particularly the true art of music. Folk tunes and dances unveil a multitude of possibilities for expression, possibilities that fascinate me. I use them—am I a thief therefore? It may be; however these rhythms belong to me from the very moment I extract my improvisations from them. Again and again I see them in my development, and I feel like the vehicle they need. Therefore I need them and consider them to be my property. Spain and America have types of folk tunes which I like to compare to Russian ones. America, however, has its surplus of music from the Negro songs and not from Europe.

"Outside of jazz, however, I despise all of modern music. I myself don't compose modern music at all nor do I write music of the future. I write for today. In this regard I don't want to quote names, but I could tell you about composers who spend all their time inventing a music of the future. Actually this is very presumptuous. Where does this still contain integrity?

"I have listened to experiments of this kind. They sound like very ordinary music, or a little bit worse. Just as though the musicians are asleep and have come into conflict with the scale. Why should one use quarter tones—I am too rich to have use of them. Those who try to use them only intend to provoke the bourgeoisie and to achieve what pleases the Bolshevists.

"For me, personally, this is very far removed, to provoke somebody with my music. If people get hysterical about my music then this is only because they don't have any understanding of it. This seems to be the simplest explanation for this. Furthermore if the audience does not understand my music, it is because it is not played in the right way. Music absolutely has to be realized exactly as it is notated. Something that unfortunately happens rather seldom. It is pronounced in the wrong way, just like my own English as soon as I am tempted to use it. Just a little while ago I listened to my *Symphonies of Wind Instruments,* which was played in such a strange manner that I myself did not know what it actually meant. A conductor has to study the psychology of his listeners so that he brings in the end his personal impression into an actual relation with the music. In the *Symphonies* I saw that the conductor occasionally started to dance around the stage stretching his arms in such a terrible manner, and this he did at a part in which two instruments had to play the most tender pianissimo. The listeners of course believed that there was something wrong, otherwise the conductor would not have made such an effort in order to produce such 'soundless' tones.

"Believe me, if a modern audience were to be presented with a concert of Bach's music performed in such a way as it is actually written, then nobody would ever listen again to Bach's music because everybody wants to have a modern attitude at any rate. But it is just this point which is the point of departure of my idea of music. This kind and the Russian church music are my sources. In *Les Noces,* for instance, I use a contrapuntal chorus, something of which nobody has an idea here. But in Russia every chorus sings this music, and it is a very common practice because these kinds of choruses have been sung in the church ever since. My music of this kind is a mixture between wind and string instruments, a mixture in which the human voices serve as wind instruments, for that is what they are in the end."

Stravinsky paused after these explanations and we talked about other things. Finally I asked him what motivated him to write the Piano Rag [The Piano Concerto?]: "That? It is now eight months old and embodies the idea of a big passacaglia or even a toccata. It is completely kept in the style of the seventeenth century, for that century lived in the same ideas as they are expressed today. As you know, nobody has played this Concerto and only I myself am able to play it. I would even like somebody else to play this Concerto, when I do not need it any longer myself.

"As you know, I am really in love with those compositions at which I am working presently. Otherwise nothing exists for me. I believe it has to be this way, because I put everything I feel into it. If I could improve my work I would certainly do so. After the fact, however, I am not always convinced that I have achieved a work of genius."

After Stravinsky had said this, he leaped from the stage with the alertness of a panther, with a nervous gesture adjusted his yellow scarf, of which he seemed to be very fond, made a short goodbye and was already gone outside the door. The secretary who was standing behind him the whole time added: "Considering his liveliness it is hard to believe that he has already a son of seventeen. He has four children altogether, and all of them are passionate musicians. Now I have to say that I must catch up with him as fast as possible because he is very much lost in thought and will forget everything. Mrs. Stravinsky has asked me particularly to take care of him because he is capable of leaving everything behind, his hat, his coat, and he is even capable of forgetting where he is supposed to go."

Authorized translation to the German by Ernst Kühnly.
[Editor's note: Originally written in English, now lost.]

Marginal Comments by Schoenberg

What is given here as utterances by Stravinsky one does not have to take too seriously because one can't. He himself is not so serious about it, otherwise he would put more weight on being quoted exactly as to what he meant to say. Most of it is nonsense which I did not expect of him, and it is difficult to distinguish what I do expect from him.

made up of pure silk (by Mr. Roerig)
or Mr. Kühnly
1932

steckt? (sticks)

If you read this interview today you cannot make the Stravinsky of today responsible for it any more, even if he did say the greater part of that conversation. For today it says already something totally different, something that moves in a totally different direction.
August 1932

Hence he has become rich through . . . (illegible)

He himself does not compose modern music at all—therefore he does not detest it. He writes unmodern music "for today."
1932

"tenderest" ei, ei! oeuf, oeuf.
1932

A counterpoint chorus: what the little Modernsky imagines to be counterpoint.
1932

Passacagalia *or* as well Toccata; "or" is nice.
the style of the seventeenth century.
always the style of a different one.
1932

he feels—ah; doesn't stop!
Well, are you really allowed to do that?
1932

I am pretty sure that only Mr. Roerig authorized this translation and not Mr. Stravinsky.
1932

Personal Portraits from the California Years

20 The Genius and the Goddess

EDWIN ALLEN

I HAD THE PRIVILEGE of meeting Igor Stravinsky when I was twenty-three in the summer of 1961 in Santa Fe, where he was conducting performances of *Oedipus Rex* and *Perséphone*. I was introduced by my friend Eleanor Bedell, who was mounting an exhibition of Vera Stravinsky's paintings in the gallery of her antique shop, one of the truly magic places in Santa Fe, made even more so by the fantastically beautiful paintings. Although the opportunity to see Stravinsky conduct was my sole motive for being in Santa Fe, being introduced to him was far beyond my aspirations. The idea even frightened me, for Stravinsky had been my musical god from the time I first heard his music, and, as I thought, proximity to the deity could only result in my certain death—if not from immediate heart failure, then from nervous excitement or some disgraceful awkwardness.

Seeing Stravinsky backstage after his performance, his shirt removed, towels being applied to his heavily perspiring, frail, but impressive body—one could have labeled each muscle—I was surprised to receive his strong handshake extended from an arm so fatigued by conducting. And the smile that broadened his face after his "How do you do?"—was it more than politeness? It actually seemed warm and friendly. So "god" had greeted me and apparently not sent me off to hell. I actually survived. Well, I was with a wonderful woman whom both Igor and Vera Stravinsky loved immensely. When she reintroduced me to Stravinsky a little later that evening at a party, this time in the company of his wife and some friends, it was proposed that I might be available to drive the Stravinskys around during their stay in Santa Fe because they had no car of their own there. I did agree to the honor, but privately I confessed to Eleanor that awe for the celebrated composer might somewhat affect the efficiency or even safety of my driving. She countered with "Don't worry; soon you will become kissing cousins." That prediction I dismissed as farfetched, but it actually came true. The following day I drove Vera Stravinsky to the market, where she was already well known to the employees. At the checkout counter, she was greeted with "Mrs. Stravinsky, welcome back. How good to see you again. And this," indicating me, "must be your son." Vera Stravinsky turned, looked at me, and having known me for less than an hour replied, "Yes, I think I would like that." Need I say that from that moment I was bonded, to Stravinsky because he was central to my intellectual life, and to Vera by the charm of that remark. But it must be said quickly that neither Igor nor Vera was ever paternal in the slightest toward me. Both my attitude and their characters prevented that. Stravinsky could never become anything other than the great man I revered, and although I am not embarrassed to say that a deep mutual affection developed between the two of us and remained thus for ten years with no harsh aspects or difficult times whatsoever, it was not a relationship of father to son or even of friend to friend. There was, of course, a great difference in our ages and our stations in life. I never lost my awe for Stravinsky, the creator of so much music I loved, and no matter how familiar I became with the man—and during the last ten years of his life I became very intimately acquainted with his world—my relationship to him was that of an adoring fan privileged to serve his idol. The utilitarian aspect of Stravinsky's friendships is well represented in the published literature. We all performed services, from Ansermet on. I can only say that it was an honor to serve, however infinitely small my contribution might have been. As for Vera being maternal, it was simply not in her character. She is the Roman goddess Venus and every bit as Olympian as her husband.

Analyzing my relationship with them into separate ones for Igor and Vera is impossible. The couple was always a unit for me. As long as Igor was living, it was ever "The Stravinskys" with whom I ate caviar, blini, borsch, and halvah and drank tea or Polish vodka or Scotch in Santa Fe, Washington, D.C., New York, or Hollywood. I saw them often, especially in New York after that first summer in Santa Fe. Our meetings then were strictly social, the opportunity to help them not fully developing until four years later when I was living in California, for a part of that time in the Stravinskys' house as a member of their household. It is still curious, and to no one more than myself, that any relationship at all developed between a young, middle-class man from Memphis, Tennessee, and the famous aristocratic Russians. Vera's remark about someone else—"Why do I like him? Probably because he likes me"—may be part of the explanation. Perhaps also Stravinsky's statement to me, "I need someone for me," provides a key. "So-and-so is for Vera," he said, "but I need someone just for me." Alas, I was incompetent for that role, as anyone would be, but I did try to provide what I could strictly out of my love for the two of them.

Anyone who knew Igor and Vera had to be impressed by one thing of paramount importance. One would had to have been blind not to observe it. The love they shared for each other was of such a quality as to be overwhelming in its impression. Never before had I seen such devotion between two people, and after Stravinsky's death, never since. There was some aura, something wondrously beautiful, emanating from the couple. Vera was not only "for Stravinsky," she was "of Stravinsky," the perfect completion of his being.

Except when he was composing or reading, Stravinsky always wanted his wife at his side. "Where is Vera?" was not an answerable question when spoken by Stravinsky, but rather a command to produce her. Failure to do so immediately, even if she was in the middle of painting or out buying herring for her husband, resulted in his great disappointment, sometimes courteously masked but at other times marked by an agitated impatience until she appeared. When she did appear, he was happy, but without her, there was always something missing for him. There was some charm at work while the two of them were together, a shared charisma that is indescribable but was felt by myself and others in their company. Their liaison, as is well known, began illicitly, but it was surely meant to be from the beginning, and even before their marriage it must have been pronounced *licit* by the only Authority who mattered. Their fifty-year romance is one of the supreme love stories of all times, and yet to be written. Vera and Igor's marriage is one of the strongest and most beautiful of all times.

Two of the functions I performed for Stravinsky when I was in Hollywood were to assist him in arranging his private papers and, on my own, to arrange the library in the house to which they had just moved. Stravinsky expressed his concern to me over the future of his archive, saying that there was only one man capable of dealing with it, his friend in Paris, Pierre Souvtchinsky. He worried about his papers. He did not want certain people to see certain things. He even went through some files at that time and discarded items. One can only speculate how many times he had weeded previously. Some of the material he disposed of—letters from Léon Bakst, for example—miraculously returned to their original files the next morning, after being discovered in the wastebasket. I did not act alone in this, but with Vera Stravinsky's blessings. The interests of posterity prevailed over Stravinsky's momentary judgment that he no longer wanted that particular bit of documentation preserved. All great men should have librarians following them around. I mention this benign deception because the familiarity I was to develop with Stravinsky's papers when they were accessible to me, prior to 1979, very much makes me wish that there had always been someone around to put things back.

Stravinsky's manner of organizing his papers almost seemed to depend more on the furniture in which it was to be filed than on any ideal classification. If the cabinets were full, as most of them seemed to be, one wonders if new material was even retained or if old was displaced. Chronology was the major category, of course, concert tours being another. Stravinsky was always proud of his being a performing artist and thought it was a family heritage. Business correspondence with publishers, recording companies, lawyers, and concert agents were other categories. "Miscellaneous" was a very popular, frequently used label. There were many programs—even multiple copies—photographs, fascinating scrapbooks, and clippings in all languages. There were noticeably few files dedicated to individuals, a fact probably not insignificant in understanding Stravinsky, who had deep love for a few friends, as evidenced musically by his many memorials from Rimsky on, but who preserved no appreciable body of personal correspondence in his private papers.

Stravinsky's manuscripts were not filed with his papers but secured elsewhere. The library of his own printed music was shelved in his studio in a cabinet occupied by the works of only two other composers—Tchaikovsky and Webern. The studio itself was decorated by souvenirs of an extraordinarily fascinating past: Cocteau's drawings, Picasso's portraits, works of his son Theodore, a photograph of his first wife Catherine, religious objects, objects remembering family, others recalling performances of stage works or concert tours. Stravinsky's eye was most discerning. The order in which he placed objects that were only decorative was just as meticulously determined as the arrangement of his tools for composition. A large collection of dictionaries was also shelved in the studio. When the studio door was shut and Stravinsky was composing, one could just hear tiny sounds from the muted piano. One walked quietly, whispered, or said nothing, tried not to make noises. Even aromas from the kitchen—often marvelous ones—could disturb him.

A cabinet outside the studio in the hallway held books written by and about him, along with the tokens of various honors and the medals he had received over the course of a long career. Next to the cabinet, shelves housed other composers' scores, of which he owned an extensive library. Many scores were in filing boxes, identified by Stravinsky's famous calligraphic hand. His collection of Russian books, which were far outnumbered by French, which in turn were far outnumbered by English, was placed just outside the bedroom in the hall. Although I had carefully arranged the Russian books according to the Cyrillic alphabet, Stravinsky's eye demanded some revision. In particular, a handsome engraving of Dostoevsky had to be visible when Stravinsky passed it in the hall. (Dostoevsky was moved to greater prominence.) When I finished arranging the entire library, Stravinsky complimented me. "A very interesting order, but not *my* order," he said, his kind smile indicating I would have to teach him where I had placed everything. I had intended to make a catalogue of the books, but we estimated that there were over nine thousand volumes and there was never time to do it. What struck me as odd about the library collection was that there were so few "Stravinsky" items in it, so little documentation of Stravinsky's world.

Stravinsky was a great reader and read as comfortably in English and German as he did in French and Russian. His lexicological interests manifested themselves constantly. An expression in English had to be repeated in French, German, Russian, and sometimes Italian, as a diverting game that could never be completed until all the languages were represented. Sometimes trips to the dictionaries had to be made, but more often Stravinsky's phenomenal memory for language quickly found the right word or phrase. Butter, for example, could not be passed at table without verbal extension: *maslo* (Russian), *beurre* (French), *Butter* (German), *burro* in Italian but definitely *not* in Spanish unless one expected to leave the restaurant on an ass. A letter from Vera begins: "*Cher* Ed, dear Ed, *dorogoi* Ed. The German is missing—to hell with them."

His verbal surprises were as delightful as fireworks, his wit so remarkable I cannot do justice to it by repeating anything he said. Often it was his manner of speaking that was wonderful. Just as he was physically the embodiment of kinetic power, so his language was explosive and always on target. When I first met him, I thought he moved like the characters in Eisenstein's films, and I thought that was just part of being Russian. But Stravinsky was especially fast, especially expressive, especially powerful. Even when his health was failing and I would walk with him for exercise, his grip on my arm demonstrated real strength.

The small man had no difficulty in maintaining true stature. No one looked down on him from whatever height. The strength of his character showed clearly in his face. His physical aspect changed only subtly in the last years. The short man alongside his tall wife presented him in a scale that might have dwarfed him. But it never did, due to the nobility of his carriage and dignity of his expression, his sense of who he was, and the great style with which he dressed. Those around him in the final years were impressed by his mellowness. The fierce composer of *The Rite of Spring* had become a gentle, sweet, old man, a pussycat. Russian kisses were accorded greeters, even if they were not intimate friends. One often sees Stravinsky smiling in photographs and films made during the final decade of his life. I can testify that this smile is genuine and no pose. It comes from the man being able to amuse himself while knowing he delighted his companions. It also comes from the great *joie de vivre* shared by both Stravinskys. That wonderful smile accompanying the witty or naughty statement is an unforgettable aspect of the man in those years.

It is difficult to speak about the sadness of the end. The period in New York was not a happy one. Often in great depression, Stravinsky sat, silent for hours or even days. If he played the piano and did not compose, he knew that it was only exercise. But exercise for what? When he realized he could no longer compose, his spirit broke. "I can no longer live this way." If we played cards, or if one simply sat holding his hand, he was consoled, but only temporarily. He took great pleasure in listening to music from recordings—and especially Beethoven, as has already been documented. But his real joy came only from Vera. The sight of the two of them together, holding hands, often only the tips of fingers touching, looking lovingly into each others' eyes, communicating silently through the bond of their fifty years of fascinating, happy, creative life together, is unforgettable. The eloquence of that infinitely sad yet infinitely beautiful picture haunts my memories. And as Vera Stravinsky now lies dying in New York, my mind's eye sees those fingers touch and those eyes meet, and despite my personal sadness at the loss, I am overwhelmed yet again by joy for those two people, both so courageous in the grips of terrible lingering deaths but never really parted because they meant as much to each other as any two humans possibly could.

This paper was first delivered on 12 September 1982. Vera Stravinsky died on 17 September 1982. [Editor's note]

21 Stravinsky at Home

LAWRENCE MORTON

I FIRST BECAME interested in Igor Stravinsky around 1931–1932, when I heard a recording of his *Symphony of Psalms,* made, I believe, in Paris. I first heard him conduct in Chicago during his American tour of 1935. I was immediately fascinated by the way in which he led the orchestra—so different in style from how Frederick Stock conducted. Stock was, of course, a very great conductor; it was he who led me into the maze of modern music. But to see Stravinsky lead an orchestra in his own works was a most memorable happening. Everything was clear, precise, and articulate, both in his gestures and (to a lesser degree) in the orchestra's response. To me, he was the very image of "modernism." I began to keep a notebook on Stravinsky in which I gathered criticisms of his work and whatever personal statistics I could find.

I finally met Stravinsky in 1941, and my earliest substantive conversation with him was on 14 October of that year at a reception following the concert at which his orchestration of "The Star-Spangled Banner" was first performed by the WPA (Works Progress Administration) Orchestra in Los Angeles. At the reception, I thanked him for giving our national anthem a very good bass line and also for the appoggiatura at the final cadence. These were not very astute remarks—and after Coventry, "the bombs bursting in air" made one wince at the text—but they set him off on discussing Berlioz, whose bass lines were, in his opinion, quite awry. He told me he had studied Berlioz in his student days and admired his orchestration. "He was a great innovator." He went on to explain that the tricks of Berlioz's orchestration were not matched by his zest for harmonic rectitude. All this was an echo of his Harvard lectures (*Poetics of Music,* 1942) and represented opinions he never revised, although in his very last year, according to Robert Craft, he took a small liking to some of the "orchestral novelties" in *The Trojans.*

Shortly after this encounter I was inducted into a civilian branch of the Signal Corps, and for the next few years, I saw very little of Stravinsky. I began to see him again in the early fifties, though I did meet him occasionally in the meantime. Once, when I went shopping for groceries on a Sunday afternoon, I saw him standing in front of a local market while Mrs. Stravinsky was inside buying delicacies. I stopped to chat with him and mentioned I had just heard a piece of his played on a radio concert. He had heard it too, he told me, and it was a very disappointing performance—"the tempos were all wrong." The complaint about tempos was, of course, perennial. He never trusted any tempo other than his own, and they, for sure, were never quite consistent. When Marni Nixon was recording his "Tilimbom" (the flute, harp, and guitar setting), some of us in the control room felt that the tempo was too fast, that there was inadequate time for articulation either of the words or the instruments. This suggestion was relayed to him over the control-room-to-stage monitor. Puzzled, Stravinsky turned the score back to the beginning, where there was a metronome mark, and then replied that it was impossible, the score says it should be a quarter-note to 108. The recorded performance is paced at 136. Subsequent performances of the orchestral version by Evelyn Lear and a later recording of the flute, harp, and guitar versions, by Adrienne Albert (both of the latter in the memorial edition of his recorded works) are paced at 136 or thereabouts. Still, the earliest version is marked 104 to the quarter and the latest version is still marked 108.

During the late 1950s and early 1960s, I was given access to certain areas in Stravinsky's studio while he was out of the city.[1] Now, without the presence of the maestro, I could look at leisure around his workroom. There was a cupboard for the published scores, files and packets of scores and sketches, each labeled and in vastly assorted sizes, side tables loaded with books, bookshelves at a higher level than Stravinsky could conveniently reach, photographs and icons and other religious objects, and all the remarkable gadgetry of his work table that everyone knows from the description in Ramuz's memoir. But any description is inadequate when one can pick up and examine each object.

I would go there with the intention of, say, looking at the sketches of *Histoire du soldat*. But that is not what I did on at least one afternoon (about twenty-five years ago) because of other fascinating things in the *Histoire* file. A good part of the sketches—perhaps about half—had been made in an already used notebook. It appeared to be an account book with a list of names, alphabetically arranged on separate sheets, down the left side of the page, and with an ordinal number after each name. But not strictly ordinal, for these were often two or three separated names followed by the same number. All were in a very beautiful and somewhat flamboyant hand.

Elsewhere, under headings of another sort, are notations of bills made out to:

> Signor Giogio Tini of San Vittore, for 19 August 1790, entered at Book A, folio 233, for the sum of 51.12 (ducats? cigliatti?)
>
> His Honor Signor the Mayor Antonio Romagnola of San Vittore, entered at Book A, folio 267, as mentioned in the annotation of Regina Romagnola, for the sum of 9.10

1. At the time, I was contemplating a book on Stravinsky. Contemplation was as far as my work progressed, though I continued to think about it until the middle sixties. One of the things that unnerved me, and that still disconcerts me, was a remark Stravinsky made to me in the fall of 1960, on the last evening we spent together in Venice just before I returned to the United States. At the entrance to his hotel, Stravinsky paused and, after the usual goodbye embraces, said, "If you are really writing a book about me, say what you have to say—but please be kind."

> Maria Barbola, wife of the late Giacomo Antonio Gianolla of San Vittore, for 4 February 1793, entered at Book AB, folio n. 28, for the sum of 85.18
>
> Teresa, the wife of Antonio Mantovanni of Sovazza, for 31 August 1787, entered at Book A, folio 110, for the sum of 38.6

San Vittore, Savazzo, and another small town called Gromo, also in the records, are in the neighborhood of Varese (Italy), and it might have been on a visit to Varese in 1913 that Stravinsky and Ravel went just to buy paper. On this visit, by the way, the two friends had to sleep together in a double bed.[2] I asked Stravinsky, "Well, how was it?" He replied that I would have to ask Ravel.

On these account books, approximately half of each page was not used for fiscal operations, and that half is what Stravinsky used for his sketches. Some of them were in horizontal position on the page, some of them vertical; some of them ran right into the ledger accounts; some were in pencil, some in ink. One sketch shows a portion of "The Soldier's March" scored for three trumpets. Another gives a list of instruments, including a piano, but no bassoon or percussion. One has the picture of four drums in profile. In another is the sketch of the proscenium of the stage.

On the alphabetical listing of the T's, there is a sketch of a passage from "Triumphal March of the Devil," from two measures after rehearsal number **8** to **9.** It is complete, with the violin part in ink and the trombone, bass, and percussion parts in pencil. On a page of B listings, the "Triumphal March" occurs again from three before **15** to one after **16.** Here both violin and percussion parts are in ink; at some undetermined point, Stravinsky evidently intended to change the barring, but the mathematics did not work out correctly, so he left it as it stands in the score. Also in the "Triumphal March," there is a passage (at **3** and passim) for the violin in double-stops where, alternately, the bottom note of one chord followed by the upper notes of the next spells out an important motif of the piece:

Example 21.1. Sketches from *Histoire du soldat* not present in the final score.

2. Igor Stravinsky and Robert Craft, *Conversations with Igor Stravinsky* (New York, 1959), p. 67. In his preface to the published sketches of *The Rite of Spring* (London, 1969), François Lesure states that the two composers made their trip to Varese in the winter of 1911–1912 and that the sketches for *The Rite* were executed in an exercise book purchased at that time. But it was in March or April of 1913 that they visited Varese, by which time *The Rite* sketches were already a year old. This does not explain why Stravinsky waited until 1918 to use the old sketchbook—that is, if it was obtained on this visit.

This is in ink, the motif above it in pencil. This is the tune that occurred to Stravinsky in a dream: a young gypsy, holding a child on her lap, was playing the violin. The child was enthusiastic about the music and applauded it. Stravinsky was also pleased and joyfully included this motif in the music of the "Petit Concert."[3] The motif is not complete, however, for it turns into another idea borrowed from "Music to Scene I" (bracketed above in Example 21.1). On still another page, still on the B listings, are the concluding eighteen bars of *Histoire*, beautifully copied as if for a final score and signed "Igor Strawinsky, 26 août 1918."

This is a fascinating document. Anything written so long ago as 1787 ought to be "historical." Perhaps it may still be, with Stravinsky's sketches, if some enterprising scholar can discover its provenance. I loved reading it for the melodious sound of Italian names and places (there were no verbs to confound me). But why did Stravinsky use this ancient notebook? Was there a shortage of paper in wartime Switzerland in 1917? Or did Stravinsky use it because he liked the feel, the texture, of the parchmentlike paper?

A footnote to the chapter on *Histoire* in *Stravinsky in Pictures and Documents* mentions that the borrowing from popular songs would make a subject for a doctoral thesis.[4] But that is no less surprising than Stravinsky's reversion to the use of Russian folk tunes as late as 1943–1944. I came across in his library a book entitled *Piesni russago nardo* [Songs of the Russian people], which I would have thought someone else might have noticed long before now. It was published by Jurgenson. No data is given, but the spelling is of course prerevolutionary (Old Style). The editor, who presumably composed the piano parts, is given as M. Bernard. Everyone who has played or even listened to the Sonata for Two Pianos is aware of some folk influence. In this book, I found two folk tunes used in the Sonata. The first of them is no. 46, "Do not sing, do not sing." It has a text about a father

Example 21.2. "Do not sing, do not sing" from *Piesni russago nardo*, ed. M. Bernard (Moscow: P. Jurgenson, n.d.), No. 46.

who has betrothed his daughter to "a foolish head." It serves as the theme for the variations of the second movement (Example 21.2). The second of the folk tunes

3. Ibid., p. 13.

4. Vera Stravinsky and Robert Craft, *Stravinsky in Pictures and Documents* (New York, 1978), p. 623, n. 280.

is no. 16, "Oh, what kind of heart is this?" with a text about a jilted lover (female). This became the tune of the trio of the last movement (Example 21.3). Both folk tunes are quoted literally, in the manner of the melodies from *The Firebird* and

Example 21.3. "Oh, what kind of heart is this?" from *Piesni russago narode*, ed. M. Bernard (Moscow: P. Jurgenson, n.d.), No. 16.

Petrushka. Although the variation theme is marked andante in Bernard's transcription, Stravinsky takes a very stately tempo, with a canon in inversion at the octave below. He takes the tune through three cycles, in increased sonority, to constitute his theme. Four variations follow, with the usual Stravinsky transformations. For the trio in the last movement, Stravinsky uses only four and a half measures, skips to the eighth and ninth, recomposes the next several bars, using previous material, and then returns to a few of the opening bars. Nothing here suggests anything like the manipulations of the elements or motifs within the folk tunes, such as we have observed in *The Rite of Spring*.[5]

What prompted Stravinsky to revert to this kind of folk tune usage? Surely it was not habit—he had abandoned folk music twenty-odd years earlier. But the Sonata was, first of all, a noncommissioned work; he began to compose it before the *Scènes de ballet* and finished it after (commissions, of course, took precedence). Stravinsky was so completely in the habit of daily composing that he probably needed something to keep himself occupied between the few commissioned works that came his way. The whole period between the Symphony in C and the Symphony in Three Movements must have been a difficult time for him. There were many adjustments to be made to turn him from a Russian-French composer into an American one. There was, for example, jazz music. He had of course made portraits of jazz during his Swiss years—*Rag-time, Piano-Rag-Music,* the small dances in *Histoire.* But the later phase brought forth the *Tango, Circus Polka, Scènes de ballet, Scherzo à la Russe,* and the *Ebony Concerto.* "I am somewhat unnerved," he wrote to Nadia Boulanger, ". . . by my lack of familiarity with this sort of thing."[6] And indeed, he sought help for at least three of these pieces.

5. Richard Taruskin later reported that further examples of Stravinsky's borrowings from Bernard had been discovered.

6. Robert Craft, ed., *Stravinsky: Selected Correspondence,* vol. 1 (New York, 1982), p. 244.

He also entertained several offers for film scores—for *Jane Eyre* and *The Song of Bernadette,* for unspecified projects at Paramount and Warner Brothers Studios, and as late as 1964 for John Huston's *The Bible.* None of them was realized.

Toward the end of 1941, Columbia Pictures Corporation, through its musical director Morris Stoloff, invited Stravinsky to discuss the possibility of his composing a score for *The Commandos Strike at Dawn,* a film based on Norwegian resistance to the German invasion. The negotiations came to nothing, but during their progress, Stravinsky began working with folk materials that seemed apt for the film. This was the genesis of the little set of four orchestra pieces called *Four Norwegian Moods.* They must not be construed as incidental music for a film, for neither their formal organization nor their instrumentation would have survived the criticism to be expected of producers, directors, and editors of motion pictures. The pieces themselves have no cinematic significance, being innocent of any pictorial or dramatic intent. At most, they might have been used to accompany scenes depicting the quiet rural life of anonymous Norwegians before war struck them.

This score has called forth a great deal of comment, including from Stravinsky: "All the themes in my *Norwegian Moods* were taken from a collection of Norwegian folk music my wife found in a secondhand bookstore in Los Angeles—and not from Grieg, as some writers on my music have stated!"[7] In the Boston Symphony program notes for the first performance, the commentator quotes Stravinsky as stating that "although based on Norwegian folk tunes, the title *Moods* . . . is purely a mode, a form or manner of style without any assumption of ethnological authenticity. . . . [I] no more than followed the tradition of folklore treatment used by Joseph Haydn in his time . . . using the folklore thematic only as a rhythmic and melodic basis."[8] Eric Walter White has stated that "there might be a case for including this work among Stravinsky's adaptations rather than his original compositions."[9] And the record annotator, Phillip Ramey, said, "The composer has adapted the style of Grieg for his own use."[10] But the most impressive comment on the *Moods* is by the German musicologist Uwe Kraemer in *Melos:* "Examination of a number of different collections of Norwegian folk music showed that they contained in part one or two melodies used in Stravinsky's work, but there is only one collection of folk tunes, *Norges Melodier,* in which one can find all the melodies adopted by the composer."[11] Kraemer goes on to describe the four volumes of this great collection, their contents, dates, edi-

7. Igor Stravinsky and Robert Craft, *Memories and Commentaries* (New York, 1960), p. 93.

8. Program of the Boston Symphony Orchestra, 13 January 1944.

9. Eric Walter White, *Stravinsky: The Composer and His Works,* 2d ed. (Berkeley and Los Angeles, 1979), p. 415.

10. "Stravinsky Conducts," Columbia Records, M 30516, record note by Phillip Ramey.

11. Uwe Kraemer, "Four Norwegian Moods von Igor Strawinsky," *Melos* 2 (March–April 1972): 80.

tors, and publishers; he quotes the specific melodies and relates them to Stravinsky's composition, noting alterations of melodic and rhythmic structures; and finally he offers a few personal comments in appreciation of the composer's mastery. Kraemer's article is admirable in almost every way—so far as it goes.

Unfortunately, it does not go quite far enough, for Kraemer did not happen upon *the* collection that Stravinsky actually used. The composer's wife, rummaging through Ring's secondhand music shop in Hollywood, is not likely to have had the extraordinary good luck of finding a scholarly work like the four volumes of *Norges Melodier,* the dates of which range from 1875 to 1924. But surely Kraemer must have realized that his claim to have found "all" the sources was inaccurate, for there are three melodies that he failed to identify.

If Mrs. Stravinsky was unlikely to happen upon *Norges Melodier* in Hollywood, so was Kraemer unlikely to have happened upon, in European libraries, the collection that Stravinsky actually used, for it is a very unpretentious volume and one so conscientiously dedicated to popular taste that it might well escape scholarly notice. Its motivation was not musicological but sentimental and evangelical, as is evidenced by the rather old-fashioned and elaborate title page (see Figure 21.1).

This publication was in Stravinsky's library in 1958. Four copies of it existed also in the Los Angeles Public Library, where I photocopied the pertinent pages some time later. A few of the students in the late Professor Ingolf Dahl's classes at the University of Southern California found it there and reported on their findings, though term papers do not make the best-seller lists. The mantle of secrecy that Stravinsky cast over his source material has long since been rent, although the information has not been widely broadcast.

I need not review here the details of Kraemer's investigations, but I would like to identify the three melodies that he did not locate. The first of these, occurring at **4** in the "Intrada," is found on page 116 of the Ditson Collection under the title of "Wedding March" [Brulaaten] and with accreditation to "Edward Grieg's Arrangement, Opus 17, Dedicated to Ole Bull" (Example 21.4).

The second of the unidentified pieces occurs in the "Wedding Dance." At **33,** where the melody is transferred to the bass instruments, Stravinsky adds as a counterpoint, for flute and strings, the opening motif of "A Humorous Dance" [Stabbe-Laaten] (Example 21.5). This tune appears twice in the Ditson Collection—on page 110, where it is given in an arrangement by Ludvig Mathias Lindeman, and again on page 111, where it is given in Grieg's elaborate arrangement from his Opus 17, again dedicated to Ole Bull. (Grieg used the tune again in his string orchestra piece, Opus 63, no. 2.) Kraemer makes no comment on this countermelody and thus assumes it to be Stravinsky's own invention.

The same assumption has been made about the third tune, the whole *meno mosso* section, also in the "Wedding Dance" (Example 21.6). What Kraemer calls "free Stravinsky" is actually *Halling* (a man's solo dance), which is found on page 87 of the Ditson Collection in a Lindeman arrangement.

THE

NORWAY

MUSIC ALBUM:

A SELECTION FOR HOME USE, FROM

NORWAY'S

FOLK-SONGS, DANCES, ETC., NATIONAL AIRS,

AND

RECENT COMPOSITIONS,

ARRANGED FOR

PIANOFORTE AND SOLO SINGING, WITH A FEW FOUR-PART SONGS.

EDITED, AND FURNISHED WITH ENGLISH TEXT, BY

AUBER FORESTIER, and RASMUS B. ANDERSON.

PART I.

SELECTIONS FROM FOLK-SONGS, DANCES, ETC., AND NATIONAL AIRS.

PART II.

SELECTIONS FROM RECENT COMPOSITIONS.

BOSTON:

Copyright, 1881, by

OLIVER DITSON & CO.

C. H. DITSON & CO., NEW YORK. LYON & HEALY, CHICAGO. J. E. DITSON & CO., PHILADELPHIA.

Figure 21.1 Title Page of *Norges Melodier* [The Norway music album].

All of Stravinsky's sources are secondary, some of them in elaborate arrangements. Of the ten melodies used, one was an arrangement by Halfdan Kjerulf, three were arranged by Carl Warmuth, four come from the Lindeman collection, and three were by Grieg—which makes somewhat disingenuous Stravinsky's disclaimer of any indebtedness to Grieg. Seven of the tunes, as Kraemer demon-

Example 21.4. *The Norway Music Album,* ed. Auber Forestier and Rasmus B. Anderson (Boston: Oliver Ditson and Co., 1881), p. 116.

Example 21.5. *The Norway Music Album,* ed. Auber Forestier and Rasmus B. Anderson (Boston: Oliver Ditson and Co., 1881), p. 110.

Example 21.6. *The Norway Music Album*, ed. Auber Forestier and Rasmus B. Anderson (Boston: Oliver Ditson and Co., 1881), p. 87.

strated, exist in the *Norges Melodier*. But only three of these were included in the first volume, published in 1875, the only one published by the time the Ditson Collection appeared in 1881.[12]

Just to be in the Stravinsky home was a delight. Arriving there, one might find the maestro engrossed in a game of solitaire, occasionally "cheating" when frustrated or mumbling obscenities in Russian. I was there one day when, playing Canfield, he uttered a frightfully vile remark just as Mrs. Stravinsky passed through the room with her gardener, who, being Russian himself, understood every word. Mrs. Stravinsky scolded her husband sharply; he was abashed. I asked him what he had said. He told me in Russian—I had a smattering of the language at the time. I asked him for an English translation, which embarrassed him still further, so I asked him to write it down. He did, and I preserve it as sole example of the scatological Stravinsky.

Dining *chez Stravinsky* was a gourmet occasion when Mrs. Stravinsky had

12. The complete list of pieces from the Ditson collection:

"Intrada"—Wedding March, p. 114; Wedding March, p. 116; Underground Music, p. 126.

"Song"—The Fisherman's Song, p. 36; Home Forever, p. 56.

"Wedding Dance"—Wedding March, p. 115; A Humorous Dance, p. 110 (or Grieg's Version, p. 111); Halling, p. 87.

"Cortège"—Return March, p. 117; Halling, p. 79.

done the cooking herself or engaged a caterer, and so were the postconcert repasts consisting, on a few memorable occasions, of cold chicken breasts and champagne. Table talk was lively. If Aldous Huxley and Gerald Heard were present, it was a wonderful experience to listen to them in conversation: Huxley, the tenor, purring his long, involuted sentences; Heard, the baritone and an orator, replying in staccato phrases, like Stravinsky's musical speech; the both of them exhibiting such skill in the manipulation of the king's English that one could just listen to the beauty of the language even without following the trend of the discussion. Generally the subject matter was global. Parentheses and footnotes were numerous. If the subject was geographical, a collection of Baedeckers was handy in the dining room bookcase, together with other reference books. But if it was lexicographical, Stravinsky would have to fetch one of the many dictionaries he kept in his study. One could say that for Stravinsky dictionaries ranked in importance just next to the Bible and other sacred writings. World literature was a frequent topic. At one time, Stravinsky was reading Turgenev simultaneously in Russian and English, and both he and his wife were deeply affected by Nabokov's translation of *Eugene Onegin.* Wine was another favorite topic—I remember Maria Huxley clutching a bottle of rare vintage to her breast to warm it and gently chiding Stravinsky for having stored it in too cold a cellar.

The Stravinskys often entertained their guests at restaurants, and only at the best ones; but they were fickle in their judgment of which one was "the best." Wherever they chose to dine, they were treated like royalty—Stravinsky was probably generous with tips. Mrs. Stravinsky, sometimes bored with the menus and the prevailing obsequiousness, would astonish the establishment by asking for a plain hamburger. When I dined alone with the Stravinskys at a restaurant, I would glance at the bill and the next day send Mrs. Stravinsky a check for my portion. For a while, the Bel-Air Hotel was a favorite dining place, and when sending my check to Mrs. Stravinsky, I enclosed some doggerel verse about the "Bel-Air, très cher." After one such *billet-doux,* Stravinsky replied in a "Twelve-tone Note"[13] (see Figure 21.2).

At lunches, much of the conversation centered around what eventually became subjects of the Stravinsky-Craft conversation books, though of course there were many other occasions for that. Critics were also a favorite topic, Stravinsky's scorn for them matching that of composers from Beethoven to Schoenberg. His published 'letters to the editor' are masterpieces of vituperation, but so full of wit and irony that the recipients should have been more gratified than aggrieved to be immortalized in a Stravinskyan malediction. Robert Craft has mentioned my having had a hand in those letters, and I am not ashamed of my participation because I have blasted the critics enough on my own account.

---

13. The writing of thank-you notes in the form of twelve-tone rows became a favorite occupation for Stravinsky. Milton Babbitt is said to have collected them. But before his dodecaphonic period, Stravinsky frequently wrote, "No time to write, only time to rush and to thank."

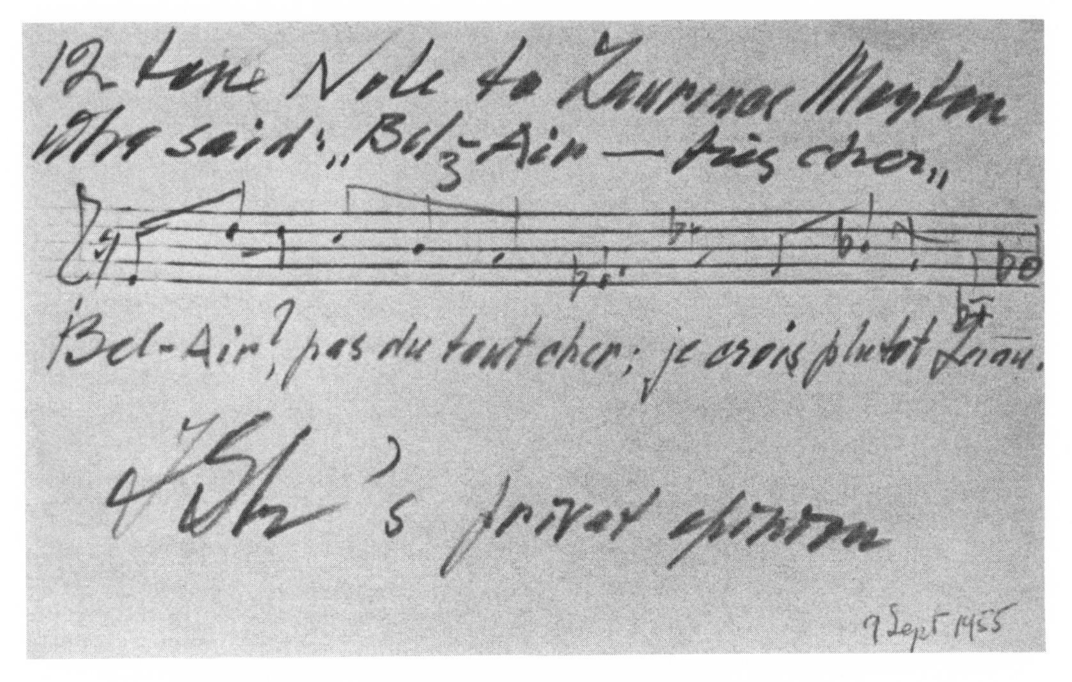

Figure 21.2 Musical sketch by Stravinsky, 9 September 1955:

12-tone note to Lawrence Morton
who said: "Bel-Air—très cher"
Bel-Air? pas du tout cher; je crois plutôt Luau.
[Bel-Air? not at all expensive; more so, Luau.]
IStr's privat [sic] opinion

On the day he finished composing *In Memoriam Dylan Thomas,* 21 March 1954, Stravinsky was eager to show the music to someone who would be interested and sympathetic. Craft being out of the city, he telephoned to invite me to look at the new score. He played it at the piano, very badly, and he sang the tenor part himself, in a composer's voice. This was not a performance, but it was accompanied by a running verbal analysis of the serial structure. Also, his fingers stuttered. At one point in the preluding dirge-canons, he paused to say in a conspiratorial whisper, "Here I cheated the row—I did not like the harmony." Subsequently, however, he found how to be honest with his series, for the canons in their final form can be parsed with academic rigor.

Stravinsky went to fetch me the proverbial Scotch while I continued to look at the score. He said to me then that it was still difficult to "unlearn" tonality and that he still felt the pull toward a tonal center. I asked him if he felt any inclination toward the twelve-tone method while he was composing the last two movements of the Concerto for Two Solo Pianos, where the involvements of the variations and the fugue often resembled the practices of serial writing. "No," he said, "because I knew very little about the twelve-tone system at that time, and I probably would have thought it very academic (Glazunov again!). Besides, what I did in my Concerto is as old as Bach. But I do resist the academic approach, except that I find it very interesting to 'experience' [that is his word, "experience"] the serial method in my *Dylan Thomas* piece, so long as the harmony is correct. I must have the correct harmony!"

Just a year earlier, when a small group of musicians gathered to read through his Septet, he had declared, particularly about the last movement, "It is fiercely tonal!" But within the next three to four years, he would announce that harmony was a dead issue and that he was, by conviction, a twelve-tone composer. But still he was a slender receiver of the gospel: "I can live without Schoenberg and without Berg but not without Webern."

When I returned home after this exciting afternoon—it was the first time I had heard Stravinsky play the piano and the first time I had witnessed the *accouchement* of a new piece—I wrote down my impressions, though I had heard it in only a piano reduction:

> Stravinsky is almost excessively watchful of the poetic text. The string quartet—he had composed nothing for it in more than thirty years, except for the prelude to scene 2, act 3 of *The Rake*—is used here with the greatest restraint and simplicity. It is kept as neutral as possible without depriving it of character. The violins scarcely touch their top string; nuances are rare; an occasional pizzicato, mutes in the postludium, and harmonics for the final cadence are the only variants from normal timbre. Yet it is through this calculated ineloquence that the strings make their presence so telling. Because their carefully woven lines of counterpoint are entirely serial, they are like mirrors reflecting back and thus illuminating the tenor's song with countless images of itself. The trombones also live on the level of the inexpressive. They play softly throughout, without dynamic variation, attacking almost every note with a tiny accent and making their mark with nothing but their wonderfully austere sonority. The two groups are never mixed, like the uncoupled manuals of an organ. In the context of all this subdued instrumentalism the tenor's song stands out in strong relief. *In Memoriam Dylan Thomas* is a beautiful tribute, far more intimate than the memorial to Debussy, and far more deeply felt than the elegiacal *Ode* for Natalie Koussevitzky. It is a smaller monument than either, but it is affecting and personal while the others are impressive and official.

In subsequent visits to Stravinsky's studio, I never paid much attention to the machinery of his serial practices. I am no Champollion of the tone row, and once I found out what he was doing with his alpha, beta, gamma, and delta rows, with his diagonals and verticals and all the other upholstery of his pieces, I was quite content with just listening to the fabulous and always fresh sounds he concocted. But I did take a fairly long look at the opening of *Threni,* largely because he had said to many of his friends that "it's a boring piece, *mais très savant*." I cannot be sure if the sketches I saw were absolutely the beginning of the piece, but they were close to it. As with *Oedipus Rex,* he was still composing to the syllable. There were many entries of the opening phrase, "Incipit lamentatio Jeremiae Prophetiae." If I read the sketches correctly, he seemed to arrive at his basic row through the setting of those words, giving the appropriate inflection to each syllable of the text. "Jeremiae Prophetiae" gave him more trouble—there are perhaps seven or eight examples of syllabification—than did the first two words. And then there were the few measures of the introduction, one of which is marked "To enlarge," which means that the equivalent of ten quarter-notes should be "enlarged" to fifteen. The "enlargement" was needed first because Stravinsky still believed in the necessity for repetition and second because there could be no Stravinsky without rests and syncopes. Here are the first and the "enlarged" second version of the introduction:

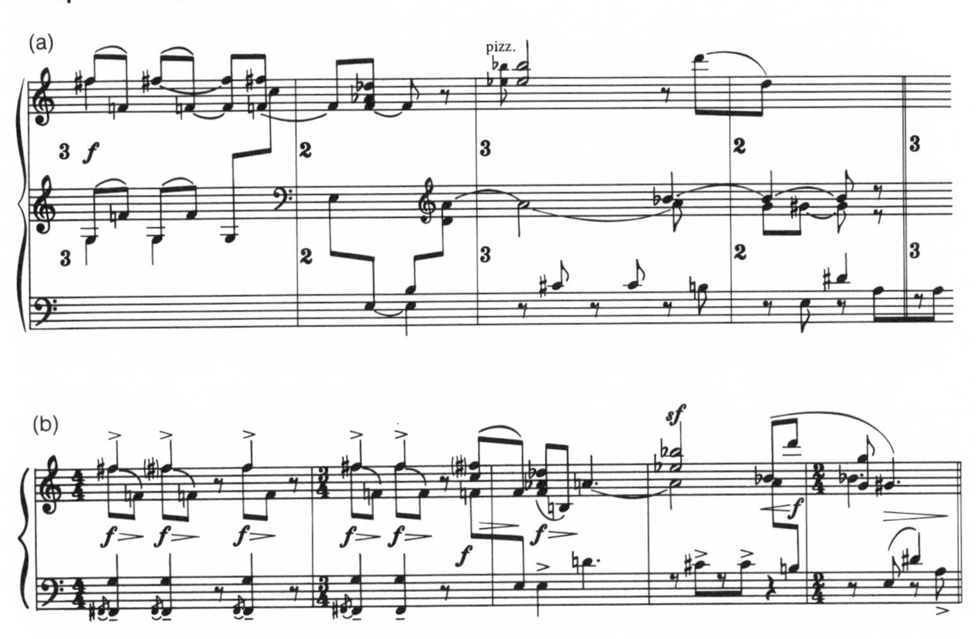

Example 21.7. Sketches from *Threni*

Greatest of all pleasures was traveling with the Stravinskys and Robert Craft. One such outing was a short excursion to Pasadena to view a Kandinsky exhibition. Another was a visit to the state fair at Pomona. Stravinsky had always been a lover of "beasties both great and small." One remembers Nicholas Nabokov's account of the birds and cats in Stravinsky's home; the pictures of Stravinsky feeding the cats in a Venetia *campiello,* and watching a giraffe in a Copenhagen zoo and wondering, "What must it be like to have a sore throat," and the trip to Kruger National Park.[14] Pomona was of course displaying only domestic animals, but Stravinsky stood in awe and admiration of the Percherons. "What wonderful testicles!" he exclaimed.

We went to San Francisco for performances of *Petrushka* (Stravinsky conducting), boarding the plane at midnight after a performance of Schütz's *Christmas Story* at a Monday Evening Concert, with "singen, singen" still sounding in our ears.[15] Later it was to Vancouver for a Stravinsky Festival and to watch the polar bears in the zoo; once again Stravinsky conducted *The Firebird* from a Kalmus pirated edition of the score. But the best trip of all was to board an Italian ship at New York for a summer vacation in Greece, Istanbul, and Italy, arriving at Venice for the rehearsals and premiere of *Canticum Sacrum.* The Stravinskys, always and everywhere, were keen, sensitive, and critical observers of everything from landscapes to mosaics. But at no point in our travels did Stravinsky neglect performing his one, great mission in life—composing. He composed everywhere, which is probably why many of his late scores are dated but not located.

In his last years, his major complaint, aside from pain and discomfort, was that he could not compose. Here are some excerpts from Robert Craft's *Chronicle of a Friendship:*

> "I want to work, and if I can't work, I want to die." Accordingly, we hoist him out of bed to a gantry-type table . . . where he transcribes Bach. . . . Some twenty minutes later we lift him back to bed . . . but he is soon up again, and up and down a total of four times during the afternoon . . . but he had to be helped this afternoon in transposing a clarinet part.
>
> "I am afraid of dreaming music, and I realize now that I will never again be able to compose."
>
> But when V. asks if he wants anything, the answer is "I want to compose."
>
> Last week, a nurse who urged him to "try" to compose was rebuffed with "I never *try.* I compose or I don't compose."

14. Nicolas Nabokov, *Old Friends and New Music* (New York, 1951), pp. 201–2; Robert Craft, *Stravinsky: Chronicle of a Friendship, 1948–1971* (New York, 1972), photographs following p. 140; Stravinsky and Craft, *Pictures and Documents,* Plate 19.

15. This was Stravinsky's favorite concert series in Los Angeles. He first attended the concerts on 6 March 1944—they were then known as Evenings on the Roof, the change of title to Monday Evening Concerts occurring at the beginning of the 1954–1955 season. Here Stravinsky heard the most recent works by Berg, Berio, Boulez, Ives, Nono, Schoenberg, Stockhausen, Varèse, and Webern, as well as older music by Josquin, Gesualdo, Monteverdi, Schütz, Couperin, and about twenty Bach cantatas—mostly conducted by Robert Craft. Stravinsky's gift to these concerts during the twenty-nine years of his residence in Los Angeles consisted of twelve premieres—six were original compositions and six were arrangements of earlier pieces. During this period, Monday Evening Concerts gave a total of seventy-two performances of fifty-eight of his works; at the present count, it stands at one hundred and eleven performances of sixty-four works. Lest this appear to be favoritism, I note that the series included forty-five works by Schoenberg and a total of one hundred and six Schoenberg performances.

> What does matter . . . is our insistence that he can, and will again, compose. At this, anyway, he smiles.
>
> I. S., at a two-year peak, composes this morning for the first time in months. . . . "I like to compose music, not to listen to it. All my life I have been pursued by 'my works,' but I don't care about 'my works.' I care only about composing. And that is finished."
>
> Still in marvelous form, he composes again today, this time for about an hour.[16]

Stravinsky courted the Muse not by invocation but by work.

One of my last chores for him was to write out, in score from his particelle, the Two Sacred Songs from the *Spanisches Liederbuch* by Hugo Wolf. I cannot now remember how many corrections had to be made—enough to convince me that he would not compose again. It was sad to contemplate. There were, of course, sporadic attempts up until a few weeks before his death. But a year and a half before this, Robert Craft had decided that he could not play Stravinsky's new Bach transcriptions in Berlin, "too little if anything of I. S. being discernible in them as they stand now, virtually unedited."[17]

So the career ended, but with *The Owl and the Pussy-Cat*. This was by no means an anticlimax to the *Requiem Canticles*, for almost from the beginning of his career—from *Renard* to *The Flood*—humor, wit, and irony were among the qualities that most dearly delighted us, even when we were deeply moved—and sometimes even to tears—at *Symphony of Psalms*, the incredibly beautiful last scene of *The Rake's Progress*, or the Dylan Thomas piece. There was in Stravinsky something of Haydn and of Mozart, a kind of play function that was part of his speech, of his response to applause, and certainly of his television appearances. People who knew him in his early Paris years (Cocteau, Souvtchinsky) have told how his performance of *Pribaoutki*—always in private or with very intimate friends—was a marvel of characterization, especially the final song, "The Old Man and the Hare." His sense of humor had been noticed by his elders in his early years when he had attended the weekly gatherings of pupils and friends at Rimsky's. An observer of the time, V. Yastrebtzov, "mentions a group of 'plaisanteries musicales,' which Stravinsky played on 6 March 1903, a 'chanson comique' . . . and a piece called *Conductor and Tarantula* . . . and an unpublished song for bass and piano entitled *The Mushrooms Going to War*."[18] And at one of these gatherings, "Nicholas Richter horrified Rimsky-Korsakov's wife by playing a cakewalk, while Mitusov and Stravinsky demonstrated how it should be danced."[19]

Such drollery did not vanish with the ending of Stravinsky's so-called "Rus-

---

16. Craft, *Chronicle of a Friendship*, pp. 366, 367, 368, 379, 381, 401.

17. Ibid., p. 370.

18. White, *Stravinsky*, pp. 27–28.

19. Ibid., p. 26.

sian" period. But in the transition to neoclassicism, it changed its pattern—from humor to wit, which is to say, for example, from Mozart's *A Musical Joke* to the last movement of almost any of Haydn's symphonies. The vehicle of this change was the *Octet,* one of the most entertaining of Stravinsky's works. It was, by the way, the first work he composed (though covertly) for Vera de Bosset.

And it was for her, too, that he composed *The Owl and the Pussy-Cat,* although she was the last person in the world who wanted or needed a dedicatory work because everything he wrote was, silently, for her. But this was a special gift, for it was the first English poem that she memorized on coming to the United States. There are no "Ich liebe dich"s in Stravinsky's work, but *The Owl and the Pussy-Cat* is a true love song, half tender, half humorous, and, as Stravinsky said, "one of the great poems in the English language."

Now, at the interval of a decade since his death, all my memories of him are happy ones, and it seems to me that it is musically just that he ended his career not with *Requiem Canticles* but with *The Owl and the Pussy-Cat* as his last will and testament.

"So he passed over, and all the trumpets sounded for him on the other side."

Appendix

Selected Source Material from "A Catalogue of Books and Music Inscribed to and/or Autographed and Annotated by Igor Stravinsky"

COMPILED AND ANNOTATED BY ROBERT CRAFT*

Books and Music Related to Specific Compositions

1. *Prayer Book of the Russian Orthodox Church.* Moscow 1922.

Signed (in Russian): "Igor Stravinsky 1926 Nice." At the back of the book, Stravinsky has inserted a paper containing a prayer handwritten in church Slavonic. Stravinsky's *Oche Nash* (1926) follows the text in this volume.

2. *Kyriale sue Ordinarium Missae.* Desclée, Rome 1909.

The Credo in this volume (p. 72–74) was the model for the Credo in Stravinsky's Mass (1944–1948). The phrasing and caesuras are the same in both settings; pitch-centricity (G) is the same in both; whole-step intervals occur at cadences in both (G F G in the *Kyriale,* B A B—cf. *"ad dexteram patris"*—in the Stravinsky); text underlay is virtually the same in both (each syllable has a separate note, the only melisma of any length is in the *"Amen"*); and Stravinsky follows the *Kyriale* in repeating the music for *"Et expecto"* and *"in remissionem."*

3. *Kyriale* (the same book in a photographed copy).

On the cover, "NB" (Nadia Boulanger). In 1944, Mlle Boulanger gave Stravinsky her copy of the original volume as well as the photocopy.

4. *Biblia Sacra, Juxta Vulgatam Clementinam.* Desclée & Cie., Paris 1947.

Stravinsky acquired the book just before composing the *Canticum Sacrum.* Signed: "Igor Stravinsky 1954." The marking in red on page 6 of "Evangelium, Secundum Mattaeum," is the composer's.

5. *Dictionnaire de Plain-Chant.* Paris 1860.

Stravinsky has underlined the text in many places, changed the music in others, and added a clausula.

6. *Russian Ballads and Folk Songs* (printed title in English on front cover). Jurgenson, Moscow 1886.

Stravinsky purchased the volume in a secondhand music store in Los Angeles in 1942. The thematic material for the Sonata for Two Pianos comes from this anthology (cf. songs nos. 4, 9, 16, and 46), as well as a motive in the third movement of the Symphony in Three Movements. He also copied and harmonized other songs that he did not use. The outer cover was made by him, and he stenciled the title on it in large red-ink letters.

7. *Russian Folk Songs* (three volumes in one), collected and arranged "for singing and piano" by Danilo Kashin. Published by Simeon Silivanovsky, Moscow 1883.

(A tear in the binding at the spine reveals part of a page from an English newspaper of 1880 or 1881.) In Stravinsky's hand, first page, in Russian: "A very rare book, one of the best collections of Russian songs." In book I, song no. 1, page 5, for soprano, alto, tenor, and bass, Stravinsky has rewritten the harmony in four places; the melodic line is stylistically similar to the melodic line in *Mavra* (particularly in the three measures before rehearsal number **38** and elsewhere in the Mother's aria). On page 75, Stravinsky has bracketed the first seven couplets of the text. In book II, page 39, Stravinsky has repositioned the words of the song in relation to the notes. The song on page 75 contains the line "I go along the street" (cf. *Les Noces,* vocal score, p. 154). The first line of the song on page 81 refers to "going down the Volga" (cf. *Les Noces,* vocal score, p. 167). In book III, the first song contains the line: "The fast river is going over the pebbles" (cf. *Les Noces,* vocal score, p. 20, "the stream running on white stones").

8. *Pyesni russkago naroda* by Sakharov. 5 volumes. St. Petersburg 1838–1839.

Bound by Stravinsky's father in red Morocco with gold lettering, Japanese end papers, and with his initials, "Ø. C.," on the spine. At one time, Stravinsky intended to use song 229 (vol. III, p. 331) in *Les Noces* and marked it in pencil.

9. *Byt russkago naroda* by Tereshchenko. 2 volumes. St. Petersburg 1848.

Stravinsky used three lines from page 332 at **93** in *Les Noces.*

10. *Complete Collection of Verse* by K. D. Balmont, 1911.

Inscribed (in Russian): "To Stravinsky from the daughter of the poet." The texts of Stravinsky's *Zvezdoliki* and Balmont Songs are included in this volume, sent to the composer by Balmont's daughter in the spring of 1961, as Stravinsky's note to her 19 June 1961 reveals. The versions he used were published in *Zeliony vertograd* (St. Petersburg: Shipovnik, 1909).

11. *Old Irish Folk Music and Songs.* Dublin 1909.

Signed: "Igor Stravinsky, London I/1913" (January 30 or 31, Stravinsky having arrived in England from Monte Carlo, where he heard a performance of *Parsifal* on January 28). The melody of the "Marche" (Three Easy Pieces) comes from this volume, which also contains Stravinsky's inserted manuscript copy of the first two measures of song no. 139.

12. *The Melodist.* "A Selection of the Most Favorite English, Scotch, and Irish Songs, arranged for the voice, flute, or violin by G. S. Thornton." New York 1820. This book was the source for the music that Stravinsky planned to write for the film *Jane Eyre.* He copied excerpts from pages 16, 19, 42, 49, 75, 85, and 88–89.

13. *Pétrarque* by Charles-Albert Cingria. Librairie Payon & Cie., Lausanne 1932.

Inscribed: "À l'auteur du Duo concertant qui va si bien avec Pétrarque celui de ce livre que rien ne motive dans la surdité de notre époque. C. A. Cingria." Stravinsky thanked Cingria as follows: "Quel beau livre que votre *Pétrarque*! Je le lis avec une joie infinie! Pas un instant de détente—j'aime ça. Merci, cher ami, de me l'avoir envoyé et si flatteusement dedicacé." The book contains the text of an early French translation of Petrarch's Latin dialogue *Joy and Reason,* which Stravinsky had begun to set for two voices and a keyboard instrument in January 1933 but abandoned in order to begin the composition of *Perséphone.* The composer has underscored passages of philosophical and aesthetic argument in Cingria's book and commented on them in the margins.

14. *Charles-Albert Cingria: Oeuvres Complètes.* 10 volumes (the complete edition, 1984, consists of 17 volumes). Edition l'Age d'Homme, Lausanne.

Stravinsky met Cingria, the Swiss writer (of Turko-Yugoslav and Polish extraction) and music pupil of Jacques-Dalcroze, in Paris in 1914. From the mid-1920s until Cingria's death in 1954, the two were close friends. In 1965, Stravinsky became a member of the honorary committee for the publication of Cingria's complete works. Stravinsky subscribed to the edition and reread the contents of the volumes that appeared in his lifetime. He did not mark the books, but he attached the correspondence to him from the Association des amis de Charles-Albert Cingria to the first book in the set. Cingria's influence on Stravinsky is most evident here in the essays on Chesterton, Claudel, Joyce, Artaud, Giacometti, and Max Jacob. Cingria's essays on Stravinsky are found as follows: volume I, on *Histoire du soldat* (1925); volume IV, the *NRF* reviews "*L'Oeuvre de Stravinsky* par de Paoli," "*Perséphone* et la critique," "Sur *Chroniques de ma vie* I," "Sur *Chroniques de ma vie* II"; volume IX, "La première de Venise" (1951), "Igor Stravinsky—Paris via Venise" (1952), "Le *Rake*'s de Paris" (1953).

15. *Poets of the English Language,* volumes I and II (J. Langland to Spenser), edited by W. H. Auden and Norman Holmes Pearson. Viking Press, New York 1950.

Auden sent the five-volume anthology to Stravinsky in 1951. The texts of the Cantata (1952), chosen by the composer from volume I of this anthology, contain his penciled markings. The texts of the *Three Songs from William Shakespeare,* taken from volume II, contain his markings (pp. 154, 171–72, 177). His markings on page 173 indicate that he had originally considered setting "Come away, come away, death."

16. *Foure Birds of Noah's Arke* by Thomas Dekkar [*sic*]. New York 1925.

Stravinsky's book markers are found on pages 12/13, 22/23 (checkmark on p. 22), and 62/63. The text of the "Prayer" in *A Sermon, a Narrative and a Prayer* follows the orthography in this volume.

17. *Apologie de la danse* by F. de Lauze. Frederick Muller Ltd., London 1952.

Signed: "IStr 1954." In Stravinsky's hand, in pencil, on the cover: "with some music by Marin Mersenne (1636)." The *Apologie* includes musical and choreographic models for most of the dances in *Agon*. Stravinsky's scansion and phrasing marks are found on some of the music examples. He began the ballet in 1953, but after composing a few numbers, interrupted work on it in order to write *In Memoriam Dylan Thomas, Canticum Sacrum,* and the "Vom Himmel hoch" Variations. He resumed the composition of the ballet in 1956 after Lincoln Kirstein sent him the *Apologie*.

18. *Cantus Lamentationum pro Ultimo Triduo Hebdomadae Majoris Juxta Hispanos Codices*. Desclée & Cie., Paris 1934.

In Stravinsky's hand, on cover: "IStr 1959." The text of *Threni* (Latin with the Hebrew alphabet) was taken from this text of the *Lamentations of Jeremiah,* though Stravinsky did not sign the cover until more than a year after he had completed the score.

19. *Everyman and Medieval Miracle Plays,* edited by A. C. Cawley. E. P. Dutton, New York 1959. Paperback edition.

The source, with one exception, of the nonbiblical texts of *The Flood*. T. S. Eliot had drawn Stravinsky's attention to this edition of the mystery plays. The book is marked extensively by R. C., an insert sheet in whose hand indicates that a Cain and Abel scene was originally planned and that the only choreographic movement was to have been "The Flood." In this edition, as in the chronology of Stravinsky's compositions, *Noah's Flood* is followed by *Abraham and Isaac,* which suggests that Stravinsky may have read both plays at the same time and have been attracted then by the subject of the (non) sacrifice of Isaac.

20. *Das Wohltemperierte Klavier* by J. S. Bach. Two volumes, Universal Edition (Czerny).

On the cover of book I: "Igor Stravinsky [in Russian] May 7, 1970." On the cover of book II: "Igor Stravinsky [in English] May 7, 1970." Stravinsky's instrumentations of four preludes and four fugues (March–May 1969) follow these texts and were to some extent plotted directly on them: in volume I, prelude IV contains red crayon markings in m. 1, 26, and 27 and pencil markings in six other measures; fugue IV contains numerous red crayon markings and pencil markings in most measures; prelude X contains pencil markings, fugue X, numerous markings in both red and black pencil; in prelude XX, Stravinsky has circled the fifths in m. 54, and, in red pencil, questioned the flat at the end of m. 11 before the end; fugue XXII is marked in red and blue pencil, suggesting that at one time he had considered orchestrating the piece; fugue XXIII is marked in red pencil; prelude XXIV and fugue XXIV are marked in red and black pencil. In volume II, prelude XI and fugue XI are marked in red and black pencil. The last music that Stravinsky played at the piano, on 1, 2, 3 April 1971 was fugue VIII from volume I, which remained open on his piano at these pages for months after his death.

Etudes and Theoretical Works on Music

21. *Technique de l'Orchestra Moderne* by Ch. M. Widor. Henry Lemoine & Cie., Paris 1910.

Stravinsky consulted this book for information about saxophones while composing *Scherzo à la Russe;* he inserted his own manuscript of saxophone ranges between pages 152 and 157. To judge from the handwriting of his marginalia, he may have purchased and read the treatise as early as 1910. The blue crayon markings in his hand on pages 194 to 201 (on violin triple-stopping) and in red crayon on pages 216 to 222 (on viola triple-stopping) might date from the time of the composition of the "Glorification of the Chosen One." He has underlined and questioned a remark on page 229 and corrected a definition on page 154. On page 132, next to Widor's expression "pâte sonore," Stravinsky wrote in the margin, "À bas pâte, à bas orchestration." On page 122, next to Widor's observation that the sonority of the bass trombone is superb, Stravinsky has added: "C'est juste." Comments by Stravinsky appear on pages 46, 47, and 106, and on a paper inserted at page 55, he has written "Sa[illegible]."

22. *Complete School of Technic for the Pianoforte* by Isidor Philipp. Presser, Philadelphia 1908.

Signed on cover: "Igor Stravinsky." Before appearing as piano soloist in his Concerto for Piano and Wind Instruments (1923–1924), Stravinsky took piano lessons from Philipp. After the attack on Stravinsky's music as "degenerate art," in Düsseldorf in May 1938, the composer again turned to Philipp for help, but of a different nature: the pianist was a friend of François-Poncet, the French Ambassador in Berlin.

23. *Exercises Preparatoires* by I. Philipp (2nd series). J. Hamelle, Paris.

Signed: "Igor Stravinsky." Pencil markings throughout in Stravinsky's hand.

24. *Differences Between 18th-Century and Modern Violin Bowing* (reprint from *The Score,* March 1957) by Sol Babitz. Early Music Laboratory, Los Angeles 1970.

Inscribed: "June 18, 1970, Happy Birthday X Igor Stravinsky. Sol Babitz." Babitz gave this pamphlet to Stravinsky in Evian in August 1970.

25. *The Violin, Views and Reviews* by Sol Babitz. American String Teachers Association, Illinois 1959.

Inscribed: "To the very cher maître, Sol Babitz, L. A. 4/4/60."

26. *Journal de Psychologie.* Paris, January–March 1940/41. Issue devoted to "La Musique architecture temporelle" by Gisèle Brelet.

Enclosures: a letter to Stravinsky from Brelet, November 10/48; and a letter from E. C. Crittenden, U.S. Department of Commerce, Washington, D.C., explaining that during one of his recent visits to Paris, Brelet (Mme Jean Terrien) had entrusted him to give the publication to Stravinsky. Though Gisèle Brelet has been overlooked by Stravinsky scholars, her writings exercised a considerable influence on him in 1946–1950, particularly "Chances de la Musique Atonale." Her letters to him (1947–1952) on the nature of genius are fervent, his replies, matter-of-fact, but the Brelet episode merits examination.

27. "Musiques Exotiques et Valeurs Permanentes de l'Art Musical" (extract from *Revue Philosophique*) by Gisèle Brelet. Presses Universitaires de France, Paris 1946 (January–March).

28. *Esthétique et Création Musicale* by Gisèle Brelet. Paris 1947.

Insert in Stravinsky's hand: "Reçu May 6, 1947." Inscribed: "Pour Igor Strawinsky, je lui restitue ces pensées que m'inspirerent sa personne et ses oeuvres, Gisèle Brelet."

29. "Chances de la Musique Atonale" (extract from "Valeurs") by Gisèle Brelet. Éditions du Scarabée, Alexandria 1947.

Enclosed: envelope from Brelet to Stravinsky.

30. "Musique et Silence" (extract from *La Revue Musicale*) by Gisèle Brelet.

Enclosed: a long letter from Brelet, 25 August 1948, setting forth her philosophy of music. Stravinsky marked the envelope "Giselle [*sic*] Brelet 1948."

31. *Le Temps Musical* by Gisèle Brelet. Paris 1949.

Inscribed: "C'est à vous, cher Monsieur, et à vos oeuvres, que je dois d'avoir pu mener à bien ce travail, puisque le temps musical, essence de la musique, est aussi l'essence de *votre* musique. Permettez-moi donc de vous offrir ce *Temps Musical* qui vous est aussi familier qu' à moi-même. Gisèle Brelet."

32. *L'Interprétation Créatrice* by Gisèle Brelet. Paris 1951.

Inscribed: "Pour Igor Strawinsky, avec l'expression de ma profonde admiration et l'espoir de vous convaincre! Gisèle Brelet, 10 juillet 1951."

33. *Hamline Studies in Musicology,* edited by Ernst Krenek. Burgess Publishing Company, Minneapolis 1945.

Signed: "I. Stravinsky July/58."

34. *Modal Counterpoint in the Style of the Sixteenth Century,* outline by Ernst Krenek. Boosey & Hawkes, London 1959.

Signed: "I Str May 1960."

35. *De Rebus Prius Factis* by Ernst Krenek. Wilhelm Hansen Musikverlag, Frankfurt 1956.

Inscribed: "For Igor Stravinsky Ad res faciendas! Affectionately Ernst, May 5, 1958."

36. *Verzierungs'-Kunst in der Gesangs-Musik (1535–1650)* by Max Kuhn (all in block letters by Stravinsky). Breitkopf & Härtel, Leipzig 1902.

Stravinsky made a notation in the margin on page 1 of the text. This book was Stravinsky's reference for the ornamentation in his "Vom Himmel hoch" variations.

37. *Gründliche Violinschule* by Leopold Mozart. J. J. Lotter, Augsburg 1770.

Taped over the portrait of Leopold Mozart on the flyleaf is a sheet of tracing paper on which Stravinsky has drawn Leopold Mozart's portrait. Comments in Stravinsky's hand, in pencil, on the inside cover.

38. *Treatise on the Ornaments of Music* by Tartini, translated and edited by Sol Babitz.

Inscribed: "To Igor Stravinsky. A Happy Birthday. June 1960. Sol Babitz."

39. *L'Art de la musique* by Guy Bernard. Paris 1960 (?).

"Au maître Igor Strawinsky avec la profonde admiration et le respectueux hommage de Guy Bernard." On page 450, in red pencil, Stravinsky has questioned two statements about himself. Enclosed: two letters from Jacques Charpier concerning the inclusion of a chapter from the *Poétique Musicale* in the present volume and a letter from Stravinsky granting permission to do this, signed in green ink, "Igor Stravinsky."

40. *La Technique de l'Orchestre Contemporain* by A. Casella and V. Mortari. Paris 1958.

Inscribed: "A Igor Stravinsky, le grand maître des musiciens d'aujourd'hui et de demain qui nous a appris l'art et la jeunesse. Avec toute l'admiration et affection, de son devoué, Virgilio Mortari. Venise. 5 octobre 1958."

41. *Lois et Styles des Harmonies Musicales* by Edmond Costère. Presses Universitaires de France, Paris 1954.

Inscribed: "Au Maître Igor Strawinsky en hommage et ma respectueuse admiration, et en témoignage et en gratitude pour l'enseignements précieux que j'ai [illegible] dans ses oeuvres, et notamment dans sa *Poétique Musicale.* Paris le 20 mai 1956 [illegible]."

42. *The History of Music in Performance* by Frederick Dorian. New York 1942.

Contains two letters from Dorian and a long and critical one from Stravinsky to him, 22 January 1943.

43. *The Musical Workshop* by Frederick Dorian. New York 1947.

Contains a letter from Dorian to Stravinsky.

44. *Acta Musicologica* by J. Warren Kirkendale. Bärenreiter Verlag, Basel 1963.

In Stravinsky's hand, in ink, on the cover: "I/1963." Enclosed: letter from the author accompanying the article on Beethoven's *Grosse Fuge.*

45. "The Goddess Fortuna in Music" (reprint from *The Musical Quarterly*) by Edward E. Lowinsky. January 1943.

Inscribed: "For Igor Stravinsky with the author's high esteem!"

46. "Adrian Willaert's Chromatic 'Duo' Re-Examined" by E. E. Lowinsky.

Inscribed: "For Igor Stravinsky with the sincere admiration of Edward Lowinsky."

47. *Secret Chromatic Art in the Netherlands Motet* by Edward E. Lowinsky. Columbia University Press, New York 1946.

Inscribed: "For Igor Stravinsky with admiration and gratitude. Edward E. Lowinsky."

48. *Dan Emmett and the Rise of Early Negro Minstrelsy* by Hans Nathan. University of Oklahoma Press, 1962.

Inscribed: "Dear master: Please accept this new book of mine as a belated gift in honor of your eightieth birthday and as a humble tribute to the incomparable, astounding harvest of your life. Hans Nathan. February 14, 1962."

49. "The Twelve-Tone Compositions of Luigi Dallapiccola" (reprint from *Musical Quarterly,* July 1958) by Hans Nathan.

Inscribed: "For Igor Stravinsky. Hans Nathan."

50. *The Technique of Variation, a Study of the Instrumental Variation from Antonio de Cabezon to Max Reger* by Robert U. Nelson. University of California Press, Berkeley and Los Angeles 1948.

Inscribed: "To Igor Stravinsky, with sincerest regards—Robert U. Nelson. April 1949." Nelson was one of Stravinsky's pupils at Harvard in 1939–1940.

51. *Samples of the Ancient Russian Singing Art* by N. Ouspensky.

Inscribed: "To dear Igor Fyodorovich for his 86th anniversary with the best wishes and deepest respect. 17–VI–1968."

52. *Fragments Théoriques I sur la Musique Experimental* by Henri Pousseur. Editions de l'Institut de Sociologie, Université Libre de Bruxelles, Brussels 1970.

Inscribed: "Au Maître incomparable, à Igor Stravinsky, en [illegible] respectueuse—affectueuse admiration. Pousseur."

53. *L'Apothéose de Rameau* by Henri Pousseur. (Article in *Revue d'Esthetique*, 2 April 1968).

Inscribed: "En témoignage de respectueuse affection. Pousseur." Label attached.

54. *En Pays Dauphinois* by Paul Pittion. Grenoble 1950.

Inscribed: "Au Maître de *Threni*, qui en 1931, était Dauphinois, ces quelques chants et danses de nos montagnes, Paul Pittion." Pittion was a choral conductor much respected by Stravinsky.

55. *Traité des Objets Musicaux* by Pierre Schaeffer. Editions du Seuil, Paris 1967 (?).

Inscribed by the author to Stravinsky, recalling a luncheon with him in Hollywood in 1945.

56. *Webern's Last Works* by Humphrey Searle. Article in *The Monthly Musical Record*, December 1946.

Stapled by Stravinsky, title underlined by him, a mistake in rhythm in the third paragraph corrected by him, and the end of the preceding article on Schumann "x"ed out by him.

57. "Serialism reconsidered" by Peter Stadlen. Reprint from *Score* magazine.

Dated by Stravinsky "February 1958" in red ink on the cover.

58. *Die Reihe*, second Anton Webern Number. Universal Edition, Vienna 1955.

Signed: "IStr."

Acknowledgments

ACKNOWLEDGMENT is made to the following publishers for use of musical examples from Stravinsky scores under their copyright:

Belwin-Mills Publishing Corp. for *The Rite of Spring* (Example 9.4, Part 3), Copyright 1974 by Belwin-Mills Publishing Corp., Melville, N.Y.

Boosey and Hawkes, Inc., for *Agon* (Examples 12.12, 13.4) Copyright © 1957 by Boosey and Hawkes, Inc.; (Bach) Choral-Variations on "Vom Himmel hoch" (Examples 13.7, 13.8a) Copyright © 1955 by Boosey and Hawkes, Inc.; Cantata (Example 13.1) Copyright 1952 by Boosey and Hawkes, Inc., New York; *Canticum Sacrum* (Examples 11.14, 13.3) Copyright © 1956 by Boosey and Hawkes, Inc.; *Duo concertant* (Example 13.10) Copyright © 1947 by Edition Russe de Musique, Boosey and Hawkes, Inc.; *Ebony Concerto* (Example 12.2) Copyright 1946 by Charling Music Corp. Renewed 1973; Copyright and renewal assigned to Boosey and Hawkes, Inc., for the U.S.A.; (Gesualdo) *Tres sacrae cantiones* (Examples 13.8b, 13.8c) Copyright © 1960 Boosey and Co., Ltd. By arrangement with Ugrino-Verlag, Hamburg.; *In Memoriam Dylan Thomas* (Example 13.2) Copyright 1954 by Boosey and Hawkes, Inc., New York; Mass (Examples 11.11, 11.14–11.16) Copyright 1948 in the U.S.A. by Boosey and Hawkes, Inc. Copyright for all countries; *Movements* for Piano and Orchestra (Examples 14.1, 15.2) Copyright © 1960 by Hawkes and Son (London), Ltd.; *The Nightingale* (Examples 7.4, 7.18–7.20) Copyright 1914 by Edition Russe de Musique (Russischer Musikverlag). Copyright assigned 1947 to Boosey and Hawkes, Inc. for all countries; *Octet* (Example 12.4) Copyright 1924 by Edition Russe de Musique. Renewed 1952, Copyright and renewal assigned to Boosey and Hawkes, Inc. Revised version copyright 1952 by Boosey and Hawkes, Inc.; *Orpheus* (Example 12.1) Copyright 1947, 1948 by Boosey and Hawkes, Inc. Renewed 1974, 1975; *Petrushka* (Examples 1.2 and 2.2 are taken from piano reductions of the score published by the Edition Russe de Musique in 1911 under no copyright. Later editions of the score are copyright 1912 by Edition Russe de Musique [Russischer Musikverlag] for all countries. Copyright assigned 1947 to Boosey and Hawkes, New York, U.S.A. New Version copyright 1948 by Boosey and Hawkes, Inc., New York, U.S.A. Copyright for all countries); *The Rake's Progress* (Example 13.11) Copyright © 1951 by Boosey and

Hawkes, Inc.; *Requiem Canticles* (Examples 11.9–11.11) Copyright 1967 by Boosey and Hawkes Music Publishers Ltd.; *The Rite of Spring* (Full score) (Examples 9.1–9.10, parts 4, 4a, 5, 7, and 8), Copyright 1921 by Edition Russe de Musique (Russischer Musikverlag). Copyright assigned 1947 to Boosey and Hawkes Inc. for all countries; *The Rite of Spring* (Examples 8.2, 8.4–8.7, 8.10–8.16) Copyright assigned 1947 to Boosey and Hawkes. New Edition 1967; *The Rite of Spring* (Orchestral parts) (Examples 9.3–9.5) Copyright 1921 by Edition Russe de Musique. Copyright assigned 1947 to Boosey and Hawkes Inc. for all countries; *The Rite of Spring* (Piano reduction) (Examples 2.3, 2.4, 7.2, 9.1, 9.2, 9.5) Copyright 1926 by Edition Russe de Musique (Russischer Musikverlag). Copyright assigned 1947 to Boosey and Hawkes Inc. for all countries; *The Rite of Spring*, "Sacrificial Dance" (Examples 8.17–8.19, 9.8, 9.9) Copyright 1945 by Associated Music Publishers, Inc. Renewed 1973, Copyright and renewal assigned to Boosey and Hawkes, Inc. for all countries; *The Rite of Spring: Sketches 1911–1913* (Examples 7.3, 9.10, part 1) Copyright 1969 by Boosey and Hawkes, Music Publishers Ltd.; *A Sermon, a Narrative, and a Prayer* (Example 13.6c) Copyright © 1961 by Boosey and Co., Ltd.; *Symphony of Psalms* (Examples 11.5, 11.6, 11.8, 11.10, 11.12) Copyright 1931 by the Edition Russe de Musique. Renewed 1958, Copyright and renewal assigned to Boosey and Hawkes, Inc. Revised edition copyright 1948 by Boosey and Hawkes Inc. Renewed 1975; *Symphony of Psalms* (Example 7.1 is taken from a piano reduction of the score that has no date or copyright notive other than Boosey and Hawkes, sole agents for the copyright owner, Edition Russe de Musique, Paris); *Threni* (Examples 11.14, 11.15, 13.5, 13.6a, 15.1, 21.7b) Copyright © 1958 by Boosey and Hawkes, Inc.; Three Pieces for String Quartet (Example 7.21) Copyright 1922 by Edition Russe de Musique. All rights assigned to Boosey and Hawkes, Inc., 1947; *Trois Mouvements de Petrouchka* (Examples 7.14–7.16) Copyright 1922 by Edition Russe de Musique (Russischer Musikverlag) for all countries. Copyright assigned 1947 to Boosey and Hawkes, Inc., New York, U.S.A.; *Variations* (Aldous Huxley in Memoriam) (Example 15.3) © 1965 by Boosey and Hawkes Music Publishers, Ltd.; Stravinsky sketches used in Charles Wuorinen's *A Reliquary for Igor Stravinsky* (Example 15.4) © 1978 by Boosey and Hawkes.

J & W Chester Ltd., London, for *Eight Instrumental Miniatures* (Example 13.9). Copyright for all countries 1963 © J & W Chester Ltd., London; *Les Noces* (Examples 11.7, 11.15, 12.13) Copyright 1950 by J & W Chester Ltd., London; Five Easy Pieces (Example 12.5) Copyright 1917 by J & W Chester Ltd.; Three Easy Pieces (Example 12.14) Copyright 1917 by Ad. Henn. J & W Chester Ltd., London; *Concertino* for String Quartet (Example 12.15) Copyright 1923 by Wilhelm Hansen, Copenhagen.

C. F. Peters Corporation for *Zvezdoliki* (Example 7.17 has no copyright notice, but the publisher is listed as Musikverlag Rob. Forberg, Bad Godesberg. Sole Agents: C. F. Peters Corporation, New York, N.Y. Catalogue No. F-94); for

Charles Wuorinen's *A Reliquary for Igor Stravinsky* (Example 15.4) © 1978 by C. F. Peters Corporation. Used by permission.

B. Schott's Söhne for *The Firebird* (Examples 7.5–7.13) All rights reserved. Used by permission of European American Music Distributors Corporation, sole U.S. agent for B. Schott's Söhne, copyright owner; Concerto in E♭ ("Dumbarton Oaks") (Example 12.9) Copyright 1938 by B. Schott's Söhne, Mainz, © renewed 1966; Symphony in C (Example 12.3) Copyright Schott and Co., Ltd., London, 1948; Symphony in Three Movements (Examples 12.6, 12.10) Copyright 1946 by AMP, Inc. New York. Copyright assigned to B. Schott's Söhne, Mainz, © renewed 1974.

Notes on Contributors

EDWIN ALLEN was a close friend of the Stravinskys from 1961 until their deaths. He is at present acquisitions librarian at Wesleyan University in Connecticut.

GILBERT AMY studied composition with Milhaud and Messiaen and conducting with Boulez. From 1976 to 1982, he was both musical director and conductor of the Nouvel Orchestre Philharmonique de Radio-France, Paris.

LOUIS ANDRIESSEN, a free-lance composer and founder of contemporary music ensembles in Holland, has just published a monograph on Stravinsky, *The Apolonian Clockwork,* together with Elmer Schönberger.

MILTON BABBITT, a 1982 recipient of a Pulitzer Prize, has taught in the music and mathematics departments of Princeton University since 1938. His articles on contemporary music have appeared in major music journals.

MALCOLM HAMRICK BROWN, a specialist in nineteenth- and twentieth-century Russian and Soviet music, teaches at Indiana University. Among many other scholarly activities, he edits the series *Russian Music Studies* for UMI Research Press.

ROBERT CRAFT, conductor and writer on music, was closely allied with Stravinsky from 1948 until the composer's death. Their collaboration involved numerous premiere performances, recordings, and literary works. He has recently published *Stravinsky: Selected Correspondence,* vols. 1,2, and 3.

LOUIS CYR studied musicology in Frankfurt, West Germany, and recently was chairman of the music department at the University of Québec, Montréal. Ordained as a Jesuit priest in 1964, he also writes on contemporary church music.

ALLEN FORTE is professor of music theory at Yale University. His published writings comprise eight books and numerous articles, including *The Harmonic Organization of The Rite of Spring.*

TAKASHI FUNAYAMA is a noted expert on Stravinsky in Japan and professor of musicology at the National University of Fine Arts and Music in Tokyo.

DAVID HOCKNEY, one of the most widely acclaimed British artists, did the set designs for the Glyndebourne production of *The Rake's Progress* (1974–1975) and the Metropolitan Opera's *Rite of Spring, Nightingale,* and *Oedipus Rex* in 1981.

SIMON KARLINSKY studied with Honegger before becoming a professor of Slavic languages and literature at the University of California at Berkeley. His published writings include numerous books on Russian writers and artists.

JONATHAN D. KRAMER, composer and music theorist, is director of electronic music and professor at the College-Conservatory of Music of the University of Cincinnati.

JEFFREY KRESKY, composer and music theorist, is associate professor of music at William Paterson College. He is the author of *Tonal Music: Twelve Analytic Studies.*

REX LAWSON, the only professional concert pianolist in the world, has recorded and performed Stravinsky's Pianola music in London and Paris.

LAWRENCE MORTON, a musicologist and writer, founded and directed the Los Angeles Monday Evening Concerts. From 1965 to 1982, he was curator of music at the Los Angeles County Museum.

JANN PASLER teaches at the University of California at San Diego. Her research and publications center on Paris in the early twentieth century and contemporary music.

ELMER SCHÖNBERGER studied musicology at Utrecht University and piano at the Royal Conservatory of the Hague. He is music editor of *Vrij Nederland* and *De Revisor* and has just published *The Apollonian Clockwork* with L. Andriessen.

BORIS SCHWARZ (d. 1983), musicologist, conductor, and violinist, was professor emeritus, City University of New York. Among his noted publications are *Music and Musical Life in Soviet Russia* and *The Great Violinists.*

ROGER SHATTUCK is a writer and cultural historian currently teaching at the University of Virginia. His many books include *The Banquet Years, Marcel Proust,* and *The Forbidden Experiment,* as well as several volumes of poetry.

LEONARD STEIN, Schoenberg's teaching assistant from 1939 to 1942 and a pianist, is currently director of the Schoenberg Institute in Los Angeles. Besides editing many collections of Schoenberg's essays, he is editor of the journal of the institute.

RICHARD TARUSKIN, associate professor of music at Columbia University and director of Capella Nova, is active both as a scholar of nineteenth-century Russian music and as a performer of early music.

PIETER C. VAN DEN TOORN, composer, theorist, pianist, and writer, recently published *The Music of Igor Stravinsky*.

GLENN WATKINS is director of graduate studies at the University of Michigan and co-editor of the works of Gesualdo. Stravinsky contributed a preface to his *Gesualdo: The Man and His Music*.

CHARLES WUORINEN, composer, pianist, and conductor, lives in New York City and performs in concerts worldwide. His *Reliquary for Igor Stravinsky* is based on the last fragments and sketches of Stravinsky.

Index

Designer: Adriane Bosworth
Compositor: A-R Editions, Inc.
Text: 10/13 Palatino
Display: Palatino
Printer: Malloy Lithographing
Binder: John H. Dekker & Sons